THE
ENEMY
WITHIN

A HISTORY OF ESPIONAGE

OSPREY
PUBLISHING

FOR SARAH

THE ENEMY WITHIN

A HISTORY OF ESPIONAGE

TERRY CROWDY

First published in Great Britain in 2006 by Osprey Publishing,
Midland House, West Way, Botley, Oxford OX2 0PH, United Kingdom.
443 Park Avenue South, New York, NY 10016, USA.
Email: info@ospreypublishing.com

© 2006 Terry Crowdy

A CIP catalogue record for this book is available from the British Library

ISBN-10: 1-84176-933-9
ISBN-13: 978-1-84176-933-2

Terry Crowdy has asserted his right under the Copyright, Designs and Patents Act, 1988, to be identified as the author of this book.

Page layout by Ken Vail Graphic Design, Cambridge, UK
Index by Alison Worthington
Typeset in Monotype Gill Sans, ITC Stone Serif, Sabon, Trajan and Hoefler Text
Originated by United Graphics Pte Ltd, Singapore
Printed and bound in China by Bookbuilders

06 07 08 09 10   10 9 8 7 6 5 4 3 2 1

For a catalogue of all books published by Osprey please contact:

NORTH AMERICA
Osprey Direct c/o Random House Distribution Center
400 Hahn Road, Westminster, MD 21157, USA
E-mail: info@ospreydirect.com

ALL OTHER REGIONS
Osprey Direct UK, P.O. Box 140, Wellingborough, Northants, NN8 2FA, UK
E-mail: info@ospreydirect.co.uk
www.ospreypublishing.com

Acknowledgements

I would like to take this opportunity to express my thanks to the British Library, Gallica, the Library of Congress, the National Archives at Kew, the National Portrait Gallery and the National Codes Centre at Bletchley Park. I would also like to thank my father, Ron Crowdy for his advice on aspects of Cold War espionage and the unwitting loan of his books. Thanks also to David Hollins and a certain Mr G., who must remain otherwise nameless, but provided much of the inspiration for my research. I would like to extend a special thank you to all my friends and colleagues who have helped over the years; in particular Ashley Kane, Tony 'Louis' Lofts, Martin Lancaster, Yves Martin and Ian Castle. None of this would have been possible without the constant support and encouragement from Anita Baker and Ruth Sheppard at Osprey; with a special thank you to Rebecca Hermann. Lastly, I must give special thanks to Sarah, who put her journalist's skills and instinct at my disposal and shared with me the ups and downs of a project that was an amazing privilege to work on.

CONTENTS

INTRODUCTION

Every action has an equal and opposite reaction

The common reading of Newton's 1687
'Law of Reciprocal Actions'

In 2001 the world was confronted with the most appalling terrorist attack to date. Islamic terrorists crashed two hijacked passenger jets into the 'Twin Towers' World Trade Center in New York City. Another hijacked jet slammed into the Pentagon in Washington, DC. A fourth flight came down in a Pennsylvanian field. It was a tragedy too big for words.

As the numbness of shock wore away, parallels were quickly drawn with the 1941 attack on Pearl Harbor. Considering the hundreds of billions of dollars the United States spends on defence each year, people wondered if anything more could have been done to prevent the attack. More pertinently, had any indication of an attack been given by the intelligence agencies? The answer was, unfortunately, yes.

Long before the attacks, America's Central Intelligence Agency (CIA) had warned that Saudi-born Osama bin Laden's network of Islamic jihadists were planning to attack the United States. On 4 December 1998, the CIA included an article in its *Presidential Daily Brief* describing how bin Laden and his cohorts were planning operations. The report claimed two members of a terror cell had made a dummy run of an attack at a New York airport, successfully evading security checks. More ominously, they reported that other members of bin Laden's network were receiving hijack training.[1] In 1999 more reports of possible bin Laden-sponsored attacks appeared, including a plot to blow up the FBI building in Washington, DC.[2] If all this was known before 11 September, why hadn't the CIA reacted more effectively?

A large part of the answer lies in the somewhat chequered history of the CIA. Although a Cold War invention, the CIA's roots began in

World War II, with the Office of Strategic Services (OSS), which was established in 1942. OSS proved itself every bit as capable as the British secret services it worked alongside. For example, OSS agents discovered that Germany was secretly obtaining vital ball bearings from Sweden after the Allies had destroyed its factories. The United States was then able to put diplomatic pressure on Sweden to halt the sales. One of its biggest coups was the recruitment of the spy 'George Wood' – in fact Fritz Kolbe – an official in the German Foreign Office. Kolbe supplied thousands of documents and reported on the development of the V1 and V2 flying bombs and the Messerschmitt Me 262 jet fighter. In addition to espionage, OSS also set a precedent for US overseas covert intervention. Perhaps less wisely in the long term, OSS provided aid and training to Vietnamese communist leader Ho Chi Minh in the war against Japan, despite warnings not to do so by France and China.[3]

At the end of World War II, the OSS was disbanded amid allegations of its becoming an 'American Gestapo'.[4] However, recognising the need for such a service, President Truman ordered the creation of the CIA in 1947. 'The Company' – as CIA operatives refer to their agency – is independent of all other government agencies and performs a mixture of clandestine missions and espionage on behalf of the US president. In the course of its history it has become no stranger to scandals, the culmination of which hampered its performance in the lead up to the 11 September attacks.

The first major scandal came with the 1961 'Bay of Pigs' affair. The CIA trained and equipped an army of Cuban exiles to overthrow Fidel Castro's communist regime, which had come to power in 1959. The operation was a fiasco and brought down the CIA boss Allen Dulles. In retaliation, Castro invited the Soviets to deploy nuclear missiles in Cuba, which brought about the Cuban Missile Crisis of 1962. Many believe that President Kennedy's handling of the 'Bay of Pigs' invasion – he would not authorize supporting air strikes – led to his assassination in 1963. There is a long held, but unsubstantiated, theory that the assassination was a mafia hit; crime bosses being unhappy at losing gambling and drug rackets in Havana.

After the involvement of ex-CIA agents in the 1972 Watergate break-ins and following a series of allegations against the agency, a Senate committee chaired by Senator Frank Church began investigating the alleged abuses of law committed by US intelligence agencies. It was revealed that the CIA had made attempts to assassinate foreign leaders, including Patrice Lumumba of the Congo and Fidel Castro. These attempts included the use of a poisoned wetsuit and exploding cigars. After the findings were presented, in 1976 President Ford issued an Executive Order banning the assassination of foreign leaders. In the 1980s the CIA again came under fire, this time for its Central American covert action programmes, its association with drug-runners and for running a private war in Angola. Shaky morale reached its nadir when in the early 1990s CIA officer Aldrich Ames was convicted of spying for the Soviets.

At the end of the Cold War, the CIA found itself on unfamiliar ground. There were big financial and personnel cuts, and as the number of agents declined, so the missions they faced became more varied. Agents found themselves shifted from crisis to crisis – one minute in the Balkans, the next in Africa. Certain corners of the world, however, were not covered at all. When it came to the Middle East, the CIA had a major problem recruiting and found itself relying on allies like Saudi Arabia for intelligence. More fundamentally, there was a sense that everything the CIA touched was bound to become a scandal in the eyes of Congress and the media. The CIA became wary of undertaking missions without a complete paper trail leading back to Washington with good legal justification for its involvement. In short, the agency would not take risks at a time when risks probably should have been taken.

Following al-Qaeda's 1998 bombings of the US embassies in Nairobi and Dar es Salaam, the Clinton administration felt bin Laden could be taken out as a justifiable act of self-defence. The CIA had already been looking to kidnap bin Laden from his Afghan base and bring him to trial in the United States before the 1998 bombings. A CIA-backed tribal group began planning the operation and mapping out bin Laden's HQ. In 1997 there was a report of an ambush by tribesmen against bin Laden on a road near Kandahar, but the operation failed because of poor tactics on behalf of the ambushing party.[5]

When CIA Director George Tenet revealed that bin Laden was attending a gathering of up to 200 jihadists at a remote camp in Afghanistan, Clinton gave the green light to attack. Not willing to risk ground forces, on the evening of 20 August 1998, 75 Tomahawk cruise missiles were launched at the terrorist camp. At the same time, 13 more

Tomahawks were fired at the al-Shifa pharmaceutical plant in Khartoum which was thought to have links with al-Qaeda. An Egyptian agent had told the CIA that a soil sample from the vicinity of the plant had tested positive for a chemical related to the production of VX nerve gas. In the wake of the 1995 Tokyo subway Sarin attack, Washington feared bin Laden might be planning something similar.[6]

Although the United States had responded to the embassy bombings, the attacks fell short of their objectives. The Sudanese government invited journalists to visit the al-Shifa plant and were shown an apparently harmless facility. No independent evidence of the CIA's nerve gas claim could be found. Worse, bin Laden survived the American attack and was seen by many in the Arab world as a hero for having done so. In fact he was probably tipped off before the attack. To reach targets in Afghanistan, the cruise missiles had to pass through Pakistan airspace. US planners feared Pakistan might think the missiles had been fired by India and retaliate. After giving Pakistan advance notice of the attack, it appears that details were leaked to bin Laden's Taliban hosts by Pakistan's Inter-Services Intelligence Directorate (ISID) – then believed to be the Taliban's 'primary patron.'[7]

At home Clinton was accused of making the attacks to distract attention from the Monica Lewinsky scandal. The incident was known as the *Wag the Dog* slur – after the 1997 film about an American president who faked a war to divert attention from a domestic crisis. Although Clinton claimed not to be affected by the Lewinsky scandal and subsequent impeachment proceedings, he was in no position to start throwing his weight around in Afghanistan, risking more adverse publicity.

Several more key opportunities to assassinate bin Laden were passed up before 9/11. On 20 December 1998 the CIA reported that bin Laden would be spending the night in Kandahar. Although the field agents indicated bin Laden should be hit, there was a fear in Washington that innocent bystanders might be killed or wounded and that a mosque might be damaged. Fear of adverse publicity stayed America's hand. The CIA then received reports that bin Laden was at a camp in the Afghan desert south of Kandahar where the risk of collateral damage was minimal. CIA sources further reported that bin Laden would be in the camp on the morning of 11 February. The attack was planned, but the mission called off. Other intelligence placed an official United Arab Emirates aircraft near to bin Laden's quarters. It was feared that an Emirati prince was with bin Laden – if the prince was killed in the attack, the United States might lose a valuable ally in the Persian Gulf. The attack was cancelled.

Finally, in May 1999 bin Laden's position was again reported. The cruise missiles were readied and the intelligence was considered as good as could be hoped for. Over the course of five days and nights the CIA received a number of detailed reports from different assets, each pinpointing bin Laden in Kandahar.[8] Again, America hesitated. Elsewhere that month, intelligence provided by the CIA had led to the accidental bombing of the Chinese embassy in Belgrade during the NATO war with Serbia – a mistake the CIA blamed on 'systemic organization problems'.[9] With this in mind the government could not risk a second blunder so soon. After that, no more missions against bin Laden were attempted until after 2001.

In the same way that questions were asked about America's failing to act in light of intelligence warnings before 11 September, when suicide bombers attacked London in July 2005 questions were asked about whether Britain's secret services had in any way come up short. Shortly after the London 7/7 bombing, *The Times* carried an interview with Prince Turki, the outgoing Saudi ambassador and former head of Saudi Intelligence. He expressed frustration that Prime Minister Blair had 'repeatedly failed to tackle radical Muslims in his backyard'. It transpired that Saudi Arabia and Pakistan considered Britain 'soft and indecisive' in dealing with extremists. Prince Turki considered the British government's response to requests to crack down on extremists 'inadequate' and accused Whitehall departments of 'trying to pass the buck'.[10] The day after this article appeared, the government announced it had detained ten suspected radicals.

Prince Turki's criticisms were nothing compared to the slating the British government received about its 2002 'September Dossier'. Before going to war in Iraq, Prime Minister Tony Blair believed a case for it should be made to the British public. He took a gamble and authorized the publication of all the available intelligence assessments, which claimed:

- Iraq was producing chemical and biological agents that could be used in weapons.

- Some of these weapons were deployable within 45 minutes of an order to use them.
- Iraq had developed mobile laboratories for military use.
- Iraq had retained up to 20 Al Hussein missiles, which could be used to deliver conventional, chemical or biological warheads within a range of 404 miles (650km).
- Iraq was trying to import uranium from Africa in order to develop a nuclear weapon.

In the document, next to the 45-minute claim, was a map demonstrating the range of the Al Hussein missiles. Within range of these weapons were countries including Kuwait, Saudi Arabia, Israel and also Cyprus – home to a British base. The text clearly suggested that British forces were just 45 minutes away from a chemical weapon attack. The importance of this intelligence was reinforced when Blair alluded to '45 minutes' four times in a speech on the dossier in the House of Commons. The message was obviously effective. On the day of the dossier's release, the front page of the London *Evening Standard* carried the headline, '45 MINUTES FROM ATTACK'. The following day, the biggest-selling UK tabloid, *The Sun*, carried the sensational headline: 'BRITS 45 MINS FROM DOOM'.

Early in June 2003, after British forces had been deployed in Iraq, a startling allegation was made about the 45-minute claim. BBC reporter Andrew Gilligan said that in the week prior to publication, the previously 'dull' Iraq dossier had been 'sexed up' by the inclusion of the 45-minute claim. Gilligan said this had happened on the instructions of the Prime Minister's Director of Communications and Strategy, Alastair Campbell. Gilligan said he based his allegation on claims made to him by 'one of the senior officials in charge of drawing up the dossier', but would not reveal his identity.

The source turned out to be Dr David Kelly, an expert in biological warfare at the Ministry of Defence and former weapons inspector for the United Nations in Iraq. In 2002 Dr Kelly was working for the Defence Intelligence Staff and, because of his expertise, was asked to proofread parts of the draft dossier being prepared by Britain's Joint Intelligence Committee. On 22 May 2003, Dr Kelly met Gilligan at London's Charing Cross Hotel. Speaking 'off-the-record' Dr Kelly told

Gilligan he had been concerned with the 45-minute claim and made the allegation about Campbell.

When the story went public, the government went on the offensive and pressed the BBC to reveal its source. On 30 June, Dr Kelly went to his manager at the MOD and reported his contact with Gilligan. He was given a formal warning for the unauthorized meeting with a journalist. The MOD then released a statement from which journalists were able to guess that Dr Kelly had been Gilligan's source. On 15 July he appeared as a witness before a committee at the House of Commons, scrutinising the Iraq war. The following day Dr Kelly gave more evidence to the Intelligence and Security Committee. On 17 July, Dr Kelly told his wife he was going for a walk. About a mile from his home he committed suicide. It was all very damaging for the government.

A committee was set up to get to the root of the dossier's claims. If officials had not sexed up the dossier, why had the intelligence been wrong?[11] Someone privy to the intelligence before the Iraq War was Robin Cook, a former Foreign Secretary under Blair. When questioned, he gave an excellent analysis of the problems of interpreting intelligence in the lead up to the war:

> ... often when you are told a piece of information you are left with very real doubts over why you are being told that information. Are you being told it to mislead you? Are you being told it by somebody who actually wants to be paid but may not actually turn out to be reliable; or is not somebody – as I think was the case with some of the Iraqi exiles pursuing their own political agenda – who wants you to hear what suits them? All these questions and motivation form very great difficulty over making your assessment of intelligence... In fairness to the intelligence community one should recognise that Iraq was an appallingly difficult intelligence target to break. We had very little access to human intelligence on the ground and no hope whatsoever of putting in Western agents.[12]

If, as Cook claimed, there had been no Western agents in Iraq, where did the 45-minute claim come from? Was the information from Iraqi dissidents, or was it false information deliberately planted by the Iraqis to mislead and deceive America and Britain? Apparently, the 45-minute claim was based on information received by the Secret Intelligence Service in August 2002 from a single source described as 'an established, reliable and longstanding line of reporting'.[13] However, although consistent with other evidence about Iraq's military capabilities, there was no other evidence to back the claim. As the Americans had found over the al-Shifa bombing, acting on uncorroborated evidence is a recipe for disaster.

Nor did the British 'uranium from Africa' claim stand up to scrutiny. The CIA sent former US ambassador to Iraq, Joseph Wilson, to Niger to investigate claims that Iraqi officials had been trying to buy uranium. Wilson reported the claims were false and the United Nations declared the supporting documents were forgeries. In the British enquiry, it was implied that British intelligence knew of the American's findings, but ignored them.[14] Despite Wilson's verdict, President Bush also referred to the claim in his State of the Union address of 28 January 2003, saying: 'The British Government has learned that Saddam Hussein recently sought significant quantities of uranium from Africa.'

In light of the evidence provided, Wilson was surprised that Bush had made this claim. In an article for *The New York Times* on 6 July 2003, Wilson said he believed the intelligence related to Iraq's weapons programme had been twisted to exaggerate the threat from Saddam Hussein's regime. Following this allegation, America's Deputy National Security Advisor, Stephen Hadley, admitted he was at fault for not deleting this part of the speech. In return, it seems the White House wanted some measure of revenge against Wilson. Later in 2003 it appears that Vice-President Dick Cheney's chief aide, Lewis 'Scooter' Libby leaked to the press that Wilson's wife was CIA agent Valerie Plame. In the United States, revealing the identity of a CIA agent is a criminal offence and after a long investigation, in 2005, Libby was indicted by a grand jury.

No sooner had this scandal blown up than the media began to focus on so-called CIA 'torture-flights'. In a process known as 'extraordinary rendition' the CIA was accused of kidnapping and illegally transferring suspected Islamic terrorists to secret prisons – known as 'Black Sites' – in third-party countries for interrogation. Many of the countries, including Syria and Egypt, have been separately accused by the US of permitting torture during interrogation. Although the US denied it, the concern was that CIA prisoners were being handed over for torture, or simply made to 'disappear'.[15] Following the allegations, the European Union wrote to US Secretary of State Condoleezza Rice expressing misgivings over reports that CIA 'torture flights' had made stops in EU countries. Stronger condemnation came in a Council of Europe report of 24 January 2006. Led by the former Swiss mafia prosecutor, Dick Marty, the report claimed more than 100 terrorist suspects had been flown to prisons and tortured. Mr Marty also stressed it was unlikely the CIA had done so without the knowledge of European governments, or at least their intelligence services.[16]

But take heart. Such secret service scandals and bungles have been causing trouble since the time of Moses, if not before. In fact, spying is recognized as the oldest profession in the world after prostitution. Throughout history, spies have gained a particularly loathsome reputation as being treacherous and morally degenerate. It is a reputation well deserved, but as General Tommy Franks, the US commander in the 2003 Iraq War said: 'To get information, we have to marry the devil or at least employ him. You have to deal.'[17]

Many believe the United States came to rely too much on spy technology and not enough on human agents. Although America spent billions on intelligence gathering every year before September 11, just 20 per cent of the budget went to the agency responsible for espionage – the CIA. The rest was spent on aerial and satellite reconnaissance and on electronic eavesdropping. Although literally billions of private emails, telephone calls and faxes are intercepted and monitored every day, the technology has yet to prove itself as effective as a well placed spy when it comes to tracking an individual, half way round the world, hiding in a cave.

Writing 2,500 years ago, the Chinese philosopher-general Sun Tzû advised that 'knowledge of the enemy can only be obtained by other men.' If this is the case, and history suggests it is, the study of espionage must come out of the shadows. One should always know one's enemy. More so if it is an enemy within.

1

IN ANCIENT TIMES

'First let each wiser art be tried;
Bribe them, or win them, or divide.'
Such was the counsel of the spy

From *The Rámáyan of Válmíki*, Book VI, Canto XX: The Spies[1]

The earliest surviving record of espionage dates from the time of Pharaoh Rameses' war with the Hittites and the battle of Kadesh (*c.*1274 BC). Although spies are best known as collectors of information, they are often used to disseminate false information in order to deliberately mislead opponents. The Hittite king Muwatallis (ruled *c.*1295–*c.*1272 BC) sent two spies into the Egyptian camp posing as deserters to convince pharaoh that the Hittite army was still quite distant. Rameses believed their story and unwittingly allowed part of his army to march into a Hittite ambush. Fortunately for the pharaoh, he captured two more Hittite spies and had his officers interrogate them.[2] Under repeated blows, the Hittite spies revealed that an ambush had been set for Rameses' advance troops. Rameses was therefore able to bring up reserves and avert disaster at what became known as the battle of Kadesh.[3]

The Old Testament is a rich source of spy stories. The first mention of spies comes as early as the Book of Genesis, when Joseph accuses his brothers – who had earlier sold him into slavery – of being Canaanite spies reconnoitring for unprotected spots along the Egyptian border. Although the brothers were simply out buying grain and the accusation was Joseph's way of scoring revenge, the story confirms that Egypt was wary of foreign spies infiltrating its borders.[4]

We then have Moses leading the Israelites on their search for the Promised Land. Having escaped Egypt and miraculously eluded the pharaoh's chariot army while crossing the Red Sea, Moses prepared to move into the land of Canaan. The Book of Deuteronomy records how

Moses, before embarking on this expedition, sent out spies after being petitioned by people who wanted them to 'bring back a report about the route we are to take and the towns we will come to'.[5] To gain this precious intelligence, Moses appointed 12 spies, who were according to the Bible from among the leaders of each of the 12 ancestral Israelite tribes. The detailed instructions given to the 12 are recorded in the Book of Numbers:

'See what the land is like and whether the people who live there are strong or weak, few or many. What kind of land do they live in? Is it good or bad? What kind of towns do they live in? Are they unwalled or fortified? How is the soil? Is it fertile or poor? Are there trees on it or not? Do your best to bring back some of the fruit of the land.'[6]

The spies set out and returned with news, carrying examples of the bountiful fruit growing in the land. Ten of them reported it was indeed a land of plenty, but the inhabitants were giants and would be too strong for the Israelites. Hearing this report, the people panicked and rebelled, refusing to go ahead with the expedition. When the two remaining spies, Joshua and Caleb, spoke in favour of the enterprise, the people grew angry and 'talked about stoning them'. The expedition was shelved and the doubting Israelites were condemned to 40 years of wandering in the wilderness – one year for each day the spies were in Canaan.

Despite this reverse, Moses continued to recognize the necessity of espionage. He used spies to much better effect in his war against Sihon, the King of the Amorites and Og, King of Bashan.[7] Having beaten Sihon at Jahaz and occupied his lands, Moses sent spies to Jazer where the surviving Amorites had settled. Armed with the spies' report, the Israelites were again victorious.

Moses was eventually succeeded by Joshua who resurrected the earlier plan to cross the Jordan and invade Canaan. Without ceremony he quietly sent two spies across the Jordan who infiltrated the strategically important fortified city of Jericho:

Then Joshua son of Nun secretly sent two spies from Shittim. 'Go look over the land,' he said, 'especially Jericho.' So they went and entered the house of a prostitute named Rahab and stayed there.[8]

Once lodged with Rahab, who was more likely the householder of an inn rather than a prostitute as the Bible reports,[9] things took a sharp turn for the worse. The two spies had come under suspicion since arriving in the city and had been reported to the king:

> The King of Jericho was told, 'Look! Some of the Israelites have come here tonight to spy out the land.' So the King of Jericho sent this message to Rahab: 'Bring out the men who came to you and entered your house, because they have come to spy out the whole land.'[10]

Luckily for the two spies, Rahab was extremely worried about the forthcoming war. She suspected it would go in favour of the Israelites and their seemingly omnipotent god. She took the spies up onto the roof of the house and hid them among stalks of flax she stored there. She then told the king's men that the Israelites had indeed been with her but had left around the time the city gates were closed after nightfall. Although she did not know where they were, she was sure that if they rode out of the city they would quickly catch up with them. The king's men rode off in the direction of the fords across the Jordan and the gates were closed behind them. Going up to the roof Rahab explained her motivation for helping the two enemy spies:

> 'I know that the Lord has given this land to you, and that a great fear has fallen on us, so that we who live in this country are melting in fear because of you. We have heard how the Lord dried up the water of the Red Sea for you when you came out of Egypt and what you did to Sihon and Og, the two kings of the Amorites east of the Jordan whom you completely destroyed.'[11]

She made a pact with the two spies. To help them escape they would arrange for her and her family to be spared when Jericho was captured. The spies gave her a scarlet thread to hang outside her window as a marker and promised no harm would come to those inside the house. In return, Rahab, whose house was built against the city wall, allowed the spies to climb out through a window and pass down a rope to safety. The two spies returned to Joshua who launched the invasion and destroyed Jericho after its walls collapsed. True to the spies' promise and by Joshua's command, the collaborator Rahab and her family were the only ones spared.

Joshua then planned the next stage of conquest, again sending out spies:

> Now Joshua sent men from Jericho to Ai, which is near Beth Aren to the east of Bethel, and told them 'Go up and spy out the region.' When they returned to Joshua, they said. 'Not all the people will have to go up against Ai. Send two or three thousand men to take it and do not weary all the people, for only a few men are there.' So about three thousand men went up; but they were routed by the men of Ai, who killed about thirty-six of them. They chased the Israelites from the city gate as far as the stone quarries and struck them down on the slopes. At this the hearts of the people melted and became like water.[12]

Having trusted the men he sent to spy on Ai, Joshua was severely embarrassed and his people afraid – he found a suitable scapegoat among the Israelites who was stoned to death. Joshua did not underestimate the men of Ai a second time. This time he attacked with 30,000 of his best troops, slaughtering all 12,000 of Ai's inhabitants before burning the city to the ground.

After Joshua's death the Israelites continued their fight against the Canaanites, putting Jerusalem to the sword and burning it. Continued fighting saw the conquest of city after city in what was called 'the hill country', but the Israelites were unable to conquer the plains because the people there were equipped with iron chariots. Instead they concentrated on the city of Bethel, with Israelite spies sent ahead to find a weakness. This they did by bribing an insider:

> The spies saw a man coming out of the city and they said to him, 'Show us how to get into the city and we will see that you are treated well.' So he showed them, and they put the city to the sword but spared the man and his whole family.[13]

The Bible also gives us the first female secret agent in recorded history – Delilah. To briefly recap the tale, Samson had been born to end the Philistines' suppression of the Israelites. He was enormously strong, so much so that he is said to have struck down a thousand men with the 'fresh jaw-bone of a donkey'. In another demonstration of his strength, Samson was discovered spending the night with a prostitute in the enemy city of Gaza. To avoid capture – or worse – he simply tore open the city gates with his bare hands and walked free. Unable to best this ultimate warrior, the Philistine rulers resorted to devious means to bring about Samson's downfall.

Their opportunity arose when Samson fell in love with a woman from the Valley of Sorek, named Delilah. The Philistine rulers went to solicit her aid, saying to her: 'See if you can lure him into showing you the secret of his great strength and how we can overpower him so that we may tie him up and subdue him. Each one of us will give you eleven hundred shekels of silver'.[14]

The result is well known: Delilah agreed and eventually teased out the secret of Samson's strength – his head had never been shaved and therein lay the root of his power. Delilah contacted the Philistines and, after Samson had fallen asleep on her lap, she called in a man who shaved off his seven braids of hair. Robbed of his strength, Samson was unable to resist capture by the Philistines, who gouged out his eyes and bound him with bronze shackles.

Female agents are also mentioned in the history of ancient China and a story survives from the end of China's 'Spring and Autumn period' (770–476 BC). The Chinese state of Wu had conquered neighbouring Yue and held captive its king, Gou Jian (ruled 496–465 BC). On his release, Gou Jian wanted revenge, but knew his country was not yet strong enough to fight Wu. Instead Gou Jian embarked on a carefully planned ruse to weaken the enemy Kingdom of Wu from within. He asked his prime minister to select ten of the most beautiful women he could find, two of whom would be sent to Wu's king Fu Chai (ruled 495–473 BC) as part of a tribute payment.

These two women would be no ordinary concubines, but highly trained and determined secret agents who were to encourage Fu Chai to expend his military resources making war on his neighbours and to alienate his skilful prime minister, Wu Zixu. Legend has it that the two candidates were Zheng Dan and Xi Shi – the latter a tea merchant's daughter who was first spotted picturesquely washing silk in a stream. For three years the women were trained in court etiquette and such entertainments as would keep the enemy king happily distracted from his responsibilities.

After bribing a corrupt Wu official, Xi Shi and Zheng Dan were introduced into Fu Chai's court. The king was so overcome at the sight of them that he ignored protocol and stood to greet them. The prime minister correctly suspected a plot and urged caution, but Fu Chai ignored him and greedily took the bait. He was besotted with the two women and soon forgot everything outside the sphere of his private chambers. Poisonous pillow talk began to weaken the standing of the prime minister, who, realizing he was the victim of elaborate subterfuge, doggedly tried to regain favour with his king. He denounced the two women but to no avail. Fu Chai grew weary of him and ordered the prime minister to commit suicide.

Without Wu Zixu's stewardship, the ungoverned country fell victim to famine. Spurred on by his two lovers, Fu Chai began a war with the neighbouring state of Qi. Seizing his chance, Gou Jian launched his long-awaited revenge attack on Wu, destroying its army in a nine-year war. At the end, Fu Chai had no option but to commit suicide, but not before he realized the two women were in fact enemy spies. He killed Zheng Dan, but Xi Shi escaped and passed into folklore as a self-sacrificing patriot and one of 'four beauties' who altered the course of Chinese history.[15]

In terms of espionage, ancient China is better known for the works of the philosopher-general Sun Tzû, who dedicated the thirteenth and final chapter of his *Art of War* to the use of spies. With the mantra 'all warfare is based on deception',[16] the theories Sun Tzû set down around 490 BC remain remarkably fresh and are required reading in intelligence agencies today.

Sun Tzû's argument for the employment of spies was based on economics. The cost of fielding an army was as enormous in ancient China as it is today. To march 100,000 men into enemy country would cost 1,000 ounces of silver a day. In addition, as many as 700,000 families would be so badly affected by the presence of an army that they would not be able to do their daily work, which would reduce tax revenues. If, through a lack of useful military intelligence, the commanding general was uncertain of the enemy's dispositions, then a war might be prolonged over several years, 'causing commotion at home and abroad'.

By finding the location, strength and intention of the enemy, spies sped wars up and thus, Sun Tzû argued, made them more humane. Considering the enormous sums of money saved by having a short war, coupled with the personal risks facing spies – almost certain death if captured – Sun Tzû declared that the payment of large sums to spies was both merited and essential. Someone who scrimped in this regard was making false economies: 'One who acts thus is no leader of men, no present help to his sovereign, no master of victory,'[17] Sun Tzû concluded.

Sun Tzû was adamant on the need for proper intelligence, or *foreknowledge* on the enemy:

> Thus what enables the wise sovereign and the good general to strike and conquer, and achieve things beyond the reach of ordinary men, is foreknowledge.
>
> Now this foreknowledge cannot be elicited from spirits; it cannot be obtained inductively from experience, not by any means of calculation.
>
> Knowledge of the enemy's disposition can only be obtained from other men.[18]

He identified five different classes of spy through which foreknowledge could be gained. It was through the simultaneous use of these different types of spies that one could achieve what he called 'the divine manipulation of the threads'. The five classes of spy included:

'**Local spies**' found among 'the inhabitants of a district'.

'**Inward spies**' found among 'officials of the enemy'. These included disaffected court officials with a grudge, such as grievance caused by a lack of promotion, or those in disgrace, not to mention those willing to co-operate for financial reward. There were also concubines, who for financial reward or out of jealousy might be convinced to betray an official. Sun Tzû urged the greatest caution in the employment of these 'inward spies' in case they were being used as a means for the enemy to plant false information.

'**Doomed spies**' were seen by Sun Tzû as an extreme yet effective means of deceiving an enemy. In this case an expendable spy was deliberately given false information. After being sent into the enemy camp, the spy was betrayed by his own side and hopefully captured. In an attempt to save his own skin, the spy would divulge the bogus information he believed true and, taking the bait, the enemy would make its plans accordingly.

Unfortunately, once the enemy realized the information given by the spy was false, he would almost certainly be put to death.

'**Surviving spies**' were those who were sent out and brought back news from behind enemy lines.

'**Converted spies**' were double agents. Sun Tzû considered these the most important type of spy as, in his opinion, they formed the key to all other espionage activities:

The enemy's spies who have come to spy on us must be sought out, tempted with bribes, led away and comfortably housed. Thus they will become converted spies and available for our service.

It is through the information brought by the converted spy that we are able to acquire and employ local and inward spies.

It is owing to his information, again that we can cause the doomed spy to carry false tidings to the enemy.

Lastly, it is by his information that the surviving spy can be used on appointed occasions.

The end and aim of spying in all its five varieties is knowledge of the enemy; and this knowledge can only be derived, in the first instance, from the converted spy.

Hence it is essential that the converted spy be treated with the utmost liberality.[19]

Lastly, Sun Tzû deals with the question of interpreting intelligence. History is littered with examples of people ignoring accurate intelligence gained through 'secret means', or, worse still, acting on uncorroborated, inaccurate reports. The fundamental skill of a spymaster is to know when to trust and when to doubt a spy. Sun Tzû placed the emphasis squarely on the assessor's own powers of judgement. The spymaster heeding Sun Tzû's advice must have a natural genius for the human character. He gave just two pieces of advice on the matter:

Spies cannot be usefully employed without a certain intuitive sagacity.[20]
Without subtle ingenuity of mind, one cannot make certain of the truth of their reports.[21]

Such intuitive gifts appear lacking in a contemporary of Sun Tzû – King Xerxes of Persia (ruled 485–465 BC). In 480 BC Xerxes was about to launch an invasion of Greece in revenge for his father's defeat at the battle of Marathon 12 years before. Having amassed an enormous army from across his gigantic empire, the 'Great King' thought he would simply trample the Greeks into submission. With an army drinking rivers dry – who needed spies?

Before Xerxes there was a long tradition of spying in Persia. The Greek historian Herodotus recorded that King Deioces (ruled 701–655 BC) had an extensive network of spies 'busy watching and listening in every corner of his dominions'. Cyrus the Great (ruled 559–530 BC) continued this practice, establishing a network of spies commonly known as the 'eyes and ears of the King'. According to Xenophon, Cyrus was a very astute user of spies. Having received some Indian emissaries, Cyrus asked some of them to spy on his Median enemies. Before their departure he revealed how much he valued intelligent spies:

> 'There are some spies who are no better than slaves, and have no skill to find out anything more than is known already, but there are men of another sort, men of your stamp, who can discover plans that are not yet disclosed.'[22]

When the Indian spies returned and made their report, Cyrus believed them because, according to Xenophon, it corresponded with information obtained from captured enemy soldiers. This cross-checking of evidence would have spared Joshua's blushes at Ai – not to mention countless others since who have trusted and acted on a single intelligence source. Cyrus was also – according to Xenophon – very fond of sending out spies in the guise of escaped slaves, a ruse also favoured by the Roman general Scipio Africanus.

Another example available to Xerxes would have been King Cambyses (ruled 530–522 BC), who conquered Egypt and was said to have sent spies into Ethiopia under the guise of emissaries bearing gifts. It was commonly assumed that official ambassadors were nothing but legal spies and the Ethiopian king played up to his audience, emphasizing his peoples' strength.

Xerxes, however, appears to have been more interested in the interpretation of his dreams than gaining hard intelligence on his enemy. According to Herodotus, Xerxes' decision to invade Greece came after he was visited by a reoccurring vision in his sleep. He did at least quiz

Demeratus, the exiled former Spartan king, about his countrymen. Even this backfired, as Demeratus sent a message home to Sparta warning that Xerxes was planning to invade Greece.

Herodotus claims Demeratus was acting out of spite by sending the message, but the elaborate measures taken to conceal the message by Demeratus suggest otherwise. Normally messages were written on wax-coated wooden tablets. To avoid his message being read, Demeratus scraped the wax off the tablet, wrote his message and then recoated the tablet with wax. The seemingly blank tablet arrived in Sparta, causing great puzzlement until Gorgo, the wife of King Leonidas, guessed there might be something hidden underneath the wax. This early warning gave the Greeks time to make preparations to meet the Persian invasion.

Although the Greeks placed enormous faith in the use of oracles and divination, they did not neglect to use human intelligence. As Xerxes prepared to invade, the alliance of Greek city states sent three spies into Asia to collect intelligence on the reputedly enormous Persian army. The historian Herodotus described how they were captured at Sardis while counting Xerxes' forces. Initially they were condemned to death, but Xerxes had other plans. He had the spies brought before him and then led round his camp where they were shown everything. They were then released and sent back to Greece unharmed. Xerxes is said to have explained his actions as follows:

> Had the spies been executed, the Greeks would not have been able to learn in good time how incalculately great the Persian strength was – and the killing of three men would not have done the enemy much harm; but if, on the other hand, the spies returned home, he was confident that their report on the magnitude of the Persian power would induce the Greeks to surrender their liberty before the actual invasion took place, so that there would be no need to go to the trouble of fighting a war at all.[23]

This attempt at psychological warfare failed and the Greeks decided to meet the Persian invasion at the strategically important pass of Thermopylae. When Xerxes arrived before the pass, he sent a spy to scout out the Greek position. In a reverse of Xerxes' ploy, the Spartan king Leonidas allowed the spy to see the Greek position, but *not* all the forces defending it:

The Persian rider approached the camp and took a thorough survey of all he could see – which was not, however, the whole Greek army; for the men on the further side of the wall, which, after its reconstruction, was now guarded, were out of sight. He did, none the less, carefully observe the troops who were stationed on the outside of the wall. At that moment these happened to be the Spartans, and some of them were stripped for exercise, while others were combing their hair. The Persian spy watched them in astonishment; nevertheless he made sure of their numbers, and of everything else he needed to know, as accurately as he could, and then rode quietly off.[24]

Xerxes was baffled by the spy's report and called on Demeratus to explain the Spartans' actions. He could not believe that the Spartans were really going to contest the pass. Demeratus explained that it was the Spartan custom to dress their hair before going into battle. Xerxes remained unconvinced and rested four more days, before on the fifth day, he grew impatient and ordered an attack.

The outcome of the ensuing battle has since passed into legend. Leonidas with his 300 Spartans and their Greek allies were able to hold the excellent defensive position at Thermopylae for three bloody days. They finally fell after being betrayed by Ephialtes, a fellow Greek who showed the Persians a track leading behind the Greek position. Although Leonidas and his men were slain, the battle is said to have cost the Persians as many as 30,000 men.

Almost a century after Xerxes' invasion the Athenian Xenophon took part in and recorded a Greek revenge attack on Persia, popularly known as the 'March of the 10,000'. Drawing on his experiences in war, Xenophon wrote 'The Cavalry General'. In it he warned generals to use spies cautiously and always in conjunction with cavalry scouts. The whole passage reads:

Before war commences your business is to provide yourself with a supply of people friendly to both states, or maybe merchants (since states are ready to receive the importer of goods with open arms); sham deserters may be found occasionally useful. Not, of course, that the confidence you feel in your spies must ever cause you to neglect outpost duty; indeed your state of preparation should at any moment be precisely what it ought to be, supposing the approach or the imminent arrival of the enemy were to be announced. Let a spy be ever so faithful, there is always the risk he may fail to report his intelligence at the critical moment, since the obstacles which present themselves in war are not to be counted on the fingers.[25]

Xenophon correctly identified one of the main problems facing a spy – the communication of secret information. We have seen how Demeratus sent a secret message to the Spartans, but Herodotus also gives us the example of Histaiaeus, who wanted to encourage Aristagoras of Miletus to revolt against the Persian king. In order to securely convey his plan, Histaiaeus shaved the head of his messenger, wrote (or perhaps tattooed) the message on his scalp, then waited for the hair to grow back. The messenger, apparently carrying nothing contentious, could travel freely. Arriving at his destination, he shaved his head and revealed the message. It was an ingenious system no doubt, but impractical for urgent messages.

With the transmission of messages came their interception and censorship. Alexander the Great (356–323 BC) is said to be the first to use postal censorship, opening his soldiers' mail during the siege of Halicarnassus in 334 BC. The siege had turned out to be more difficult than anticipated and as it dragged on morale among Alexander's troops began to dip. To raise spirits, Alexander allowed his men the unusual privilege of writing home to their families. Unknown to his men, Alexander had the messages scrutinized before they were sent back to Macedonia. All those who had questioned Alexander in their letters were sent back home before they could cause trouble.

Seven years later, when Alexander passed through the Hindu-Kush, he came into contact with the ancient civilizations of India. Unlike Sun Tzû, who drew a distinct line between intelligence gathering and the use of divination or spells to forecast an enemy's intentions, the Indians relied on a heady mix of spells, poison and devious chicanery to illicit secret information. The classic texts of ancient India are full of references to espionage, indicating it was carried out in an organized manner as early as 7000 BC, if not before.[26]

In the Vedic era (1200–500 BC), espionage appears to have been the sole preserve of the priestly Brahman caste, with Varuna, the all-knowing god, in charge among spies: 'Varuna's spies, sent forth upon their errand, survey the two world-halves well formed and fashioned.

Wise are they, holy, skilled in sacrifices, the furtherers of the praise-songs of the prudent.'[27] The reason for using priests was simple – they were both literate and trusted.

Later spies were drawn from every class and level of society and all were considered 'the eyes of the king' both at home and abroad. The great Hindu epic the *Mahabharata* offers the following instructions for kings on espionage, all of which are recurring themes in Indian sacred literature:

> He [the king] should employ as spies men looking like idiots or like those that are blind and deaf. Those should all be persons who have been thoroughly examined (in respect of their ability), who are possessed of wisdom, and who are able to endure hunger and thirst. With proper attention, the king should set his spies upon all his counsellors and friends and sons, in his city and the provinces, and in dominions of the chiefs under him. His spies should be so employed that they may not know one another. He should also … know the spies of his foes by himself setting spies in shops and places of amusements, and concourses of people, among beggars, in his pleasure gardens and parks, in meetings and conclaves of the learned, in the country, in public places, in places where he holds his own court, and in the houses of the citizens. The king possessed of intelligence may thus ascertain the spies despatched by his foes. If these were known, the king may derive much benefit.[28]

Spies should also be sent abroad, according to another part of the *Mahabharata* – the *Sambhava Parva*:

> After testing their faithfulness thou shouldst employ spies in thy own kingdom and in the kingdoms of others. Thy spies in foreign kingdoms should be apt deceivers and persons in the garb of ascetics.[29]

Many of these ancient principles were codified some time shortly after Alexander the Great's incursion into the subcontinent in the *Arthasástra*, a guide to kingship.[30] Written, or at least compiled by Kautilya (sometimes referred to as Chanakya or Visnugupta), the *Arthasástra* covers almost every eventuality in the employment and usage of spies, both as a method of internal policing and as a potent weapon in war. In places it reads as an assassination manual, providing a lethal menu of poisons and the method of their concoction.

Most importantly, the *Arthasástra* counselled kings to properly qualify intelligence reports before acting on them. When a report was received from a spy, the officers of the institutes of espionage (the *samsthánámantevásinah*) would send out other spies to verify the information provided. When the same information was received from three independent sources, it could be held as reliable, not before. If on the other hand the three sources differed wildly, the spies concerned were to be secretly punished or dismissed.

Kautilya divided agents into two distinct groups: The first were 'institutes of espionage' (*samstháh*), permanent spies financed by the state and formed to 'ascertain the purity of character of the king's servants.' The *sancaras*, on the other hand, were 'wandering spies' who moved around the country depending on operational needs. Neither of the two groups were aware of the other's existence.[31]

The samstháh consisted of five branches, including 'a fraudulent disciple', someone skilled at guessing the minds of others and on the watch for whatever wickedness he or she could find, and 'the recluse', someone initiated in asceticism and possessed of 'foresight and pure character'. The recluse was provided with money, disciples and land allotted for cattle rearing and agriculture, the proceeds from which would fund a network of sub-agents under his control. His particular focus was on crimes committed against the king's wealth. 'The householder' was chosen from a cultivator 'fallen from his profession'. In the same way as the recluse, the householder would receive an allocation of lands through which he would fund other cultivators who would work as agents. 'A merchant' formed the fourth institute and followed the same model.

The last branch of the samstháh was a spy living under the guise of 'an ascetic practising austerities'. Disguised with shaven or braided hair and surrounded by a host of disciples, this spy would take up residence in the suburbs of a city 'and pretend as a person barely living on a handful of vegetables or meadow grass taken once in the interval of a month or two,' although in secret the spy could eat as he fancied. Merchant spies would join in on the act and worship him as one possessed of 'preternatural powers'. This would encourage people to throng to him so that they would explain away their innermost secrets while their futures were foretold through palmistry. From the information gleaned by such spies, the king would better understand 'whether there prevails content or discontent among those who live upon the grains, cattle, and gold of the king'.

The 'wandering spies' were in general 'of good family, loyal, reliable, well trained in the art of putting on disguises appropriate to countries and trades, and possessed of knowledge of many languages and arts'. Their principal aim was to spy on the movements of the king's ministers, priests, generals, senior officials and, of course, his heirs.

There were four categories of wandering spy. There were the 'class-mates' – orphans brought up by the state and put to the study of science, palmistry, sorcery, the duties of the various orders of religious life, sleight of hand, the reading of omens and augury. Then there were the poisoners, selected from among those 'who have no trace of filial affection left in them and who are very cruel and indolent'. A *bhikshuki* (mendicant woman) was a poor widow from the religious Brahman caste, very clever and wanting to earn her livelihood as a female ascetic. Such women were highly honoured in the king's harem and would also frequent the residences of the king's prime ministers, thus making them very well placed.

The most dynamic of the wandering spies, were the *tíkshna* (lit. firebrands) or fiery spies. The tíkshna were described as 'such brave desperados of the country who, reckless of their own life, confront elephants or tigers in fight mainly for the purpose of earning money'. When not picking fights with wild animals, fiery spies could be trusted to accomplish tricky assassinations with 'weapons, poison, and other means'. A favourite lure was to make an appointment for the victim with a harlot, or dancing girl, in some secret house where the spy would be able to hide in underground chambers or secret wall compartments. When the unsuspecting lover arrived, the fiery spy would be waiting to make the kill or abduct him.

In ancient India spies also played the role of saboteurs in wartime. In case of invasion, spies were to carry the fight behind enemy lines, maintaining their disguises and falling into the rear of the enemy as it advanced. Disguised as vintners, spies were to generously distribute liquor mixed with the poisonous juice of the madana plant to enemy soldiers. Spies disguised as food vendors were to vie with each other in proclaiming the excellence of their produce, which was of course poisoned. Spies dressed as servants would sell poisoned grass and water to cripple the enemy horses and elephants. Spies disguised as cowherds were to release such animals that would attack horses, mules, camels and buffaloes, having smeared the eyes of those animals with the blood of a musk-rat. Huntsmen spies were to release 'cruel beasts' out of traps, while snake-charmer spies were to release highly poisonous snakes into the midst of the enemy army. More orthodox methods of subversion included the destruction of stores and crops, burning enemy camps and assassinating enemy generals.

In addition to these acts of guerrilla warfare, spies were seen as an important psychological weapon against enemy morale. To demonstrate their association with the gods, kings were encouraged to visit a temple and publicly hold conversations with the gods, whose voices would be played by hidden spies. For example, a tunnel would be made so a spy could safely crawl into the centre of a sacred fire, then seemingly appear out of the flames and address the ruler as the 'voice' of the god. Other spies hid underwater with primitive breathing apparatus made from animal intestines. They would release burning oil into the water and then suddenly appear themselves, imitating the gods and goddesses of Nágas (snakes). To add to the magical effect they could release smoke from the mouths of their costumes and smear their bodies with special burning oils that did not harm their skin. They were to pose, sharpening their iron swords or spikes, shouting 'We are going to eat the flesh of the king.'

Spies, wearing the skins of bears were to pose as demons, pacing up and down outside an enemy city with smoke pouring out of their mouths, filling the air with 'the horrid noise of antelopes and jackals'. Other spies were to arrange for blood to pour from the statues of gods in temples outside the cities. Anyone coming out to look at the miraculous sight was to be 'beaten to death by others with rods, making the people believe that he was killed by demons'. Even the enemy king was to be duped by spies disguised as soothsayers and astrologers who, having lured him into a private place to hear their predictions, would have him beaten to death by hidden assassins.

Before the arrival of the besieging army, spies disguised as priests would appear before the enemy city blowing their conch shells and beating their drums, proclaiming that a powerful army was coming close behind them. It was hoped that this sudden revelation would be enough to make the enemy army disperse, or at least give up key gates and towers.

Once a siege had begun it was assumed that the king would have spies disguised inside an enemy city. Prior to the siege these would have been sent weapons hidden in the carts of agriculturalists and merchants. Once so armed, the spies in the city were to look for opportunities to support the besieging force outside. They were encouraged to cause fires by tying 'inflammable powder' to the tails of mongooses, monkeys, cats and dogs, which were then sent to pass over the thatched roofs of the houses. Alternatively a 'splinter of fire' could be kept burning in the body of a dried fish that was given to a monkey or a crow, which would go up onto the roofs to eat its meal. Once the animal discovered its food was on fire, it would naturally drop the burning fish, which would fall down onto the thatch.[32]

The ancient Indians perfected the use of female spies and agents, utilizing the glaringly obvious fact that through the lure of sex even the most powerful of men were vulnerable. In particular, women were at the forefront of counter-espionage operations. Foreign spies were known to frequent liquor bars, so, operating in the guise of actresses, female spies skilled in linguistics would seek them out, get them drunk and murder them. Poison was the weapon of choice for female spies and there were a number of ingenious methods of delivery. Women posing as food vendors could cause havoc to an enemy army by selling poisoned food, while others stationed in a harem could blow a poisonous powder over a sleeping man, or, less subtly, throw a poisonous snake at him.

Perhaps the most cunning means of delivering a poison was the use of *vishakanyas* or 'poisonous damsels'.[33] The vishakanyas were female courtesans who from early childhood were given doses of poisonous herbs or the venom of snakes and scorpions. By the time they reached adolescence, although they themselves had become immunized, they were deadly poisonous to those who had contact with them – especially intimate contact. As with the legendary Sumerian female demon Succuba, to whom they have been compared, a night of passion with a vishakanya was likely to be fatal.

We also know that the practice of enciphering messages was known in India at this time. We have seen several examples in Herodotus where messages were concealed, but enciphered messages have a big advantage. Even if the message is intercepted, its true meaning is not to be revealed. Writing in code appears to be something practised by women, for the *Arthasástra* mentions that female spies (the mendicant women) were to use 'secret messages' to send intelligence reports back to their controllers. Even the *Kama Sutra*, which was written about 500 BC, says that women should be skilled in 'the art of understanding writing in cypher', although it must be said that this was primarily to maintain a veil of secrecy over their love affairs.[34]

Departing India, it is perhaps fitting to conclude our journey through ancient times with the case of Judas – the man whose name is still synonymous with treachery and betrayal 2,000 years after his passing. In the Christian calendar, the Wednesday before Easter Sunday was traditionally known in England and Ireland as 'Spy Wednesday'. This was the day that Judas Iscariot agreed to betray Jesus.

According to the Gospel of John, as Jesus' popularity increased, the Jewish authorities began to view him with increased suspicion. In Luke's Gospel the 'teachers of law and the chief priests' started looking for an excuse to arrest Jesus and sent spies to entrap him. Hoping that Jesus might say something against the Romans and give them an excuse to hand him over to the governor as a troublemaker, the spies asked Jesus to comment on the conflict of interest between following 'the way of God' and paying taxes to the Romans. Realizing that the question was a set up, Jesus thwarted the spies. He asked them to show him a Roman coin and asked the spies whose portrait was on the back of it? 'Caesar's,' replied the spies. 'Then give to Caesar what is Caesar's, and to God what is God's.'[35]

To assess the potential threat of this 'Messiah', a meeting of the Sanhedrin was called – the Jewish 'Great Council' with jurisdiction over religious matters. The chief priests were worried that Jesus' increasing popularity might result in a Roman clampdown on the Jewish nation. Therefore Caiaphas, the high priest, concluded it would be better to get rid of Jesus quietly than to risk conflict with Rome.

Hearing of the plot against him, Jesus went to ground, withdrawing with his disciples to a village called Ephraim on the edge of the desert. As the time for the Jewish Passover approached, people began to gather in Jerusalem for their ceremonial cleansing, and the speculation on Jesus' whereabouts began to gather momentum. The chief priest ordered anyone knowing the location of Jesus to report it so he could be arrested. Privately, though, Caiaphas was concerned that if Jesus was arrested publicly during the feast, he would have a riot on his hands. He needed what Matthew called 'some sly way' to arrest Jesus and have him killed.[36] This 'sly way' presented itself when Judas came forward and offered to betray Jesus. From that point on, albeit only briefly, Judas became a secret agent of the high priests, an 'inward spy', to use Sun Tzû's definitions. But why did he do it?

Six days before Passover, Jesus arrived at Bethany. While staying at the house of Simon the Leper, Jesus was anointed by a woman with an expensive perfume. Matthew records an argument that broke out over the perfume: 'When the disciples saw this, they were indignant. "Why this waste?" they asked. "This perfume could have been sold at a high price and the money given to the poor."'[37] The Gospel of John is more specific on this item of discord. According to John 'Mary' (most presume Mary Magdalene) took 'an expensive perfume; she poured it over Jesus' feet and wiped his feet with her hair. And the house was filled with the fragrance of the perfume. But one of his disciples, Judas Iscariot, objected, "Why wasn't this perfume sold and the money given to the poor? It was worth a year's wages." He did not say this because he cared about the poor but because he was a thief; as keeper of the money bag, he used to help himself to what was put into it...'[38]

Judas illustrates a motive common among spies: greed. We perhaps can take Luke's description of Satan entering Judas as a metaphor for his succumbing to avarice, rather than actual demonic possession. Bypassing any theological implications, the next event recorded by Matthew was when Judas 'went to the chief priests and asked, "What are you willing to give me if I hand him over to you?" So they counted out for him thirty silver coins. From then on Judas watched for an opportunity to hand him over.'[39]

The actual betrayal took place on the Mount of Olives at a place called Gethsemane. Judas knew Jesus often met there with his disciples and it was a quiet place where there would be few witnesses. At night, after Jesus and his disciples had taken supper together, they went to Gethsemane. While Jesus was talking with his followers Judas led a detachment of temple officials and guards carrying lanterns, swords and clubs. To identify Jesus from the others, Judas had a prearranged signal – he would walk up to Jesus and say 'Greetings, Rabbi!', then kiss him. All this went according to plan, except for a brief scuffle when Jesus' supporters drew swords and Simon cut off the right ear of a servant to the high priest. Jesus was led away for trial and crucifixion. As for Judas – like many who betray their own – he was overcome by remorse. We are told he later hanged himself.[40]

2

THROUGH DARK AGES

'Beware the ides of March'

From Shakespeare's *Julius Caesar* (I, ii, 33)
The one intelligence report Caesar ignored

Having seen the extent of espionage in ancient times, it should be no surprise to find further examples in Roman history. From the 3rd century BC, when Rome began to expand its hegemony over the Italian peninsula, there are many incidents of espionage and the use of secret agents. For instance, Consul Quintus Fabius Maximus sent his brother – an apparent master of disguise and fluent in Etruscan – on a secret mission to win support for the Roman cause. Disguised as an Etruscan peasant, he is said to have gained access to areas Roman agents had previously failed to penetrate.

Spies also helped bring about a quick end to the siege of Nequinium in 299 BC. According to Livy, two townsmen whose houses adjoined the city wall made a tunnel through which they deserted to the Roman outposts. They offered to conduct a detachment of Roman soldiers through the tunnel, thus placing them inside the town wall. The Romans were suspicious of the offer and so, keeping one of townsmen as a hostage, the other led two Roman spies into the city. The spies made a short reconnaissance and returned with a favourable verdict. Three hundred soldiers were sent through the tunnel at night and seized the nearest gate. Once it fell the remainder of the Roman army raced in and the city surrendered.[1]

Rome's first major brush with espionage took place during the Second Punic War (218–201 BC) when the Carthaginian Hannibal (*c.*247–183 BC) invaded Rome from across the Alps. Carthaginian spies were at large and working across Italy and even inside Rome.

Evidence of this is found in Livy, who recorded that 'a Carthaginian spy who for two years had escaped detection was caught in Rome, and after both his hands were cut off, he was sent away.'[2]

With Hannibal still in Italy, in 204 BC Rome sent an expeditionary force to North Africa under the command of 32-year-old Publius Cornelius Scipio (235–183 BC), later dubbed 'Africanus' for his exploits. Scipio landed in North Africa with 20,000 men but quickly found himself up against an army of 90,000. While the Carthaginians gathered in two camps, Scipio built a secure base named Castra Cornelia. From there he devised a plan to destroy the numerically superior enemy.

From the evidence, we can see that Scipio valued spies and the information they brought from the enemy camps. The historian Polybius reveals how Scipio Africanus debriefed his agents returning from the enemy camps during the night, when his own camp was quiet:

> it is the custom among the Romans at supper-time for the trumpeters and buglers to sound their instruments outside the general's tent as a signal that it is time to set the night-watches at their several stations. After this, calling the spies whom he used to send to the enemy's camps, he questioned them closely and compared the accounts they gave of the approaches and entrances of the camps...[3]

While appearing eager to negotiate with the Carthaginians, Scipio staged an ingenious ruse. Envoys were sent to meet with enemy commanders Hasdrubal and Syphax, but Roman centurions went along disguised as camp servants and slaves. On one such visit the Roman spies deliberately let a horse loose and ineptly gave chase to it round the Carthaginian camp, no doubt to the amusement of watching enemy soldiers. However, while giving chase, the Romans were carefully noting the layout and construction of the camp. Livy explains how similar missions were carried out:

> Whilst the envoys were in conference these men strolled about the camp noting all the adits and exits, the general arrangement of the camp, the positions of the Carthaginians and Numidians, respectively, and the distance between Hasdrubal's camp and that of Syphax. They also watched the methods adopted in posting the watches and guards, to see whether a surprise attack would be better made by night or by

day. The conferences were pretty frequent, and different men were purposely sent each time in order that these details might become known to a larger number.[4]

On one occasion the plan nearly backfired when Scipio's envoy, Gaius Laelius, went to meet with the Numidian prince Syphax. One of the Numidians thought he recognized a disguised centurion, Lucius Statorius, from a time they had been in Greece together. To prove he was mistaken, a quick-thinking Laelius had the impudent 'slave' flogged for daring to carry himself like a Roman. Statorius humbly submitted to the punishment, something the watching Numidians thought a Roman centurion would never have allowed.

Having gained detailed intelligence, Scipio was able to make his move. The Carthaginian camps were almost wholly built of wood. The Numidians had constructed huts made from wattled reeds roofed with grass matting. Breaking off negotiations suddenly, the Romans launched a horrifying night attack, setting both enemy camps on fire. In one night 40,000 men either burned to death or were put to the sword.

In 203 BC Hannibal was recalled from Italy to deal with Scipio. As was his habit, Hannibal sent out spies, hoping to find out where the Romans were encamped and how their camp was set up. These spies were caught and brought before Scipio who, rather than punishing them, decided they could perform him a useful service. He ordered a tribune to show them the camp and point out clearly its exact arrangements. After this had been done Scipio asked the spies if the tribune had explained everything to their satisfaction. When they answered that he had done so, Scipio furnished them with provisions and an escort and told them to report carefully to Hannibal everything they had seen. On hearing the spies' report, Hannibal was pleased to learn that the Romans were very weak in cavalry. He decided to give battle. What the spies had not learned was that Scipio was expecting a reinforcement of 6,000 horse within two days. The two armies met at the battle of Zama and Hannibal was heavily defeated, in large part due to Scipio's superiority in cavalry.

Victory against Carthage set Rome as the dominant power in the Mediterranean and to some extent its empire grew faster than its bureaucracy could develop. This was especially the case with regard to an official secret service, something republican Rome lacked entirely. We have seen how in previous empires, Persia for instance, the king had governed with the benefit of wide-ranging and powerful intelligence services – the 'eyes and ears of the king'. These services had developed around autocratic figures in whom all information was centred – and this was Rome's problem. In those formative years of empire, Rome was a republic and governed by its Senate. There was no single autocrat under whom a secret service could be built. The only intelligence networks were really the private enterprises of individual politicians or generals. As the fortunes of these individuals waxed and waned, so their spy networks came and went. Another problem was one of public image. Unlike India, where espionage was acknowledged as a vital tool of statecraft, the use of spies was viewed as an affront to the noble ideal of being a Roman. Conveniently ignoring Scipio's antics in North Africa, Rome, they said, won its battles fair and square.

In truth, by the 1st century BC Rome was rotten to the core. The arch exponent of its corruption was Marcus Licinius Crassus (c.115–53 BC), a businessman who had gained his reputation by crushing the Spartacus slave revolt in 71 BC. Crassus set up an enormous network of spies focused primarily on gathering economic intelligence. Crassus was the richest man in Rome, if not the empire, because he heard news first and thus reacted fastest. He made his fortune in real estate, slaves and perhaps the most dubious fire-fighting service in history – it would only put out a fire if the owner of the property first agreed to sell the building to Crassus at a much reduced rate.

Backed by his financial might (he was nicknamed 'The Rich') Crassus entered the political arena, becoming consul with Pompey in 70 BC. In 59 BC the two were joined by Julius Caesar (100–44 BC) and formed the famous First Triumvirate, which ruled Rome virtually unopposed. In 55 BC Crassus again shared the consulship with Pompey and looked for military glory when he was appointed governor of Syria. In a campaign against the Parthians, Crassus took on more than he could manage and was completely routed at the battle of Carrhae in 53 BC. Killed by the Parthians, there is a tradition that on receiving Crassus' body, the Parthian king had molten gold poured down his throat as a punishment for his greed.

Crassus' partner Julius Caesar was another exponent of intelligence gathering and spy craft. To complement the interrogation of prisoners and local people, during his campaigns in Gaul he employed a variety of scouts. The *procursatores* were uniformed scouts positioned immediately in front of the army on the march, while the *exploratores* were longer-range, mounted military scouts. For deeper penetration and for spying missions, at least ten *speculatores* were attached to each Roman legion. The speculatores were elite scouts who could often speak Gallic and would make use of disguises. They were also known to use codes and ciphers to protect secret information. In each case Caesar was insistent that the commanders of scouting missions had direct access to him so he personally was kept abreast of the latest reports.

Caesar's successor, Augustus (ruled 31 BC–AD 14), made valuable progress in the dissemination of reports and intelligence. Like the Persians before him he added a state-run messenger service – the *cursus publicus*. Now at least there was an official means for Rome to communicate with the extremities of its growing empire. The couriers were often drawn from the army, in particular speculatores who were used on special missions.

In the imperial period very few Roman emperors died of natural causes, with the vast majority falling victim to assassination. This situation created a certain amount of paranoia and turned the focus of espionage activity towards potential enemies within, rather than those outside, the boundaries of empire. The emperors' principal means of information were *delatores* – informers – with soldiers of the Praetorian Guard acting as undercover agents to arrest traitors and other suspects.

Out of the collective paranoia also developed a form of secret police known as the *frumentarii*. This organization was originally formed during the reign of Emperor Domitian (ruled AD 81–96) out of non-commissioned officers and centurions who were primarily responsible for the purchasing of grain (*frumentum*) for the individual legions. Drawn from each of the Roman legions for 'special duty', the frumentarii were quartered at the Castra Peregrinorum on Rome's Caelian Hill. They were commanded by the *princeps peregrinorum*, a senior centurion directly responsible to the emperor.

The frumentarii first worked as tax collectors and couriers, and were also responsible for regulating the city of Rome's grain supply. Under the reign of Emperor Hadrian (ruled 117–138), who halted the expansion of the Roman Empire and began to look inward instead, the frumentarii developed their reputation as a form of secret police force.

There were an estimated 200 frumentarii operating at any one time.[5] Unlike typical secret policemen, the frumentarii were quite open about their existence and even wore a special uniform marking them out as such. Under Hadrian they were put to work as spies against the imperial court. By the late 2nd and early 3rd centuries they were closely watching generals, senators and Christian dissidents. Through tax collection and arrests, by the end of the 3rd century the frumentarii were universally despised around the empire. It is not beyond reasonable doubt to suspect that some were corrupt and very much a law unto themselves. On the other hand, the frumentarii may not have always been the brightest. Apparently a Christian named Dionysius was being hunted by the frumentarii, but escaped because they didn't think of searching his home, where he hid for four days.[6]

Because of the abuses, Emperor Diocletian (ruled 284–305) disbanded the frumentarii, but was not so naive as to leave Rome without a replacement. Instead he used *agentes in rebus* (general agents), the only major change being that these agents were from civilian not military backgrounds. The general agents were much more numerous than the frumentarii had been, and their corps included on occasion about 1,200 men. Despite the change, the abuses continued, but the agentes in rebus continued to function as late as 700 in the Byzantine Empire.

As the Roman Empire broke apart in Western Europe, it continued relatively unchanged in the East. The capital of the Eastern Empire was Byzantium, which was also known as Constantinople after its founder, Constantine, the first Christian emperor of Rome. Although the Byzantines in fact spoke Greek, they considered themselves every bit as Roman as their Latin counterparts, perhaps even more so after the last Western Roman emperor, Romulus Augustulus, was deposed in 476 by the Hun chieftain Odacer.

Into this confused age came Byzantine emperor Justinian (ruled 527–565), who is most famous for his legal codes, which had a profound effect on the development of European laws during the Middle Ages. The primary historical source for the Justinian era is Procopius (c.500–560s). Some time around 550, after writing several 'official' histories of the period, he set down an altogether different version of events in *The Secret History of the Court of Justinian*. A veritable feast of sex-scandals and intrigue, *The Secret History* was only published posthumously, and for centuries blushing historians shied away from translating some of its more risqué passages. Procopius said of it:

You see, it was not possible, during the life of certain persons, to write the truth of what they did, as a historian should. If I had, their hordes of spies would have found out about it, and they would have put me to a most horrible death.

Explaining how they were neglected in Justinian's time, Procopius reveals something of the role performed by the frumentarii and agentes in rebus. In order that they might quickly be informed of enemy invasions, uprisings or any other unexpected troubles, Roman emperors had maintained a system of public couriers. Procopius explained how these couriers brought in news of the actions of governors and other citizens and ensured that the annual taxes were brought in without delay or danger. He described how the couriers would travel a series of stages (normally five to eight stages per day) with fresh horses kept at each stage post. With the best mounts made available to them, the Roman couriers were able to travel up to ten times faster than was considered the norm.

Justinian, so Procopius claims, did away with many of the stage posts and in some regions forced the couriers to make their journeys by sea in small boats – no matter how severe the weather. Although the staging posts along the road to Persia were maintained, those elsewhere in the East as far as Egypt were so reduced that only one could be reached in a day's travel. Instead of finding horses at these posts, couriers were met by slow-moving asses. Consequently, news from the most distant parts of the empire travelled very slowly and often arrived too late after the event to be of any use.

Justinian also made cuts in the hiring of spies. As emperor he inherited a long-established system dating back to the time of the Medes, which Procopius describes as follows:

The spies were organized as follows. Many men were formerly supported by the treasury, who visited the enemy, especially the Persian court, to find out exactly what was going on; on their return to Roman territory, they were able to report to the Emperors the secrets of the enemy. And the Romans, being warned, were on guard and could not be taken by surprise.[7]

However, Justinian did away with 'the practice of hiring Roman spies, and in consequence lost much territory to the enemy'. On the other hand, his empress, Theodora excelled herself in their employment. Theodora is an interesting case. Whereas her eldest sister, Comito, was one of the leading *hetaerae* (courtesans) of the day, and as well versed in music and poetry as in the carnal arts, Theodora lacked any such sophistication. By all accounts she was nothing but a common prostitute. According to Procopius' sensational indictments, she gained a reputation for appearing in bawdy comedies or performing lewd, exotic dances. For example, her show-stopper was to have slaves scatter grains of barley over her naked body then unleash specially trained geese to peck her clean.[8]

Despite her deserved reputation, or perhaps even because of it, Justinian fell deeply in love with Theodora, changed the law so that he might marry her and even began a tradition of Byzantine emperors marrying commoners. Needless to say, once made empress in 523, Theodora became sensitive to references to her early life, so much so that she kept a large retinue of spies to inform her of those gossiping against her. Procopius' *Secret History* records some of her more notable victims, but also summarized her general method of dealing with dissenters in the following way:

> No other tyrant since mankind began ever inspired such fear, since not a word could be spoken against her without her hearing of it: her multitude of spies brought her the news of whatever was said and done in public or in private. And when she decided the time had come to take vengeance on any offender, she did as follows. Summoning the man, if he happened to be notable, she would privately hand him over to one of her confidential attendants, and order that he be escorted to the farthest boundary of the Roman realm. And her agent, in the dead of night, covering the victim's face with a hood and binding him, would put him on board a ship and accompany him to the place selected by Theodora. There he would secretly leave the unfortunate in charge of another qualified for this work: charging him to keep the prisoner under guard and tell no one of the matter until the Empress should take pity on the wretch or, as time went on, he should languish under his bondage and succumb to death.[9]

In the centuries after Justinian's passing, the emperors of Byzantium appear to have resurrected the secret services to some degree. This change was made in view of an ongoing conflict with the emerging forces of Islam. For example, in the 8th century, Anastasius was forewarned of a siege, which allowed him to improve Constantinople's already formidable defences and fill the granaries before the Saracen siege was put in place. With fast-moving Saracens making frequent raids into the Empire, Emperor Nicephorus II Phocas (ruled 963–969), was well aware of the need to act speedily on intelligence received, writing the instruction: 'Never turn away freeman or slave, by day or night, though you may be sleeping or eating or bathing, if he says that he has news for you.'[10]

In the early days of conflict with the Muslims, there is a well-known account of the Byzantines using Christian Arabs as spies. Shortly before the siege of Damascus in 634, a Roman commander named Qulbuqlar sent a Christian Arab to spy on the Muslim camp and assess the quality of their army. Being an ethnic Arab, the spy had no trouble passing through the camp unnoticed. According to Muslim accounts the spy came back with disheartening news for Qulbuqlar: 'By night they are like monks, by day like warriors. If the son of their ruler were to commit theft, they would cut off his hand; and if he were to commit adultery, they would stone him to death. Thus they establish righteousness among themselves.' The Byzantine general replied to his spy: 'If what you say be true it would be better to be in the belly of the earth than to meet such a people upon its surface.'[11]

Emperor Leo VI (ruled 886–912), who considered the Saracens to be the most formidable enemy of the Eastern Empire, wrote an instruction for his generals known simply as *Tactica*. In this he recommended his generals use every stratagem or ambush possible to gain an advantage over their adversaries, in particular sending negotiators over to the enemy with no other object but to spy on their armies.[12]

It is also interesting to note how Leo VI considered Frankish knights to be utterly hopeless when it came to setting outposts and reconnaissances. This is perhaps a little unfair, as spies were certainly known to the great Frankish leaders, Clovis and Charlemagne. We also have positive evidence of their employment in the aftermath of the battle of Tours in 732, the pivotal battle that halted the Islamic conquest of Western Europe. According to the *Chronicle* of Isidore of Beja, the morning after the battle the Franks saw the tents of the Muslim camp had not been struck. Expecting another battle, the Franks sent forward spies to discover what the Saracens were preparing to do. They were astonished when the spies reported that the camp was empty and the Saracens had retreated under the cover of night. Wary of falling into a trap, the Franks sent scouts everywhere but found no trace of the enemy army.

The Muslim armies had a long history of using spies themselves, dating back to the time of Muhammad. Not long after the time of Procopius, the Prophet Muhammad was born in 570 at Mecca in Arabia. Working as a trader, Muhammad married at the age of 25 and went on to develop an interest in spiritual matters. In 610 he had his first revelation, in which it is said the Archangel Gabriel revealed he was to be a prophet. The revelations increased over a number of years before Muhammad proclaimed he would be the last in a number of prophets, including Adam, Noah, Abraham, Moses and Jesus. Equally the text of the Koran was proclaimed the last Book of God.

Over the next decade, Muhammad preached his views, which did not seem to go down too well with the majority of his fellow Meccans. Through informants, in 622 Muhammad learned of a secret plot to murder him and so was able to plan his escape to the northern town of Yathrib (Medina) where 70 of his followers had settled in advance. When the plotters arrived at Muhammad's home they found his cousin Ali had taken his place in bed. The angry Meccans set off in pursuit, but were unable to find the prophet who had taken refuge in a cave. Eventually Muhammad escaped and reached Yathrib where he resumed his teachings.

In 624 Muhammad and his supporters went to war with the Meccans. Muhammad's spies informed him that a rich caravan en route to Mecca was his for the taking. Unbeknown to Muhammad, the caravan realized it had been spotted and so sent to Mecca for reinforcements. Luckily for Muhammad, his spies then caught two Meccan soldiers and brought them in for interrogation. The two soldiers confirmed an army of 950 soldiers was fast approaching the Muslim position. Forewarned, Muhammad led his numerically weaker army to a position in a valley from where they controlled the water reservoirs. Despite odds of three to one, the Muslims routed the Meccans at the ensuing battle of Badr, giving Muhammad his first victory. Undaunted, the Meccans returned a year later with a much larger force. At the battle of Uhud the Muslims were driven back and Muhammad wounded, but they still clung on in Medina. Two years later, at the so-called battle of the Trench, the Meccans were roundly defeated and Islam was firmly established in Arabia.

Muhammad's sights now turned to the capture of Mecca itself. This was achieved in 630, largely due to several years of intelligence gathering and infiltration, beginning with the sending of an ambassador named Othman. Despite a rumour that Othman had been murdered, he returned to Muhammad with a representative from Mecca who negotiated a treaty. While protected by the treaty Muhammad managed to infiltrate Mecca with many of his followers, forming what became an effective fifth column inside the city.

Dating from the time of the battle of Badr there is an interesting tale of ten spies recalled by the Islamic traditionalist, Al-Bukhari (810–870). It suggests no disgrace or contempt was attached to those who spied in the service of Islam and portrays them as heroic and as deserving of praise as any foot soldier.

According to the story, Muhammad sent out ten spies under the command of Asim. Although their exact mission is unrecorded, we know they journeyed to Had'a where their presence was reported to a branch of the Hudhayl tribe. About a hundred archers set out after the Muslim spies, following their tracks until they found where they had stopped to eat a meal of dates. Before long Asim and his nine companions saw their pursuers and attempted to hide. They were spotted and surrounded. The archers called on the spies to give themselves up and assured them of their safety. Asim stoutly refused and was shot down by arrows along with six others. The remaining three surrendered, but when the first two were bound with bowstrings the third refused to submit and preferred being put to death. The two remaining spies were taken to Mecca and sold into slavery and disgrace.[13]

After Muhammad died in 632, Syria, Egypt, Iraq and Persia were quickly conquered by his successors. The most famous Muslim general of the age was Khalid ibn al-Walid (c.587–642). Initially an enemy of the Muslims and having come within an ace of killing Muhammad at the battle of Uhud (625), Khalid accepted Islam in 629, three years before the Prophet's death. Dubbed 'The Sword of God' by Muhammad, Khalid went on to become one of the most successful generals in the history of warfare.

The noted medievalist Sir Charles Oman put the successes of the early Islamic generals down to fatalist fanaticism on behalf of Muslim soldiers and their 'extraordinary powers of locomotion'.[14] He appears not to recognize the guile and craft evident in many of their victories. During the siege of Damascus (634–635), Khalid received a traitor from the city who revealed to him that there was a celebration in the city marking the birth of the Roman governor's son and the people were all drunk. Accepting the information in return for rescuing the traitor's bride, Khalid and a few picked men were able to scale the city wall and open a gate to allow the Muslim army in.[15]

After the fall of Damascus, the Byzantine emperor Heraclius (ruled 610–641) gathered an enormous army up to 200,000 strong with which he hoped to re-conquer Syria. Khalid learned of this army through the interrogation of Roman prisoners and through his numerous agents, some of whom were inside Heraclius' army. As the intelligence picture began to develop, Khalid realized that the Islamic forces were too spread out and vulnerable. He therefore suggested that the Muslim army fall back from Syria and Palestine and concentrate before meeting the Roman forces. Although numerically far superior, the Romans were soundly beaten at the battle of the Yarmuk on 20 August 636, leaving Syria firmly under Muslim control.

Moving away from military espionage, the early Islamic world made an important contribution to the related subject of code breaking. Between 750 and 950 Baghdad was ruled by what is known as the Abbasid Caliphate. With a population in the region of a million souls, Baghdad was one of the planet's great centres of cultural and scientific achievement. Living in these brilliant times was the Iraqi scientist Abu Yusuf al-Kindi (born c.800). While working on translations of Greek philosophy in the Baghdad institute and library known as the 'House of Wisdom', al-Kindi made an important advance into the world of code breaking, known as frequency analysis. He realized the obvious fact that in any piece of given writing certain letters occurred more frequently than others. Therefore, if you knew the language of a piece of encrypted text was in, you could compare it with a piece of plain text. If for example 'e' was the most commonly occurring letter in the plain text, you could predict the letter representing 'e' would be most common in the encrypted text.

In sharp contrast to the achievements of the Abbasid Caliphate come the forebears of modern Islamic terrorists – the notorious sect of Assassins. An extremist sect of Ismaili Shi'ite Muslims, the Assassins established a reign of terror in the Middle East that lasted from 1090 to 1256. Their speciality was the murder of prominent rival Shia Muslims. Daggers were the weapon of choice and attacks were by preference made in public places for maximum shock value – inside mosques during Friday prayers was the prime time for their suicide or 'martyrdom' attacks.

Their enemies called the agents of this sect the *Hashshíshín* – from which Christian Crusaders derived the word 'assassin'. There is some conjecture on the origins of this name. The traditional translation is 'eaters of hashish', which stems from the belief that their Grand Master fed members the drug to show them the paradise awaiting them after martyrdom. Others believe the term was used by opponents of the sect, implying the Assassins' extreme behaviour was caused by the consumption of mind-bending narcotics. At the risk of ruining a good story, the phrase might simply have meant 'followers of Hassan' – the first Grand Master. The group actually named itself *al-da'wa al-jadída* (the new doctrine) and its members were referred to as *fedayeen* – a word still very much in use today, deriving from the Arabic *fidá'í* or 'one who is ready to sacrifice their life for a cause'.

In 1090 Hassan-i-Sabah (*c*.1034–1124) took possession of the fortress of Alamut in the mountains south of the Caspian Sea. From there a chain of Assassin strongholds spread like a cancer through the region. Duly concerned, the Seljuk sultan Sindjar decided to make a stand against them, albeit a short-lived one. Deriving his power from intimidation and fear, Hassan sent one of his agents to deliver an unmistakable 'back-off' message to Sindjar. What occurred brings to mind the famous scene in the movie *The Godfather*, when a movie producer wakes up to find that mafia henchmen have placed a horse's head in his bed while he slept. Hassan's agent crept unnoticed into the room and placed a dagger in the floor next to the sleeping Sindjar. When the sultan awoke and saw the dagger – which could have just as easily been planted in his chest – he half died of fright. The message was clear – Hassan's reach extended long and far from his mountain hideaway.

Curiously, the Assassins were a big influence on the Knights Templar, who copied some aspects of the Assassin organization and perhaps even their costume – white cloaks with red devices.[16] Better known is the description of 'the Sheikh of the mountain' given in the

Travels of Marco Polo. The Venetian explained how the leader of the Assassins would use spies to check on the progress of his recruits and identify the best among them:

> He would send some off on a mission in the neighbourhood at no great distance with orders to kill such and such a man. They went without demur and did the bidding of their lord. Then, when they had killed the man, they returned to court – those of them that escaped, for some were caught and put to death. When they had returned to their lord and told him that they had faithfully performed their task, the Sheikh would make a great feast in their honour. And he knew very well which of them had displayed the greatest zeal, because after each he had sent others of his men as spies to report which was the most daring and best hand at murdering. Then, in order to bring about the death of the lord or other man which he desired, he would take some of these Assassins of his and send them wherever he might wish, telling them that he was minded to dispatch them to Paradise: they were to go accordingly and kill such and such a man; if they died on their mission, they would go there all the sooner.[17]

The Assassins finally came unstuck in 1256 when the Mongols wiped them out. The conflict began when the Assassins murdered a Mongol prince because he forbade conquered Muslims from observing certain religious practices. The Assassins' Grand Master then sent 400 agents to kill the Mongol Great Khan, Mongke. Unsurprisingly, the Great Khan replied in kind, sending his brother Hulegu to wipe every Assassin off the face of the earth. With a siege train of Chinese engineers, the Mongols began the systematic destruction of Assassin strongholds. Just prior to the campaign, rule of the Assassin sect passed to a young Grand Master, Rukn ad-Din, who tried to placate the Mongols when they attacked Alamut. The Grand Master was given permission to negotiate directly with Mongke, but was brutally put to death by his Mongol escort.[18]

The destruction of the Assassins was not the first time the Islamic world had experienced the wrath of a Mongol army. The first Mongol ruler, Mongke's father Genghis Khan (1167–1227), is well known as the most successful and ruthless conqueror the world has ever seen. When Genghis' conquests brought him into contact with the Khwarizm

Empire (Persia) he proposed opening trade with its shah, Allah ad-Din Muhammad. To this end, in 1218 he sent a caravan of 450 merchants to the frontier town of Utrar. Unfortunately, when it arrived in the city the governor, Inalchuk Khwadir Khan, suspected the Mongol merchants were in fact spies, confiscated their camels and goods, then had them executed without trial.

One survivor managed to escape and informed Genghis Khan of what had occurred. Considering his reputation, the reaction of the Great Khan and self-styled 'Emperor of Mankind' was surprisingly restrained. He sent an ambassador and two Mongol soldiers to the Khwarizm shah and demanded that the governor be punished. It is unclear what thoughts – if any – were guiding the shah, but his response was to behead the Mongol ambassador. He then insulted the two soldiers by burning off their beards and sending them back to Genghis carrying the ambassador's head.

Perhaps Genghis Khan would have invaded the Khwarizm Empire at some point anyway, but the treatment of the Mongol ambassador made the annihilation of the huge empire an absolute certainty. Genghis launched this attack and before long, the Khwarizm Empire was devastated, the shah fleeing to live out the remainder of his days in poverty on an island in the Caspian Sea.[19] Inalchuk, the governor of Utrar, was less fortunate and was captured alive by the Mongol warriors. Not the forgiving type, Genghis Khan had Inalchuk executed by the novel means of having molten silver poured into his eyes and ears.[20]

The irony behind this story is that Inalchuk was probably right. It is almost certain that at least some of the Mongol merchants were spies. It was a classic Mongol ploy. Genghis Khan, or Temujin as he was named at birth, was well acquainted with the art of espionage. In 1177, he and his brother killed their half brother for spying for a neighbouring tribe. Long before the 'Mongol Horde' – in fact the most efficient military machine on the planet – came visiting, merchant spies would have been active in the area. While peddling their wares, these spies would patiently gather intelligence on the territory, spot potential pastures for the Mongol horses, estimate garrison strengths, and so on. Once the conquest was decided upon, long-range scouts would be sent hundreds of miles ahead of the main body, their reports being communicated by an unrivalled system of post riders called the *yam*, with riders capable of covering up to 150 miles (241km) a day.

When the Mongols prepared to invade Europe they were faced with the obvious difficulty of any clash between different ethnic groups. There was simply no way an Asiatic Mongol could have gone about unnoticed in a European town or village. To get round this problem, in 1221 Subedei negotiated a secret treaty with the Venetians. In return for intelligence on Western Europe, the Venetians found themselves the benefactors of what amounted to a Mongol protection racket. This gave them a virtual trade monopoly with the Mongol Empire, which controlled the Silk Road trade route from China to Europe. From the intelligence provided by Venice and with the help of spies hired by Mandarin Chinese working for the Mongols, maps of Hungary, Poland, Bohemia and Silesia were drawn up.[21] Fortunately for Europe the Mongol generals' attention was drawn elsewhere, or the course of history might have followed a very different route.

Although less famous than Genghis, the last of the great nomadic leaders, Timur (1336–1405), more than merits a mention. Better known as Tamerlane, this European version of his name derives from the Persian Timur-i lang – 'Timur the lame' – a reference to an arrow wound he received rustling sheep in his early twenties. Timur – which means 'iron' in his native tongue – was born at Kesh, about 50 miles (80km) south of Sarmarkand and he claimed to be descended from Genghis Khan. Like the famous Mongol ruler, Timur rose from being a nomadic chieftain to a conqueror in the same league as Alexander the Great.

Although his conquests were notoriously savage, Timur was no unsophisticated thug. He was described as being highly intelligent and appears to have used the Mongol tactic of having a contingent of spies disguised as merchants. When Timur first proposed an invasion of India, his princes pointed out the numerous difficulties he faced – the rivers to cross, the mountains and deserts to traverse, thousands of enemy soldiers and India's war elephants dubbed 'the destroyers of men'. Timur was not so easily put off. His spies had told him that India was on the verge of anarchy, with a hated sultan in Delhi and provinces in open rebellion. Timur followed Alexander's route across the Punjab, but where the Macedonian halted, Timur pushed on until he captured Delhi.

The invasions of the steppe horsemen did not always meet with success. In fact, Japan twice survived Mongol invasions, in 1274 and then again in 1281 when the Great Khan, Kublai, was thwarted – if the legends are correct – by typhoon winds breaking up his invasion fleets.

These winds were thought to be heaven sent and so received the name *kamikaze*. It was in memory of this 'divine wind' that Japanese suicide pilots were named in the closing stages of WWII, hoping to repeat against Allied ships what nature had done to the Mongols.

Medieval Japan was nominally ruled by an emperor, but real power was held by military dictators known as *shoguns*. Below them were the knights, or samurai, who followed a strict code called *bushido* (lit. the way of the warrior). As in all feudal, militaristic societies, there was a very real need for spies, assassins and others capable of undertaking special operations against rival warlords and clans.

The concept of military espionage was introduced to Japan by the diplomat Kibi Makibi (693–775) on his return from China. Sun Tzû's *Art of War* was translated in *Shoku Nihon-gi* (747), an official history of early Japan. This work had a lasting impact, particularly in the field of espionage. In the Japanese version we find the five species of spy classed as: *Inkan* (local spy), *Naikan* (inward spy), *Jukan* (converted spies), *Shikan* (doomed spy) and *Shokan* (surviving spy). There are records of spies in use from early samurai war tales, in particular *Shomonki,* composed shortly after 940, which tells of a naikan hired to perform an assassination.

From the 14th century we find espionage being carried out by specially trained individuals generically called *shinobi*, but better known as *ninja*.[22] In modern fiction and popular culture ninja are well enough known as agents of the criminal underworld, as stealthy assassins clad in black pyjamas and hoods, armed with deadly throwing stars, performing gravity-defying leaps and other superhuman feats. For Western audiences, their first introduction to the ninja was in the 1964 James Bond novel *You Only Live Twice,* which was made into a film of the same name in 1967. Since then they have continued to feature through to the present day in a multitude of kung-fu movies and 'Manga' comics.

In fact the ninja were a very real force in feudal Japan, with their own villages and code of ethics – *ninpo*. Very much like the mafia code, the most important rule of ninpo was maintaining the veil of secrecy. The severest crime was to leave the village without authorization, after which a ninja would be outlawed and have family members sent out to bring him back dead or alive.

From the mid-15th century certain samurai clans had begun to practise the art of *ninjutsu* from which the word ninja derives. Ninjutsu is sometimes translated as 'the art of invisibility'. Magic played an important role in Japan at the time and ninja were accredited with magical powers, utilizing curses, talismans and spells. However, not taking 'invisibility' in the literal sense, some describe ninjutsu as 'one who is concealed' or more cryptically, 'one who endures'. In practical terms the art included methods of stealth and entering, avoidance skills, escape and concealment, misdirection techniques, not to mention the art of disguise and impersonation.

These last two skills were immensely important for those on espionage missions. Casting aside the mental image of ninja warriors, an armed black-clad ninja would have looked as out of place walking through a town in medieval Japan as he would today. For that reason ninja employed the age-old technique of disguising themselves as itinerants, who would not cause suspicion wandering from place to place. Particular favourites were dancers, *ronin* (masterless samurai), various types of musicians, priests and merchants. One of the favourite disguises suited for ninja was as a *yamabushi* – a mountain-dwelling monk whose loose-fitting robes were a perfect place to disguise weapons.

In terms of combat skills, the ninja had to be versatile and inventive, using what was to hand and what could be easily concealed. In addition to the mastery of the samurai sword, spear and bow, ninja would be taught to use specialized weapons including knuckledusters, knives, darts, throwing stars and chain-and-sickle instruments. They would also make use of gunpowder to produce a range of fireworks and bombs in pottery and iron casings. Some say that ninja fighting techniques developed from the fighting techniques of peasants who, banned from using swords by the rigid caste system, developed other means of protection against marauding samurai and pirates. Others give an even more ancient origin for ninja fighting skills, claiming that they originated from the Chinese Lin Gui clan. Translating as 'demons of the forests', the Lin Gui are said to have been secretive group of mercenary assassins working during the Shang Dynasty (1700–1100 BC).

One of the ninja's principal means of attack was arson, particularly during siege warfare, which was a speciality of theirs. In 1562 Kaminojo castle was entered by a large group of 80 ninja, with up to 200 extra soldiers in support. They had split up and assembled in different places outside the fortress before sneaking in at night. Once inside they did not give the customary war cries, but simply began attacking the defenders and firing the towers. Accounts say the ninja were dressed like the castle guards, but had been given a password to distinguish between one another. The confusion was complete: 200 guards were burned to death in the fire and the castle quickly fell.[23]

Another celebrated ninja feat concerned a siege, this time on the Shimabara peninsula in 1638. In 1637 Christianity had been outlawed in Japan and the country was thereafter closed to foreigners. However, a combination of Christians and peasant farmers revolted and shut themselves up in Hara castle. The local shogun, Tokugawa Iemitsu (c.1604–51), mounted an expedition to quash the rebellion and hired ninja from Koga. In a clear indication of their skills, these ninja were able to make a detailed reconnaissance of the castle, its moat, the surrounding roads, the height of the walls and the shape of its loopholes.[24] Wearing disguises, the Koga ninja were able to approach right up to the castle and even gain access to it. Once inside they stole supplies and obtained the passwords.

Shortly after, the ninja were ordered to spy on the castle garrison and find out if, as was suspected, it was running low on supplies. The ninja were told it was a dangerous mission and that only a few of them would make it back alive, but volunteers 'prepared to die' were forthcoming.[25] To allow the ninja to approach the castle in darkness, guns were fired at the defenders, who quickly doused all the torches. When the sentries began to relax their guard later in the night, the ninja scaled the castle walls dressed in the uniforms of its defenders. Once inside the walls, one of the ninja, Arakawa, fell into a pit. He was rescued by a comrade called Mochizuki and continued his mission, stealing a Christian banner as proof they had got so far. When the garrison reignited the torches the two ninja made a dash through the middle of the guards and down over the walls. As they escaped they were subjected to a hail of missiles and both were badly injured. This would be the last time ninja were employed in war. After the Shimabara Rebellion Japan entered an era of peace which would last until the mid-19th century and the arrival of the United States Navy.

3

SPY, BRITANNIA

'I pray you, though, tell
your folk and home, lest hence ye fare
suspect to wander your way as spies
in Danish land. Now, dwellers afar,
ocean-travellers, take from me
simple advice: the sooner the better
I hear of the country whence ye came.'

Passage from the oldest English epic, 'Beowulf', composed in the
8th century by an unknown Northumbrian bard[1]

The history of the British Isles is underpinned with a rich heritage of espionage operations and secret service actions. A fiercely independent island race, Britons are proud of their traditions of fair play, tolerance and freedom of speech. It is a paradox, then, to find among these same people, such a virulent penchant for 'dirty tricks'.

Probably the greatest modern 'conspiracy theory' outside the existence of extraterrestrial life concerns the death of Princess Diana in August 1997. Accident or not, such was her celebrity that many people cannot accept Diana died because she was not wearing a seatbelt. It has been alleged by businessman Mohammad Al Fayed that Diana and his son Dodi were victims of a plot by the British secret service – it has furthermore been claimed that driver Henri Paul had links with the same organization. Former MI6 agent Richard Tomlinson, who was imprisoned in 1997 for breaching the Official Secrets Act by publishing a book on his time with the secret service,[2] claims Mr Paul was regularly paid for supplying information about guests at the Paris Ritz. Also central to the conspiracy is a note written in October 1996, given by Diana to her butler, Paul Burrell, in which she seemingly predicted her death in a car crash.[3] Burrell also claimed that Queen Elizabeth II cryptically warned him from being too close to the Princess – 'Be careful Paul... There are powers at work in this country, about which we have no knowledge.'[4]

The story of these 'powers at work' in Britain begins in 55 BC, when Julius Caesar brought the British Isles into recorded history for the first time. Waging a campaign to bring Gaul under Roman rule, Caesar made two expeditions against Britain. Before setting off on what he called 'The First Invasion', Caesar found almost nothing was known about the island. The Gallic traders he interviewed could report only on those parts of the coast facing Gaul and even then their knowledge was, from the military strategist's point of view, utterly incomplete. Writing in the third person, Caesar commented:

> And so, although he interviewed traders from all parts, he could not
> ascertain anything about the size of the island, the character and strength
> of the tribes which inhabited it, their manner of fighting and customs, or
> the harbours capable of accommodating a large fleet of big ships.[5]

Faced with this lack of basic intelligence, Caesar sent a warship under the command of Volusenus to make a general reconnaissance as quickly as possible. The mission lasted four days but at no time did Volusenus dare put himself ashore for risk of capture by the natives. He made his report to Caesar who continued with his preparations to sail with two legions in 80 transports protected by a screen of warships.

While Caesar had little idea of what to expect on the other side of the Channel, he admitted that the Britons knew he was coming. Although he tells us that a number of envoys were sent by British tribes, offering hostages and submission to Rome, the reception Caesar received on the island's beaches suggests an element of propaganda in his prose. An absence of proof does not mean the ambassadors sent to offer the hostages were not secretly spying on his build-up. Suitably forewarned of the Roman expedition, the Britons were able to muster their forces on the coast in time to dispute Caesar's landing. The Romans landed in full view of their enemy and met fierce resistance, which was only overcome with great difficulty.

Caesar soon left Britain, returning again the following year for a second unsuccessful attempt. In fact, Britain would remain unconquered until Emperor Claudius' expedition landed almost a century later in

AD 43. Caesar had experienced the problems faced by every would-be conqueror of Britain over the next two millennia. Apart from the obvious problems of crossing a turbulent and unpredictable stretch of sea, the need to assemble a great number of ships made it impossible to keep invasion plans a secret. It also proved very difficult to infiltrate the island with spies.

In AD 410, the last Roman legions were withdrawn from Britain and Emperor Honorius informed the Romano-Britons that they should look to their own defence against the Saxon raiders. Thus began a period of strife known as the Dark Ages, which lasted until punctuated by the Norman Conquest of Britain in 1066. From what evidence survives we can deduce that this turbulent age proved fertile ground for spies and associated plotters. From the 5th-century rule of Kentish king Vortigen, who urged King Constans to hire Pictish spies to head off rebellion in the north,[6] to the reign of King Canute (ruled 1016–35), who maintained spies in the Norwegian and Swedish armies, espionage was no stranger to British shores.[7]

Although perhaps dismissible as legend, perhaps even myth, according to Geoffrey of Monmouth spies also had a hand to play in the death of Uther, the father of King Arthur. While Uther was at St Albans, spies disguised as beggars entered the city working for the Saxon king Colgrim. Establishing that Uther was ill and required a particular type of water from a certain spring, the spies laced the well with a lethal dose of poison.[8] Legend or not, the story gives us an example of how spies were employed at the time.

More probable, although still in the realms of popular legend, is the story of the king who was his own spy. In 878 England faced a great Danish invasion led by Guthrum. In opposition was Alfred the Great, King of Wessex (ruled 871–899), who, it is said, dared not trust anyone but himself when it came to counting the size of the Danish forces. Legend has it that Alfred assumed the garb of a minstrel and visited the Danish camp where he played a harp and sang Saxon ballads. Impressed with his talent, Guthrum is supposed to have invited Alfred into his tent to entertain him with his harp playing.

Alfred spent a week in the Danish camp learning everything about the size and preparedness of their forces. Realizing that the Danes relied on small-scale raids to provision their men, Alfred focused on attacking these raiding parties to good effect. Suitably weakened, the

Danes lost the battle of Edington and Guthrum was captured. On meeting Alfred and learning he was the minstrel, Guthrum was so stunned he converted to Christianity and consented to the division of England into two kingdoms – Wessex and Danelaw.

It is clear in the run up to the battle of Hastings in 1066 that King Harold (c.1022–66) used spies to find the strength of William of Normandy's invasion army. From Norman sources there is a story that William caught an English spy watching his troops in Normandy and sent him back to Harold with a message that Harold should not waste money on spies because he, William, would be bringing his army to England by the end of the year and Harold would be able to see its strength for himself.[9]

Before the battle, Harold is said to have stopped 7 miles (11km) short of the Norman encampment and sent French-speaking spies to ascertain the size of William's army. The spies, however, did not realize that the Norman knights were soldiers on account of their being clean shaven and having short hair. Consequently they reported back to Harold that there were more priests in William's camp than there were fighting men in Harold's. Fortunately the Saxon king knew the Norman custom and corrected his spies.

After Hastings, with England under Norman rule, a series of dynastic struggles commenced, which were made all the more crucial by a simultaneous jockeying for position between church and state. As the centuries rolled by, events were further complicated by England's quest for domination over the entire British Isles, bringing conflicts with Wales, Scotland, Ireland, always France and then increasingly Spain. In this blizzard of intrigue, conflict and persecution, the use of spies eventually developed into what many consider the first modern secret service.

The first of the dynastic disputes involved King Henry I (ruled 1100–35) who succeeded to the throne in 1100 largely because his brother, William Rufus, had died without an heir and his elder brother, Robert, Duke of Normandy, had not yet returned from the Crusades. Henry quickly made peace with his elder brother and, through marriage, also with Scotland. But he continued to feel his throne was vulnerable because of the powerful and reputedly sadistic Robert de Belême, Earl of Shrewsbury.

According to the historian Ordericus Vitalis, Henry used 'private spies' to watch Robert and prepare a list of indictments against him. Based on the spies' reports Henry I summoned Robert to his court and accused him of committing 45 offences 'in deed or word' against him and his brother, the Duke of Normandy. Robert stalled and asked for time before responding to the charges, then fled. An irate Henry I finally cornered Robert at Shrewsbury Castle before banishing him to Normandy.[10]

Perhaps more fundamental was the later clash between Henry II (ruled 1154–89) and his former chancellor, Thomas à Becket. This clash of ideas was the first of a series of conflicts that would see England ultimately reject the power of the Roman church. Henry II had made Becket Archbishop of Canterbury in 1162. In a nutshell, Henry II believed he ruled in the name of God, not in the name of the pope – Becket disagreed. To resolve the matter, in October 1164 the archbishop was summoned to Northampton to stand trial for misappropriating funds while he was chancellor. Beckett claimed the council had no right to try him and after a stormy exchange he fled the country to avoid Henry II's spies. During six years of exile Becket kept up a secret correspondence, intriguing with supporters in England against the king. Reconciliation was attempted in 1170, but, ultimately inflexible, Becket was brutally murdered by supporters of the king in Canterbury Cathedral.

It comes as no surprise to see the Plantagenet king Edward I[11] (ruled 1272–1307) use a spy to finally apprehend his implacable Scottish enemy, William 'Braveheart' Wallace. The identity of the spy who betrayed Wallace has long been a bone of contention, for it was never recorded to whom the '40 Marks' of blood-money were paid. Many suspect that the culprit was Jack Short, Wallace's servant who betrayed him to Sir John Menteith, a Scottish baron who recognized Edward's reign. Menteith certainly appears to have supervised the actual capture in 1305, receiving £151 and a grant of land for his troubles – with a further 100 marks divided between those who made the arrest. In the Hollywood version, Wallace's betrayer is none other than the father of Scottish legend Robert the Bruce. This appears unlikely as the Bruce's father died in Palestine on crusade 15 months before Wallace's arrest.

Aside from bludgeoning England's Celtic neighbours, Edward Plantagenet is notable for introducing the 'Ward and Watch' system. This was something akin to the Persian 'eyes and ears of the king' and provided a system of surveillance, which served as a form of counter-espionage service. In 1283 Edward had proclaimed that the City of London was to have a night watch – then in 1285 expanded the watch throughout the kingdom. The watch was to be kept at the gates from dusk 'til dawn. All strangers were to be detained and delivered to the local sheriff the next morning. If necessary, watchmen could summon help by sounding the 'hue and cry' after which all freemen between the ages of 15 and 60 were required to band together in pursuit of a suspect, or, to use the parlance of the American West, form a posse. This means of surveillance, which was still in use in the 19th century, was further solidified in 1434 by Cardinal Beaufort who introduced the institution of state informer.[12]

In other examples, during the Hundred Years' War (1337–1453) between England and France there was a huge increase in the number of spies employed in Europe. Records show that the French heroine Jeanne d'Arc was betrayed by a paid agent of the English, Bishop Pierre Cauchon de Beauvais. During the Wars of the Roses (1455–85) it was said that the espials of Richard III 'ranged and searched in every quarter' and had 'the eyes of a Lynx, and open ears like Midas'.[13]

In the later medieval period there was a marked escalation in the employment of ambassadors sent to spy on foreign courts. Previously, foreign ambassadors were received very quickly and sent packing before they had much chance to see anything of real value. However, during the Middle Ages, the practice of sending 'resident ambassadors' changed intelligence gathering dramatically. Although out of politeness this new breed of ambassador was not meant to behave as a spy, most did. They had been placed abroad with the sole intention of gathering intelligence, which they did by setting up their own networks of informers and agents.

Curiously, the English were slow on the uptake of placing resident ambassadors abroad. With the exception of two at the Papal Court, the first resident ambassador was not sent abroad until 1505. Instead the English relied on old-fashioned espionage for intelligence and were greatly assisted by their possession of the French port of Calais. This foothold on the European mainland allowed agents to be safely infiltrated and a special boat service was used to bring news quickly across the Channel to Dover. Calais proved a valuable watching post for French military build-ups and came into its own during wartime, when spies were sent out on reconnaissance missions. Under the reign of both Henry VII (ruled 1489–1509) and Henry VIII (ruled 1509–47) the Calais intelligence service was run by an Italian 'professional diplomat' named Thomas Spinelly.[14]

Spies were mostly itinerants – people whose professions allowed them to travel without raising suspicion. These included merchants, priests and musicians (minstrels). Other spies adopted the costumes of monks, pilgrims and hermits as cover. The best spies were those who were personal servants, grooms, ushers and the like. These could either be planted in the service of an opponent or be found among existing staff and tempted with bribes to spy on their masters and mistresses.

Although the rewards could be good for a successful spy, with fixed, regular monthly payments a common perk, the punishments meted out to captured spies were particularly brutal, even by medieval standards. Execution was certain, but only after the application of various degrees of torture, which had been authorized as a legal means of interrogation by Edward IV.[15] An agent of Catherine d'Anjou found himself locked in the Tower of London and was interrogated by having hot irons applied to the soles of his feet – under such torture most victims would confess to anything put before them, no matter how trumped-up the charge.[16] Edward IV and Henry VII often led the interrogations personally.

Espionage continued under Henry VIII but took a back seat to the most important issue of the day – Henry's bloody quest for a male heir. When Pope Clement VII would not permit Henry to divorce Catherine of Aragon in order to marry Anne Boleyn, Henry broke off from Rome and declared himself head of the English church. In 1534 this was confirmed by an 'Act of Supremacy', swiftly followed by a new, severe 'Act of Treason', which outlawed any opposition to the break with Rome.

In 1535, as supreme head of the church, Henry appointed Thomas Cromwell as his Principal Commissary in ecclesiastical matters. In short, Cromwell's mission was to coerce or batter the clergy into submission. A royal commission was set up, the agents of which were sent to visit monasteries and report on their condition. This mission began in Oxford in September 1535 and resulted in the closure of 376 monasteries and the seizure of riches from religious shrines.[17] In the process, England became a police state and Henry a brutal despot.

One of the commissioners' most sickening abuses was the execution of the 84-year-old abbot of Glastonbury, Richard Whiting. Although the abbot had in fact accepted the supremacy of the king, one night while he slept, the commissioners searched his study and claimed to find a manuscript arguing against the divorce of Henry VIII and Catherine of Aragon. It appears that the manuscript was a forgery planted by Cromwell's spies. Nevertheless, Whiting was chained to a cart and taken to London to stand trial for treason. In a sign of the times, Whiting, who was both deaf and sick, was allowed no counsel and was found guilty. His body was quartered, with a piece each sent to Wells, Bath, Chester and Bridgewater. The abbot's head was hung from the gate of Glastonbury abbey.[18]

So far did royal spies infiltrate the kingdom that people stopped writing, gossiping, going to confession or even sending presents to one another. Everyone knew that the slightest slip of the tongue would see the finger of suspicion pointed at them. It was, many felt, 'as if a scorpion lay sleeping under every stone'.[19]

There was poetic justice behind Cromwell's demise. Enjoying his new-found importance, Cromwell advised Henry VIII to marry Anne of Cleves. When this marriage proved a disaster like the rest, Cromwell's head was on the block – literally. In an ironic twist of fate he was arrested on charges of heresy and treason. Secret agents working for his rival, the Duke of Norfolk, planted incriminating letters in Cromwell's home confirming the charges. Cromwell was executed outside the Tower of London on 28 July 1540.

Many consider the reign of Henry's daughter, Elizabeth I (ruled 1558–1603), the Golden Age of England. Whatever her merits may have been, hers was a reign oozing with the blood of her enemies. Elizabeth was the daughter of Henry and Anne Boleyn and only came to the throne through the misfortune of others. When Henry VIII died in 1547, the throne passed to Elizabeth's nine-year-old half-brother, Edward VI. Smallpox and tuberculosis caused Edward's death at the age of 15 (1553), so, according to Henry VIII's wishes, the throne should have passed to Elizabeth's elder half-sister, Mary Tudor. However, because Mary was a devout Catholic, the English Protestants offered the throne instead to Lady Jane Grey, the granddaughter of Henry VII. Unfortunately for Lady Jane, her succession was deemed to contravene an Act of Parliament and was annulled nine days later. As Henry VIII had intended, the throne passed to Mary, who instantly set upon a course of reconciliation with Rome. In achieving this joyful harmony, the queen gained the disturbing soubriquet 'Bloody Mary'.

First to the block was Lady Jane. Mary then unleashed her own version of the Spanish Inquisition, burning heretics at the stake in droves. It was lucky for English Protestantism that Mary's reign was but short lived. After just five years on the throne, in 1558 she died and the throne passed to Elizabeth.

Crowned on 15 January 1559, Elizabeth re-established the Protestant church and in so doing opened a whole new conflict with Rome and Catholicism. First Elizabeth was excommunicated. Then the pope strongly hinted that anyone assassinating her was guaranteed to go straight to heaven. The Catholics even had a replacement waiting in the wings – Mary Queen of Scots. All they needed was Elizabeth dead.

With plot after plot to foil, most authorities claim that the Elizabethan era marks the true beginning of the British secret services. But is this claim justified? The chief spymaster of Elizabeth's reign was Sir Francis Walsingham (c.1530–90), her First Minister and member of her Privy Council. Certainly Walsingham was head of a formidable network of spies, but it was a network built around him, not the state. With only occasional exceptions, this service was not state-funded. Generally speaking, Walsingham paid his spies from his own purse and died with enormous debts because of it. Most importantly, when Walsingham died, so did the service – there was no official framework in place to ensure it survived him intact.

Walsingham was a commoner by birth, but of a good enough family to study at King's College, Cambridge. He did not take his degree, but instead went abroad to 'places unknown' in 1550 to broaden his horizons through travel. He returned in 1552 and went to study law at Gray's Inn, one of four 'Inns of Court' around the Royal Courts of Justice in London. The Inns were fashionable places for the sons of noblemen and country gentlemen, with only a handful of members ever actually becoming barristers.

As a Protestant of strong conviction, Walsingham left England during the reign of Bloody Mary and resumed his foreign travels in order to avoid persecution. He went to the Italian city of Padua where he enrolled in its university to study law. The university was one of Europe's great centres of learning and by December 1555 Walsingham was appointed *consularius* – the official representative of all resident English students. In the Tudor period, Padua was a magnet for English scholars, eager to learn and feed off the energy of the Italian Renaissance – this was, after all, the era of Leonardo da Vinci (1452–1519), Michelangelo (1475–1564) and Machiavelli (1469–1527).

Machiavellian is a word often used in context with Walsingham and it is believed he came into contact with the Italian's writings while in Italy. The Florentine Niccolò Machiavelli was responsible for a number of important works, including the notorious *Il Principe* (The Prince), which was partly based on the exploits of Cesare Borgia, the illegitimate son of Pope Alexander VI. Similar in nature to Kautilya's manual on statecraft, *Il Principe* also drew on the experiences of historical figures, in particular those recorded by the Roman historian Livy. By way of an example, a typical piece of 'Machiavellian' advice is found in Chapter 18 of *Il Principe*: '… men are so simple, and yeeld so much to the present necessities, that he who hath a mind to deceive, shall alwaies find another that will be deceivd.'[20]

Under the heading of the 'Secrete conveing of letters'[21] Machiavelli discusses the diverse means of communication used by those under siege. He introduces the reader to the world of cipher writing, explaining messages were not sent 'by mouth'. As a further precaution, the enciphered messages were hidden in a variety of ways: within the scabbard of a sword, or placed in an unbaked loaf, which was then cooked and given to the messenger. Some spies were known to hide messages 'in the most secret place of their bodies' while others hid them in the collar of a pet dog. Machiavelli also revealed how others disguised their secret messages by use of secret ink, writing in between the lines of an ordinary letter. This way the sender did not have to trust the carrier with their secrets.[22]

In Renaissance Italy cryptography became an everyday tool of machinating diplomats. In turn, intercepted ciphers required experts to crack them. Foremost among these was Giovanni Soro, cipher breaker-in-chief to Venice from 1506. Even the Vatican would send him messages to test their impenetrability.[23] While in Italy Walsingham picked up what was considered *the* manual on code breaking by Leon Battista Alberti, the inventor of the cipher disk. Alberti's main contribution to the world of secret codes was to switch between two cipher alphabets in the same message in order to baffle attempts at frequency analysis.

Other advances in cryptography that Walsingham would have been aware of included the insertion of blanks into numeric ciphers. In this case each letter of the alphabet could be issued a value – for instance 'A' might become '23', while '86' might represent 'B' and so on. To confuse frequency analysts, other numbers would be inserted that had no value whatsoever. Some numbers would indicate that the letter preceding it should be repeated – an ingeniously simple way of avoiding writing the same letter twice in a row. As the ciphers became more sophisticated, some numbers or symbols were a shorthand code for key words or names. In this case '43' might indicate a commonly used word such as 'the' while the number '76' could mean 'the Queen' or a place name, like 'Rome' for instance. The variations were endless – but not impregnable.

Although his stay in Padua must have been a great influence on the future spymaster, he did not remain there long. At the time he was being made *consularius*, the 'Dudley Plot' to depose Bloody Mary failed. As a Protestant, Walsingham got out of Italy, spending much of his time in Switzerland. His self-imposed exile continued until Queen Mary died. Returning to England Walsingham came under the patronage of William Cecil, later Lord Burghley (1521–98), who had been responsible for all matters of secret intelligence. However, as he went on to lead Elizabeth's government, Burghley began farming out much of the intelligence work to Walsingham.

After a period as ambassador to France, Walsingham became Elizabeth's Secretary of State, a post he would retain until his death in 1590. As Secretary of State, Walsingham's prime concern and his major achievement was quite simply keeping Elizabeth alive.

There had already been several attempts to replace Elizabeth with Mary Queen of Scots. The Ridolfi Plot of 1571, involving Philip II of Spain and Pope Pius V, led to the execution of the Duke of Norfolk in June 1572. Then in 1583, Walsingham's agents had arrested Francis Throckmorton, who, under torture, revealed a Catholic conspiracy to place Mary Queen of Scots on the throne. On both occasions, Parliament had called for Mary to be executed, but Elizabeth had overruled them. Walsingham agreed with the parliamentarian view that the only way to stop Catholic plots against Elizabeth was to get rid of Mary. The trouble was in convincing Elizabeth to recognize this and getting her to act. Although Mary was under effective house arrest from 1568, Elizabeth did not want blood on her hands. What Walsingham needed was implicit proof that Mary was involved in a plot to kill Elizabeth.

Such an opportunity presented itself in December 1585, when a Catholic named Gilbert Gifford arrived at the port of Rye. It is unclear if he was acting from conscience, avarice or fear, but Gifford went to Walsingham and revealed he was acting as a messenger between Mary and her supporters on the Continent. He offered to work as a double agent and demonstrated all the right credentials, telling Walsingham: 'I have heard of the work you do and I want to serve you. I have no scruples and no fear of danger. Whatever you order me to do I will accomplish.' Walsingham sent Gifford to his code-breaking expert, Thomas Phelippes, who took hold of the secret correspondence and set to work deciphering it.

Walsingham's plan was quite simple. Gifford was sent to the French ambassador, Baron de Châteauneuf, to reveal a means of delivering messages to Mary in secret. He had bribed a sympathetic brewer who would conceal letters in beer barrels being delivered to Chartley, where Mary was being held. Because of his time on the Continent and the contacts he had made there, Gifford was able to convince Châteauneuf he could be trusted. However, before Châteauneuf's messages were delivered to Mary, Phelippes saw them first. After he copied them, another of Walsingham's men, Arthur Gregory, expertly resealed the envelopes with counterfeit wax seals. They were then taken to the brewer who had them put in a watertight bag and inserted into the bung of the beer barrel. Mary's replies followed in reverse. When Phelippes quickly broke Mary's cipher, Walsingham was privy to her secrets. All he needed was a conspiracy to pounce on.

There were plenty of English Catholics who were unhappy, but to find one actually prepared to murder the queen was another thing entirely. Fortune must have been smiling on Walsingham then, for in March 1586 at the Plough Inn, London, a plot was formed, led by the outlaw priest John Ballard (or to use his alias – 'Captain Fortesque', gentleman soldier) and Anthony Babington, an impulsive 24-year-old law student at Lincoln's Inn. With Ballard was his companion, Bernard Maude, who had obtained passports for them to travel to Paris. There in the French capital they planned to meet Mary's supporters and the Spanish ambassador, Don Bernardino de Mendoza. The first item on their agenda was the Catholic invasion of England. Poor Ballard had no idea his dependable Maude was an English government spy.[24]

Towards the end of May 1586, Ballard and Maude returned from France and excitedly told Babington the news. By September at the latest, a force of 60,000 French, Italian and Spanish troops would be landing in England. But before they could land, certain undertakings had to be fulfilled. Ballard said that he and Maude would travel to Scotland and raise a rebellion there, while Babington led an uprising of English Catholics. Thirdly, someone would have to assassinate Elizabeth – only then would the continental troops come ashore.

The person nominated for the regicide was John Savage, who while studying at Rheims had taken a vow to kill Elizabeth. From his time on the Continent Gilbert Gifford already knew of Savage's vow. So, with the interception of Mary's mail fully in swing, Gifford was sent to shadow Savage and incriminate him in the plot.

With Savage and Ballard under close surveillance by double agents, only Babington was still relatively unknown to Walsingham. The opportunity to place an agent with him arose in June when Babington tried to obtain a passport. There are several theories why Babington was planning a trip abroad at this juncture, even that the whole passport application was a red herring to throw Walsingham off his scent. The most plausible explanation is that his friend, Thomas Salusbury, realized that Ballard was nothing but trouble and was trying to get Babington as far away from the priest as possible. Their first attempt to secure a passport failed, but then Salusbury used a friend named Tindell to contact Robert Poley, a man reputed to have connections with Walsingham, who held ultimate sway over passport applications. In fact Poley was a fully fledged Walsingham stooge.

Poley heard Babington's request for a passport and agreed to help, for a sum. Told by Walsingham to ingratiate himself with Babington, Poley offered to go abroad with Babington as a companion-servant. Babington appears to have been totally taken in by Poley, who by the end of June had arranged for Babington to meet Walsingham to discuss his passport request. During this, the first of three meetings, Walsingham appeared to be sounding Babington out to become an informer for him while abroad. This was all very normal – all loyal Englishmen travelling abroad were expected to pick up little snippets of intelligence in return for a passport. In truth Walsingham had no intention of letting Babington anywhere near the Continent. He either wanted Babington to turn Queen's evidence, betray his fellow conspirators and implicate Mary, or be arrested as a conspirator himself.

A second meeting was held on 3 July at Walsingham's house, when the spymaster pressed Babington over what sort of services he was prepared to perform in return for the passport, hoping he might inform on Jesuit missionaries.[25] The meeting concluded with Walsingham convinced that Babington was of no use to him. Instead he would be set up as the fall guy. Gilbert Gifford had recently returned from a mission to Paris and Walsingham sent him to Babington to reveal the Catholic invasion was still very much on schedule. Gifford told Babington to communicate to Mary the details of what was being planned, using of course his 'secure' means of communication – the beer barrel express.

On 6 July Babington sent a letter that proved to be his death warrant. He named Ballard as the bringer of news from abroad, but no others. As for the details of the plot, Babington informed Mary that he with ten gentlemen and a hundred of their followers would come to rescue her. For the murder of Elizabeth – 'the usurper' he called her – he claimed to have six 'noble gentlemen' all of whom were his private friends. This of course was not strictly true, as Savage was the only one committed to the deed thus far. Most importantly, Babington asked for Mary's approval and her recommendations concerning the arrangements he had made. If Mary said 'yes' to the plot, Walsingham's elaborate snare would be sprung.

Mary's reply came out of Chartley on the night of Sunday 17 July. She had already sent two letters in May that strongly incriminated her – one to the Spanish ambassador, Mendoza, giving her support to an invasion of England, and the other to a supporter, Charles Paget, asking him to remind Philip of Spain of the urgency for invasion. Both letters had reached Walsingham, but neither implicated her in the way the letter to Babington did. In it Mary wholeheartedly endorsed Babington's plan and even gave advice on how best to proceed. When referring to the assassination of Elizabeth, Mary stressed the importance of her being quickly rescued lest her keeper learned of the plot and took measures to prevent her rescue.

After it was decoded by Phelippes, the letter was taken by Walsingham to Elizabeth. Not satisfied with it, Elizabeth asked that a postscript be added that might reveal the identity of the six would-be assassins. Walsingham had Phelippes copy out the whole message again, this time inserting the appropriate pieces.[26] The postscript read:

> I would be glad to know the names and quelityes of the six gentlemen
> which are to accomplish the dessignement, for that it may be I shall be

able uppon knowledge of the parties to give you some further advise necessarye to be followed therein ... as also from time to time particularlye how you proceede and as soon as you may for the same purpose who bee alredye and how farr every one privye hereunto.[27]

On 29 July the letter finally arrived with Babington, who slowly began to decipher it. The following day, a message from Walsingham arrived requesting another meeting. The spy Robert Poley began hinting to Babington that he should tell Walsingham everything about the plot. Realizing that their plan to raise England and Scotland in rebellion was a fantasy, Babington, Savage and Ballard agreed that they should tell Walsingham everything, but try to shift all the blame onto Maude and Gifford. Poley was sent to arrange the meeting.

Walsingham, meanwhile, had been playing a waiting game. He wanted to see how Babington would reply to Mary's letter, but he was beginning to fear the plotters might be about to flee. On 4 August he finally struck, arresting Ballard as he went to visit Babington.[28] When Babington learned of Ballard's capture he was at a complete loss and turned to Poley for advice. Babington asked if he should turn himself in and blame Ballard, or go on the run. Poley advised him to do neither, but to remain where he was. He would go and petition Walsingham for Ballard's release.

When Poley did not return that evening, Babington wrote him a farewell note and prepared to flee. However, Walsingham had sent another agent, John Scudamore, to keep track of Babington. The two went to dinner together and towards the end of the meal a note arrived for Scudamore. A glimpse of the handwriting told Babington all he needed to know – the message was from Walsingham. Babington calmly stood up and, leaving his sword and cloak at the table, he went off to pay for the food. Once out of sight, he ran for his life.

Warned by Babington as he stopped to change clothes, the conspirators went their separate ways in order to avoid arrest. Babington held out in St John's Wood with several companions. They reached a Catholic family by the name of Bellamy, where they received food and attempted to disguise themselves as labourers by cutting their hair and staining their skin. However, by 14 August they had been spotted and were arrested then returned to London. So pleased was Elizabeth, she ordered the church bells rung in celebration, with bonfires lit and psalms sung in thanksgiving.

Before being brought to trial on 13 September 1586 facing charges of high treason, the conspirators had the ordeal of interrogation to face. As a Catholic priest, Ballard could expect every device and means of torture to be placed at the hands of his tormentors. His interrogation began on 8 August and by the time of the trial he could no longer walk and had to be carried into the Westminster courtroom. One of the accused had died during the interrogation, or, to use the improbable official verdict, had strangled himself. All bore the marks of torture, but Babington and Savage were treated less harshly. In return Babington provided two long confessions, no doubt with Walsingham aiding his recollection of events. All must have been sickened to realize how they had been set up and played by Walsingham.

The trial was of course a mere formality. All were condemned to die and, as a deterrent against further plots, Elizabeth asked if some crueller than usual punishment might be devised for them. When Lord Burghley assured her that the existing methods were quite sufficient, he was making the understatement of the millennium. On 20 September Babington, Ballard, Savage and four others were tied face down onto hurdles at the Tower of London and dragged by horses through the streets of London to the place of execution. A disturbingly graphic, probably first-hand account of the execution was given by William Camden in his *Annales*:

The 20th of the same month, a gallous and a scaffold being set up for the purpose in St. Giles his fieldes where they were wont to meete, the first 7 were hanged thereon, cut downe, their privities cut off, bowelled alive and seeing, and quartered, not without some note of cruelty. Ballard the Arch-plotter of this treason craved pardon of God and of the Queene with a condition if he had sinned against her. Babington (who undauntedly beheld Ballard's execution, while the rest turning away their faces, fell to prayers upon their knees) ingenuously acknowledged his offences; being taken downe from the gallous, and ready to bee cut up, hee cried aloud in Latin sundry times, *Parce mihi Domine Iesu*, that is, *Spare me Lord Jesus*. Savage brake the rope and fell downe from the gallous, and was presently seized on by the executioner, his privities cut off, and he bowelled alive. Barnwell extenuated his crime under colour of Religion and Conscience. Tichburne with all humility acknowledged his fault, and moved great pitty among the multitude towards him. As in like manner did Tilney, a man of a modest spirit and goodlie personage. Abbington, being a man of a turbulent spirit, cast forth threates and terrors of blood to be spilt ere long in England.[29]

The carnage unleashed upon these seven men stretched the public's desire for justice to the limit. Apparently, when the executioner plunged his hand into Babington's body to pull out the heart, the plotter still appeared conscious and was seen to murmur, causing the crowd to gasp. So violent were their ends that the Queen ordered the other seven men be hanged until dead before the ritual disembowelling began. Their sentence was carried out the following day.

With incontrovertible proof and the confessions of the Babington plotters, Walsingham now turned to his real prize, the trial of Mary. Despite Walsingham's proof, Elizabeth was still reluctant to take action against her. A trial was eventually held at Fotheringhay Castle on 14 October 1586. The prosecution began with a discourse on the Babington conspiracy, concluding that Mary 'knew of it, approved it and had promised her assistance'. Mary began her defence courageously, denying she knew Babington, that she had never received any letters from him, nor written to him, nor plotted against the Queen. If there was written evidence in her own hand contrary to her statement, she demanded it be produced. She did admit some English Catholics were unhappy, but pointed out that shut up in her virtual prison, she could neither know nor hinder what was being attempted in her name.

The prosecution revealed Babington's confession of a correspondence with Mary. When copies of Babington's letters to Mary were read out, she admitted Babington may well have written them, but could the council prove she had received them? They could. Proof came when more of Babington's confession was read out, in which he confessed that Mary had written back to him. Mary burst into tears, but claimed her cipher had been used by others to forge the letters – something which was partially true.

The confessions of Savage and Ballard were then read out. They had confessed that Babington had told them of certain letters he had received from the Queen of Scots. Mary continued with the line that it was easy to counterfeit ciphers. She then turned her guns on Walsingham, who found himself 'taxed' by her words. As a lawyer, he was prepared for this sort of argument and he protested his mind was free from all thoughts of malice:

> I call God to record that as a private person I have done nothing unbeseeming an honest man, nor as I bear the place of a public person have I done anything unworthy my place. I confess that being very careful for the safety of the Queen and Realm, I have curiously searched out the practises against the same.[30]

Mary continued on the attack and told Walsingham that she was only reporting what she had heard said of him. To discredit Walsingham's evidence she declared spies were 'men of doubtful credit, which dissemble one thing and speak another'. Flooding with tears she begged Walsingham not to believe those who declared she had consented to Elizabeth's destruction. Through the tears she said: 'I would never make a shipwreck of my soul by conspiring the destruction of my dearest sister.' It was the performance of her life, but it was all in vain.

After much deliberation, it was decided that Queen Elizabeth's safety could not be guaranteed so long as Mary Queen of Scots survived. Her execution took place on 8 February 1587 in the Great Hall at Fotheringhay. She dressed as if on a festival day and was led to the scaffold, upon which were a chair, a cushion and a block, all draped in black cloth. After prayers, Mary laid her head at the block and remained very still, repeating to herself, 'In manus tuas, Domine.'

While one of the executioners held her steady, the other struck, but missed the neck. Struck in the back of the head, Mary was heard to whisper 'Sweet Jesus' before the second blow fell. Even this blow did not sever the head completely. A third blow was required before the head rolled completely free. The incident proceeded further into farce when one of the inept executioners went to lift up the head to acclaim the words 'God save the Queen' – he lifted it by the hair, only to find Mary had been wearing a wig. Her head fell to the floor with a thud and according to one witness, Robert Wynkfielde, Mary's lips continued to move up and down for a quarter of an hour after the execution. Then Mary's pet dog appeared from hiding under her petticoat and began lapping up the blood.

Running concurrently with the plot to snare Mary, Walsingham had been successful in obtaining intelligence on the Spanish preparations for invasion. The first of his successes was in the running of the double agent, Sir Edward Stafford.[31] Sent to France as Elizabeth's ambassador in 1583, Stafford was quickly snapped up by the Spanish who exploited his precarious financial position. In return for Spanish bribes, Stafford disclosed the contents of official British papers. Walsingham was wise to the temptations offered to ambassadors working abroad and was doubly suspicious of Stafford, who appeared a little too eager in his acclamations of loyalty to Elizabeth. Walsingham sent an agent named Rogers to spy on the ambassador and quickly established that Stafford was indeed selling secrets. Bigger news was to follow. Stafford was in contact with agents of Mary Queen of Scots and was acting as a go-between for French and English Catholics.

Armed with even a fraction of this evidence, Walsingham could easily have obtained Stafford's recall and a one-way trip to the Tower. The fact he did not do this proves Walsingham's mastery of the art of espionage. By retaining Stafford, Walsingham embarked on a classic deception ploy. He fed the ambassador with false intelligence, which he knew would quickly find its way to the French and Spanish. By July 1586 Stafford actually began reporting good intelligence to Walsingham. The ambassador revealed the Spanish were gathering an army strong enough to mount an invasion of England to depose Elizabeth and restore Catholicism.

If true, this was important news to say the least. But Walsingham knew he could not trust Stafford and so needed another source of information.[32] Although many gave him intelligence on the Spanish Armada, the key to success was Anthony Standen.[33] A curious ally, Standen was in fact a Catholic refugee and former supporter of Mary Queen of Scots. Although Walsingham was wary of him, Standen became his chief source on the Armada.[34] Operating in Florence under the alias of 'Pompeo Pellegrini', in February 1587 Standen reported that he had befriended Giovanni Figliazzi, the Florentine ambassador to Madrid. Although Standen feared Philip II might offer to employ Figliazzi, he need not have worried. The Florentine ambassador's declaration that he was 'addicted' to Walsingham prompts suspicions that Figliazzi and Walsingham knew each other from earlier in their careers.[35]

After receiving a 300 crown loan from Walsingham to fund the network, Standen recruited a Flemish agent whose brother – as luck would have it – was a secretary to the Grand Admiral of the Spanish Fleet, the Marquis of Santa Cruz.[36] Using Figliazzi to pass his reports back to Standen at Florence, this unnamed Flemish agent obtained a complete inventory of the ships, manpower and stores required for an invasion of England.

Armed with this intelligence Walsingham was able to act. The use of this intelligence is recorded by Richard Hakluyt in his 1589 work *The Principal Navigations, Voyages and Discoveries of the English Nation*. To repeat his archaic prose:

> Her Maiestie being informed of a mightie preparation by Sea begunne in Spaine for the inuasion of England, by good aduise of her graue and prudent Counsell thought it expedient to preuent the same.[37]

In plainer words, Elizabeth ordered Francis Drake to launch a preemptive attack. To the astonishment of the Spanish, Drake arrived in Cadiz harbour on 29 April and spent the afternoon cannonading and burning everything in sight. The Spanish lost 37 ships and enormous quantities of stores. Continuing his raid, he netted the *San Felipe,* a Spanish treasure ship laden with a cargo in the tens of millions of pounds in today's prices.[38] Drake had, they said, singed the Spanish king's beard.

Walsingham was able to assess the damage inflicted by Drake through a grain merchant in the Low Countries named Wychegarde, who spied on behalf of England despite losing his cargo in Drake's attack. Wychegarde also produced an accurate assessment of the Spanish land forces gathering in the Low Countries under the Prince of Parma. Having been seized by pirates and deposited in Boulogne with just his underwear, Wychegarde made his way home across land and accurately counted just 5,000 veteran Spanish troops. Unfortunately this assessment was disregarded as it did not tally with other reports, which put the figure much higher at 18,000 men. In fact, Walsingham's biggest failing in the war with Spain was his inability to get a spy inside Parma's headquarters, or to intercept his correspondence with Philip II.[39]

About the time of Drake's raid, Walsingham drew up a document he called a *Plot for Intelligence out of Spain*. Because it was difficult to get information directly out of Spain, this seven-point intelligence masterpiece called for the targeting of the Venetian ambassador by Stafford and the French ambassador to Spain. Spies would be placed in French ports observing visiting Spanish ships, while two special spies – French, Flemish or Italian – would be sent to find out what was happening on the Spanish coast. These two spies would be furnished with letters of credit so they might appear as merchants while performing the operation. Walsingham also wanted to try and place two *intelligencers* in the court of Spain, one to the port of Finale and another sent to Genoa. Other intelligence-gathering posts would be set up in Brussels, Leyden and Denmark.

In addition, Standen continued to report on the build-up of the Armada and in June 1587 correctly estimated that it would be unable to set sail until early in 1588. Walsingham dutifully reported this intelligence to Burghley, but asked that everything possible be done to protect its source. Standen also reported that Philip II had gone to Genoese money-lenders to make good the damage done by Drake. With this intelligence, Walsingham was able to put pressure on Genoa to refuse Philip the loan he so desperately needed. An even bigger coup may have been performed in February 1588. Walsingham had an agent in Malaga named Nicholas Ousely, who, in addition to sending ciphered intelligence reports hidden inside barrels of wine, is rumoured to have fatally poisoned the Spanish Grand Admiral, the Marquis of Santa Cruz at Lisbon.[40]

However, it must be said that despite all the secret service work, when the Armada finally sailed later in 1588 it was as much destroyed by Spanish incompetence and storms as by English cunning. When Walsingham died of natural causes in 1590 there was, quite understandably, much rejoicing in Spain. In terms of espionage he left no heir, but Lord Burghley, who had first passed the torch to Walsingham, now intended the office to go to his son, Robert Cecil. In the immediacy of Walsingham's death, there appears to have been something of a 'turf war' to take control of his interests. Although Cecil was the leading candidate, other contenders included Elizabeth's Vice-Chamberlain, Sir Thomas Heneage, and the Earl of Essex, both of whom were dabbling with secret matters of their own.

This jostling for position may have had an unlikely casualty in the guise of the playwright Christopher Marlowe (1564–93). Of the countless figures on the periphery of the Elizabethan secret service, much is made of Marlowe's connection with espionage – perhaps too much. If it had not been for his celebrity as a writer and the dubious circumstances of his death, Marlowe the spy might not have been remembered at all.

The details are sketchy, but most commentators agree that Marlowe entered Walsingham's secret service while studying at Cambridge University. From 1584 Marlowe appears to have been absent from Cambridge for several lengthy periods. When it came time to receive his master's degree, the university refused him on the grounds that he was suspected of having travelled to Rheims, the French city where Englishmen went to be trained as Catholic priests. The university reversed its decision after the Queen's Privy Council explained that he had not been to Rheims but instead had been performing good services for Her Majesty. This service may have been posing as a Catholic in order to infiltrate their underground network in England.

Marlowe's violent murder lends to his cult status among purveyors of fine conspiracy. He met his end in an upstairs meeting room by the Thames at Deptford. He was with three men, all of whom had secret service connections of their own: Robert Poley, Nicholas Skeres and Frizer. Drawing together all the pieces, Poley, who we know from the Babington plot, was now working for Heneage. Skeres had also formerly spied for Walsingham, but now served Essex. Frizer was a 'servant' of Thomas Walsingham, a cousin of the great spymaster. Quite where Marlowe fitted into this picture is unknown, but it is possible that all the interested parties had decided to silence him in case he defected to the Catholics. Over drinks and a game of backgammon, Frizer pulled a knife on Marlowe and stabbed him through the eye. Frizer claimed he acted in self defence and received a royal pardon with surprising haste.[41]

Another Cambridge man and dabbler in espionage was Lord Burghley's nephew, Francis Bacon (1561–1628). Although more famous for his philosophical works, like his elder brother, Anthony, Francis attended Cambridge and became a member of Gray's Inn. Between 1581 and April 1582 Francis went on a tour of Italy, Spain, Germany and Denmark. This trip was in part organized by Anthony who had been abroad since 1578 on various intelligence missions of his own. Francis compiled a lengthy intelligence report, which was presented to Burghley and the queen.

The ultimate irony of Elizabeth's reign was that upon her death in 1603, the throne passed to the son of Mary Queen of Scots, James I (ruled 1603–25). Suspicious of the power previously wielded by Walsingham, his reign is said to have marked a low tide in the employment of spies.

Instead, he adopted the Spanish practice of relying on ambassadors for foreign intelligence, in particular the services of Sir Henry Wotton (1568–1639). Going abroad at the age of 22, Wotton travelled extensively through France, Germany and Italy. While in Florence he was sent on a secret mission to James, using the alias of Octavio Baldi, warning of a Jesuit plot to poison him. In reward, James knighted Wotton and appointed him ambassador to Venice. The old republic continued to prove itself an effective listening post against plots emanating from Spain, and Wotton was also able to monitor the Jesuits with a network encompassing all Italy, making great use of postal intercepts.[42]

One notable incident of James I's reign concerned the Gunpowder Plot of 1605. The plot has similarities to the Babington plot. A group of Catholic conspirators met on 20 May 1604 at the Duck and Drake Inn on the Strand. The conspirators included a ringleader, Robert Catesby, and Guy Fawkes, a Yorkshireman in service with the Spanish army. Together they decided to blow up the Houses of Parliament and rented a cellar underneath the House of Lords, in which they stacked 36 barrels of gunpowder – more than enough to send the whole edifice sky-high. In the meantime, Fawkes travelled to Flanders to solicit foreign aid. While there he was spotted by spies of Robert Cecil, now Earl of Salisbury and James I's First Minister.

In October, Fawkes was chosen to light the fuse, before escaping to Europe. However, someone betrayed the conspiracy on the night of 26 October. Guy Fawkes was arrested in the cellar while preparing to light the fuse and was taken in for questioning. Perhaps mindful of the fate met by Babington, the other conspirators fled and with good reason. On 6 November James I authorized torture on Fawkes, but failed to extract any information for two days. However, it was only a matter of time before eight others were rounded up and the trials began on 27 January 1606. All were found guilty and, like the Babington plotters before them, were brutally hanged, drawn and quartered.

It was not until after the English Civil War (1642–49) that anything like a return to Walsingham's day occurred. After the execution of Charles I in 1649 and the rejection of Charles II, England came to be ruled by Oliver Cromwell (1599–1658) as Lord Protector. In 1653 Thomas Scot was replaced as director of intelligence by the recently appointed Secretary of State, John Thurloe (1616–68). A lawyer like Walsingham, Thurloe shared his predecessor's enthusiasm for uncovering plots, this time aimed at Cromwell by Catholic Europe and, in particular, by Charles II, son of the executed monarch. So vehement was Charles's desire for a restoration of the monarchy that he let it be known a knighthood awaited Cromwell's assassin.

In order to thwart these plots and conspiracies, Cromwell ensured that his spymaster-general was adequately funded. Later, in the reign of Charles II (ruled 1660–85), the diarist Samuel Pepys recorded in an entry of 14 February 1668: 'Secretary Morrice did this day in the House, when they talked of intelligence, say that he was allowed but £70 a-year for intelligence, whereas, in Cromwell's time, he [Cromwell] did allow £70,000 a-year for it.'[43]

Thurloe built up a formidable network of spies throughout Europe who, not being ambassadors, were much harder to detect. He revitalized the cryptographic service, which was put under the astute leadership of the mathematician John Wallis (1616–1703). In 1655 Thurloe took charge of the post office, enabling him to intercept the letters of royalist supporters and other conspirators.

His successes were many, including foiling Leveller plots to assassinate Cromwell. Edward Sexby (1616–58) was an English Puritan and Leveller, who had fought on the side of Parliament during the Civil War, but who considered Cromwell a tyrant. In 1655, he was discovered plotting against Cromwell and had to flee to the Continent, where he began negotiating with Spain and English royalists for the invasion of England and Cromwell's overthrow. In Flanders he met a fellow Leveller, Miles Sindercombe, who returned to England with a plan to assassinate Cromwell.

Sindercombe soon found out that assassinating public figures is one thing, but escaping from the scene of the crime with one's life intact is something different entirely. It was this element of 'self preservation' that rendered Sindercombe's efforts ineffectual. Aided by two companions, Sindercombe hatched a plan to kill Cromwell while he walked from Westminster Abbey to the Houses of Parliament. A house overlooking the entrance to the abbey belonged to a Royalist sympathizer. On the day in question, Sindercombe and his two henchmen arrived at the house with a blunderbuss concealed inside a musical instrument case.[44] Fortunately for Cromwell, the crowds were so great that Sindercombe could not get a clear view for a shot. Unwilling to go outside and fire the shot from close range – to do so meant certain capture, torture and execution – the plotters packed up and left.[45]

A second attempt was staged. This time Sindercombe planned to fire on Cromwell's carriage on its regular Friday journey to Hampton Court. He hired a room in Hammersmith, which overlooked the road at a narrow point where Cromwell's coach would have to slow down. Having bribed one of Cromwell's escort troopers, John Toope, for details of Cromwell's itinerary, Sindercombe laid in wait all day, only to learn that Cromwell had made the journey by boat.

With his patience running out, Sindercombe planned to shoot Cromwell in London's Hyde Park. It had been noted that Cromwell often took exercise in the park and was only lightly guarded. Sindercombe's accomplice – an old soldier named John Cecil – was chosen to commit the deed. To facilitate Cecil's escape, the park gate was broken and a fast horse was provided. However, when push came to shove, Cecil's courage appears to have failed him. He returned to Sindercombe with the sheepish excuse that the getaway nag had been too ill for him to ride.

Lastly, the plotters decided they would kill Cromwell by blowing up the Palace of Westminster. To that end they placed a bomb in the palace chapel but were betrayed to Thurloe by John Toope, the Life Guard trooper they had earlier bribed.[46] Thurloe caught up with Sindercombe & co. on 8 January 1657 and had them imprisoned in the Tower. To avoid the humiliation of public execution Sindercombe committed suicide and, as befitted a suicide, was buried anonymously under a public highway.

Sexby met his end after producing a pamphlet called *Killing Noe Murder* in which he justified political assassination as a means to defeat tyranny. There were no prizes for guessing which tyrant he had in mind while penning the piece. On a visit to England in 1657, he was captured and sent to the Tower. After interrogation, Sexby apparently went insane and died of fever in January 1658. The following year, Thurloe's spies infiltrated and thwarted another plot, this time by a group known as the Sealed Knot. A combination of exiled royalists and dissatisfied parliamentarians, the Sealed Knot planned for a national rebellion set for 1 August 1659. However, with Thurloe well informed by his spies of the group's plans, the army was mobilized in readiness and the revolt was crushed.

With such successes, it is surprising to learn how Thurloe was himself betrayed by his secretary, Samuel Morland (1625–95). When the Cambridge-educated Morland learned that Thurloe was plotting to assassinate Charles II, he became a double agent, leaking out the details of the plot to the royalist camp. Another blow came from the former scout-master-general in Scotland, George Downing (1624–84), after whom Downing Street, London, is named. Cromwell had sent Downing to Holland on a diplomatic mission, which appears to have provided a cover for him to spy for Thurloe on English exiles and the Dutch military. However, with the restoration of the monarchy in 1660, Downing sent Charles II Thurloe's papers. For this Downing was knighted while Thurloe was arrested on charges of high treason. It is an indication of the spymaster-general's worth that he was released after just a few months on the condition that he would make his services available, should the new government require them.

4

ESPIONAGE IN THE AGE OF REASON

That man certainly deserves to be well rewarded,
who risks his neck to do your service.

Frederick the Great on spies[1]

The 18th century, where we find the seeds of so much we take for granted in the modern world, was an age of enlightenment, where Reason battled for supremacy over superstition and ignorance. It was the age that gave us Voltaire and Rousseau, not to mention the American Revolution, which marks the beginning of the modern age. It was an era born out of a morass of war, plague and disease. The preceding century was scarred by the Thirty Years' War (1618–48), a conflict that left Germany in ruins with anything up to 30 per cent of its civilian population slain.

During these dark times the foundation of France as a modern state was laid by Cardinal Richelieu (1585–1642), who through sleight of hand, cunning and the use of spies ensured the omnipotence of absolute monarchy. His work was continued by Mazarin (1602–61), his protégé and the de facto regent for Louis XIV (ruled 1643–1715) – who became known to history as 'The Sun King'. Louis was the pinnacle of absolutism and must have seemed a living god to those who saw his palace at Versailles. How many would have guessed within a century of his passing that *his* France would be ruled by the heirs of the commoners he taxed almost out of existence?

In terms of warfare, much of what was put into practice at the end of the century was a result of lessons learned during the course of it. In the 18th century we find the art of war defined by soldiers who took time to scrutinize and dissect every facet of the military being. It is little wonder that this century produced one of the great captains of history – Napoleon Bonaparte (1769–1821) – not to mention the army he led so victoriously.

Before Napoleon, one of the great military innovations of the 18th century was the development of what was called *petit guerre*. This was a war between outposts and patrols, the screens thrown out to protect an army's march or its encampments. Pioneered by Balkan irregulars in Austrian service, the light troops performing this function made it considerably harder for spies and scouts to get close enough to the main body of the enemy army to discover its intentions. The officers commanding these troops were also instructed to use spies to their own advantage, to find out what was 'over the next hill' or to pinpoint local enemy positions. This local or 'tactical' espionage was in contrast to the 'strategic' espionage performed by spies in the pay of the commander-in-chief, who were more concerned with the goings-on in enemy headquarters.

In this period, military thinkers defined the purpose of espionage within the sphere of military operations. We are particularly indebted to the works of Comte de Saxe (1696–1750), who is most noted for his service in the French army of Louis XV (ruled 1715–74) and his victory over the British at Fontenoy (1745). Using his long experience of war, de Saxe set down a military treatise entitled *Mes Révieres* – a chapter of which he dedicated to the employment of spies and guides. The short text is worth reporting in full:

> You cannot give too much attention to spies and guides. Monsieur de Montécuculli[2] says they serve like the eyes in your head, and are just as necessary to a general. He is right: One cannot spend too much money to have good ones. These people must be chosen from the country in which the war is fought. Intelligent, clever and wise people must be employed. They must be dispersed all over, with the officers, the generals, among sutlers, and especially among contractors for rations; because, by the provisioning, the depots and the bread bakeries, it is easy to judge the designs of the enemy.
>
> These spies must not be known to each other. They must have different orders; those who are suited for the purpose, will smuggle themselves into the [enemy] ranks; others will accompany the army as sellers and buyers. These must each know one of the first type, to receive from them that which must be carried to the general who pays

them. You must give this task to someone who is faithful and intelligent, making him report every day, and to be sure that he is not being bribed.'[3]

Perhaps the most famous piece of military writing from that era was penned by Frederick the Great, King of Prussia, one of the most successful military commanders in history. He fought two major wars, the War of Austrian Succession (1740–48) and then the Seven Years' War (1756–63), during both of which he employed spies to excellent effect. After inflicting a huge defeat on the French at Rossbach on 5 November 1757, Frederick wrote of the enemy commander: "Marshal Soubise is always followed by a hundred cooks; I am always preceded by a hundred spies.'[4]

The twelfth Article of his often quoted *Instructions for Generals* was entitled: 'Of Spies, how they are to be employed on every Occasion, and in what Manner we are to learn Intelligence of the enemy.' Based on first-hand experience, the Article is again worth presenting in its entirety:

If we were acquainted beforehand with the intentions of the enemy, we should always be more than a match for him even with an inferior force. It is an advantage which all generals are anxious to procure, but very few obtain.

Spies may be divided into several classes: 1st, common people who choose to be employed in such concern; 2dly, double spies; 3dly, spies of consequence; 4thly, those who are compelled to take up the unpleasant business.

The common gentry, viz. peasants, mechanics, priests, &c. which are sent into the camp, can only be employed to discover where the enemy is: and their reports are generally so incongruous and obscure, as rather to increase our uncertainties than lessen them.

The intelligence of deserters is, for the most part, not much more to be depended on. A soldier knows very well what is going forward in his own regiment, but nothing farther. The hussars being detached in front, and absent the greatest part of their time from the army, are often ignorant on which side it is encamped. Nevertheless, their reports must be committed to paper, as the only means of turning them to any advantage.

Double spies are used to convey false intelligence to the enemy. There was an Italian at Schmiedeberg, who acted as a spy to the

Austrians, and being told by us, that when the enemy approached we should retire to Breslau, he posted with the intelligence to Prince Charles of Lorraine,[5] who narrowly escaped being taken in by it.

The post-master at Versailles was a long time in the pay of Prince Eugene.[6] This unfortunate fellow opened the letters and orders which were sent from the court to the generals, and transmitted a copy of them to Prince Eugene, who generally received them much earlier than the commanders of the French army.

Luxembourg[7] had gained over to his interest a secretary of the King of England, who informed him of all that passed. The king discovered it, and derived every advantage from it that could be expected in an affair of such delicacy: he obliged the traitor to write to Luxembourg, informing him that the allied army would be out the day following on a large foraging party. The consequence was that the French very narrowly escaped being surprised at Steinquerque, and would have been cut to pieces if they had not defended themselves with extraordinary valour. It would be very difficult to obtain such spies in a war against Austria: not that the Austrians are less alive to bribery than other people, but because their army is surrounded by such a cloud of light troops, who suffer no creature to pass without being well searched...

When we wish to gain intelligence of the enemy, or give him a false impression of our situation and circumstances, we employ a trusty soldier to go from our camp to that of the enemy, and report what we wish to have believed. He may also be made the bearer of hand-bills calculated to encourage desertion. Having completed his business, he may take a circuitous march and return to camp.

There is yet another way to gain intelligence of the enemy when milder methods fail, though I confess it to be a harsh and cruel practice. We find out a rich citizen who has a large family and good estate, and allow him a man who understands the language of the country dressed as a servant, whom we force him to take along with him into the enemy's camp, as his valet or coachman, under pretence of complaining of some injuries which he has received; he is to be threatened also at the same time, that if he does not return after a certain period, and bring the man with him, that his houses shall be burned, and his wife and children hacked in pieces. I was obliged to have recourse to this scheme at ...[8] and it succeeded to my wish.

I must farther add, that in the payment of spies we ought to be generous, even to a degree of extravagance. That man certainly deserves to be well rewarded, who risks his neck to do your service.[9]

These observations were expanded after the Seven Years' War, in Leroy de Bosroger's 1779 *Principes de l'art de la guerre*.[10] In the section 'Article II – Knowledge of the enemy's forces', Bosroger goes over much of what de Saxe and Frederick recorded, but then added some clauses of his own. In an interesting development, Bosroger shows how matters relating to espionage were being dealt with not by the army commander or sovereign personally, but delegated to a diligent staff officer on their behalf. This is the beginnings of army staff development, something which would prove a huge influence on the Napoleonic Wars and beyond.

According to Bosroger: 'It is ordinarily an assistant to the General Staff[11] of the army who is charged with this district.' On the qualities of such an individual, Bosroger asserts the officer 'must be a man unbiased and intelligent, who has enough knowledge to distinguish what deserves to be believed, from that which might be suspect.' He also gives advice on the subject of double agents and how to use them to plant false plans in the hands of an enemy. Double agents, Bosroger says, 'go to the highest bidder, and if the enemy pays better than you... they will serve them to your detriment. Those who are pledged to both parties can render essential services when they are paid well enough to be sure of them.'

Two spies in particular stand out in 18th century, both of whom were extraordinary men in their own right and who are more famous for other reasons. The first is the Venetian seducer-extraordinaire, Giovanni 'Jacques' Casanova (1725–98), and secondly, the Chevalier d'Eon (1728–1810), the patron saint of cross-dressers in whose memory the term 'eonist' was used before the word transvestite became vogue in the 20th century.

Casanova was born into a family of actors and it appeared that the legendary Lothario looked destined for a career in the church – but he could not help himself and one scandal after the other put paid to all such notions. His nomadic youth led him far and wide and then back to Venice where until 1755 he made his money posing as an alchemist and practitioner of the occult.

In that year he was betrayed by a spy named Manuzzi to the Venetian State Inquisition, which arrested him on charges of devil worship. He was imprisoned in the infamous and supposedly escape-proof dungeons in the loft space of the Doge's palace – known colloquially as 'the Leads'.

After 15 months' imprisonment Casanova made his escape with a fellow inmate, Father Balbi. Having made a hole in the ceiling, Casanova and his accomplice climbed up onto the lead tiles that formed the palace roof. Strange as it may seem, having succeeded in breaking out of their cell, Casanova and Balbi now contrived to break back into the palace through an open window. Once back inside, the two escapees found themselves in a locked archive room. Casanova smashed a hole through the door through which both men climbed. They then found themselves faced by a much larger door, the sort of which would require gunpowder to force open. Being outside the prison section of the palace and being relatively well dressed, the quick-witted Casanova went to a window and was seen by a man in the palace courtyard, who, thinking they must have accidentally been locked into the room the night before, went to get the key holder. With the door open, Casanova and Balbi fled to the nearest gondola and made their escape. Casanova fled to France, where his published account of the escape was a sensation. Basking in the limelight, Casanova made a fortune by starting a lottery, which further served his keen predilection for gambling.

During his stay in France, Casanova turned his hand to espionage and was employed as a spy by Louis XV's Foreign Minister, Cardinal Francois de Bernis (1715–94). Casanova's first mission was to travel to Dunkirk where the British fleet lay anchored. A large garrison of British troops controlled Dunkirk at that time, the port having been ceded to England by the 1713 Treaty of Utrecht. When Casanova accepted his role of secret agent, however, France and England were beginning the bloody Seven Years' War (1756–63). His memoirs leave a detailed account of this mission and give us important clues as to how such secret operations were carried out at the time. His controller was the Abbé de la Ville, who asked if Casanova 'thought himself capable of paying a visit' to British warships in Dunkirk, making the acquaintance of the officers, and investigating the provisioning, armaments and crews. Casanova accepted the challenge readily.

Working undercover, Casanova would not be provided with the usual letters of introduction and passports necessary to move freely about France. Casanova was told: 'As this is a secret mission, I cannot give you a letter of commendation; I can only give you some money and wish you a pleasant journey.' The Abbé did at least offer the Venetian some advice to help him on his way:

'As you are on a secret mission, my dear Casanova, I cannot give you a passport. I am sorry for it, but if I did so your object would be suspected... You quite understand how discreet your behaviour must be. Above all, do not get into any trouble; for I suppose you know that, if anything happened to you, it would be of no use to talk of your mission. We should be obliged to know nothing about you, for ambassadors are the only avowed spies. Remember that you must be even more careful and reserved than they, and yet, if you wish to succeed, all this must be concealed, and you must have an air of freedom from constraint that you may inspire confidence.'[12]

To cover his tracks, Casanova obtained a passport from a different acquaintance, under the pretext of accompanying some English friends to Calais. Furthermore, he called on a banker to arrange a letter of credit on a Dunkirk bank, stating that he was making the trip 'for the sake of pleasure'. If stopped on the way, these documents would prove enough to see him through.

Arriving at Dunkirk, Casanova went to exchange the credit note with a banker who out of politeness asked the Italian to sup with him that evening. This invitation gave Casanova his lead into local society and introductions to the banker's other guests, including several British naval officers. Casanova proclaimed himself a brother-in-arms to them, telling them he had served in the navy of the Venetian Republic, before launching into a discourse on naval architecture and Venetian naval manoeuvres. Within three days Casanova was on excellent terms with all the captains of the British Dunkirk Fleet.

Able to begin his mission against the English 'Jacks' in earnest, Casanova put aside his 'usual companions' of pleasure, gaming, and idleness and set to work. He recalled:

Four days after I had been at Dunkirk, one of the captains asked me to dinner on his ship, and after that all the others did the same; and on every occasion I stayed in the ship for the rest of the day. I was curious about everything – and Jack is so trustful! I went into the hold, I asked questions innumerable, and I found plenty of young officers delighted to shew their own importance, who gossiped without needing any encouragement from me. I took care, however, to learn everything which would be of service to me, and in the evenings I put down on paper all the mental notes I had made during the day. Four or five hours was all I allowed myself for sleep, and in fifteen days I had learnt enough.[13]

It was only when Casanova began his return trip to Paris that the mission became complicated. Despite good advice to 'avoid trouble' he seemed unable to proceed through any town without drawing every possible attention to himself. In one episode, a customs and excise official searched Casanova's carriage and found some contraband snuff. It was confiscated and a large fine was levied. Indignant with rage and fuelled with an almost maniacal sense of self-importance, Casanova refused to pay and demanded to see the local superintendent in order to complain about 'his scoundrelly myrmidons'. After much bickering and posturing, on the intervention of an Italian guest of the superintendent the fine was waived and Casanova continued on his way.

Eventually returning to Paris, Casanova first handed his report to de Bernis who read it through and suggested some editing. When he mentioned the troubles he had experienced returning to Paris, de Bernis was amused but did point out 'the highest merit of a secret agent was to keep out of difficulties; for though he might have the tact to extricate himself from them, yet he got talked of, which it should be his chief care to avoid.'[14]

A month later Casanova received the considerable sum of 500 louis and heard that the First Lord of the Admiralty had 'pronounced my report to be not only perfectly accurate but very suggestive'. Reflecting on this episode later in life, after the French Revolution had occurred, Casanova declared the use of spies such as himself as corrupt. The mission had cost the admiralty 12,000 francs, when it could have been done for nothing if a naval officer had been given the mission instead. Instead, with scant regard for the damage it was doing to the national finances, French ministers preferred to lavish money on their sycophants and hangers-on, or 'creatures' as they were called.

A contemporary of Casanova, the Chevalier d'Eon, led an amazing life. A dragoon and war hero, a noted fencer and duellist, diplomat and Freemason, d'Eon is best known for the very public confusion over his gender. In his lifetime it was generally believed that he had been born female, but had worn male clothing from a very young age. In the 1770s, while d'Eon was in Britain, speculation about his gender reached fever pitch and became the subject of wagers – with speculations even traded on the London Stock Exchange. In 1777 an insurance company asked for an investigation, the findings of which declared d'Eon was female.

In France too, d'Eon was forbidden to appear out of women's clothing in any part of the country – Queen Marie Antoinette sent him dressmakers and maids. The *chevalier* became a *chevalière*! Moving back to London, in 1787 d'Eon opened a fencing school and supplemented his income by offering to fight a famous French duellist. A match took place at London's Carlton House between d'Eon – wearing a dress and lace bonnet – against Monsieur de Saint-George, and was witnessed by the Prince of Wales. When he died on 21 May 1810, a medical examination confirmed that he was male, not female or hermaphrodite as some suspected, a revelation they say caused King George III a terminal bout of madness. Aside from all issues relating to the chevalier's gender, it should also be known that d'Eon was a spy – and a very good one at that.

However, before his career as a spy can be properly examined, we must first learn about *le secret du Roi* – the King's Secret. The king in question was Louis XV of France and his 'secret' was a shadow cabinet that met in his private apartments at Versailles, through which he pursued policies against those of his official ministers. When he came to the throne in 1743 it was very much in the shadow of his predecessor Louis XIV – the aforementioned Sun King. But rather than being the absolute monarch he aspired to, Louis XV found himself virtually powerless in matters of state. To wrest the initiative from scheming ministers and mistresses of court, Louis XV formed a *cabinet noir* – a 'system of espionage' headed by Robert Jeannel, the postal director who had the letters of Louis' rivals opened and copied.[15]

Before the Seven Years' War, the cornerstone of Louis XV's foreign policy was to secure the Polish crown for a French candidate – a policy supported by his cousin, Prince de Conti, who considered himself the leading candidate. Unfortunately, Russia had similar interests in Poland and as the Seven Years' War approached, diplomatic relations between Paris and St Petersburg were at an all-time low, the last French ambassador having been thrown out by the Anglophile Grand Chancellor, Alexis Bestucheff.

Inside Russia, the Empress Elizabeth Petrovna found herself at odds with Bestucheff. The empress was in fact pro-French, but with no French ambassador or agent it was impossible for Louis XV to communicate with her. An envoy, the Chevalier de Valcroissant, had tried to make contact, but Bestucheff had arrested him and thrown him into prison. Any diplomatic activity would have to be conducted secretly, hence the formation of *le secret du Roi*, with Conti at its head.[16]

In 1755, a secret agent was chosen to open communications with the empress. This spy was a 'creature' of Prince de Conti. Charles de Beaumont – as d'Eon was known at the time – was deemed to have all the right qualities befitting a secret agent. He was intelligent, active, an expert fencer, cultured and, as a portrait of him at the age of 25 shows, completely believable 'in drag'. Conti's plan was for Beaumont to travel to Russia disguised as a lady in waiting, 'Mademoiselle Lia de Beaumont'.

With 'her' would travel 'Chevalier Douglas', a Scottish émigré named Douglas MacKenzie taking refuge in France. Douglas was also a secret agent. Posing as a mineralogist he had been ordered to collect information on the Russian resources, intentions and the size of its army. While doing so 'Lia' would present the empress with a personal letter from Louis XV, inviting her to open a secret correspondence.

The mission began and Lia secured a position as *lectrice* to the empress, who had a fondness for French literature. At some point Lia revealed Louis' letter and also the nature of the deception – that he was a man. The empress played along with the ruse and wrote to Louis, a letter which Beaumont took back to France with him. Encouraged by this success, in the spring of 1756 Louis sent Beaumont back to St Petersburg to help consolidate a treaty between Russia and France. This time Beaumont dressed as a man and played the part of Lia's brother (sometimes reported as 'uncle'), who was employed as assistant to the French ambassador.

Beaumont remained in Russia through most of the Seven Years' War, returning to France in 1761 whereupon he was appointed captain of dragoons. Serving only a single campaign, Beaumont was an aide-de-camp to Marshal de Broglie and received two wounds. In recognition of his bravery and for his services in helping secure peace with Russia, Beaumont was awarded the Cross of Saint-Louis and the title Chevalier d'Eon.

In September 1762 d'Eon was sent to Britain as secretary to the Duke of Nivernais, the negotiator charged with establishing British terms to end the war. After being pelted with potatoes at Dover, the two Frenchmen found themselves in happier circumstances, mixed up in agreeable London society. D'Eon became a favourite of Queen Charlotte and, if rumours were to be believed, attended private, after-dark audiences with her.

During the negotiations Nivernais was visited by British Under-Secretary of State, Robert Wood. An indiscretion on Wood's part alerted d'Eon to a startling opportunity. Inside the Englishman's portfolio were the final instructions and ultimatum, which was destined for the Duke of Bedford, the British ambassador to Versailles. Knowing Wood liked a drink, d'Eon had Nivernais invite him to dinner. While the Englishman was plied with wine by Nivernais, d'Eon opened the portfolio, copied the dispatch to Bedford and sent it off to Versailles with all speed. When the duke began his negotiations, the French ministers knew what he would hold out for and were thus quickly able to come to terms. When the peace was signed in Paris on 10 February 1763, d'Eon was chosen to carry the ratification by George III from London.

The end of the Seven Years' War did not mean the end of *le secret*. Louis XV wanted revenge and set a secret plan to invade England. D'Eon became a middle man between his cousin, the Marquis de la Rozière, and the Count of Broglie, now head of the king's espionage service. Rozière was charged with gaining intelligence on the English coast and its tides, as well as the state of English military readiness. In addition to passing on Rozière's intelligence, d'Eon was charged with some espionage of his own; namely to probe the British court. To this end he was made *ministre plénipotentiaire* in Britain, pending the arrival of the ambassador, Count of Guerchy. This was to prove the high-water mark of d'Eon's clandestine career.

When Guerchy arrived, d'Eon was heavily in debt. As it became clear France would not meet the chevalier's creditors, he began collecting secret documents with which to blackmail his way to solvency. Refusing to return to France, in 1764 d'Eon published a book that humiliated Guerchy and hinted at scandal in high places in England and France. The book was a roaring success, but d'Eon was not so stupid as to reveal the king's secret plan to invade England – and this probably saved his life. A decade later, an agent was sent to negotiate for d'Eon's documents. Pierre Augustin Caron de Beaumarchais arrived in London incognito and offered d'Eon a settlement of 1,500 louis up front, with further sums in the form of a pension. The chevalier agreed and burned the incriminating letters.

Shortly after Beaumarchais returned to Versailles in triumph, Louis XV died on 10 May 1774. He was succeeded by his grandson, Louis XVI, who, in one of his first acts, dissolved *le secret du Roi*. He also tried to tempt d'Eon to return to France before he disclosed his espionage activities in England. Attempting reconciliation with the English, Louis XVI did not want the invasion secret to become public knowledge. In the end d'Eon accepted Louis XVI's guarantees of safety and a pension, provided he could return to France and live as a woman. The king agreed and for the short term at least, harmony reigned. But while d'Eon found temporary reconciliation, across the Atlantic dramatic events began to unfold in Britain's American colonies.

As commander-in-chief of the Continental army during the American Revolutionary War, and as the first President of the United States, George Washington (1732–99) holds a lofty position in the history of America. As late as 1976 he was still being honoured when, in an attempt to clarify the seniority among the pantheon of American generals, President Ford declared Washington the most senior US military officer of all time.

To complement his 'father of the nation' position, the Washington legend has been underpinned with a strong moral code. Not long after his death in 1799, Parson Weems published the famous story of how young Washington had cut down his father's cherry tree. When questioned on the fate of the tree, young Washington replied: 'I cannot tell a lie. It was I who chopped down the cherry tree.' The story, true or not, was intended as an inspirational parable for children and parents alike. As the first President of the United States elected under the US Constitution, Washington did indeed set a fine example. By standing down from the presidency, he set an important precedent: the highest office would not be 'for life'. In such respects he marked himself different from both Napoleon and Cromwell.

On the other hand, to achieve what he did, Washington must have had a ruthless streak within him. He was a man of his times. The famous Virginian was a slave-owning planter and freemason who grew Indian hemp, which many believe he smoked to relieve dental troubles.[17] Like many of the 'founding fathers', his religious beliefs are a matter of some controversy and, perhaps most un-American of all, he was an enthusiast of cricket. Washington was, after all, descended from Englishmen. Perhaps this English gene, ticking away inside him, imparted to him something of Walsingham and Thurloe.

Washington was every bit as astute as any leader before him, or since, in the art of espionage and deception. This skill was a vital attribute to the American commander, because the Revolutionary War was not a regular war – it was really a civil war. At the time there was a thin dividing line between being 'British' and 'American', with many seeing themselves as being both, or neither. It was not as if the redcoats were without support in the colony; quite the opposite. While supporters of the revolution were known variously as Patriots, Whigs or simply rebels, its opponents were called Tories.

It is unclear where Washington derived his penchant for underhand tactics, but they seemed to come naturally to him. Prior to the revolution he had served as a colonial officer during the French and Indian War and gained some insight into irregular warfare, albeit on the receiving end. During the Braddock Expedition of 1755 – a British attempt to retake the Ohio country from the French – Washington was involved in the disastrous battle of Monongahela. The British column he belonged to was ambushed by French soldiers and allied tribesmen. Washington was lucky to survive the retreat, having his coat pierced by musket balls four times. He had more success in the Forbes Expedition, which successfully drove the French away from Fort Duquesne.

There now comes one of those small turning points in history, which later snowball into a matter of huge significance. Throughout Washington's military career, he desired a commission in the regular British army. This promotion never came and in 1759 Washington resigned from the army, married and went back to living the life of a genteel, slave-owning, Virginia planter. Ponder for a moment what would have been the outcome of the Revolutionary War with Washington on the British side? Instead, Washington was available to become commander-in-chief of the Continental Army on 15 June 1775. Realizing the Americans would be no match for the British regulars in toe-to-toe pitched battle, Washington opted to slowly wear the British down, while his army gained support. He could only hope to achieve this by out-thinking and out-spying the British.

Unfortunately for Washington, the British already had a head start on him. General Thomas Gage (1719–87) had commanded the British forces in North America since 1763 and was well aware of the growing rebellion and the likelihood of war. In response, Gage had established a network of spies among the Patriots and was thus able to counteract their military preparations by raiding arms caches.

Annoyed by the success of Gage's raids, the Patriots created a small surveillance committee within Boston's secret 'Sons of Liberty' organization. Over the winter of 1774–75 this committee met at the Green Dragon Tavern on Union Street. Thirty-strong, the group patrolled Boston at night looking for signs that the British were preparing to raid patriot military stores. The members of the Green Dragon group are often referred to as 'the Mechanics'. One of their leaders was Dr Benjamin Church, a noted author of Patriot propaganda. He was also General Gage's highest-paid spy.

A Harvard graduate, Church had studied medicine in England and married an English wife. On his return to America he continued to live the high life and found himself increasingly in debt. Spying offered an attractive second income, which allowed him to maintain a mansion and a mistress. Such high living was well beyond his means and should have been noticed by his colleagues. Indeed, fellow Mechanic Paul Revere had his own spies inside General Gage's headquarters and knew there was a traitor among the Mechanics. Unsure who that traitor might be, the Mechanics turned to the Bible. At the beginning of each meeting at the Green Dragon, each of the Mechanics would swear on a Bible not to reveal the group's secrets. A noble idea perhaps, but not one to deter someone as unscrupulous as Church.

Following the battles of Lexington and Concord, on 21 April 1775, after the patriots had driven the British troops back into Boston, Church entered the besieged city to meet Gage. Unluckily for Church, he was seen talking with Gage in an overly familiar manner. On Church's return, Revere confronted him with this. The doctor told Revere he had been indeed been arrested and interrogated by Gage for several days but had been set free. Suspicions were averted for now.

In May 1775 Church informed Gage that he was being sent to the Continental Congress in Philadelphia, to arrange for it to recognize the various militias at Boston as its army. He accomplished this task well and on his return, the Massachusetts militias became the Continental Army under the command of George Washington. Church was appointed chief physician of the army.

Church finally became undone after he sent an enciphered letter to a Major Cane in Boston, 'on his magistys service'. Three times Church failed to get this message through to the British lines, so he asked his mistress to deliver it to either Captain Wallace of HMS *Rose*, the Royal Collector Charles Dudley or George Rome, a merchant-ship owner. Instead she went to a local baker called Godfrey Wainwood who said he would deliver the letter on her behalf.

Wainwood agreed but did nothing about it until late September 1775 when Church's mistress sent him a note reminding him to send the letter. Wainwood became suspicious. How could she have known the letter had not been delivered? Wainwood took the letter and was presented to General Washington. Washington examined the letter and asked for the woman to be arrested. After a lengthy interrogation, she revealed Church was the author. This disclosure led to Washington ordering Church and his papers be seized.

Church readily acknowledged the letter and said the enciphered text was a harmless note to his brother-in-law in Boston. Why then, Washington wondered, did Church attempt to send the letter via a British warship, rather than send it under a flag of truce from Cambridge? Why, if it was so harmless, did Church refuse to provide the cipher key? A classmate of Church, Reverend Samuel West, stepped forward and offered to break the cipher. A second person, Elbridge Gerry, a member of the Massachusetts Provincial Congress, teamed up with Colonel Elisha Porter to make an independent examination of the letter. It turned out to be a simple mono-alphabetical cipher and was easily broken.[18]

The letter gave details of artillery, casualties, troop totals, provisions, stores, recruitment and gunpowder manufacture. In it Church also pleaded with Cane for the British to come to an arrangement with the rebels rather than declaring war on them. Washington confronted Church, who said the letter was not an intelligence report, but Washington was not convinced. In his defence, Church claimed he was trying to overstate the strength of the rebel army in an attempt to gain concessions from the British. Washington convened his officers to discuss what to do with Church. They all agreed that the issue should be presented to the Continental Congress.

The Church case presented Congress with a problem. No one had considered what to do with captured civilian spies or traitors. A committee was formed to consider what would be the proper punishment for those passing intelligence to the enemy. On 7 November 1775 the Continental Congress added the death penalty for espionage to the Articles of War, but the clause was not applied retrospectively and Dr Church remained in jail, without pen or ink and unable to speak to anybody without there being a sheriff or magistrate present. However, the following year Church was released on health grounds. He took a ship to the West Indies, but was never heard of again and was presumed lost at sea.

The modern United States Army intelligence service dates from 1776. In that year George Washington asked Lieutenant-Colonel Thomas Knowlton (1740–76) to command an elite detachment of volunteers to carry out dangerous secret missions. Known as 'Knowlton's Rangers', the group comprised of 150 officers and men and was the first American special forces unit. Serving with the Rangers was Captain Nathan Hale (1755–76), a graduate of Yale College and the first martyr of the revolution.

After the battle of Brooklyn on 27 August 1776, Washington's defeated troops were forced to evacuate Long Island to the new British commander, General Howe. Nathan Hale volunteered to go behind enemy lines on an intelligence-gathering mission. With no experience in undercover missions, he adopted the cover of a Dutch school teacher and armed himself with his diploma from Yale as proof, before setting out. Nothing is known about what Hale managed to achieve, except on 21 September he was arrested on suspicion of espionage. Hale admitted he was a serving officer in the Continental Army and in so doing sealed his fate. On the orders of General Howe, Nathan Hale was hanged the following day outside the Dove Tavern, which is now the intersection of Third Avenue and Sixty-Sixth Street.[19] According to tradition, before execution Hale was allowed to make a speech which included the now immortal words: 'I only regret that I have but one life to lose for my country.' Although Hale had proved to be a singular disaster as a spy, as a martyr he was without peer.

Far more successful in terms of intelligence provided was the so-called 'Culper' spy ring. This network operated in and around New York City, which had been seized by the British shortly after Nathan Hale's execution. It was formed in 1778 and was controlled by Major Benjamin Tallmadge, a cavalry officer working from an outpost on the Hudson River. A former classmate of Nathan Hale, Tallmadge was a native of Brookhaven, Long Island. Through his local contacts he recruited 28-year-old Abraham Woodhull as his principal agent, based in Setauket. Using the pseudonym 'Samuel Culper', Woodhull recruited an agent in New York City called Robert Townsend who operated as Samuel Culper Junior.

To the detriment of his nervous system, Townsend recruited numerous agents throughout the city and gathered vital intelligence for the rebel cause. One of these agents was the Tory printer James Rivington. Despite Rivington's anti-Patriot publications, he and Townsend went into business together in 1779, opening a coffee shop. This establishment was used as a listening post to glean intelligence from overheard conversations of British patrons. To further cement his cover, Townsend would write articles for Rivington's *Royal Gazette*.

Although Washington advised the group to use secret ink in their correspondence, Tallmadge also introduced a numerical substitution code. Each of the 763 numbers used in the code was assigned either to a word, phrase or name. The surviving examples include '711' for George Washington, '745' for England, '38' for attack, '727' for New York, and so on. To ensure speedy communication between Culpers Sr and Jr, a Setauket tavern keeper named Austin Roe was recruited. In order to keep the tavern supplied, Roe frequently travelled into New York City. This allowed him to collect messages written in secret ink from Townsend, which he then deposited in hiding places on Woodhull's farm. These deposits, known as 'dead letter drops' in the trade, ensured Woodhull never had to leave the farm and raise suspicion. As soon as Woodhull received a report out of New York City by this means, he used a final link in the chain to get the message across Long Island Sound – a boatman named Caleb Brewster.

To arrange for Brewster to collect the messages, a system of semaphore was used. Another member of the chain, Anna Strong, would put a black petticoat onto her washing line when there was a message to be delivered. To indicate which cove the boatman should use, in addition to the petticoat, Strong would hang an arrangement of handkerchiefs. Receiving this signal, Brewster would take the coded messages across to Connecticut to Tallmadge, who would transmit them to Washington without delay. As can be imagined, this chain did not spring up overnight, but took a long time to perfect. However, it delivered several huge intelligence coups which went a long way towards securing victory for the revolution.

In July 1780, the Culper ring reported that the British were planning to attack the French expeditionary force, which had landed at Newport, Rhode Island, on 10 July. The French involvement in the American Revolutionary War can in large part be put down to the work of the Committee of Secret Correspondence, which had been formed in November 1775. This group was made up of five members, each appointed for the sole purpose of corresponding with supporters of the revolution in Britain and elsewhere.

In March 1776 the committee appointed Silas Deane as its agent in France. Posing as a Bermudian merchant, Deane's mission was to gain secret assistance from the French. Still smarting from its losses to Britain in the Seven Years' War, France became a clandestine supporter of the American rebels, providing them with covert aid through a 'front' company called Roderigue Hortalez et Compagnie. This clandestine support became open with the signing of the French–American treaty of alliance on 6 February 1778. The alliance was further strengthened in 1780 when Lieutenant-General Rochambeau was sent to support Washington with 6,000 French troops.

The British wanted to attack Rochambeau while his troops were still recovering from their arduous sea crossing. To that end 8,000 men were sent from New York to Whitestone, Long Island, from where they would embark and be taken to Rhode Island. This information was transmitted by the Culper ring to Washington, who received it on the afternoon of 21 July. In an attempt to pin the British down at New York City, Washington immediately drew up plans for a fictitious attack on the city, which he signed and then had delivered to a British outpost. At the same time he sent out orders for his army to manoeuvre in the direction of Manhattan to add weight to the bogus plans he had just delivered. Inside New York City, British general Henry Clinton saw he had no option but to recall the 8,000 men in expectation of Washington's attack. The French expeditionary force was thus saved from probable destruction.

The Culper ring also played a prominent role in exposing the treason of American general Benedict Arnold, and to the capture and execution of British intelligence officer Major John André. British troops were quartered in Townsend's (Culper Jr) home in Oyster Bay. One evening, when a British colonel was holding a dinner, Townsend's younger sister,

The oldest visual record of a spy? Scenes from an Egyptian temple relief carving of the battle of Kadesh. The two kneeling figures are Hittite spies being beaten by Rameses' officers.

Caught in a honey trap. Delilah betrays Samson to the Philistines, providing them with the secret of his colossal strength.

Betrayed by a kiss. Judas had told the temple guards that he would identify Jesus from his followers by kissing him.

Julius Caesar understood the need for military intelligence perfectly well and employed numerous spies and scouts. Strange then that he fell victim to a conspiracy. It is said that he was warned of the danger by a soothsayer, but was then convinced into rejecting the advice as pure superstition. He was stabbed 23 times on the day predicted by the soothsayer.

The wife of Emperor Justinian, Empress Theodora was reputedly among the most ruthless tyrants that ever lived. She maintained her own network of spies, informing on those who alluded to her scandalous past.

Genghis Khan. His notoriety often clouds the recognition his genius for war deserves. A true father of his nation, in 2003 it was estimated that the Great Khan had 16 million living male descendants.

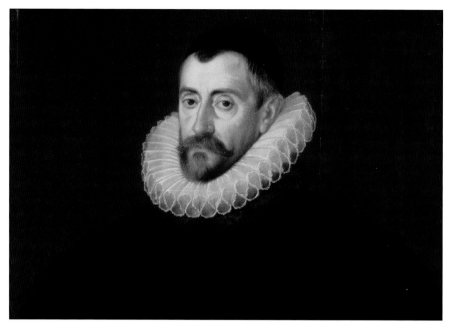

Sir Francis Walsingham, Secretary of State and spymaster to Elizabeth I, *c.*1585. Through his Machiavellian dealings, Walsingham managed to secure the conviction and execution of Mary Queen of Scots and had spies watching the build up of the Spanish Armada.

Mary Queen of Scots is beheaded at Fotheringhay Castle, 1587. The executioner is about to deliver the first of three blows in the bungled execution.

Frederick the Great leads his soldiers against the Russians at the battle of Zorndorf in 1758.

Marshal of France, Maurice de Saxe (1696–1750), victor over the British at Fontenoy (1745), where French officers courteously invited the British to 'fire first'.

George Washington, general in the American Revolution and first President of the United States, 1789–97.

Portrait of General Charles Pichegru (1761–1804). From the early stages of the French Revolutionary War it appeared that a soldier would replace Louis XVI as ruler of France.

Joseph Fouché, Duke of Otranto (1759–1820), Minister of Police under Napoleon.

Napoleon I, Emperor of France.

Austrian general Melas prepares to sign the Convention of Alessandria, presented to him by General Berthier, on 15 June 1800.

Arthur Wellesley, First Duke of Wellington, by Sir Thomas Lawrence.

Wellington's chief of communications during the Peninsular and Waterloo campaigns, George Scovell (1774–1861).

Sarah, saw a stranger come into the house and place a letter addressed to 'John Anderson' on the pantry shelf. The colonel's guest, John André, placed the letter in his pocket. Later in the evening, she overheard the colonel and André discussing the American stronghold at West Point, where considerable stores were located. Thinking this was important, Sarah had a messenger sent into New York City for supplies. The messenger took a note from Sarah to her brother, mentioning West Point as a British objective and also the names André and Anderson.

When this information was communicated up the chain to Tallmadge he was dumbstruck. He had recently received a message from the commander of West Point, General Benedict Arnold, that a friend of his called John Anderson might be passing his way. As a favour, Arnold asked that Anderson be given an escort of dragoons, as he would not know the countryside. Tallmadge realized Arnold was up to something and so set out in pursuit of this John Anderson to gather proof.

Passed up for promotion, badly wounded in action and upset by the alliance with France, Benedict Arnold was a time bomb in the American ranks waiting to go off. To shorten the fuse, while recuperating in Philadelphia Arnold met Peggy Shippen, whom he married in April 1779. Shippen was an 18-year-old socialite from a family with well-known Tory sympathies. In order to keep his wife in the manner to which she was accustomed, Arnold began living beyond his means and getting into debt. Prior to meeting Arnold, Shippen had been courted by Clinton's secret-service chief, Major André. It is not too much a leap of faith to suggest that Shippen talked Arnold into opening a secret correspondence with André, in order to remedy his situation. Arnold wrote to André and proposed a deal. For £20,000 he would deliver West Point over to the British.

On 20 September 1780, André travelled up the Hudson River in the sloop *Vulture*. He was rowed ashore at Stony Point where he set off to meet with Arnold. While this meeting was conducted over the course of 21 and 22 September, *Vulture* came under fire from an American shore battery and was forced to leave André behind. In order to escape, Arnold provided André with civilian clothes and a passport under the name of John Anderson. He also provided André with six papers showing the British how to take West Point. These papers were hidden in André's stockings.

On 23 September, André was stopped by three armed men near Tarrytown, New York. Thinking the men were Tories, André revealed he was a British officer. They told him they were Americans and he was now their prisoner. André said he was really American and showed them his passport, but the men were suspicious. Searching him they found the papers, after which André tried bribing them to let him go. Unusually they did not accept the bribes.

The militiamen still did not know the significance of their capture. They turned him over to a lieutenant-colonel of dragoons, John Jameson, who unwittingly decided to send 'Anderson' to Benedict Arnold at West Point. Fortunately for the Americans, he did send the papers found on the prisoner directly to General Washington. At this point Tallmadge intervened and stopped the prisoner from being sent to Arnold. When the truth of André's mission became known the British officer was tried on 29 September. He was found guilty of being behind enemy lines in disguise and under a false name. After the fate of Nathan Hale, Tallmadge's former classmate, death could be the only sentence.

Washington sent Clinton a message that André would be hanged at 5.00pm on 1 October. Clinton appealed on the grounds that André had landed under a flag of truce and the execution was delayed a day while Washington sent a delegation to discuss this. In the meantime Benedict Arnold had escaped and gone over to the British. He wrote to Washington and explained that André had indeed landed under a flag of truce so should be spared. Washington was in no mood for bargaining with traitors and so offered Clinton a deal. André would be spared the gallows in return for Arnold being sent back to him. Clinton would not agree to this and to the regret of many on both sides, André was hanged at noon on 2 October. What goes around comes around.[20]

5

VIVE LA RÉVOLUTION?

*The names are called over, the heads fall, and
pouf, pouf, the thing is done!*

Quote attributed to Citizen Héron, Robespierre's chief of secret police

The French Revolution of 1789 caused a veritable tsunami of paranoia among the ruling classes of Europe. True, America had recently become a republic and the world had not come to an end, but this was different. The French Revolution put a real and immediate threat of democracy on the doorstep of every European country – Britain included.

In the role of a real-life Scarlet Pimpernel, the Gascon Baron de Batz (1760–1822) was author of several attempts to rescue the ill-fated French king and queen. De Batz hatched a plot to snatch King Louis while he was being taken to the dreaded guillotine. On the day of the execution, 21 January 1793, de Batz ambushed the guards escorting the king. Unfortunately for de Batz, republican spies had infiltrated his plot and ensured that there were only a handful of supporters to heed his call to attack. De Batz managed to fight his way out of the mêlée and, with his king dead, instead devoted himself to saving the deposed queen, Marie Antoinette. He enlisted the support of a captain in the National Guard, whose company often guarded the queen. The night of 22 June 1793 was selected to stage the escape and disguises were made for the fleeing royals. However, republican spies again learned of the plot and changed the guard. A price was put on de Batz's head.

The fact he managed to survive in the capital is a testament to the power of gold over the Republic's discredited paper money. While bribing republican agents to overlooking his presence, de Batz hit upon an extreme idea to destroy the revolution from within. Using his ample funds, he promoted the most outrageous political extremists and terrorists so that ordinary Frenchmen would become sickened with the Republic and crave the return of the monarchy. On 17 November 1793 he was arrested for taking part in a scam to defraud the French India Company.

Although 55 of his associates were executed, de Batz escaped the guillotine largely because the government feared what damaging things he might say if put on trial. After the fall of Robespierre's government on 27 July 1794, he was again free to roam. Before sliding off into obscurity, de Batz had one last throw of the dice. On 4 October 1795 he was involved in stiring up a large Royalist mob, which threatened to overthrow the republican regime. The revolt was famously put down in the streets of Paris by artillery fire directed by an ambitious young Corsican officer – Napoleon Bonaparte.

The multitude of royalist spies and agents active at the time were complemented by the shortest adult spy in recorded history. A servant of the Orléans family before the revolution, the spy Richebourg (1768–1858) was reputedly just 23in (58cm) tall. During the revolution he smuggled messages for royalist agents by posing as an infant wrapped in swaddling clothes, carried in the arms of his 'nurse'.

Such was the level of paranoia inside France that during the 11-month reign of 'the Terror' up to July 1794 somewhere in the region of 17,000 people were sent to the guillotine. During this time police spies and informants were everywhere in the streets, cafés and at public spectacles, watching and listening, waiting for even the most innocuous hint of anti-republican sentiment. Every day in Paris, the floors of the prisons groaned under the weight of newly arrived suspects denounced by these secret police agents. The guillotine eventually had to be moved when the ground could no longer soak up the blood and members of the government grew sick of watching decapitations.

Chief of the secret police was Héron, dubbed 'Robespierre's bulldog' by his victims. History records him as a paranoid lunatic. It is said that he never left home without a veritable arsenal concealed about his person – a large hunting knife, two daggers, loaded pistols and two blunderbusses hidden beneath a bulging cloak. His thugs were posted in the corridors everywhere around the infamous Committee of Public Safety, the extremist political group with such brotherly notions as 'freedom must be established by violence' and 'the time has come to organize the despotism of liberty'. When the committee needed an enemy eliminated it was Héron they called for. He described his work simply: 'The names are called over, the heads fall, and pouf, pouf, the thing is done!' Héron's duplicity is revealed when we learn that he was charged by Robespierre with spying on the government's Committee of General Security, who in turn employed Héron to spy on Robespierre![1]

Following the king's execution, the revolutionary government was wary it might suffer the fate of the ancient Roman Republic – something they called 'Caesarism' – in other words, a military coup d'état. The first attempt at this came in 1792 after the collapse of the Bourbon monarchy on 10 August. In a bid to restore the constitutional monarchy, the Marquis de Lafayette tried to make his troops swear an oath in support of the king. They refused and Lafayette was forced to surrender to the Austrians. The government responded by sending representatives 'on mission' to spy on France's armies and its generals for signs of weakness or counter-revolution.

Nevertheless, a second, potentially more serious coup was attempted in April 1793 by General Charles Dumouriez (1739–1823), commander of the republican army fighting in Holland. Since the declaration of war with Britain on 1 February 1793, the British government had taken a pragmatic approach to restoring stability to Europe. Unenthused by the prospect of a democratic republican neighbour, the British government preferred France to be governed like itself, by a constitutional monarchy. This did not necessarily mean a restoration of the Bourbon monarchy, who were still enormously unpopular in France. It should also be remembered, with some irony, that the Bourbons had recently supported republicans against Britain in the American Revolution – they ought not to have harboured too much hope of British aid.

With the Bourbons out of favour, eyes turned to a commoner, by preference a popular and successful soldier behind whom the country could unite. The prime candidate was General Dumouriez, a former minister of war who it was believed already harboured his own ambitions of taking up the crown.[2] Dumouriez had opened a secret correspondence with the Austrian general Karl Mack (1752–1828) and also with London.[3] Having worked out a plan to march on Paris, Dumouriez found his plans were thwarted when his troops refused to follow. On 5 April 1793 General Dumoriez fled, first to Ostend, where he was refused a passport by the British, and then to the Austrians.

The trail went cold until August 1794 when a memoir reached the British Foreign Office alleging two members of the French Convention had made an overture for peace and a restoration of the monarchy if amnesties were granted for their part in the regicide of Louis XVI.[4] If this document was true, it might prove possible to destroy the revolution from within. It was decided to send an emissary to Switzerland to investigate the letter and set up a secret-service network. The organization of spies in France came under the remit of the Alien Office. This body had been set up after the British government had passed an 'Alien Act' on 8 January 1793. This act had initially been intended to regulate and place surveillance on the large numbers of French émigrés and other foreign nationals coming from the Continent to escape the revolution and war, thus providing a counter-espionage agency.

The man chosen by the Alien Office as spymaster for Switzerland was a magistrate named William Wickham (1761–1840). Having been educated at Oxford, Wickham had taken a law degree in Geneva in 1786 and then married Elanore Bertrand from Geneva. Before joining the service in August 1793, Wickham had written to the Home Office stressing the importance of Switzerland in any forthcoming war with France. Centrally placed in Europe, he described it as the perfect staging post to assemble an army that could strike at France's eastern border, or southwards to support operations against France's Mediterranean coast.[5] Switzerland was also the perfect place to infiltrate spies into France and correspond with them. Given his background and interest in the region, Wickham appeared the obvious choice.

Wickham left Britain on 16 October and travelled to Switzerland, joining the ambassador, Lord Robert Fitzgerald, at Lausanne.[6] His initial investigations showed the report of French instability was optimistic at best and there was no evident desire to return to the pre-1789 monarchy. Nevertheless, the British government was still keen to see who the key figures in Paris were and if there was any chance of reasoning with them. To that end Wickham began to assemble his intelligence network, which pushed on into the French capital. Recognizing Wickham's energy and not privy to the true nature of his work, Lord Fitzgerald stood down as ambassador, allowing Wickham to take the position. He took up his official residence in Bern on 12 January 1795, sending to London for more funds and his Swiss wife.

Through his secret network, Wickham was alerted that the French commander on the Rhine, General Charles Pichegru (1761–1804) had been in contact with a Swiss border guard, Captain Victor Roland, a confirmed royalist.[7] From first impressions it appeared that Pichegru was unhappy with the direction France had taken and might be open to offers. A soldier before 1789, Pichegru rose to prominence as the commander of a National Guard battalion. When his commander, General Hoche, was arrested in December 1793, Pichegru became commander-in-chief of the Army of the Rhine-and-Moselle, then the Army of the North in February 1794. With success after success, he became a celebrity and received the title 'Saviour of the Homeland'. However, somewhere amid the constant campaigning, Pichegru's doubts and unease began to surface. In their continued discussions, Pichegru told Roland he would help restore the royal family if it consented to a constitutional government.

Facing Pichegru on the opposite bank of the Rhine was an army of French émigrés commanded by Louis Henri Joseph de Bourbon, Prince de Condé (c.1756–1830). The prince had been one of the first princes to emigrate from France after the fall of the Bastille in 1789 and was one of the principal exponents of counter-revolution. While living in the German city of Worms, in 1791 he formed what was known as the 'Army of Condé' and sided with Austria. By the time Wickham arrived in Switzerland, this army consisted of just 5,000 volunteers and was as short of cash as it was down on its luck. In late May 1795 Wickham cryptically informed the prince that a Swiss officer had established a safe and reliable means of contact with a French general. Unknown to Wickham there were already plans to make contact with Pichegru.[8]

Two days before, Condé had met with a secret agent named the Comte de Montgaillard (1761–1841) with whom he had discussed the possibility of an approach to the republican commander. Montgaillard was a self-styled secret agent and intriguer, at once allied to all men and causes – his allegiances shifted depending on the payday. He came from an impoverished noble family in the Languedoc region of south-western France and enrolled himself as a Bourbon secret agent soon after the outbreak of revolution. After the downfall of the monarchy, Montgaillard travelled to England on 20 September 1792, where he stayed for just six weeks. His first intention was to join the Army of Condé, but instead he returned to France in November 1792.

Between then and 1795, Montgaillard denied almost everything said about him.[9] It is said he lived quite openly in Paris during the Terror, which has led to speculation that he worked as an agent for Maximilien Robespierre (1758–94), the leading light among the Jacobin 'Terrorists'. As an agent, in May 1794 Montgaillard is supposed to have been charged with a mission to Austrian headquarters, during the course of which he met the Duke of York and Emperor Francis II of Austria. Montgaillard claimed he left Paris because it was not safe and was in the Allied camp at the emperor's request. The Duke of York then sent him to London – something Montgaillard at last confirmed – where he met many of the principal 'names' in British public life, including William Pitt and the Duke of Gloucester. However, he was suspected of being a Jacobin spy by the British and deported – Montgaillard denied this and said he left of his own free will.

Returning to the Continent, he went to Switzerland and from there was introduced to the Prince de Condé, head of the exiled royalist army. Montgalliard informed Condé that the British were only lukewarm on the idea of a Bourbon restoration and so he would have to take positive steps to ensure its success. Montgaillard proposed 'buying' General Pichegru and suggested a third party be used to act as an agent to sound out the general on their behalf.[10] This was because Pichegru's every move was shadowed by three political representatives who were agents of the government sent to monitor his reliability. If Montgaillard made the approach directly, he might well be recognized.

For an agent, Montgaillard suggested they use a Swiss man named Louis Fauche-Borel (1762–1829), a bookseller and publisher from Neufchatel. In late July 1795, Fauche-Borel received his instructions. In return for his services, on the re-establishment of the monarchy he would be made a millionaire, be given the directorship of the royal presses and be made inspector general of the royal libraries. If his mission failed, he would still be paid 1,000 louis in reward for his trouble. It was a win-win situation for the ardent monarchist.

Fauche-Borel now had to work out how to approach Pichegru and deliver Condé's message without the three deputies finding out. Pichegru was not easy to gain access to as he was an army commander and as such was surrounded with men. Fauche-Borel had no option but to follow the general and hope an opportunity arose.

On 11 June Fauche-Borel learned that Pichegru was travelling to the Upper Rhine region and would be stopping at an inn near Huningue. Entering the inn, Fauche-Borel found Pichegru with General Ferrand. Fauche-Borel made eye contact with Pichegru, who by now had noticed this mysterious figure following him all over the place. Pichegru turned to Ferrand and in a raised voice said, 'I'm not having dinner here; I will dine in Blopsheim, at Madame Salomon's'. Passing close to Fauche-Borel, Pichegru glanced at him 'significantly.' With Ferrand standing next to him, Fauche-Borel offered to give the general his coat because it was raining torrents outside. 'No, don't worry,' replied Ferrand, 'the general is not scared of rain.'

After dinner that evening, Fauche-Borel took a coach to Blopsheim. He presented himself at the château and asked to speak to Pichegru, claiming to have carried out his orders to supply champagne for his headquarters. The general was taking coffee when Fauche-Borel was presented to him. Fauche-Borel proceeded to tell him about some manuscripts he had of the philosopher Rousseau which were in Basle, in Switzerland. Seeing Fauche-Borel's obvious anxiety, Pichegru said: 'You can speak to me, what is it?' Fauche-Borel told him he was on an important mission. 'On behalf of whom?' quizzed the general. Fauche-Borel replied: 'Prince de Condé.' Intrigued, Pichegru asked the royalist: 'And what does he want of me?'

Fauche-Borel proceeded to explain how Condé wanted to join forces with his army and re-establish the Bourbons on the throne and return peace to France. Naturally suspicious, Pichegru asked to see Fauche-Borel's passport and confirm he was not an émigré but a Swiss printer. He said to Fauche-Borel: 'Return to the Prince, report that I want a letter confirming your mission ... I know his handwriting ... and telling me exactly what he wants from me. Be here the day after tomorrow at five in the morning.'

Hardly able to contain his excitement, Fauche-Borel scuttled off to Montgaillard, who spent the night composing a long letter to the general based on Condé's attentions. Fauche-Borel then went to Mulheim to find the prince and give an account of what had occurred. Condé wrote to Pichegru, giving him the codename 'Z' (and using 'Y' for the Austrians). He then told Fauche-Borel to inform Wickham what was going on, but not to tell Wickham that Montgaillard knew anything about it, as Wickham was suspicious of him.

When he arrived back at Blopsheim, Pichegru had gone, so Fauche-Borel was forced to follow him to Illkirch, near Strasbourg. He arrived saying he had seven cases of champagne for the general, and was admitted. 'Ah good, have you seen the Prince?' asked Pichegru. 'Yes General, here is his letter.' Pichegru read the letter and, after lighting his pipe, again asked Fauche-Borel what the Prince wanted. 'General,' replied Fauche-Borel, 'to join his army with yours; that you give him Huningue, that the white flag floats over Strasbourg and that you proclaim the King.' In reply Pichegru assured Fauche-Borel that the prince could count on him and outlined a plan where the two armies could reach Paris in 'fourteen marches'. He also hinted a deal would have to be done with the Austrians, who would be behind them.[11]

Thereupon began what Wickham called 'the Grand Plan'.[12] Secret discussions would continue with Pichegru and his deputy, General Moreau, both of whom appeared to genuinely favour a constitutional monarchy. At the same time, through their secret means, the British would promote uprisings in the predominantly royalist provinces in the south and west of France. With the country in a state of turmoil, a coup would be staged in Paris supported by at least one French army. To achieve this, a secret correspondence was established between Pichegru and the Austrian general Klinglin, both of whom met secretly in January 1796.

Communication was made through spy couriers. Packets were taken by Pichegru's aide-de-camp, General Badouville (alias *Coco*), to Strasbourg, then given to an intermediary named Demouget (alias *the Ferret*). From there they were smuggled across the Rhine. We are lucky to have many examples of the conspirators' secret codes, as much of the correspondence was captured at a later date. If an agent ferrying the information from one side of the Rhine to the other was caught, the arresting party would find a note reading something like the following extract from 2 January 1796:

452534:135.23520299114536.9600.4499
5677.52455294.9911990 4456990895231
250. votre oublie 452534:18474259904456
99140521489520 117 671189 Flute 99520[13]

Other letters would be written in plain text, but with names and certain key words substituted by codenames or enciphered. The following extract is a good example of this, with the codenames shown in italics:

> J'espérais, mon cher *Persée*, vous écrire, hier matin. Mais enfin *Louis* m'est venu de la ville, et a resté chés moi jusqu'a 4 heures, avec deux des ces amis, aussi 11.27.52.45,94.16. de *Bluet*, dont l'un surtout, me parait un homme de mérite, il se nomme 66.52.45.56.25.99.23.56.14.10 tous ont le plus grand desir de vous voir et irons chés vous incessament![14]

The letter makes much more sense when the codenames are revealed. *Persée* (Perseus) was Klinglin, *Louis* was Fauche-Borel and *Bluet* (Cornflower) was Wickham. The text does in fact read (after translation):

> I had hoped, my dear Klinglin, to write to you yesterday morning. But finally Fauche-Borel came to me from the city and remained at my home until 4 o'clock with two of his friends, also agents of Wickham, one of whom especially appears to me a man of merit named Fenouillot. All have the greatest desire to see you and will be with you shortly![15]

Just as the pieces of the plot appeared to fall into place, the project was holed below the water line by one of those within. Wickham had been uncomfortable with Montgaillard's involvement in the conspiracy from the start and had been warning Condé not to trust him. As far as was possible Wickham had frozen the count out of the picture, in particular when it came to the distribution of secret funds. Ignoring any loss of prestige, Montgaillard was hurt financially, unable to cream off his little 'commissions'. An unpaid, jilted spy is a dangerous creature and if Wickham and Condé ever made a mistake they should have paid Montgaillard with a generous pension and shipped him off somewhere out of the way. Either that or arranged an 'accident' for him. They did neither.

By June 1796, Montgaillard felt it was useless for him to spend any more time in Germany and decided to go to Venice to seek out the commander of the French army in Italy, Napoleon Bonaparte. Travelling to Munich, Montgaillard received passports from the Austrians after telling them he intended to join General Dagobert Wurmser, the Austrian general facing Bonaparte. Instead he travelled to Venice, then still technically a neutral state, arriving on 2 September with his companion the Abbé du Montet.[16]

In Venice he presented himself to the plenipotentiary of the French Republic, Lallement, and proceeded to tell him 'secrets' that were of interest to the future of the state. Lallement's role in Venice was similar to Wickham's mission in Switzerland. In addition to his ambassadorial role, he spent a lot of his time running spy networks, sending important intelligence to Bonaparte. It is alleged Montgaillard offered to spy on behalf of the French Army, but it is uncertain if this offer was genuine or simply a ploy to ingratiate himself with the republicans at a later date. It should be mentioned that while speaking to Lallement, Montgaillard was also visiting the British representative in Venice, Francis Drake. To him Montgaillard suggested offering Bonaparte the same deal offered to Pichegru, namely paying him off to serve Louis XVIII (ruled 1814–24).[17]

Having hatched this new project, Montgaillard planned to travel to Milan around mid-December. Before going, he made a call to a member of the Russian legation in Venice, the Empress Catherine's special advisor on French affairs, the Comte d'Antraigues. This title was yet another front, as Montgaillard knew d'Antraigues was in fact Louis XVIII's top-secret agent in the city.

Emmanuel-Louis-Henri de Launay, Comte d'Antraigues (1753–1812) had fled revolutionary France and launched a career as a secret agent. On leaving France d'Antraigues acquired both Spanish and Russian nationalities. He took up a post in Venice as Empress Catherine's advisor on French affairs. From Venice d'Antraigues formed an important link in the secret chain of spies getting information out of Paris. Royalist spies sent from Britain to Paris would pass their correspondence to the Spanish ambassador in Paris. In turn he would forward their messages on to Spain's man in Venice, Don Simon de las Casas, who passed them to d'Antraigues.[18]

The exact nature of Montgaillard's meeting with d'Antraigues will later take on huge importance. We do know that Montgaillard explained his project to convert Bonaparte to the royalists' cause. To help achieve this, Montgaillard asked for the 'modest sum' of 36,000 francs with which to open negotiations. D'Antraigues was sceptical and said he would not give a penny without direct orders from Louis XVIII, then sent to Germany for advice. While waiting for word from the royalist pretender, Montgaillard went back to Drake and asked him for the money. He even wrote to Fauche-Borel and asked him to go to

Milan and repeat what he had done with Pichegru, but this time with Bonaparte (codenamed *Éléonore* in Montgaillard's letters).[19] The Swiss publisher-turned-spy ignored him.

Montgaillard quit Venice in December 1796. Most of his papers were left behind with his accomplice, Montet, but he did take two letters from Condé, one from Louis XVIII plus 36 pages of copies showing how far negotiations with Pichegru had developed.[20] His plan to reach Milan ran into complications as Austrian troops were massing to relieve the fortress of Mantua, which was under French siege. Unable to slip through their lines, he was arrested and taken to General Josef Alvinzy at Trent.

Alvinzy was unwilling to let Montgaillard continue with his mission and instead forbade him from taking any other road than that leading to the Tyrol and the headquarters of Archduke Charles at Offemburg. Before leaving, Alvinzy confided in Montgaillard that he was having enormous trouble getting messages through the siege lines to Wurmser in Mantua, which was on the verge of falling to the French. To smuggle messages through, Austrian spies resorted to the following means. A short message, no more than a few lines long, was written on a small piece of paper, which was rolled up. This piece of paper was then encased in a wax ball, which was swallowed by the spy carrying the message. Unfortunately for the Austrians, Bonaparte learned of this method and when he next caught a spy, he retrieved the message through forced 'evacuations'. According to Fauche-Borel, the battle of Rivoli (14 January 1797) was lost because of these interceptions.[21]

Thwarted in Italy, Montgaillard returned to Germany and sought out the Prince de Condé. This time he resorted to pure and simple blackmail to get his money. To begin with he asked the prince for the enormous sum of 500 louis as compensation for the 'personal services' he had rendered the royalist cause and to pay off a number of agents he had employed on the left bank of the Rhine. The prince coldly told Montgaillard he did not want to pay him as he already had enough outgoings. Furthermore, if Wickham did not want to pay him either, Montgaillard would have to go to Louis XVIII directly. However, if he took that course of action he was unlikely to be received warmly there either. The prince told Montgaillard they knew he had been to see Lallement in Venice and d'Antraigues had written to Louis XVIII at Blankenburg expressing 'very strong things' against Montgaillard. He went to visit the pretender nonetheless.

Some time between 22 and 24 January 1797, Montgaillard had an audience with Louis XVIII, in which the pretender revealed he had great confidence in Pichegru and Moreau, but said little else. He did learn that much of the secret correspondence between Paris and the Rhine was being stored by Wickham in a depot in Hamburg. Montgaillard imparted these facts in an account of his voyage to Blankenburg and the audience with Louis XVIII in a letter to Lallement. Returning to the Prince de Condé, Montgaillard was by now so short of funds that he was forced to sell his coach, one which had been bought for the service of 'the principal agents of the King'. Faced with impoverishment he let it be known he was going to return to France, to reconcile himself with the republicans and tell the government everything he knew about the royalists' secrets. As if that were not enough, he threatened to take all his correspondence with him, if he was not paid 500 louis.

This was bad news for the royalists. On 17 March 1797 Condé wrote to Fauche-Borel asking him to go to Berne and talk Montgaillard out of betraying them. He was also to warn Wickham and Pichegru what might be about to happen and to urge them to take precautions. It was known that Montgaillard's papers were stored somewhere in Basle and Fauche-Borel was asked to seize them. If he failed there was a general acceptance that Montgaillard would have to be paid the money.

The loyal Fauche-Borel caught up with his prey in Neufchatel at the Falcon Inn. The evening before, a letter had been delivered to Montgaillard from Prince de Condé asking him to return the 17 signed letters in his possession and announced Fauche-Borel had been authorized to pay him 500 louis on their receipt. Montgaillard told Fauche-Borel to get the money quickly as he was leaving the next morning at 6.00am.

At 5.00am Fauche-Borel went to Montgaillard's room and found him still in bed. He had been intending to make the transaction, but next to the bed Fauche-Borel saw a red leather briefcase, which he naturally assumed contained the prince's letters. He grabbed the case, taunting Montgaillard 'now you can do what you like' before running off to shouts of 'thief' and 'assassin', which woke everyone in the hotel. A chase began, which ended when Fauche-Borel ran into the home of the mayor, Monsieur de Pierre. The two men eagerly opened the case, but they only found two letters from Condé and one from Louis XVIII, presumably the same ones Montgaillard had intended to show Bonaparte. Already in an agitated state Fauche-Borel blew up on this discovery. He went straight back to Montgaillard, asked for the 17 letters and when they were not forthcoming, he punched him. 'If you have a drop of French blood in your veins, you will demand satisfaction from me' challenged Fauche-Borel. Montgaillard did not take up the offer of a duel and wormed his way out of a confrontation with his former protégé.

Calming the situation down, Montgaillard explained to Fauche-Borel that the letters were not in his possession, but were in safe keeping with 'the widow of Serini' in Basle. Knowing the person in question, Fauche-Borel appears to have been placated. In what seems a terribly naive thing to do, Fauche-Borel made Montgaillard sign a declaration saying he would not put the papers to ill use and would give them back to the prince. He then credited him with the 500 louis, less the 75 louis which Montgaillard owed him.

The war effectively came to an end with the signing of an armistice at Leoben on 18 April 1797 between the Austrians and Napoleon Bonaparte. After the fall of Mantua on 2 February, Bonaparte had been able to advance out of Italy into Austria and now threatened Vienna itself. With the outcome of the war being settled in favour of the republicans, the royalist camp now replaced their plans for invasion with victory by the ballot box. They asked Wickham for 'immense sums' to fix the forthcoming French elections in their favour.[22]

The previous year, on 14 March 1796, Pichegru had been sacked by the French government for his lack of action in the war. This was not as big a blow as it at first might seem. Pichegru was able to go to Paris, where he was still popular for his victories in Holland, and command of the army passed to his ally General Moreau. It all fitted in rather neatly into Wickham's grand plan – Pichegru could launch the coup d'état in Paris, supported by the Army of the Rhine under Moreau. However, when Pichegru arrived in Paris, he found the politics of the capital were far more muddled than expected. By June, he quit the capital and returned to his estate for a long period of procrastination.[23]

On 4 April the elections were held in France and the royalist faction gained a huge majority in the House of Deputies. On 1 June 1797 Pichegru finally made a move and was made president of the Council of 500, the other legislative body. The bodyguard troops guarding the council were supplied from the 'reliable' generals Moreau and Desaix. One of the five directors in power at the time, Paul Barras – the man who secured Bonaparte's command of the Army of Italy and introduced him to his wife Josephine – saw the writing on the wall. To avert a royalist coup, Barras needed a republican overthrow of the present government. First he needed troops, which were sent to him by Bonaparte in July and, second, now Pichegru was a civilian, he needed hard evidence to arrest him.

This proof came in the guise of a little piece of 'insurance' planted by Montgaillard. On 16 May 1797, Napoleon Bonaparte had overthrown the government of Venice following an anti-French uprising over the Easter period. As the French came in, Drake and the British legation had fled, as had the royalist agent d'Antraigues, who sought refuge with the Russian legation. At first it appeared that d'Antraigues would escape, but on 21 May the Russian party was stopped at Trieste by General Bernadotte. Despite his pleas for diplomatic immunity, d'Antraigues was arrested and had his papers seized.

Bonaparte then had d'Antraigues' papers opened in the count's absence. Witnessed by his chief of staff, General Berthier, and General Clarke, among the papers they allegedly found was an unsigned paper called 'my conversation with Comte de Montgaillard, on the 4th of December 1796', which made reference to an arrangement between General Pichegru and Louis XVIII.[24] Unfortunately for Bonaparte, by opening the papers without d'Antraigues and an independent witness being present, the count could no longer be tried under civil law. If the count refused to cooperate, Bonaparte only had two real options left – to have him tried under a court-martial and shot, or to let him go. Neither option appealed.[25]

In an interview on 1 June at 3.00am, Bonaparte thought he could reason with d'Antraigues and asked him to recognize the paper and witness it with his signature. The count refused. Leaving in a huff, Bonaparte sent d'Antraigues to the citadel in Milan where he lingered in a cell for a week before being moved with his family to the palace of Marquis Andreoli. There he was interrogated by a staff officer named Couthard. Apparently Bonaparte authorized Couthard to use force to make d'Antraigues sign the paper. Despite this, the count would only admit to meeting Montgaillard, whom he described as an 'adventurer' and issuing him with a Spanish passport to allow him to travel through Italy. He refused to sign the letter and so Bonaparte, not wishing the count's death on his hands, sent it off to Barras in Paris, signed by Berthier.[26]

If the letter was a forgery as d'Antraigues always claimed, where did it come from and how did Bonaparte know about Montgaillard's meeting with the count? According to the memoirs of Fauche-Borel, when Montgaillard left Venice to attempt to meet Bonaparte, his partner in crime, Montet, remained behind with secret instructions. After 16 May, Montet went to see Bonaparte and revealed the Pichegru plot, naming d'Antraigues as being one of those 'in the know'. Fauche-Borel claims to have spoken with d'Antraigues on the subject and was assured the paper was not in his handwriting. It was therefore probably written by Montgaillard following the count's refusal to grant him the 36,000 francs he had asked for.

Armed with this letter, forgery or not, Barras struck on the morning of 4 September (18 Fructidor in the French revolutionary calendar), calling in Bonaparte's troops and arresting Pichegru with a number of other leading royalists. As ever, in the wake of the coup everyone looked to save his or her own neck, Moreau in particular. On 5 September he disclosed the secret correspondence between Pichegru and Klinglin, which his troops had captured in a wagon on 22 April.[27] The d'Antraigues conversation was hastily appended to the deciphered messages and published for all to see. Moreau was sacked, but Pichegru was finished.

The former hero of Holland was convicted of treason and exiled with 15 others on 22 September to the prison at Sinnamary, near Cayenne in Guyana. Pichegru's torment began with him being clapped in irons in the hold of the ship on a long sea voyage lasting until 21 November. Surrounded by swamps and tropical forest, life expectancy was so short in this South American hellhole that it was nicknamed 'the dry guillotine'. It is perhaps to Pichegru's credit then that he did not break, but instead looked for a means of escape.

Fortunately for him the British government had no intention of deserting their man, and a year to the day after he was deported, Pichegru would turn up in London. His escape was the stuff of legend. On his arrest, the British government sent word to a French privateer owner named Tilly-Blaru to make a rescue attempt. Tilly-Blaru had contacts with the prison and so, on 3 June 1798, he arrived with a shipment of Bordeaux, which he freely distributed to the guards. While the garrison drank themselves silly, an accomplice arrived with a canoe concealed in an inlet below the fort. Eight prisoners escaped, including Pichegru, and although the canoe was overloaded and on the verge of sinking, they made it to a settlement up the coast in Dutch Guyana. There a British frigate picked the party up and brought them back to London.

Rather than count his lucky stars for having survived the ordeal, Pichegru decided to have one last shot at the title. Having saved the Directory in 1797, Bonaparte mounted a successful coup d'état of his own in November 1799. Even after his victory at Marengo (14 June 1800) he was by no means universally popular. Royalist agents stalked his every move, looking to assassinate him. They very nearly pulled it off when a large bomb was exploded on 24 December 1800 as Bonaparte was travelling to the opera. Bonaparte turned the incident to his advantage by blaming Jacobins and had a number of them deported.

In London plans were made to reunite the great alliance of Pichegru and Moreau. Unfortunately the two generals had fallen out after Moreau had sent the Directory the Klinglin papers. However, Moreau was needed because he still commanded the respect of his soldiers on the Rhine – and any coup would need the backing of an army. Another sticking point was the outcome of the conspiracy: Pichegru was firmly in the Bourbon camp, but Moreau wanted power for himself. To try to reconcile these differences, on 5 June 1802 the Swiss spy Fauche-Borel was sent from London to Paris to meet with Moreau. He met with generals Moreau and Macdonald but was arrested on 1 July and imprisoned at the Temple.[28]

On 16 January 1804, Pichegru finally made his move and landed in France. He was met by another key agent in the bid to restore the monarchy, Georges Cadoudal. It appears that the plot was doomed from the start and that Pichegru had been duped by French agents into thinking Moreau would help. This was confirmed when Pichegru and Moreau did meet in a carriage on the Champs Elysées and clearly disagreed with one another.[29] What is more, the French secret police were well aware of the conspiracy and were just waiting for the right moment to pounce.

About to break under interrogation in the Temple prison, one of the conspirators attempted to hang himself in his cell. Just as Bouvet de l'Hozier was on the point of death, a prison guard came into the cell by chance and cut him down. After recovering, he made a full confession and so, on 13 February 1804, Moreau was arrested. On 26 February Pichegru was pulled out of his bed and detained. Cadoudal was caught trying to escape and killed a gendarme in the arrest. In all there were 356 arrests. Moreau was acquitted, but Pichegru was found dead in his cell. Although the verdict was suicide, he was apparently strangled by four Mamelukes on the orders of Bonaparte.[30] Finally, just to teach the royalists a lesson over their continued plots, Bonaparte had the Bourbon Duc d'Enghien kidnapped on 15 March 1804, tried without a defence and executed by firing squad.

Meanwhile, although d'Antraigues had refused to sign the paper containing the infamous 'conversation' with Montgaillard, it was d'Antraigues' name that sent Pichegru to Sinnamary and thwarted Louis XVIII's plans to restore the monarchy. It is fair to say that d'Antraigues found himself out of favour with the Bourbon camp for some time.[31]

It was not until 1 November 1800 that he found secret-service employment again when the tsar made him a councillor of state. He moved first to Vienna and then in June 1802 to Dresden in Saxony, which had become the centre of anti-French diplomacy and intrigue. D'Antraigues remained one of the key players in both the Russian secret service and the counter-revolutionary movement, finding informers on the local French embassy and Austrian chancellery. Expelled from Saxony in 1804, d'Antraigues moved to London where he became such an important link in Anglo-Russian co-operation that in 1807 Foreign Secretary George Canning went so far as to offer d'Antraigues the title of 'Director of British Intelligence'. The count declined any official title, but continued to collect reports from his spies and informants on behalf of the British.[32]

D'Antraigues' greatest coup came in 1807 when he betrayed the tsar to the British. After the French had defeated Russia at the battle of Friedland (14 June 1807), Napoleon and the tsar signed the Treaty of Tilsit on 25 July 1807. So secret were the contents of this treaty that only Napoleon, Tsar Alexander and the King of Prussia were privy to its details, which were not published for another 84 years. In a bid to thwart spies, the actual signing took place on a raft in the middle of the River Niemen.

A short time after the signing took place d'Antraigues revealed the contents of the treaty in a letter to Canning. Purportedly from a Russian general close to Alexander, the contents of the letter were a bombshell for Britain. Not only had France and Russia agreed to support each other in case of war, but the two emperors had agreed to threaten war against Denmark, Sweden and Portugal if they did not close their ports to British shipping. If this happened the Baltic Sea would be closed to British shipping and the loss of Portugal as a trading partner would severely hurt British commerce. With foreknowledge of the emperors' intentions, in September 1807 Canning sent a task force to Denmark to prevent their fleet falling into Napoleon's hands. Denmark only handed over their ships after Copenhagen had been bombarded.[33]

Following the Tilsit revelation, d'Antraigues' future in Britain was guaranteed and he was granted a pension of £400 per annum. In 1812, d'Antraigues took on an Italian servant called Lorenzo, a deserter from the French army in Spain. Three months later, on 22 July 1812. Lorenzo assassinated the count and countess in their home in Barnes. After committing the deed, Lorenzo shot himself, leaving investigators clueless as to the motive. In a macabre ceremony, local legend has it that Lorenzo was buried at a crossroads with a stake hammered through his body to prevent his ghost from returning. Meanwhile d'Antraigues' son Jules accused Napoleon of ordering the murder. However, it is more likely to have been orchestrated by Louis XVIII, settling scores and removing a potential obstacle to his future plans.[34]

No account of espionage in the revolutionary era would be complete without an introduction to the career of Joseph Fouché (1763–1820), one of the greatest users and organizers of spies in history. Originally marked out for a career in the church, Fouché found himself in Nantes at the beginning of the French Revolution. Firmly embracing the revolution, he was returned as a deputy to the National Convention in 1792 and voted in favour of the execution of King Louis XVI.

His notoriety began during the Terror when the Convention demanded the annihilation of a royalist uprising in Brittany and the Vendée. Fouché's own particular target was at the very core of the royalist uprising – the church. From the autumn of 1793 Fouché advocated the complete de-Christianization of France, ransacking and looting churches and promoting the Jacobins' own brand of religion – the cult of the Goddess of Reason. Fouché was then sent to Lyons, which had dared to revolt against the revolutionary government. It was there that he gained the nickname 'Mitrailleur de Lyon'. When the queues to the guillotine grew too long, Fouché administered revolutionary justice with artillery loaded with *mitraille* (canister shot).

In June 1794 Fouché fell out with Robespierre and was ejected from the Jacobin club. This proved an enormous stroke of luck because the Jacobins were soon expelled from power in the 'Thermidor' coup d'état. While Robespierre was sent to the guillotine, Fouché drifted back into the shadows for a time. He returned to help Barras in the 'Fructidor' coup of 1797. After ambassadorial missions to Italy and Holland, he was made chief of police. In this new post his first victims were members of the resurgent Jacobin Club and royalists still reeling from the arrest and deportation of Pichegru.

When Bonaparte came to power he retained Fouché, although their relationship was at best one of mutual suspicion. While feeling the need to retain Fouché's underhand talents, Napoleon was privately concerned how much Fouché's spies had told him. It is fair to say that Napoleon employed him, if nothing else, in order that nobody else could. In fact, Napoleon organized his own secret police force, which was intended to rival and check up on Fouché's network. However, Fouché soon possessed a list of its agents and decided to play a trick on them. He planted a false story with one agent that Napoleon's secretary, Louis de Bourienne, had been heard in a Paris hotel on the Rue de Varenne telling people that Napoleon wished to make himself king. Napoleon's police chief, Jean-Andoche Junot, jumped at the bait and included the accusation in his bulletin. When he came to make his daily morning report, Bourienne asked Junot to remove the report, but the police chief refused, saying his agent was a credible witness.

Unfortunately for Junot, on the night in question, rather than spreading rumours about the First Consul, Bourienne had in fact been working with him until three in the morning. Reading the report, Napoleon was amused at Bourienne's discomfort, but berated Junot, calling him an 'ass' and an 'imbecile' for allowing such ridiculous inventions. Napoleon had immediately realized Fouché was behind the set up – further proof of how dangerous he had become.

At the same time, because Napoleon was often abroad on campaign, he needed a man like Fouché who would keep France under close surveillance and inform him of any plots brewing. With the establishment of the Napoleonic empire, Fouché turned France into a police state, with an intricate web of informants making Napoleon's reign more absolute than anything the Bourbons had enjoyed before 1789.

Fouché was deputized by four Councillors of State. These councillors corresponded on matters of police and state security with the local prefects in France's 96 departmental regions. Every *département* was divided into four or five districts, each under the control of a sub-prefect. Within these districts, each community of 5,000 inhabitants had a police superintendent and a mayor, both of whom were appointed by the central government. Through this chain of command, Fouché was able to monitor the prisons, the Gendarmerie (military police) and the movements of strangers, immigrants and other suspects. At every level spies reported back to the prefects, to the councillors of state or to Fouché directly and, to make them accountable for the denunciations they made, they had to sign their reports. Beyond France's frontiers, spies were placed or informants found in every major foreign city and court. Foreign newspapers, intercepted letters and other documents, both public and private, found their way to Fouché. The expense was enormous, swallowing up millions of francs each year.

Six days out of seven Fouché would report to Napoleon, who was frequently absent from the capital on military campaign. The topics covered in these reports were comprehensive to say the least. They included:

- Palace gossip
- Audience reaction to new plays
- Stock market prices
- Desertions from the army
- Arrests of foreign agents
- Results of interrogations
- News of crime
- Offences by soldiers
- Fires
- Rebellion against the Gendarmerie
- Intercepted correspondence
- Visiting personages
- Public reception of news of victories
- Shipping news
- The indiscretions of Fouché's enemies
- Contractor's tenders

- Agitation against the draft
- Suicides
- Prison epidemics
- Progress of construction.
- Unemployment figures
- Extracts from inter-ministerial correspondence
- Persons detained or under special surveillance[35]

Above all, Fouché was, if anything, a survivor. He spied on everybody: on royalists, democrats, fellow ministers, Napoleon's wife Josephine and the First Consul himself. But in 1810 it was discovered that Fouché had been corresponding with the British – he was dismissed and replaced by General Savary who had until then headed Napoleon's military intelligence services. The ex-minister declined to brief his replacement in all but the most obvious facts. He withheld most of his papers, in particular the confidential correspondence that had passed between himself and the emperor. Although he claimed to have burned them, these papers were Fouché's insurance policy – or so he thought. He calculated that Napoleon would, at a loss without the lists of spies and informants, recall him to his post. Unfortunately for Fouché he had underestimated Savary's own capacity for ruthlessness. Savary found some papers that Fouché had overlooked, and managed to piece together a list of his own, revealing who Fouché's agents were. Within a year Savary's network rivalled anything Fouché had amassed.

When Napoleon first abdicated in 1814, Fouché attempted reconciliation with Louis XVIII, who at long last came to the throne. However, it was only when Napoleon returned from exile in Elba that Louis XVIII offered Fouché the police ministry. Fouché declined the king's offer and was instead given the post by Napoleon. Although Fouché appeared loyal on the surface, he privately thought Napoleon's return was a mistake that would ultimately prove short lived. As Napoleon planned the campaign that ended at Waterloo on 18 June 1815, Fouché was intriguing with everyone, Wellington included. After Napoleon abdicated for a second time the minister of police tried to ingratiate himself with the new regime by hunting down Bonapartists. However, his past at last caught up with him and he was convicted of regicide in 1816 and forced into exile. Living in obscurity, he died in Trieste on Christmas Day, 1820.

6

NAPOLEON'S 'SECRET PART'

*We name the 'secret part' everything relating to
espionage. Nothing is more important in an army
than the organization of this service.*

General Paul Thiébault, 1813

From the battlefield to the bedroom, almost every facet of
Napoleon Bonaparte's life and career has been trawled over by
battalions of historians. However, in matters of secret service
Napoleon's activities, although often alluded to, have rarely been
exposed. While he is remembered as the greatest general of his age,
perhaps he should also be proclaimed its spymaster supreme. For like the
kings of ancient Persia, Napoleon the autocrat was served by a myriad
of agents, informers, plotters and spies at every level, home and abroad.

Napoleon first demonstrated his understanding of military espionage
during the Italian campaigns of 1796–97. Before his arrival, Italy was
already a hotbed of intrigue, revolution and secret societies. Since 1789
French diplomats posted to Italy had encouraged the formation of
revolutionary clubs along Masonic lines. Their most active disciples were
from the liberal professions – doctors, lawyers, merchants, 'enlightened'
nobles, soldiers and priests with leanings towards Jansenism. These clubs
appeared most along the border with France, in the country of Piedmont,
then ruled by the King of Sardinia, Victor Amadeus (ruled 1773–97).
Calling themselves 'Patriots', the Piedmontese revolutionaries wanted
the French to help them establish a sister republic. Taking advantage of
these sentiments, the French *chargé d'affaires* at Genoa, Tilly, established
contact with three Patriot clubs in Turin. Although these formed the hub
of revolutionary activity in Piedmont, secret meetings were also held in
Alba, Asti, Vercelli and Novara.

At the beginning of 1794, the French advanced into Liguria, the narrow coastal strip between Genoa and Nice. Under Tilly's direction, the Turin Patriots conspired to raise Piedmont in revolt. Unfortunately, on 24 May the chairman of one Turin club, Dr Barolo, betrayed the conspiracy and denounced his fellow Patriots. A crackdown ensued, which saw the arrest of around 40 Patriots, some of whom were sentenced to death. The survivors fled and in the most part joined an already large number of Italians gathering around Nice or in the city of Oneille.[1]

There they found fellow political exiles including Filippo Buonarroti (1761–1837), a sort of unofficial ambassador of Italian revolutionaries to France. Buonarroti's long-term objective was to create a 'Republic of Turin'. Key to his plans was the creation of a provisional government, thus avoiding the need for French military occupation. Despite the failure of the 1794 uprising, Buonarroti wanted to stage another coinciding with a French invasion – a plan supported by French general Pierre Augereau (1757–1816).

From the French point of view, this influx of active, politically astute Italians gave them a ready pool of agents. This was realized by General Scherer, who by the beginning of 1795 had built an impressive intelligence service in preparation for the invasion.[2] His 'secret correspondence' was overseen by a committed Piedmontese revolutionary, Adjudant-Général Rusca. Operating from an advanced position at Savona, Rusca was seconded by a number of skilful men, including the exiled Turin lawyer Angelo Pico, a member of the treacherous Dr Barolo's Turin club who had managed to escape after arrest. Between them, Rusca and Pico assembled a network of agents in southern Piedmont. Both were assisted by another of Dr Barolo's former club mates, Felice Antonio Campana, who acted as their linkman in Nice, fulfilling the functions of secretary. Scherer also had an agent in Genoa named Régis running a separate network up through the Bochetta Pass into the region between Alessandria and Tortona. In addition to the army general staff's headquarters intelligence service, Scherer had each of his major-generals form their own intelligence networks covering their immediate fronts. When Napoleon took over command of Scherer's army on 27 March 1796 he inherited this spy network ready built and very active.

As Bonaparte was young and relatively inexperienced, the French government thought he might benefit from two experienced 'chaperones'.

The first of these was a political representative, Antoine-Christophe Salicetti (1757–1809), a lawyer-turned-politician and fellow Corsican. The other was an experienced staff officer, General Alexandre Berthier (1753–1815), who had been drawn from the Army of the Alps. Prior to 1796, Berthier had worked on developing a system for running an efficient army staff. When it came to intelligence gathering – or more specifically, what was called the 'secret part' – Berthier suggested keeping a register dedicated to all secret matters. This register would normally be maintained by an *adjudant-général*, a staff officer equivalent in rank to a colonel. Unfortunately Berthier did not stipulate what this register should contain and none of his registers appear to have survived – presumably each was destroyed at the termination of a campaign.

This secret register contained the instructions given to spies, their reports, information obtained by questioning local inhabitants, the reports of officers sent on reconnaissance and the topographic reports provided by engineer officers or other specialists. In addition, it contained information gleaned from the interrogation of travellers, prisoners of war, enemy deserters and from reading intercepted mail. Finally it would contain the secret correspondence with diplomatic agents working in foreign cities who organized their own spy networks. It was, in short, a central record of all intelligence.[3]

More is known on the affairs of the 'secret part' from the works of General Paul Thiébault (1769–1846), who published a service manual for general and divisional staffs in 1813.[4] This was an expansion of his *Manual des Adjudans généraux* (1800) in which he discussed the functions of the 'secret part' at great length. What makes his work so important is that we know it came from first-hand experience: Thiébault had dealt with the 'secret part' while serving on the staff of General Massena in 1796. According to Thiébault, one officer on the general staff was responsible for the register. He would maintain an 'active correspondence' with the chiefs of staff at divisional level, who were responsible for local intelligence gathering and espionage – especially in the case of the advance-guard divisions spearheading the army. Each morning the head of 'the secret part' would receive reports from the divisional chiefs of staff and then make a report to the chief of the general staff who would, in turn, present an intelligence summary to the commander-in-chief.

Explaining the need for spies, Thiébault wrote: 'To achieve the goal, which is always to mislead the enemy on what he wants to know and to learn what he has an interest in hiding, one can only use spies.'[5] Writing on the nature of spies and their employment, Thiébault suggested using the largest number of spies possible, ensuring that they were given the clearest, most concise and complete instructions and that a record was made of all their declarations.

On the different types of spy, Thiébault identified five classes of them. The first class were those with a complaint about the opposing government. These spies were usually educated and in a position to make accurate judgments. Thiébault stressed nothing should be neglected to discover them, and to give them all the guarantees they required.[6]

In contrast, the second class included those who became spies out of a sense of duty to better serve their country. In spite of the obvious risks they faced, these spies would find some pretext for crossing over to the enemy, usually employing a means of disguise. Thiébault maintained these spies should be well rewarded, but more with honours than money.

The third class, which Thiébault described as 'always the most numerous', could contain people of any nationality or sex. Potential agents could be found from among:

> monks and priests; conniving, gallant, or even impassioned women; people who have some favour to obtain from the government; people who made bad deals, or who, corrupt in their opinion, do not have any other honest means to exist in the world; officers of the enemy army, who having debts, or who enjoy gambling or ostentation, do not have the means of supporting their lifestyle, to fulfil their engagements, or to satisfy their tastes: ... the majority of these people without principles, that is to say, without honour, will sacrifice their country to their debauchery, just as they sacrificed themselves: Their greed will triumph over all; they will always go to the highest bidder and one will usually need only gold to learn from them everything that is in their capacity to discover.[7]

As an afterthought, Thiébault recommended using women and priests in Catholic countries to gain useful information. He reasoned these two groups had ways of gaining information 'like no others' and that in general, people would not be wary of confiding in them.

The fourth class of spy were those individuals who were professional spies and who, to double their pay would, Thiébault bemoaned, 'serve both armies and tell everything they have learned from one [side] to the other'. Such men ought to inspire much caution and Thiébault warned his men 'to prevent spies of this species unnecessarily remaining with the General Staff, circulating round the army, or building up relations, meeting each other or conferring' and also to 'observe all those with whom they communicate'. They should always be questioned separately and in secrecy where they might be engaged in an elaborate game of bluff, the aim of which was to deceive the enemy commander. When discussing matters of importance, the interrogator was warned to appear distracted, as if disinterested. Instead he was to dwell on 'futile things', trying to put false ideas into the spy's mind. Hopefully the spy would be duped and report his false observations back to the enemy commander. Thiébault thought these spies should only be used at the most vital moments, but warned that the enemy had probably filled the spy with false information of his own. 'In this respect,' concluded Thiébault, 'success goes to the most skilful.'

The fifth and last species of spy were those who spied out of fear. These were easily recruited, but because they were mostly taken from the poorly educated classes, they would be limited to shedding light only on 'material things'. It was important to remember that these spies would never report anything other than what they believed would guarantee their safety – i.e. what the interrogator wanted to hear. They included peasants whose loyalty could be guaranteed by arresting their families or seizing their property, and who were sent into enemy territory under the pretext of selling their produce. Merchants or foreigners who, while going about their business had passed though enemy-occupied territory, were also to be quizzed. Accurate intelligence could be obtained by arresting them, confiscating their goods and by retaining them until their declarations could be checked. Also worth attention were 'the principal inhabitants of occupied enemy towns and villages'. These were to be threatened and forced to reveal everything they had seen or heard. Enemy deserters were also to be questioned with a great deal of attention, but prisoners of war were considered less reliable. However, even these could still be used to confirm facts and information already received from other sources.

Thiébault offered advice on substantiating intelligence reports. He rarely relied on the opinion of a single spy, feeling it necessary to check the depositions of one spy against the other and to only count on the pieces of information reported by coincidence between spies who did not know one another. If a single spy had to be relied upon, one should warn him that he would be detained until his report was checked and that his life depended on its veracity.[8]

There is a strong stress put on the questions spies should be answering. Thiébault lists 11 topics, which, if properly ascertained, would give intelligence on the location, strength, condition, morale and probable intentions of the enemy army. The 11 most important subjects for spies to report on were:

1. The headquarters of the enemy commander-in-chief and divisional generals.
2. The location, names and characters of the enemy generals.
3. The location and strength of the artillery parks and cavalry reserve.
4. The names and strength of each corps, its nationality and the number of guns.
5. If the enemy is concentrating or dividing its troops.
6. The measures taken for provisions, transportation and for hospitals.
7. How their troops are nourished, clothed, paid; their morale; how many are sick; the prevalent diseases; the mortality rate, etc.
8. If the enemy moves his troops by day or night; by masses, corps or in detachments.
9. The reinforcements the enemy expects.
10. If military reviews are inspections or field manoeuvres.
11. Are fortifications are being built and how many workmen are involved?

Finally from Thiébault are what might be considered some general maxims on the employment of spies. In treating with spies a central theme had been their payment, something Thiébault did not neglect:

As for the manner of acting with the spies, it must always be the same. One will undoubtedly proportion the reward to the service, but one must always give to them what has been promised to them and above all one will not treat them less well than the enemy does. Thus one will be always liberal and on occasions one might be prodigal.[9]

Like Sun Tzû, Thiébault suggested the greatest wisdom be employed when using spies to the maximum advantage, profiting from everyday human failings to gain an advantage in war.

> Such are the means that the nature of things and events can offer. The manner of discovering them and of employing them with the most utility cannot be taught; art develops talent, guides it, but it does not create it... One conceives ... how much natural tact and knowledge of men and things are necessary in the conduct of everything relating to this service, to employ the ambitious, to intimidate or interest apprehensive or covetous people and finally, to benefit from every weaknesses one can discover.[10]

Returning to Italy in the spring of 1796, the spy Angelo Pico was hard at work, expertly using disguises and the cover of gypsy caravans to move about Piedmont unnoticed. When Napoleon attacked, Pico's network helped guide the French columns forward and reported on Austrian troop build-ups. At the same time – just as Buonarroti had planned – rebellion broke out in Piedmont. Following the French forces, two Patriots – Ranza and the exiled Turin clubbist Bonafous – proclaimed a revolutionary municipality in the city of Alba. Together they put out a call for Piedmontese and Lombard soldiers to desert their regiments and form revolutionary legions. Further uprisings occurred in Cuneo and Verceilli, but just as the hopes of Piedmontese radicals were on the verge of being realized, their hopes were dashed in what must have seemed to them the most unexpected manner.

What the Italian patriots had failed to grasp was that France was in Italy not to liberate Italians but to attack the Austrian army and take pressure off the French armies along the Rhine. The whole operation was intended as a diversion, not a crusade, and neither Paris nor Bonaparte wanted the chaos of another revolution on their hands.

Just 18 days into the war, on 28 April 1796 Bonaparte signed an armistice with King Victor Amadeus at Cherasco. In return for peace, Napoleon received three fortresses, Cuneo, Tortona and Alessandria, the guarantee of safe passage for his soldiers through Piedmont and the passage of the River Po at Valenza. For his part Victor Amadeus was allowed to keep his throne – there would be no 'Republic of Turin'. After the armistice came the backlash: the city of Alba was retaken by royal troops who went on to put down all signs of insurrection. Bonaparte pushed on and took Milan.

After the seizure of Milan on 16 May 1796, Bonaparte made some positive steps to streamline his secret intelligence service, which was unchanged since Scherer's time. Napoleon placed cavalry officer Jean Landrieux in charge of the 'secret part', which became known officially as the *bureau secret*. Operating under the title 'commander of the cavalry depots', Landrieux's real mission was clearly defined from the outset. In Milan he was given the equivalent of 10,000 francs to found a bureau of secret affairs and set up the means to place agents not only in the enemy army but within the French army too. Furthermore he was to infiltrate Naples, Rome, Florence, Turin, Venice, Vienna and even the French government in Paris. The bureau was not to have any political agenda or affiliations, either with royalists or republican factions, and Landrieux was to report to Bonaparte directly, although Berthier appears to have been privy to the information.[11] The extent of the operation is clear from Landrieux's description:

> All the Kings, all the conquerors, all the generals, since the beginning of the world, have used more or less the means that Bonaparte ordered me to employ. I had put myself without scruple to the job and this work, which often gave several reports per day with which the commander-in-chief occupied himself a great deal and which, without the knowledge of almost all his headquarters, had become immense.[12]

For practical reasons Landrieux divided the secret bureau's work into two departments. One would deal with general military affairs while the other was for purely political matters, including the surveillance of the occupied territories and the repression of popular movements. This 'political wing' was presided over by Salicetti who was greatly assisted by an agent named Galdi who procured him informants and spies from all walks of life, including prostitutes. Landrieux described it as a council of 'high police' and gave it the sinister appellation *l'assemblée nocturne*. Sessions were held late at night outside the Milan opera house because, Landrieux tells us, the generals were freed up from their duties at this late hour.

They were as active spying on the intentions of the government in Paris as anywhere else. Through its informants, Bonaparte was able to find out which officers and politicians posted to Italy were government spies.[13] Once informed that a government stooge was en route, Bonaparte would arrange for him to be reassigned to a different army or better still, 'buy' him and his services, as happened with General Clarke. Using Berthier as a mouthpiece, Bonaparte was free to more or less dictate the secret reports Clarke sent to Paris, portraying him in a positive light.[14]

When it came to military intelligence, however, like most soldiers Landrieux was against the idea of involving civilian police:

> Can an army do without a secret bureau? Which good General did not have one? Is it necessary to surround oneself with civilian policemen? They would understand almost nothing... A soldier must be in charge of this part, and he must, as much as possible, employ only soldiers.[15]

Although most of the secret bureau's exploits are now forgotten, Landrieux gives enough examples for us to understand its work. For example, Landrieux explained how he taught officers seconded to him to deliberately allow themselves to be captured. Once behind the enemy lines, the captured officer would be on the look out for useful information. At the time, captured officers were usually exchanged quickly between warring armies, but Landrieux would only make exchanges when a captured subordinate mentioned a pre-arranged codeword in his correspondence. When the officer told Landrieux 'not to forget the cartel' the secret service chief knew that the captured officer had something important to communicate. Landrieux would then arrange for him to be swapped with a captured Austrian officer.[16]

Landrieux also explained an operation against Austrian agents. To make good their army's military loses, Austrian spies kept boats on the lakes north of Milan, which were used to transport escaped prisoners of war to Valteline. From there the prisoners were given money and escorted through the Grisons country back to the Tyrol where they could rejoin their regiments. The system was so effective that Landrieux estimated that barely a quarter of the prisoners announced in the bulletins actually arrived in France – although he admitted part of the problem was that the bulletins lied about the number of prisoners in the first place.[17]

Landrieux sent a cavalry officer named Etrée to Bergamo to find proof against an Austrian agent named Andréo who was working on the escape route. From the papers discovered on his person, it was established that Andréo was a spy and he was shot on his arrival in Milan. Not realizing Andréo had been executed, a number of people came to speak on his behalf the following day. Landrieux made a careful note of their names, suspecting that many of them might also be Austrian spies. He was very suspicious of a certain Foscarini, a Venetian official sent on a mission to Milan in order to secure Venice's neutrality in the war between France and Austria. In truth Foscarini was a spy, successfully reporting on French agents sent into Venetian territory.

Important as Landrieux was, French historian Jean Savant perhaps overstated things when he described Landrieux as 'the man who knew everything'. He probably knew about Bonaparte's contacts with French diplomats, including Tilly in Genoa, Lallement in Venice and Théobald Bacher, a diplomat stationed in Switzerland since 1792 with a vast network of spies stretching from northern Italy up through the German States. However, it is unclear how much Landrieux knew about Napoleon's most secret operations.

Using special agents who were paid directly by Berthier, Napoleon secretly negotiated with some of his Austrian opponents, using agents to deliver huge bribes to 'throw' the fate of battles or to ensure some troops were 'delayed' in arriving. Savant describes two such bribes that went to Austrian generals: 100,000 francs to Argenteau and 50,000 to Lauer. Apart from these 'grand traitors', Bonaparte is said to have paid even more to the Venetian official Giovanelli to set up what became the Verona uprising of 1797.

On 6 March 1797, while Landrieux and General Charles Kilmaine (1751–99) were at dinner in Milan, Berthier paid them an unexpected visit. He revealed that as part of their ongoing secret discussions, Austrian agents had put forward a proposal to help end the war. If the French were 'masters to dispose of the Venetian States' the Austrians – who had long coveted Venice – might be able to come to an arrangement over Lombardy, Mantua and at the same time Belgium.

Although the French already had small garrisons in the major mainland cities, the idea of selling out the world's oldest republic to the Austrians was unpalatable to say the least. Therefore Bonaparte needed an excuse to depose of the Venetian government, after which he could do with the territory as he liked. Needless to say, Landrieux's bureau was put to work on the matter straight away. In fact, Landrieux had to a degree anticipated this move and had already sent agents to Bergamo, Brescia, Salo, Verona, Vincence and Padua to seek out opponents of the Venetian government.[18]

As with Piedmont, the French would utilize Italian revolutionaries to raise rebellion in each of Venice's 14 mainland provinces. Landrieux began at Bergamo, which had long experienced revolutionary tensions. The Venetian governor there, Count Ottolini, had learned that revolutionaries were planning an uprising in his city by Milan-based Venetian spies such as Foscarni. This had been confirmed on the night of 12 January 1797, when Bergamo's Riccardi theatre was burned down – apparently by revolutionary freemasons. Subsequent to this an increasingly jittery Ottolini had brought in 450 extra guards and doubled their patrols.

Landrieux began his search for an *agent provocateur* who was audacious or mad enough to enter the town and begin inciting rebellion. Although Landrieux had never been short of spies, none volunteered for this particular mission. They told him: 'A spy is not accustomed to serving except with his eyes and ears.'[19] The former French commander at Bergamo, Adjudant-Général Couthard, suggested a man to Landrieux. Lhermite was by all accounts a brigand who fled France after being condemned to the prison galleys for theft. It was his very criminality that made Lhermite so perfect for the job Landrieux had in mind. For the past several years Lhermite had eked out a living by trafficking fake gems and knew pretty much every crook and thug in Bergamo. Landrieux accepted the recommendation, but had a poor opinion of the man, recalling: 'my field observers or *mouchards* [Fr. slang for 'informants'] ... could be considered men of rare probity when compared to Lhermite. What a labyrinth is the human head!'[20]

Lhermite set to work and on 11 March, 700 people signed a petition calling for the removal of Ottolini. Another of Landrieux's agents, Marchesi, described the mob as being armed to the teeth to defend themselves because Ottolini had sent out couriers to raise the provincial militia. During the night the Venetian standard was lowered from the castle and next morning troops from the French garrison began to secure strategic points around the city.[21] Realizing that the game was up, Ottolini fled to Venice.

Landrieux soon regretted hiring Lhermite altogether. After the coup the agent was instrumental in setting up the municipal government, causing acute embarrassment by having it offer Landrieux and

Kilmaine 5,000,000 francs to share in gratitude. This offer directly implicated Landrieux and the French as being behind the affair. 'Have you seen anything more imbecilic than that spy of Couthard's?' Landrieux wrote to Kilmaine, '… he has a reputation as a swindler … The people of Bergamo must have the greatest confidence in me and we cannot be associated with a scamp.' Matters became worse when it was revealed that Lhermite had somehow found time to pull off a major jewel heist while masterminding the coup: he was now a wanted man by the Bergamese authorities. Lhermite vanished, then turned up in Milan, lodged with an unwitting supply officer. On his arrival he had extorted 30,000 francs from the committee of police for his espionage services. When an arrest warrant was issued he took refuge in Spain.[22]

Things went more smoothly when Landrieux turned his attentions to raising Brescia. Again, a great deal of preparation had gone into the operation. Writing to Bonaparte on 21 January 1797, Landrieux revealed that he had sent agent Venturi to Brescia some time after the battle of Castiglione (5 August 1796). From Venturi, Landrieux learned that Venetian spies were being sent to Milan to monitor those Patriots corresponding with citizens of Brescia. More ominous still was the warning that four Frenchmen had been assassinated. In retaliation Landrieux sent more 'trusted people', but on 23 January he regrettably informed Bonaparte that one of his best spies, Lavocato, had been stabbed to death the day before. With its streets and cafés filled with hostile spies, Bresica was no longer safe. The people of Brescia, who were generally well disposed towards the French, were scared of going out into the street lest they were suspected of spying for the French and sent to the Inquisition at Venice. In response Bonaparte ordered Landrieux to expel all Venetian citizens from Milan – Foscarini included.[23]

Brescia rose up on 17 March. Landrieux's chief agent in Brescia was one of the Lecchi brothers – five of whom were in French service, while his sister was mistress to French general Joachim Murat (1767–1815).[24] Another of his agents operating in Brescia, Nicoloni, also pulled off a stunning coup, serving up Crema to the French. Posing as a messenger from Venice, Nicoloni conned a hapless sentry into lowering the city drawbridge one night. With the gates opened, 500 French grenadiers charged in and secured the city while the garrison slept on blissfully unaware.

While Landrieux had been working on Bergamo and Brescia, the spy Pico had been ordered to raise a revolt in Verona 'at any cost'. Landrieux appears to have known what Pico was up to as he mentioned corresponding with him around this time. In what was by then a well-developed routine, Pico – now a captain on Berthier's general staff – planned to use Italian Jacobins to kick off a revolt and throw out the Venetian governors. Unfortunately the plot was discovered and Pico, along with almost all his Jacobin accomplices, found himself thrown into prison.

With time at a premium Bonaparte resorted to bribery, paying off an unsavoury Venetian official named Giovanelli to stage an uprising against the French garrison in Verona. The exact arrangement is unknown, but the payoff was huge – something in the region of the tens of millions of dollars in today's prices.[25] In making the deal it is improbable that Bonaparte realized just how much trouble he would get for his money. On Easter Monday, 17 April 1797, the people of Verona attacked the French. Instead of the loud riot Bonaparte expected, there was a massacre. Although it was later estimated that 400 had been killed, the first hurried estimates reported up to 3,000 French casualties, including many sick and wounded murdered in their hospital beds. It was exactly what Napoleon needed and within a month, on 12 May, Venice was in his hands.

Landrieux first heard of the uprising from one of his spies, a certain Countess Pellegrini. She put the blame squarely on Landrieux, whom she had warned to expect trouble eight days before the massacre. However, Landrieux had indeed passed on the warning to the garrison commander, General Balland, and could not understand why he had not taken preventative steps.[26] He began to smell a rat and the scent led to Giovanelli.

Landrieux wrote to Kilmaine:

Giovanelli betrayed Venice. The Senate is not composed of imbeciles, and they well know that two thousand Frenchmen are not all of the French, and that those remaining will hunt them down without mercy. The Senate did not order this. This crime has been committed only to render the name of Venice odious to the rest of the universe... But who could have employed Giovanelli to have done it? It is neither you nor me. Who is it then?[27]

The unpalatable truth began to surface when Landrieux learned that General Balland had been accused of treachery by his colleague General Lahoz – an accusation which led to the two men drawing swords on one another. In his defence, Balland said he had seen a letter from Bonaparte, signed by Berthier, in Giovanelli's hands. Lahoz refused to believe that Bonaparte or Berthier would have any dealings with Giovanelli, a known 'brigand,' a 'maniac' and sworn enemy of the French. Landrieux believed Balland's version of events and suspected Giovanelli was an agent of Bonaparte.

It was a serious charge – did Bonaparte plan the massacre of his own troops or not? Landrieux suspected not because Giovanelli fled once the rioters in Verona eventually capitulated to the French army. He concluded that Bonaparte had wanted a disturbance that would provoke Balland's garrison, not one that would lead to the murder of French troops. However, strangely enough, once Bonaparte overthrew the Venetian Senate and imposed his own puppet government, Giovanelli was made part of it. Later, under the empire, Giovanelli became one of the top dignitaries in the Kingdom of Italy. Perhaps Bonaparte knew more than he let on? The truth may never be known, but from then on Landrieux's relationship with Bonaparte soured considerably. The head of the secret bureau began to suspect that Bonaparte harboured plans of becoming sovereign of Italy.

Not long after Verona, in May 1797 there was a popular uprising in Genoa. A delegation of protestors came to Milan to ask Bonaparte for assistance against the aristocratic government there. The French government was against regime change in Genoa and so Napoleon brusquely refused them, giving them 24 hours to get out of Lombard territory – or else. Instead the delegation went to Landrieux who agreed to help them.[28] He nearly came unstuck when allied troops from the Lombard Legion entered Genoa on the side of the protestors. If the Genoese government survived and complained to Paris, then Landrieux would be in a very sticky position. He feared having gone behind Napoleon's back and saw no other option but to flee and take refuge in Austria. He went as far as putting his wife and four-month-old baby into Kilmaine's care, then plundered the secret expenditure chest to fund his retirement. Fortunately for Landrieux, the rebellion succeeded and, let off the hook, he was able to breathe a huge sigh of relief.

The strain of secret operations had finally begun to tell on Landrieux and he asked for a period of leave, which Napoleon eventually granted. He was replaced by Adjudant-Général Boyer (1772–1851) who took over the secret service chest. Soon after leaving, a piece appeared in a Milan journal claiming to be written by Landrieux. The piece was lengthy and outlined French secret operations in relation to Venice. In his memoirs Landrieux denied writing the piece, but did not deny its veracity. The only other people who knew about these things were Berthier and Bonaparte. Had they leaked the information to frame him? Landrieux never held an official position again.[29]

One of the little-known stories of the Napoleonic Wars is of a spy who went by the name of Francesco Toli. Like Angelo Pico, Toli appears to have been one of the Turin 'Patriots' – a young barrister who idealistically embraced their cause but was forced to flee during the crackdowns. Toli claimed to have procured himself an appointment with the French army's staff where, because he was a native-speaking Italian, he was employed with spies, probably translating reports before going on missions himself.[30] With his name first appearing around the time of the battle of Bassano (8 September 1796), Toli is credited with providing information that allowed Napoleon to get reserves to the battle of Rivoli (14 January 1797), affording him a complete victory.

After securing a treaty with Austria in 1797, Napoleon went to Egypt in 1798. Before his return in 1799, an Austro-Russian army invaded Italy and pushed the French back to a small enclave around Genoa. During this reversal of fortunes, Toli switched sides. He threw himself at the mercy of the Austrian chief of staff, General Zach, who was at that time about to lay siege to the French garrison at the fortress of Cuneo. He agreed to take false orders into Cuneo, instructing the garrison commander to seek the best terms possible as there was no chance of relief. In fact the relief column was just a matter of days away – its guns could be heard in the distance as the Cuneo garrison marched off into captivity.[31]

When the Austrians learned that the recently returned Napoleon was going to attack Italy in the spring of 1800, Toli was employed by them in scouting out the strength and location of the French Army of the Reserve. Although Zach had guessed Napoleon would attack in May when the snow on the mountain passes cleared,[32] he did not know the exact route Napoleon intended to follow, there being a number of major passes through which he could debouch.

When it became increasingly likely that the French would use the Great St Bernard Pass, Toli was sent to explore the area. Unknown to him, on 14 May the French advance guard had already begun its advance up to the mountain pass. Toli – disguised as a priest heading for a monastery on the summit – was spotted and fired on by a French patrol. Finding the way ahead blocked, Toli took another route and, in what must have been an epic ordeal, took 60 hours to cross over the icebound peaks. Exhausted and injured, he climbed down the rocks towards the Etremont valley, before taking the path to Bagnes. At Mauvoisin he encountered a picket of 30 soldiers guarding the bridge, but was able to crawl past them unnoticed at daybreak. When in sight of the town of Osières, his luck ran out when a French cavalry patrol intercepted him. Toli pleaded to be taken before Napoleon.

The First Consul was sitting down to dinner when Toli was brought before him. After examining the spy, he said to him in Italian: 'François Toli, you served me at Mantua and Rivoli. You then took the pay of Wurmser as well as mine. What did you come to find in Switzerland?' 'General, Moreau did not think to employ me and Massena is closed in [Genoa]. I sold myself to Vukassovich,' replied the spy, before continuing: 'One must live well.' 'How much does the Austrian General pay you?' quizzed Bonaparte, to which Toli only lowered his head. 'Speak and I will reward you. But if you stay mute, the French will shoot you in ten minutes.' Toli remained silent, prompting Bonaparte to call to one of his aides: 'Here is a spy. Ready the firing squad.' At this the Italian's resistance broke: 'Vukassovich was committed to Milan three weeks ago and paid one hundred Florins in advance for information on the strength of the republican battalions massing in Switzerland.'

Napoleon looked down at a map. 'How did you get here? The passes are guarded.' 'You well know, General, that I know my craft,' Toli replied. He then explained his ordeal, upon which the First Consul congratulated him on his courage. 'Do you want one thousand Francs a month to serve me? Serve me as faithfully as you did in 1796?' Toli nodded. 'Yes, you accept,' exclaimed Napoleon triumphantly. 'Then I will let you know the news.'[33] The First Consul explained the situation of the army and listened to Toli's reports. He then asked

Toli to find out the latest news from Melas' headquarters and to meet him in Milan.

On 4 June, Bonaparte received Toli in the Lombard capital at 11 o'clock. According to Napoleon's secretary, Bourienne, Toli hinted he was looking for a way out of the spy game:

> 'General, when the war recommenced, I entered the service of Austria because you were far from Europe: I attach myself to the fortunate; I have always found my account in so doing: but I am tired of my profession; I wish to leave this business, make up my little fortune and live in tranquillity. Sent into your lines by General Melas, I have it in my power to render you important service. But I must report to my employer. You are sufficiently strong to communicate to me some real information, which I may impart to him.'

Clearly there was risk that Toli was playing a double game for Melas. Heeding the advice of Frederick the Great and others, to cement his loyalty Bonaparte offered Toli the huge sum of 1,000 louis, which he would pay only after Toli had done 'good service'. Bourienne recorded the subsequent transaction of information:

> I then wrote, from the mouth of the spy, the names of the Austrian corps, their force, their position, the names of their Generals, etc. The First Consul marked with pins, upon a map, all the disclosures made, relative to localities. The spy afterwards added Alessandria was not yet provisioned, and Melas was far from expecting a siege; that there were many wounded in the place and medicines wanting. Berthier, in return, received the authority to give him a note, pretty nearly correct on our position.[34]

Leaving Milan, Toli reported back to Zach, who realized that Napoleon was attempting to cut the Austrians off from their lines of communication with Vienna. In response he diverted two divisions from the siege of Genoa and sent them to help defend Piacenza. However, they were delayed in leaving and ran into a strong French force at the battle of Montebello on 10 June. After this the Austrians were forced back on Alessandria. Zach decided his last hope was to trick Napoleon by using Toli to deliver false news to the French headquarters indicating the Austrians were awaiting the arrival of more troops from Genoa before attempting a break out to the north across the River Po. Toli delivered this information to Napoleon on 13 June.

The French commander compared the information with other intelligence and was not convinced. Napoleon had sent cavalry patrols north of the Austrian position and they had not reported any Austrian movement – if the Austrians were about to cross the Po they would have their cavalry patrols up there scouting the terrain. Perhaps Napoleon suspected that the Austrians had fed Toli false information? However, if the spy was to be believed, there would be Austrian troops to the south in the direction of Novi by the end of the day. He ordered General Desaix to take an infantry division south to intercept them; meanwhile the rest of the French army would probe forwards into the centre of the plain between Alessandria and Tortona.

On 14 June, the Austrians attacked the French forward positions at Marengo. Napoleon was taken off guard by the ferocity of the Austrian attack and spent the day slowly retiring on his reserves. Fortunately for the French, Desaix's division had been recalled from its false errand in time. In the evening Desaix launched a powerful counter-attack against the heavily depleted Austrian centre. By nightfall the French had reoccupied all the lost ground. Next day the Austrians agreed to an armistice, which confirmed Napoleon's victory and opened the way for him to be crowned emperor four years later.

Before disappearing into obscurity with bulging saddlebags, Toli paid one last visit to the French headquarters. Bourienne provides the epitaph to the story:

> The 1000 Louis were paid after the battle of Marengo, for the information had proved exact and important. The spy afterwards informed me that Melas, enchanted with his manner of serving the Austrians, had also handsomely rewarded him. 'I am now,' he added, 'able to bid adieu to my villainous trade.' This little event the First Consul regarding among the favours of his good fortune.[35]

After Marengo, both as First Consul of the Republic, then after December 1804 as Emperor of France, Napoleon needed to broaden his intelligence services considerably. In effect he used the same system he set up with Landrieux. Although on a much larger scale, the roll of the 'secret part' was much the same as before and entrusted to Savary, later the Duke of Rovigo. Matters of 'high police' on the other hand were left in the hands of the infamous Joseph Fouché, Duke of Otranto.

General Anne Jean Marie René Savary (1774–1833) was born into a military family. During the Revolutionary Wars he was an aide to General Desaix and served on the Rhine, in Egypt and at Marengo. When Desaix was killed at Marengo, Napoleon took Savary into his service and was rewarded by unswerving loyalty. As one of Napoleon's chief 'fixers' a black cloud lingers over Savary's reputation. He played a leading role in several unsavoury affairs, including the illegal capture and execution of the Bourbon Duc d'Enghien in 1804 and the underhand acquisition of the Spanish throne at the conference of Bayonne in 1808. However, he was principally employed as head of intelligence in Napoleon's Grand Headquarters[36] and it was in that capacity that he ran one of the best-known spies in history – Karl Ludwig Schulmeister (1770–1853), known more simply as 'Monsieur Charles' by the French.

The son of a pastor, Schulmeister spent most of the Revolutionary War supplementing his income as an ironmonger by smuggling. Living on the border of France and Germany, ample opportunities came his way to ferry contraband across the Rhine. Schulmeister proved an intelligent and ruthless gang leader, killing a customs officer who came to arrest him. Of course, his illegal activities on the German side of the river made him the perfect spy for French commanders.[37] In 1794 he first teamed up with Savary, who was then serving in General Desaix's advance guard division. In 1798 business was so good that he bought a house in Strasbourg, running a grocery store and tobacconist's as a front for his operations.[38] He also worked as an informer for Fouché at this time, monitoring French émigrés moving in and out of Switzerland.

In 1805 Napoleon began planning to campaign in Germany for the first time. As his previous European campaigns had been limited to Italy, he needed to maximize his knowledge of the terrain and the enemy army ranged against him. In his capacity as head of intelligence, Savary went to Strasbourg and held what amounted to an open day for all the spies in French pay. Legend has it that Schulmeister turned up and so dazzled Savary that he was taken to meet Napoleon in Strasbourg on 1 October 1805. There are several popular stories about what happened next.

According to one, Savary presented the spy, saying: 'Here, Sire, is a man all brains and no heart.'[39] In another account, Bonaparte asked: 'What are your references?' 'None, I recommend myself alone' replied the spy confidently. 'Then, I cannot employ you,' retorted Napoleon tersely and withdrew behind a folding screen. Unperturbed, Schulmeister disguised himself and went before the Emperor a second time. 'Who are you? What are you doing here?' quizzed Napoleon. 'I am Schulmeister.' A suitably impressed emperor agreed to employ him.[40]

Although perhaps less colourful, the truth behind Schulmeister's appointment probably had more to do with his role in the arrest of Duc d'Enghien. It is alleged that Savary co-opted Schulmeister into the operation and through him sent d'Enghien a forged letter purportedly from a young woman from Strasbourg he was attached to. This letter told d'Enghien she had been arrested and was being held in a house in Belfort near the frontier. When d'Enghien took the bait and went to rescue the girl, he would have to pass into French territory – and therein lay the trap. As a member of the deposed Bourbon monarchy, the duke would be liable to face the death penalty on his return to native soil.[41] In fact the plan was superfluous, as the duke was simply kidnapped from neutral territory, tried without defence and shot at the Château de Vincennes.

At the beginning of the 1805 campaign, Napoleon was faced with a coalition of Austrian and Russian field armies. While the Russians were still a month's march away, an Austrian army under General Mack was located in the Bavarian city of Ulm. Wanting to defeat the Austrians before the Russians arrived, Napoleon developed a plan to encircle Mack at Ulm. It was imperative, therefore, that Mack remained where he was and was unaware of the French columns moving across his line of retreat. Achieving this deception would be the task given to Schulmeister.

Posing as a noble of Hungarian descent, Schulmeister travelled to Vienna, claiming Napoleon had expelled him for his pro-Hapsburg views. In September he had in fact been expelled from the Department of the Lower Rhine by the local prefect, but it is unclear if this was related to his smuggling operations, or to provide him with an alibi with the Austrians. In any case, his next move was to ingratiate himself with Mack, which he did by presenting letters purportedly from Berthier's staff. The French spy gained the total confidence of Captain

Wend, the commander of the Austrian army's intelligence services.[42] Through conversation with Wend, Schulmeister was able to give Napoleon in-depth appraisals of Mack's intentions. Dishing up lie after lie, Schulmeister deceived Mack entirely. His first concoction was that the French would march eastwards through the Black Forest and then advance along the Rhine towards the Danube. Having fixed Mack's gaze in the wrong direction, Schulmeister further muddled his vision with false reports on the size of the French army.

When Mack at last decided to advance out of Ulm on 11 October, he unexpectedly ran into French opposition in the guise of General Dupont's division. Schulmeister quit Ulm and went to Stuttgart, from where he began sending Mack messages of the most urgent nature. He told Mack that Napoleon's army was in retreat, claiming a revolution had broken out in Paris and that the English had landed an army in northern France – it was all lies. In short, despite all the better advice, Schulmeister convinced Mack that he should return to Ulm and await events. Like Zach in the Marengo campaign before him, Mack trusted the spy, complied and unwittingly allowed the French to complete their encirclement. On 20 October, with his army encircled, Mack capitulated in disgrace. His forces, including 33,000 men, 18 generals and 60 guns, defiled past a jubilant Napoleon. It was one of the greatest triumphs of deception in military history.[43]

The day after the surrender, Schulmeister returned to Savary looking for a new assignment. He told the intelligence chief that he had friends in Vienna, including an inspector of police and one employed on the Austrian war council. He also had planted an agent – a man named Bendel – with Archduke Ferdinand, who had escaped from Ulm and was now being hotly pursued. On 23 October Schulmeister set out from Ulm for the Austrian camp at Muldorf. Once there a friend of his named Lieutenant Rulzki introduced him to a number of Austrian generals and staff officers including Kienmayer, Werneck and Merveldt. Through his discussions with these men Schulmeister was able to advise Napoleon that the Russian commander, General Mikhail Kutusov (1745–1813), would not accept battle before he had concentrated all his corps.

At this point Schulmeister's luck finally ran out. Until then everyone in Austria had considered Mack the architect of disaster at Ulm, but people now began to suspect that Schulmeister – now prancing round in an Austrian uniform – may have had a hand in it.[44] He was arrested and sent to Vienna, whereupon his famed good fortune returned. The French arrived in the city on 13 November just in the nick of time to save him from almost certain execution. To rub salt into Austrian wounds, Schulmeister was appointed commissioner general of police in the Austrian capital. He remained there until 12 January 1806, when he returned to Strasbourg, his previous expulsion order having been smoothed over by Savary. Having been paid by both Napoleon and Mack, Schulmeister's earnings had been considerable. He treated himself to a fabulous château with ornamental gardens featuring a giant statue of Napoleon.

In 1806 when Napoleon went to war against Prussia, Savary again employed Schulmeister. In a similar arrangement to Pico and Toli, Schulmeister – now known simply as Monsieur Charles – held the rank of captain and served on Savary's staff. In addition to the usual intelligence operations, Schulmeister exhibited bravery in the field, capturing the town of Wismar at the head of just 13 troopers. The following year he gained a nasty scar when hit on the forehead by a musket ball at the battle of Friedland (14 June 1807). The former smuggler was then made responsible for the protection of Napoleon and Tsar Alexander at a conference in Erfurt held in 1808.

A recurring theme for spies is their desire for recognition. Like a master criminal having pulled off the crime of the century, simply living peacefully in retirement on ill-gotten gains is never enough. Such people want the world to know of their brilliance, their cunning and audacity. Unfortunately in the case of spies, their ambitions are normally quashed by the ego of the general they serve. Successful generals want their victories to be attributed to their own brilliance, cunning and audacity and have almost always downplayed what was owed to 'the secret part'. This is because of the reputation that spies have traditionally held in Western culture. They are abhorred – like Judas. Schulmeister was no different in this regard. Although a millionaire several times over, he coveted the cross of the Legion of Honour in recognition for his actions. Napoleon, however, was adamant that money was the only reward for a spy.

After the end of the Napoleonic empire in 1815, Schulmeister and Savary were left unemployed and mistrusted. Loyal to the end, Savary wanted to follow his master into exile on Saint Helena. Refused, he took refuge in England, returning to France three years after Napoleon's death in 1821. He eventually reconciled himself with the new regime and returned to military service, dying in 1833. Schulmeister was reduced to near poverty after the Austrians flattened his estate, apparently using an entire artillery regiment to destroy his mansion. He set himself up as a tobacconist in Strasbourg where he lived until death came in 1853. Although he had never received the Legion of Honour, he did enjoy one final moment of recognition. In 1850 Prince Louis Napoleon, nephew of the former emperor, paid Schulmeister an impromptu visit while visiting Strasbourg. None of his neighbours had any idea why.

7

UNCIVIL WAR

*'Sir,' said I, 'it is impossible that a colonel of
light cavalry should condescend to act as a spy.'*

From *The Adventures of Gerard* by Arthur Conan Doyle

As old legends go, this is one of the best. During the Napoleonic Wars, a French ship sheltered from a storm in the British port of Hartlepool. Next morning both storm and the enemy ship had gone. However, a monkey had been washed ashore dressed in some sort of uniform – presumably the French ship's mascot. At the height of an invasion scare, the people of Hartlepool – having never seen a monkey, but having heard Frenchmen were short and hairy – arrested the ape on charges of espionage. Unable to provide a coherent defence, and presumably thinking that the monkey was speaking French, the unlucky ape was found guilty and hanged from the yard of a fishing boat.[1]

More seriously, when Napoleon placed his brother Joseph on the throne of Spain in 1808, he accomplished the unthinkable: Spain and Great Britain became allies against France. The ensuing conflict to liberate Portugal and Spain from French occupation was a catastrophe for Napoleon, who compared it to an 'ulcer'. Although not as spectacular a disaster as his invasion of Russia (1812) or the battle of Leipzig (1813), the war in the Iberian Peninsula sapped his strength, resources and morale for five years. For the average French conscript, a posting to Spain was seen as a one-way ticket to hell. Aside from the regular forces under Wellington,[2] fierce Spanish partisans known as 'guerrillas' fought what they called *guerra a cuchillo* – 'war to the knife'. It was a war of brutal savagery; of assassination, torture and revenge.

When Wellington landed in the Iberian Peninsula with 30,000 men in July 1808, he was heavily outnumbered and, by all accounts, without even a proper map. Nor did he know much about the French forces of occupation, except that they outnumbered him and had been largely undefeated for the best part of two decades. Even his allies were unknown quantities. He did not know what support to expect from the Portuguese, and as for the Spanish, Wellington knew – for reasons both historical and religious – that even the most generous Spaniard would view the British as a lesser of two evils. Wellington's first priority, therefore, was the need for accurate intelligence.

Britain's military intelligence services were then at an embryonic stage. Faced with the threat of French invasion, in 1803 the Secretary-at-War had created a Depot of Military Knowledge within the Quartermaster General's branch of the Duke of York's London headquarters. This depot's primary purpose was to purchase and copy maps while building a library. It also collected information from overseas agents useful to the movement of British troops about the globe. Unfortunately, because the war with France resumed a matter of weeks after its establishment, many of the personnel earmarked to serve in it were sent on active duty instead.

In the absence of any specialized field service, Wellington became his own chief of intelligence. Those he employed for secret service work were people he personally trusted. The fewer the better, these intelligencers were a motley bunch of British officers, Spanish irregulars and clergymen. Unusually for the British army of the time, Wellington completely understood the need to win the intelligence war against the French. In a Sun Tzû-like moment of reflection, Wellington wrote: 'All the business of war, and indeed all the business of life, is to endeavour to find out what you don't know by what you do: that's what I called "guessing what was at the other side of the hill."' This informed guesswork took him from victory to victory. It was said that his intelligence was so effective that he would have discovered the French army if it had been 'in the bowels of the earth'.[3]

Without a chief of staff, he used his quartermaster general, Sir George Murray, to co-ordinate the movements of his army – movements which required new, accurate maps to be drawn. This task was undertaken by a group of individuals known as the 'exploring officers'. As the campaign progressed, these exploring officers became responsible for gathering military intelligence. In general they operated alone or occasionally with local guides. To produce the level of intelligence Wellington expected of them, they were each by necessity a combination of excellent horseman, linguist, reporter and even artist, able to sketch the terrain ahead of the army. To avoid execution if captured, they generally retained their uniforms. It was still dangerous work and most of the exploring officers were either killed or captured at some point.

The most famous among them was Colquhoun Grant (1780–1829), an officer Wellington considered 'worth a brigade'.[4] On 16 April 1812, he and his guide were captured by French soldiers while hiding in a tree. Grant was found with notes on the composition and strength of the French forces, but although his guide was executed, the uniformed Grant was spared. Taken into captivity he was invited to dine with the French commander, Marshal Marmont. Thinking Grant would offer him an insight into his commander, Marmont was disappointed when Grant refused to discuss Wellington. The following day, Marmont offered Grant his parole, which meant he promised not to attempt escape and would wait to be exchanged with a captured French officer.

Wellington rued the fact that Grant gave his parole, saying he would have offered the guerrilla chiefs a tidy sum for rescuing him.[5] In fact Grant had thought of a ruse to continue his operations from behind enemy lines. While on parole he reasoned he could maintain his surveillance of the French army and would find a way to send messages back to Wellington. Unluckily for him, the French were not new to these games and had Grant sent away from the frontline into France.

Grant learned that Marmont had recommended he be handed over to the police agents of Joseph Fouché once in France. In Grant's opinion this negated his parole agreement and so he escaped. Posing as an Irish officer in French service, Grant travelled to Paris where he made contact with a British agent and even managed to send Wellington information on Napoleon's preparations to invade Russia. After gaining an American passport, he eventually escaped from France in a fishing boat and within 18 months of his capture, Grant was back in the Peninsula heading Wellington's intelligence service.

Less celebrated than his exploring officers, Wellington had a number of churchmen who served as secret agents. Before the Peninsular War began in early 1807, the Spanish king Charles IV agreed to provide Napoleon with a corps of 14,000 men. These troops were sent to garrisons in Hamburg and Lübeck under the command of General Romaña. Fearing retaliation when he invaded Spain, Napoleon had Romaña's troops split up and posted to a number of Danish islands with the excuse that they had to help guard against British attacks.[6]

Romaña was openly pro-British and so London hatched a scheme to rescue him and his men, before transporting them to Spain where they could help fight the French. This scheme relied on an agent making contact with the dispersed Spanish. Already four spies had been killed looking for Romaña.[7] The Duke of Richmond suggested a fifth candidate from the Scottish monastery at Ratisbon, Father James Robertson. Wellington interviewed the fluent German-speaker on 31 May 1808. 'Tell me, Mr Robertson,' opened the British general, 'are you a man of courage?' 'Try me, Sir Arthur,' he replied. 'That,' Wellington concluded, 'is what we mean to do.'[8]

Robertson landed in Germany on board a smuggler's boat and was met by another ship, the captain of which had been bribed to take him to Bremen. Posing as a German cigar merchant, Robertson obtained a passport allowing him to pass through Napoleon's empire. From a Spanish chaplain he learned that Romaña was based on the island of Fünen, which he reached after travelling through Lübeck, Kiel and then Copenhagen. Under the pretext of selling his wares, Robertson managed to arrange a meeting with the general.

Prior to Robertson's arrival, the Spanish general had learned of the French invasion of his homeland and also the Madrid uprising against the French on 2 May. On 22 July the local French commander, Marshal Bernadotte, asked Romaña to pledge allegiance to Joseph Bonaparte, the newly installed king of Spain. At this crucial hour Robertson told Romaña of the rescue plan, to which the Spanish general agreed. Romaña ordered his men to concentrate on the island of Nyborg under the pretence of swearing their loyalty to King Joseph.

Unfortunately, Robertson had no instructions for alerting the British navy. He was caught on a cliff top by a Danish soldier waving a handkerchief to a British frigate. Robertson was taken into custody, but managed to convince the Danes he was a German merchant simply trying to sell cigars to the British sailors after having done so to the Spanish. Released, he managed to get a message through to the British base on Heligoland. Receiving the message, Admiral Keates raced to Nyborg and by 27 August the Spanish soldiers had begun to embark. At this point Marshal Bernadotte arrived to hear the oath to Joseph being sworn. He was horrified to learn that 9,000 of Romaña's men had escaped on British ships. All he could do was take the remaining 5,000 Spaniards prisoner.

Another of Wellington's 'religious irregulars'[9] was the 72-year-old Reverend Dr Patrick Curtis, a professor of Natural History and Astronomy at the University of Salamanca. Known to the people of Salamanca as Don Patricio Cortés, he headed his own network, which extended throughout occupied Spain and north across the Pyrenees. During the course of the war, there were only four names on the college books, Burke, Shea, O'Grady and O'Kelly – all of whom were absent, working as guides and interpreters for the British army.[10] Although the French had their suspicions, it was only after the battle of Salamanca (22 July 1812), when Wellington met Curtis, that his cover was blown. When the French briefly retook Salamanca in 1813 Curtis was forced to flee, and thus a valuable set of eyes behind enemy lines was lost.

After the autumn of 1809, Wellington's 'exploring officers' began building their own networks of Spanish informers and spies. Their payments were generous – perhaps too generous. Eager for British silver, these spies gave reports which were at best ill informed and at worst utterly fictitious. To keep out of trouble, low-grade spies have a habit of reporting what their masters want to hear. At best Wellington knew where the French were, or how strong they might be at a particular point, but he had very little indication of their intentions. In the absence of any high-level traitors, Wellington relied on captured despatches to learn what the French intended. These dispatches were acquired by the guerrilla bands who made a particular point of intercepting French messengers – over 200 staff officers were killed in the Peninsular War.[11]

Because of the guerrillas' efforts, French communications were paralyzed in the Peninsula. Detachments garrisoned themselves in blockhouses and were unable to keep the roads clear. The normal French system of building telegraph towers could not be realized in Spain, as each station would find itself constantly attacked. Instead the French relied on messages written in plain text or a simple numerical cipher. They also used local Spanish spies to carry messages in places where even a strongly escorted messenger might fail to pass. But even these were rooted out by inquisitive and watchful guerrilla bands who knew the British paid a good price for news.[12]

Once delivered, most messages required some form of decipherment. This challenge proved a major headache for Wellington who later claimed he would have given £20,000 to anyone who could have deciphered them.[13] He was initially reluctant to send the messages back to London or Cadiz for decipherment, both because of the long delay and also because of security. It was imperative that the French did not realize he was reading their messages. If someone back in London accidentally let slip about the codes, before long it would end up in the newspapers and the French would find out.

With no decoding expert on his staff, almost everyone in headquarters had a try at code breaking. The most successful was Captain George Scovell (1774–1861), whose primary function on the staff was commanding a corps of Army Guides and managing the army's communications. His main qualification for code breaking was his excellent knowledge of French and sheer enthusiasm. Initially the codes were of a simple construction based on 50 numbers, but then the French introduced a much more complex cipher (the Army of Portugal code) with 150 numbers. This in turn was replaced with 'The Great Paris Cipher' based on 1,400 numbers, some of which were 'blanks' inserted to confuse any attempt at breaking it.

With the introduction of this code in 1811 Wellington sent to London for help,[14] but by December 1812 Scovell had broken enough of it to understand a letter from King Joseph to Napoleon. The contents of this letter greatly assisted Wellington at the battle of Vittoria on 21 June 1813. After Vittoria British soldiers captured Joseph's carriage in which Scovell discovered an intact copy of the complete Paris cipher. Unfortunately, Joseph guessed the British might have done this and after the battle he warned Napoleon against using it.

While in the Peninsula, Wellington asked Scovell to provide the British army with a cipher of its own. His method was ingenious in its simplicity. Both the sender and recipient were to be provided with identical dictionaries. The code gave the exact location of the word in the dictionary, for example, 46B6, meaning page 46, column B, line 6. If the French managed to intercept the message, they would first have to deduce the nature of the code and even then, if they did not possess that exact edition of the same dictionary they would still be at a loss.[15]

In military terms, Wellington's finest hour came not in the Peninsular War, but at the battle of Waterloo on 18 June 1815. Alongside the Prussian army under Blücher, Wellington found himself facing Napoleon for the first time. When he first learned of the direction taken by the French emperor toward Brussels, Wellington famously declared: 'Napoleon has humbugged me, by God!' So what had gone wrong with his intelligence?

Many of the same names as in the Peninsular War, including Grant and Scovell, were in place during the Waterloo campaign. Although Wellington was unable to use military scouts across the French border without a formal declaration of war, he was amply provided with spies inside France. While fulfilling his duties as ambassador to France in 1814, he built a good network of informants in the French government, many of whom were still in place after Napoleon's return from exile on Elba. Wellington received regular news from the capital and fully expected ample warning if Napoleon was going to attack.[16] He also received reports from the king in exile, Louis XVIII, and even Fouché, now hedging his bets and claiming himself all things to all men. So – again – what went wrong?

It was a question of focus. Wellington had beaten a host of Napoleon's subordinates, but had never come up against Napoleon himself. Napoleon had built his reputation by manoeuvring quickly to cut armies off from their lines of communication and retreat. In this case, Wellington believed his Achilles heel was the English Channel. If Napoleon swung north, the British would be cut off from Antwerp and the boats home.

With this in mind, Wellington placed his forward intelligence post on the Paris–Brussels road, near the French border at Mons under the command of Major-General Dörnberg. From there Dörnberg sent out spies over the border and questioned travellers coming in. Clearly some of these travellers were French spies sent by Napoleon to spread rumour and plant false ideas, but it appears Wellington received enough good information to have made the correct dispositions.[17] However, because the reports did not tally with his expectations, Wellington discounted them. As it turned out, this was not the Napoleon of his younger days. The French emperor tried to bulldoze a path between Wellington and Blücher, pushing back the years in one last hurrah. That he failed was partly because Napoleon's own spies left him with the impression that he would catch the allies off guard.[18] These failings in the intelligence game on both sides ensured Waterloo was, as Wellington so famously stated, 'the nearest run thing you ever saw in your life'.

All told, the Revolutionary and Napoleonic Wars marked an enormous punctuation mark in the history of the West. In the vacuum of peace that followed, men hung up their sabres, retired to their writing bureaus and began trying to make sense of it all. One of the most interesting pieces of this great debriefing was de Brack's *Avant-postes de cavalerie légère* (1834), which, as the title suggests, was a guide for light cavalry officers serving in an army's forward posts.

De Brack was influenced by the work of another Napoleonic veteran, Comte de la Roche-Aymon, author of a service manual for light cavalry on campaign. In his manual, Roche-Aymon declared his preference for using priests and monks for spies, calling them the best sort and the safest. De Brack, however, is a goldmine of everyday practicalities for advance-guard officers on how to run spies. Using a question-and-answer format, de Brack opens his lesson with something of a revelation. In reply to the question 'does an officer of the advanced-guard employ spies?' de Brack's answer is a surprising one: 'Yes; but unfortunately only too seldom, because he does not have enough money to pay them well.'[19]

De Brack goes on to instruct his novices to 'put great care, great finesse, into the use made of these spies'. In selecting them it was first necessary to 'know his family, his neighbours, and through them, his morality and the relations which he might have with the enemy'. The biggest fear was that the spy might pass secrets to the enemy, or worse still lead enemy troops to their camp. De Brack explains the need to be on high alert on the return of a reconnaissance party or spy, lest he had been followed by the enemy. In order to safeguard oneself from treachery, de Brack went for a carrot-and-stick approach. If the spy was loyal he ought to be promptly rewarded. If he was disloyal he should be made aware that his family and goods were threatened. After this general advice, he covers the following scenarios:

Is it necessary to first test a spy with small missions that are not very important and not very dangerous?
Yes: and upon his return be faithful to meet exactly, and promptly, the commitments undertaken towards him. When one recognises intelligence and devotion in these less dangerous missions, one charges him with more important ones.

When one has much information to collect on the enemy, does one use the same spy?
It is first necessary to appreciate the degree of intelligence in the man to whom you entrust a mission. If his intelligence is limited, restrict the work you give him. It is dangerous to put all your secrets in the same hand. It is thus better, by all accounts, to employ several spies whom you send out at different times, whom you direct on different points, and that they have no knowledge of each other.

If you have reasons to distrust one of them. Should he be arrested?
Not always; but better to give him a false mission...

Do you give written instructions to a spy?
For a false mission, yes; and in this case, you conceive them so that if the enemy seizes them, their reading it serves your plans.

And for a true mission?
Never; the instructions should only be verbal...

From among which men do you chose your spies?
As much as possible from among those the enemy least distrusts; thus, postmasters, postilions, the drivers of public carriages and merchants who are known in the country, can be extremely useful, because they will be naturally less suspicious than men who, if they were captured, could not justify their trip, nor be vouched for by anybody.

How do you recognise enemy spies sent to you?
By the way they watch things. By the attention they pay to what is going on in your bivouac. By the frivolous pretexts they take to enter it. By their emotion if you arrest them. By the uncertainty of their answers, if you question them, and especially if they believe you recognise them. Often by the money which they have the clumsiness to carry about them. With the eagerness they destroy an instruction which they are carrying...

How should one advise the soldiers, when espionage is feared?
One must forbid them having too intimate a relationship with the inhabitants; to distrust their questions; never to answer them when they

open a conversation, and can look on our position. One must also order them to arrest people who give them drink and question them...[20]

Another soldier putting pen to paper was de Brack's contemporary, Marshal Bugeaud (1784–1849). France's most distinguished soldier during the reign of Louis-Philippe, Bugeaud had served under Napoleon, but he is better known for the conquest and colonization of Algeria. Having fought an often elusive enemy in North Africa, Bugeaud fully realized the importance of espionage in military operations. He championed the need for each army corps to have its own espionage service and for all staff officers to send out spies and to monitor their reports.

The fact that Bugeaud felt it necessary to go over this well-trodden ground makes one suspect that French officers were not taking the subject seriously. Bugeaud confirms this when he complained that French officers were lagging behind their British, Russian and American counterparts. These, Bugeaud noted, were adept at using disguises and other ruses to penetrate enemy designs. In Bugeaud's opinion, French officers should be well versed in recruiting spies from among Jews, women and hawkers, asking for the publication of a handbook to give them guidance on the subject.

Unfortunately, such matters fell on deaf ears. In the Saint Cyr military academy, trainee officers were taught about intelligence matters only in terms of geography and military statistics. Worse was to follow. Enter Carl von Clausewitz (1780–1831), author of a book heralded in some quarters as the 'most influential work of military philosophy in the Western world' – *Vom Krieg* (On War), published posthumously in 1832. Clausewitz appears to have had a problem with intelligence. Reports are mostly false, he concluded and the negativity in them is amplified by the natural timidity of men, because 'everyone is inclined to magnify the bad'. A chief should therefore rely on his own 'better judgements' and ignore the reports, like a rock standing against the sea.[21]

Clausewitz was not talking about spies specifically in this case, but *all* reports. In fact, he does not really talk about espionage at all. When the word 'spy' does crop up, it is followed very quickly by the word 'unreliable'. When applied to secret intelligence gained through the use of spies, Clausewitz's Canute-like advice goes against the face of what almost every successful commander in history knows to be true. Gone is the subtlety of interpreting often contradictory intelligence reports and discerning the correct course of action – wars were to be won by a display of brutal strength alone. Clausewitz saw war as a science, not an art.

By now there will be little surprise to learn another of the 'great' military thinkers of the post-Napoleonic world was blowing hot and cold on the use of spies. In Baron de Jomini's *Art of War* he recognized four means of obtaining information on enemy operations: espionage, reconnaissances, the interrogation of POWs, or lastly, by using 'the hypotheses of probability'.[22] At first he appears to favour espionage:

> Spies will enable a general to learn more surely than by any other agency what is going on in the midst of the enemy's camps; for reconnaissances, however well made, can give no information of anything beyond the line of the advanced guard.[23]

However, he then describes severe limitations with using espionage:

> An extensive system of espionage will generally be successful: it is, however, difficult for a spy to penetrate the general's [cabinet] and learn the secret plans he may form: it is best for him, therefore, to limit himself to information of what he sees with his own eyes or hears from reliable persons. Even when the general receives from his spies information of movements, he still knows nothing of those which may since have taken place, not of what the enemy is going finally to attempt ... but must still ask himself the questions, where are they going, and what enterprise are they engaged in? These things the most skilful spy cannot learn.[24]

It appears Jomini had been kept in the dark about Napoleon's use of spies. Surely Jomini had heard of Schulmeister's exploits in 1805 when he penetrated General Mack's headquarters?

Part of the problem for historians was that battle reports were largely written by the generals who fought them. When victorious they received plaudits, titles and estates to comfort their retirement. Vain creatures humans are, where spies or devious stratagems had been used to good effect, it was rarely admitted lest the truth dulled the general's glory or, worse still, implied he had acted without honour. In defeat, it was just as unlikely a general would admit having been duped by a spy.

So, when the accounts were written, objectivity was not always the foremost concern. When writers like Jomini and Clausewitz sat down to explain the Napoleonic system, they either did not have the whole picture to work from, or they were too embarrassed to reveal underhand methods of waging war.

The British appeared equally averse to learning from the Napoleonic Wars. Chosen to lead Britain's contingent in the Crimean War (1854–56), Lord Raglan (1788–1855) was a Waterloo and Peninsular War veteran, but again, he failed to grasp the importance of secret intelligence. In a review of Kinglake's *The Invasion of the Crimea* in *The Times*, Raglan was severely criticized for arriving in the Crimea without having found out the strength of Russian forces. The reason for this intelligence black hole was because:

> Lord Raglan was averse, forsooth, to employ spies to ascertain the numbers of the enemy, because it was repulsive to the feelings of an English gentleman! We can only say that if he was, he had learnt very little from the Great Duke.[25]

The Crimean War was waged to prevent Russia from taking Constantinople and closing the Black Sea to Britain and France. When the coalition partners landed their troops in the Crimea to attack the Russian base of Sebastopol in September 1854, the region was as unknown to them as it had been to Jason and the Argonauts searching for the Golden Fleece. Britain's Depot of Military Knowledge, founded in 1803, had never been properly resourced. In the 'Great Peace' that followed Waterloo, it had become known as the Topographical Department and was almost entirely useless in providing relevant intelligence.

The only small ray of light came from information provided by Charles Cattley, the former British consul at the Crimean port of Kertch. Having only recently been expelled, Cattley was able to supply useful intelligence on the Russians. To Raglan's credit, once in theatre he had Cattley form a Secret Intelligence Department (SID) in October 1854. Provided with a secret expenditure fund, Cattley hired spies, chiefly from among Tartars, to create an espionage service against the Russians.[26] Unfortunately, having made a good start, Cattley was stuck down and died of cholera in 1855. SID continued after Cattley's demise, but it is thought the Russians had the upper hand in terms of espionage. The British believed the Russians had infiltrated their spies throughout the camp and even inside British regiments. These agents were mostly hidden among the thousands of camp followers and sutlers, of whom nothing was known, and ethnic Greeks disguised as Tartars. But worse than Tartars, the British press was responsible for a number of sensitive leaks on troop landings, movements, orders of battle, numbers of sick, supply problems, articles on appalling living conditions and so on.[27]

Much the same as ambassadors, journalists had come to be recognized as a form of legitimate spies. Wellington had complained about them in the Peninsular War, but because their reports took so long to reach their editors in London, stories rarely compromised operational security. In the Crimea, however, the introduction of the electric telegraph meant that reporters could file their copy in record time. When combined with photography – the Crimea was the first photographed war – and the new vogue for investigative reporting, Raglan went into meltdown. Although newspaper editors in London vowed to self-censor, nothing sold like a good military scandal or blunder. The best-known reporter in the Crimea, William Howard Russell (1820–1907) of *The Times*, lifted the lid on the awful conditions the soldiers were forced to live in and the inadequate medical facilities provided for them. While the British military establishment cringed at such revelations being made public, the tsar is said to have exclaimed: 'We have no need of spies, we have *The Times*.'[28]

This problem with journalists 'spying' on armies continued in the American Civil War (1860–65). Up to 150 war correspondents followed the Union Army, along with photographers and artists, serving the big Northern dailies. War was being reported faster than at any time in history and in much more detail. Troop movements, plans and orders of battle were served up to a news-hungry public back home. They also became one of the Confederate Army's main sources of information. The Washington and Baltimore newspapers were arriving on the desk of Confederate President Jefferson Davis within 24 hours of being printed, while those of New York and Philadelphia arrived a day later.

Attempts were made to limit the damage, with sometimes farcical results. On 2 August 1861, General McClellan made Washington correspondents agree not to report sensitive information without the permission of the commanding general. Two months later, Secretary of

War Simon Cameron happily gave the *New York Tribune* a complete order of battle run-down of the Union forces in Missouri and Kentucky. In 1862 an attempt by the War Department to introduce telegraph censorship met with hostility and the Lincoln administration was accused of using security as an excuse to stifle public debate on the running of the war.

The problem appears to have become less acute after it was required for journalists to submit their reports to provost marshals before filing them. General William T. Sherman, a man with little time for reporters, went a step further and insisted that correspondents were 'acceptable' to him before they were allowed to work at the front. By 1864, the press co-operated better and Sherman's famous 'march to the sea' was done without being reported. The problem seems to have been very much one-sided. While Union commanders were frustrated by the presence of journalists at the front, the Confederates excluded them from the frontline altogether. The need for strict censorship appears to have been better understood by those few Southern newspapers continuing to run during the war.[29]

One of the most colourful secret service figures in the American Civil War was Allan Pinkerton (1819–94), the Scottish-born founder of the detective agency bearing his name. Famous for railroad protection and running down such notorious desperados as the James Gang, the Wild Bunch and Butch Cassidy, the company logo was an all-seeing eye with the motto 'we never sleep' – hence the expression 'private eye'.

In January 1861, Samuel Felton, president of the Philadelphia, Wilmington and Baltimore Railroad, hired the Pinkerton agency to protect his company from sabotage by secessionist sympathizers in the Baltimore area. Pinkerton agreed the contract and took six of his operatives to infiltrate the secessionists. Alongside Pinkerton was detective Timothy Webster, an English-born New York City policeman and without doubt the agency's top undercover man. Webster passed himself off as sympathetic to the South and enrolled in a rebel cavalry troop formed to resist 'Yankee aggression'. Another agent, Harry Davies, was already familiar with many of the leading secessionists, having previously lived in the South. It was Davies who first discovered a plot to assassinate President-elect Abraham Lincoln (1809–85).[30]

The sixteenth president of the Union, Lincoln had been elected on 6 November 1860. Although billed as 'Honest Abe', many saw his winning the presidency as akin to the coming of the Antichrist. In Baltimore an excitable Italian barber at Barnum's Hotel named Cypriano Fernandina formed a conspiracy to assassinate Lincoln. The Italian's motives are unclear, except to say that many of his best customers were secessionists. According to Davies, Fernandina had called a secret ballot from which eight assassins had been chosen. Before his March inauguration, the Republican president-elect had to travel to Washington by train, working to a publicized timetable. When he stopped at Baltimore, a fracas would break out to divert police attention away from Lincoln and the assassins would strike. Learning of this plot Pinkerton went straight to Philadelphia to consult with Felton.

Meanwhile, Lincoln had left his home in Springfield, Illinois, on 11 February. He arrived at Philadelphia on 21 February and was introduced to Pinkerton, who outlined the plot. It took some effort to convince Lincoln that someone was willing to assassinate him, but eventually he came round to the idea and agreed that Pinkerton should make arrangements for his safe transport to Washington. Deviating from the schedule, Lincoln left a dinner in Harrisburg early and boarded a special train provided by Felton. To prevent secessionist spies transmitting details of his unscheduled departure, Pinkerton had the telegraph lines cut. At Philadelphia, Lincoln joined the night train to Washington. Along the route between Philadelphia and Washington, Pinkerton and Felton placed reliable men posing as members of a work gang whitewashing railroad bridges apparently in an attempt to make them fireproof. These men were given lanterns in order to signal that the train had safe passage through their sector.

Throughout the journey, Lincoln posed as an invalid travelling with his sister, a role played by Kate Warne. A Pinkerton agent since 1856, Warne is celebrated as America's first female private detective. Pinkerton claimed Warne approached him wanting to be a detective, but others think Warne was looking for a job as a secretary. Although there were no vacancies, Pinkerton employed her anyway because he took a shine to her. She then became Pinkerton's mistress and would pose as his wife on certain missions.[31]

The president-elect made it to Washington unharmed and when the plotters realized they had missed their chance, they melted away. Many believed the whole Baltimore conspiracy was a stunt engineered by Pinkerton himself. Pinkerton was a good businessman. If he was paid to uncover conspiracies, then conspiracies he found. If the conspiracies were magnified to ensure the customer felt that he or she was getting value for money, well … business is business, as they say.

After the first shots of the war were fired, Pinkerton again offered Lincoln his services. The detective was invited to Washington and asked for his advice in dealing with Southern sympathizers, but was not given the contract he was seeking. Instead Pinkerton was asked to form a secret service for the army of General McClellan who commanded the Military Department of the Ohio. Setting up shop in Cincinnati and using the alias of E. J. Allen, Pinkerton launched his agents into the Confederacy on McClellan's behalf.

Posing as a Georgia gentleman, Webster was the first agent to move south, heading in the direction of Memphis. Even Pinkerton got in on the act and crossed the Ohio. He had a lucky escape when a German barber from Chicago recognized him, but did not denounce him. Another of Pinkerton's Englishmen, Pryce Lewis, set off in June 1861, travelling through the Confederacy as a neutral tourist. Near Charleston he was stopped and interrogated by a Colonel Patton. Grandfather to General George S. Patton, the Confederate colonel was so sure of Lewis' credentials that he took him on a tour of the fortifications he commanded.

On 22 July 1861 McClellan was given command of the Army of the Potomac and charged with protecting Washington. He immediately invited Pinkerton to follow with his secret service. The most pressing need at that time was for a counter-espionage service, as both Baltimore and Washington were alive with rebel spies and supporters. While Pinkerton dispatched Webster and the agent Carrie Lawton to Baltimore to infiltrate rebel cells, he concentrated on snaring the top rebel spy in Washington. This agent was supposed by many, including Assistant Secretary of War Thomas Scott, to be the politically well-connected socialite widow Rose O'Neal Greenhow (1817–64).

Greenhow had been recruited as a spy at the beginning of the war by West Point graduate Thomas Jordan, a US officer who joined Confederate General Beauregard's staff. Before leaving Washington, Jordan provided Greenhow with a simple cipher and instructions to contact him using his alias – Thomas J. Rayford. In July 1861 she scored a significant coup when she sent a copy of Union General McDowell's orders for the Army of the Potomac, which was to advance into Virginia. Forewarned,

General Beauregard caused the Union army an embarrassing defeat at Bull Run on 21 July.[32]

Pinkerton put Greenhow and her contacts under close surveillance. By all accounts Greenhow unsuccessfully tried to pull strings with government friends to have Pinkerton called off. Then, one rainy August evening, Pinkerton and three agents, including Pryce Lewis, tailed an officer to Greenhow's home. When an upstairs light came on, Pinkerton had his men form a human pyramid with himself at the apex. Glimpsing into the room, Pinkerton saw the young officer handing Greenhow a map and heard him give instructions on how to read it. Then the two went into a back room, where Greenhow no doubt favoured the traitor with a reward. An hour later, the officer departed Greenhow's home with a kiss. Pinkerton had the officer arrested and, when confronted with the evidence, he later committed suicide in his cell. Meanwhile an embarrassing list of prominent figures were seen coming and going from the Greenhow home, including former president James Buchanan.

Having heard enough, Scott ordered Greenhow's arrest. On the day of the arrest, Greenhow was found in her parlour reading a book. While Pryce Lewis stood guard over her, Pinkerton searched the house and recovered an amazing hoard of classified Union documents including plans of Washington's defences and fortifications. Prize among them was Greenhow's diary, which detailed the full extent of the Confederate spy ring. In terms of counter-espionage, the find was priceless. It gave the names of Greenhow's contacts, her informants and means of delivering messages to the Confederacy – numerous arrests followed. At one point in the search, Greenhow pulled a pistol on Lewis, but failed to cock it properly. Otherwise the only real trouble came from her eight-year-old daughter, who hid up a tree outside the property and called down a warning to anyone she recognized approaching the house: 'Mother has been arrested!'[33]

With Greenhow in custody the problem arose of what to do with her? She was too well connected and too much a celebrity to send to the gallows, but the number of prominent soldiers, politicians, bankers and so on involved with this conspiracy made her presence acutely embarrassing for President Lincoln. This problem was exacerbated when Greenhow continued sending messages to Richmond from jail, including an unflattering account of how Pinkerton had arrested her. In the end, after a trial, Greenhow was sent to Richmond where she continued her celebrity lifestyle. She was later sent on a mission to London, where she had an audience with Queen Victoria and to Paris where she was received at the court of Napoleon III. After writing her memoirs she returned to the Confederacy in 1864 on the blockade-runner *Condor*. Chased by a Union gunboat, *Condor* ran aground and Greenhow drowned.[34]

While Pinkerton had been busy with Greenhow, Timothy Webster had been making a name for himself among Confederates and their Maryland acolytes. Working so far undercover, Webster was actually arrested by a Federal detective who believed he was a Confederate spy. Webster could not hope for better credentials to maintain his cover. While under arrest, he met with Pinkerton who arranged for him to 'escape' while being transferred to Fort McHenry for internment. Hand-picked guards even fired shots after the escaping Webster, all to give the agent more credibility. Arriving at a safe house in Baltimore, Webster had become a hero of the cause. Even when a man denounced him after seeing Webster with Pinkerton, the Union agent simply punched the man in the jaw and called him a damned liar.

From Baltimore to Richmond, it seemed Webster had the run of the Confederacy. His intelligence reports from behind enemy lines were exhaustive and accurate. Set up in a top Richmond hotel, Webster was so believable that the Confederate Secretary of War entrusted his personal letters to him for delivery to Baltimore. This of course allowed Pinkerton to read the letters, which lead to a number of high-profile arrests.

In support of Webster, other Pinkerton agents were sent south, including John Scobell, a former Mississippi slave recruited to the agency in the autumn of 1861. Scobell performed a variety of roles, sometimes posing as a cook or labourer, other times acting as a servant to Webster or Carrie Lawton. Another of his means of gaining intelligence was through his membership of the Legal League. This was a secret African-American organization in the South, the members of which often helped Scobell by providing couriers to carry his information across Union lines.[35]

However, as the war entered its second year and McClellan was planning another offensive, Webster began to suffer from illnesses brought about by his constant exposure to the elements. After feeling the effects of rheumatism while accompanying Carrie Lawton on a mission to Richmond, Webster fell seriously ill and stopped reporting. Desperate for news on the eve of the new offensive, Pinkerton made the cardinal error for spymasters. He became impatient.

When Pinkerton asked Pryce Lewis to replace Webster, the Englishman baulked at the idea and refused the assignment. Then, when Pinkerton convinced him otherwise, he told Lewis that another agent, John Scully would be joining him. Their cover would be as smugglers carrying a letter to Webster from Baltimore. It was an ill-conceived plan.

On the afternoon of 27 February 1862, the two Union spies were at Webster's sick bed when the Confederate detective Captain Sam McCubbin entered the room only to check on Webster's progress. The feeling of relief was only temporary, for McCubbin was followed by the son of a former senator, whom Lewis and Scully had guarded after Pinkerton had ordered their family arrested. Before they had a chance to escape, Lewis and Scully were seized and taken before General Winder, head of Confederate secret police, who suspected they were both spies.

Lewis tried to play it cool, insisting he was a friend of Webster calling in to see how he was doing. After the senator's son gave a positive ID on the two Pinkertons – whose names were already known to the Confederates – Lewis tried to escape on the night of 16 March, having filed the bars on the prison windows. Unfortunately Lewis was picked up 20 miles (32km) from Richmond on the Fredericksburg road. He was returned to jail and clapped in irons.

On 1 April, Scully and Lewis were found guilty of spying and sentenced to be hanged four days later. Lewis had one last card to play. The Confederacy was trying to gain recognition from Britain and he and Scully were still subjects of Queen Victoria. Lewis gave the prison chaplain a letter for the British consul, asking for the Crown's protection. Although the consul arrived and promised to help, Scully was near breaking point. Dissolving into tears, Scully admitted he had written to Winder and, if pardoned, would reveal everything he knew. This course of action was confirmed when the guards removed Lewis from the cell so that Scully would not be influenced by him.

Not long after, Lewis saw a carriage arrive at the prison and was horrified to see Webster and Lawton being led out as captives. Scully had betrayed them. Expecting to be executed at 11.00am on the morning of 4 April, Lewis was told that President Davis had delayed the execution for two weeks. This was to allow for a trial, with both

Scully and Lewis called as witnesses against Webster. The Confederates were furious they had allowed themselves to be duped by Webster and wanted swift revenge. While Scully spilled the beans, Lewis tried his best to protect Webster. The trial was a foregone conclusion. The increasingly frail Webster was sentenced to death with all haste, lest Webster died of his illness first. Lawton was sentenced to a year's imprisonment as his accomplice, while Scully and Pryce Lewis were spared the gallows as British subjects.

When Pinkerton learned of the trial from a Southern newspaper he was beside himself with anguish. The matter went as far as Lincoln, who wrote to President Davies pointing out that Confederate spies had not been executed in the North. With this came the obvious threat – if Webster was executed, Southern spies could expect the same treatment. The pleas went unheard and Webster was given a public execution. With no proper executioner, it took two attempts to hang him. On the first attempt the noose was too loose and ended up round Webster's waist and on the second attempt, it was so tight it almost throttled him before the trapdoor was released.

The loss of Webster seemed to mark the beginning of the end for Pinkerton as secret service chief. As a general, McClellan was heavily criticized for being over cautious. One of the main reasons given for this caution was Pinkerton's mistakes in reporting the Confederate order of battle, which he constantly over-exaggerated. In March 1862, McClellan advanced with 85,000 troops against Richmond. Encountering resistance at Yorktown, McClellan quickly halted and settled down for a month-long siege. Against him were no more than 17,000 troops, but Pinkerton's intelligence was faulty. During the course of the siege the Confederates received reinforcements, bringing their strength up to 60,000 men. At the same time McClellan's forces grew to 112,000 strong, but he still believed the Confederates to have twice as many troops as was the case. When McClellan finally broke through and resumed his advance on Richmond, the Confederate army was reinforced by General 'Stonewall' Jackson. Its actual strength was in the region of 80,000 men: Pinkerton reported it to be 200,000 and McClellan decided to retreat.[36]

On 5 November, Lincoln replaced McClellan and in so doing ended Pinkerton's active involvement with the war. The detective's fault was not in an inability to gather intelligence, but in his appreciation of it. As Landrieux had written of his time in Italy, the head of a military secret service had to be a soldier because a civilian policeman would 'understand almost nothing'. Pinkerton was living proof of this. He had been successful at counter-espionage, which was above all, police work, but it was commonly agreed that Pinkerton was an abject failure with military intelligence. This failure also proved in the long run, very bad for business. Washington disclaimed any responsibility for Pinkerton's expenses, arguing that he was the private employee of General McClellan. He was replaced by a Secret Service Bureau under Lafayette Baker (1826–68) who was appointed by Secretary for War Stanton.

Previous to this assignment, like Webster, Lafayette Baker had been working as a spy behind enemy lines. His *modus operandi* was to pose as an itinerant photographer, which he did with aplomb, despite his camera being broken and without film. On his travels he met Jefferson Davies and interviewed General Beauregard. Finally he was rumbled at Fredericksburg when one inquisitive spark wondered why he was the only photographer never to have any photographs with him. The jig was up and Baker escaped back to Union lines.[37]

Perhaps the most significant example of military espionage in the war came during the build-up to the battle of Gettysburg (1–3 July 1863), the largest battle ever fought on American soil. In brief, the Confederate general Robert E. Lee had invaded the Union with the 75,000-strong Army of Northern Virginia. While advancing along the Shenandoah Valley towards Harrisburg, Pennsylvania, Lee was reliant on a cavalry screen to protect his march. Under the command of General J. E. B. Stuart, the Confederate cavalry went raiding instead, leaving Lee and the entire army blind. While Lee waited vainly for news from Stuart, the commander of I Corps, General James Longstreet, sent a spy to accomplish what Stuart had not.

This spy was identified by Longstreet in his memoirs as a scout named only as 'Harrisson'. It was not until the 1980s that he was finally identified as Henry Thomas Harrison (1832–1923), a native of Nashville, Tennessee. In 1861, Harrison joined the Mississippi State Militia as a private and was often employed as a scout. In February 1863 he came to the notice of the CSA Secretary of War, James Seddon, who brought him to Richmond and employed him as a spy. In March Seddon sent Harrison and several others dressed as civilians to General

Longstreet, recommending he use them as scouts. To test them, Longstreet sent them on missions, including finding a passage through the swamps in the direction of Norfolk. Of those sent, Harrison was marked out as 'an active, intelligent and enterprising scout' and was retained in Longstreet's service.

It is worth noting here that although Longstreet politely refers to Harrison as a 'scout' he was dressed as a civilian, thus making him in the eyes of the law a spy. As is so common in the story of espionage, spies were distrusted and thought to be double traitors, giving away as much information to the enemy as they received back from them. Even Longstreet was cautious when dealing with Harrison lest he was betrayed. When he sent Harrison to go to Washington and to glean as much intelligence as possible he would not answer Harrison's query about where he should report to after the mission was accomplished. In one version of the conversation, Longstreet told Harrison the headquarters of I Corps were large enough for any intelligent man to find. Another version, given by Longstreet's chief of staff, Gilbert Moxley Sorrel, has the general saying: 'With the Army; I shall be sure to be with it.' Wryly, Sorrel noted such a precaution was unnecessary as Harrison 'knew pretty much everything that was going on'.[38]

According to Sorrel, Harrison's instructions were to proceed into the enemy's lines and to remain there until the end of June, bringing back as much information as he could. He returned on the night of 28 June, finding Longstreet's headquarters at Chambersburg, Pennsylvania. 'Travel-worn and dirty',[39] he had been arrested while trying to cross back through the Confederate picket lines and was taken to Longstreet's camp by the provost guard. Sorrel recognized him and debriefed him immediately. Harrison's report was long and, as events would prove, completely accurate. He explained how the Union Army of the Potomac had quit Virginia and started in pursuit of Lee in great numbers. Two Federal corps had been identified around 50 miles (80km) away at Frederick and George Meade had recently been placed in command of the army, in place of General Hooker. Recognizing the importance of the report, Sorrel took Harrison to Longstreet and woke him up. Hearing the news, Longstreet lost no time in sending Harrison directly to General Lee's camp with one of his staff officers, Major John W. Fairfax.

Arriving at Lee's tent, Fairfax entered and announced that one of Longstreet's scouts had arrived with information that the Union army had crossed the Potomac and was marching north. Lee had spent the day fretting over Stuart's lack of communication and Fairfax's report appears to have startled him. 'What do you think of Harrison?' asked Lee. 'General Lee,' replied Fairfax, 'I do not think much of any scout, but General Longstreet thinks a good deal of Harrison.' 'I do not know what to do,' came Lee's blunt reply after a moment's reflection. 'I cannot hear from General Stuart, the eye of the Army. You can take Harrison back.'[40]

Later that night, after absorbing the shock that he was in severe danger from an unknown force, Lee sent for Harrison. In what must have been a lengthy interview, Lee patiently listened to Harrison's entire report: how he had left Longstreet at Culpeper and had gone to the Union capital, Washington, where he had picked up gossip in saloons. Hearing the Union army had crossed the Potomac in pursuit of Lee, Harrison recalled how he set out for Frederick, mixing with soldiers during the day and moving on foot by night. At Frederick he had identified two infantry corps and had heard of a third nearby, which he had been unable to locate. Learning that Lee's army was at Chambersburg, he found a horse and hurried back to reveal the position of the Union army. On the way there, he learned that at least another two corps were in the vicinity and that General Meade had taken control of the army.[41]

With no other option but to believe Harrison, Lee gave the orders to concentrate in the direction of Gettysburg. Many applaud Harrison for saving the Confederate army from being attacked in the rear, but ironically, in so doing, he also led it to disaster. Against Longstreet's advice, after unexpectedly encountering lead elements of the Federal army at Gettysburg, Lee attacked Meade for three days of confused and bitter fighting. The battle was a heavy defeat for the Confederacy, losing men and commanders it could ill afford to replace. At the end of it Lee was forced to retreat back across the Potomac.

Later in the year Harrison obtained permission to return to Richmond. Before leaving headquarters he told Sorrel he was appearing on stage in the role of Cassio, in Shakespeare's *Othello*. When Sorrel asked Harrison if he was an actor, the spy explained he was not, but he was doing the performance to win a $50 wager.[42] Sorrel saw the performance – Cassio was unmistakably Harrison – and noted that the entire cast seemed quite drunk. Although perhaps just harmless fun, Sorrel decided to investigate Harrison's indulgencies more closely. When he found Harrison had a reputation for heavy drinking and gambling, Sorrel concluded he was not safe to be employed as a spy. Harrison was dismissed from Longstreet's service in September and sent back to the Secretary of War.[43]

The American Civil War was notable for the number of female agents on both sides. Already we have seen Rose Greenhow, Kate Warne and Carrie Lawton. To these must be added 'la belle rebelle' Belle Boyd (1844–1900) who at 17 shot an overly exuberant Federal soldier on her doorstep when he tried to raise the Union flag over her Virginia home. During the Shenadoah Valley campaign of 1862, Boyd famously ran across a battlefield to deliver vital intelligence to 'Stonewall' Jackson. He was so impressed with her exploits, he made Boyd captain and honorary aide-de-camp on his staff. Boyd later travelled to Britain where her autobiography became a bestseller.[44]

Sarah Emma Edmonds (1842–98) enlisted in the Union army under the name Frank Thompson. Volunteering for a mission behind enemy lines at Yorktown, Edmonds gained entrance to Confederate camps near Yorktown, Virginia, disguised as an African-American slave, having bought a wig of 'negro wool' and stained her skin with silver nitrate.

She was assigned to work on construction of the Confederate ramparts opposite McClellan's position and noted how logs were being painted black to look like guns. Unfortunately, the heavy work took its toll on Edmonds' disguise. As she began to sweat, the silver nitrate began to fade. Popular legend has it that a slave noticed Edmonds' skin was becoming paler and pointed this out. Edmonds coolly replied that she always expected to become white one day, as her mother was a white woman. This excuse was apparently accepted. On the second day of her mission, Edmonds was sent out to the Confederate picket line to replace a dead soldier. From there she made her escape to Union lines.[45]

Pauline Cushman (1833–93) also merits an honourable mention. An actress from New Orleans, Cushman followed the Confederate army 'looking for her brother', but in reality spying for the North. She was captured and sentenced to be hanged, but was rescued by Union troops in the nick of time. President Lincoln made her an honorary major. Also of great service was the freed slave Mary Touvestre, who was housekeeper to a Confederate engineer in Norfolk, Virginia. She stole a set of plans for the first Confederate ironclad warship and took them safely to Washington.

But of all the female agents – Greenhow included – the connoisseur's choice must be 'Crazy Bet' Elizabeth Van Lew (1818–1900). From a Northern family settled in Richmond, Van Lew did not hold with the Southern way of living. When her father died, she used her inheritance to free the family slaves, an act which gained her a reputation among polite, Southern society as something of an eccentric.

After the arrival in Richmond of Union soldiers taken prisoner at Bull Run, Van Lew obtained a pass from General Winder to visit them. While providing them with food, medicine and clothing, Van Lew began collecting messages from the prisoners, which she had smuggled to their homes. This simple act of generosity soon developed into an espionage network, known as the Richmond Underground. This comprised of an elaborate network of spies, messengers and escape routes for prisoners she helped break out of prison. By way of an example, in 1864 Van Lew was responsible for the escape of 109 prisoners, half of whom she quartered at home while waiting to be smuggled back north. Of course, Winder was not entirely unaware of Van Lew's activities. From 1862 he had her under surveillance, but without success. Aware she was being watched, Van Lew began to act very strangely, confirming suspicions she was unbalanced, if not actually insane.

Van Lew's spy ring was centred on one of her former family slaves, Mary Elizabeth Bowser. Early in the war, Van Lew obtained Bowser employment as a servant in the home of the Confederate president. As an African-American female servant, she was ignored by the president's guests who did not suspect Bowser was carefully eavesdropping on their conversations, or reading documents on Jefferson's desk while going about her chores. To collect reports from Bowser, Van Lew recruited a local baker who made deliveries to the Confederate 'White House'. The baker collected the messages for Van Lew, who enciphered them and passed them to an old man – another former slave – who took them to the Union's General Grant, hidden in his shoes. Again, because the man was seen as a slave, he passed unnoticed under the auspices of carrying flowers.

In 1864 Winder made another attempt to catch Van Lew red-handed. He ordered her property searched by troops, who found nothing, despite there being prisoners hidden in a secret room on the third floor. After the raid, Van Lew went into an apoplectic spasm in Winder's office, declaring him not a gentleman and forcing an apology from him. A few short months later the war was over and General Grant made a special point of visiting Van Lew, thanking her for the excellent intelligence he had received from Richmond. Unsurprisingly, Van Lew's neighbours were less than pleased to learn the full extent of her treachery. 'Crazy Bet' spent the next 35 years of her life despised as an outcast and a traitor.

8

THE GODFATHER
OF SECRET
SERVICE

*But even the best-informed chief of the best
secret intelligence service can never predict the
future! The best I could do was to guess what, in
view of all the information I had received, would
be the most probable outcome.*

Wilhelm Stieber[1]

Having provided us with Clausewitz, Germany supplied an antidote in the guise of Wilhelm Stieber (1818–92). Not from Prussia himself, Stieber was born in Merseburg, Saxony, and had an English mother named Daisy who claimed descent from Oliver Cromwell. In 1820 the family moved to Berlin where his father held a position in the church. Naturally enough, Stieber was also expected to enter the church and so his father paid for him to study theology at Berlin University. While there he became interested in the case of a young Swedish janitor who had been accused of burglary. In those days anyone could defend an accused person in court. So, believing him innocent, Stieber took up the case and won the Swede's acquittal.

This first taste of legal process opened Stieber to the possibility of a future outside the church. While his father continued to subsidize his studies, Stieber secretly began taking courses in law, public finance and administration. When Stieber eventually revealed his preference for a career in law, his father all but disowned him. Stieber was thrown out of the family home and his funds were cut off. This was a pivotal moment in the young man's career. To continue with his studies, Stieber needed an income.

This necessity led him to work as a secretary to the criminal court and Berlin Police Department. Through this vocation Stieber was introduced to the work of Berlin police inspectors, who occasionally took him on arrests. He was immediately hooked on criminal investigation, so, after graduating as a junior barrister in 1844, Stieber applied for and was granted a place as a Berlin police inspector. He was quickly given a chance to impress. The Minister of the Interior asked for Stieber to be sent undercover into Silesia to conduct an investigation into an alleged 'workers' conspiracy'. Posing as a landscape artist named Schmidt, he quickly identified the ringleaders of the so-called 'Silesian Weavers' Uprising' (4–6 June 1844) and under orders from Berlin had them rounded up and arrested.

However, it was during the riots of 1848 – the year of revolutions – when Stieber really came to the fore. With Berlin on the verge of rebellion, King Friedrich Wilhelm IV (ruled 1840–61) rode out onto the streets of the capital in an attempt to calm his subjects. He was quickly surrounded by an unruly mob and appeared in danger of being pushed from his mount. There are many different versions of what happened next, but Stieber's memoirs recall how he seized a banner from one of the protestors and stood in front of the king's horse, making a path through the crowd for him to pass. Shouting 'The King is on your side – Make way for your King!' Stieber managed to get the king back to the palace gates where the guards carried him to safety. In some accounts Stieber is said to have arranged the whole thing as a stunt to gain popularity with the king. Stieber claims the man he saved was in fact an actor posing as the Prussian monarch. Whatever the truth, the event certainly brought Stieber into the spotlight. When in November 1850 the notorious revolutionary Gottfried Kinkel was sprung from jail, a section known as the 'Criminal Police' was formed with cross-district jurisdiction – Stieber was its commander.

More significant was the king's approval of Stieber's assignment to monitor German communists attending the international industrial exhibition at London's Crystal Palace in October 1851. Stieber travelled to London again using the alias of Schmidt, but this time posing as a newspaper editor covering the exhibition. Enjoying the right to freedom of speech and assembly in the liberal British capital, a German newspaper editor named Karl Marx had been organizing an 'International Communist League'. Stieber went to visit Marx, claiming to be carrying family news to a fictitious colleague, Friedrich Herzog, who was believed to be a member of the Communist League. Unsurprisingly, Marx had never heard of Herzog and unwisely told Stieber to consult with a German named Dietz who held records of the communist movement.

Before Stieber went looking for Dietz he chatted to Marx for a while. Talking of his own background, he told Marx he had studied medicine and was editor of a Berlin medical publication. On learning he had a medical background, Marx asked Stieber if he knew a good cure for haemorrhoids. He went on to say that it would be impossible for him to sit and write except for a medication made up by Dietz, himself a former apothecary. Confirming this was the same Dietz holding the League's records, a plan hatched in Stieber's mind. Bidding farewell to Marx he went to Dietz's address, but not before forging Marx's signature on a note reading: 'Please bring me some medication and the files at once.' Posing as a physician named Dr Schmidt, Stieber duped Dietz into handing over four volumes of information on the Communist League's activities across the globe.

From London Stieber travelled to Paris where the communists appeared strongest and best organized. A few days after arriving, a man turned up in his apartment calling himself Cherval. He was a communist and had been sent to retrieve the stolen records. When Stieber refused to hand them over, Cherval drew a dagger and attacked him. Knocking his assailant unconscious with a chair, Stieber handcuffed him and interrogated him. Cherval was in fact a German who had adopted a French name on arriving in the country. Stieber promised to drop the charges relating to his attack if Cherval would spill the beans on his co-conspirators. The communist obliged and a number of significant arrests were made.

Returning to Germany, Stieber's information led to yet more members of the Communist League being arrested. In reward for his efforts, in January 1853 Stieber was made director of the Security Division at Berlin. Thereafter he embarked on a number of police-related cases which are outside the scope of this study except in one respect. Through his investigations he became fascinated with the world of high-class prostitutes and their rich clientele, who were often high-ranking officers and members of government. He quickly realized that these men would be extremely vulnerable if the prostitutes were agents of a foreign power:

To my amazement, I discovered that among the prostitutes who frequented these brothels, there were actually many who had acquired a certain amount of education through their constant association with their highly-placed visitors, so they could recite lines by Virgil and Horace and often commanded an entire catalogue of legal and military concepts; and to my horror, found among them women who appeared to have been predestined to become spies... Some of them had already made a regular business out of enticing intimate, compromising information out of married men in the highest reaches of society and then extorting large sums of money from them by threatening to reveal these secrets to their wives.[2]

Thinking it best to have these women on his side, to win them over Stieber helped establish a 'Prostitutes Recovery Fund'. The whole vice trade became much more regulated and in return for his favour, prostitutes began to supply Stieber's officers with information relating to crimes. Before long they had became the best police spies in the city.

Everything was going well for Stieber until 1857, when the king was declared insane after suffering a brain tumour. The throne passed to a regent, the king's liberal-minded brother Wilhelm. With his royal protector out of the picture, Stieber's many enemies had him imprisoned and ransacked his apartments looking for documents that might compromise their own positions. Unfortunately for them Stieber escaped from his cell and rescued the documents, which he knew would save his neck. Arguing his case in public through the newspapers, Stieber claimed that to accuse him of wrongdoing was to accuse the king himself. His accusers quickly drew a line under the business and Stieber was largely exonerated, albeit left without an appointment and put on half pay.

Continuing his work against communists and anarchists, Stieber went to St Petersburg. With him he took his dossiers on Russian revolutionaries working abroad in London and Paris. Arriving at a time when the Russian secret services were at an embryonic stage, Stieber was asked for advice on dealing with radicals living abroad. Stieber's solution was to track down ex-pat Russian criminals, forgers and blackmailers and, in return for immunity from prosecution, these would be paid to spy on the radicals.[3]

But Prussia was never far from Stieber's mind. His rehabilitation came when in 1863 he uncovered a plot to assassinate the newly appointed Prussian prime minister, Otto von Bismarck (1815–98). He was introduced to Bismarck by August Brass, founder of the *Norddeutsche Allgemeine Zeitung,* who recommended him despite his unpopularity.[4] The plot may have been a ruse on Stieber's part, but Bismarck took it seriously enough. An assassination attempt was indeed attempted by a Russian revolutionary named Bakunin, but with the benefit of hindsight it does appear a somewhat stage-managed affair. Bakunin ended up shooting a dummy of Bismarck, and Stieber's men were miraculously right on hand to arrest him. Charges were not pressed against the Russian, who was quietly slipped out of Prussia never to return. Stunt or not, Bismarck was impressed and from that moment, Stieber became his chief problem-solver.

Bismarck set a special mission for Stieber, one far more important than any he had thus far attempted. Bismarck's greatest legacy would be the unification of the independent German states into a single political entity – Germany. However, at the time these independent German states looked to Austria for leadership rather than Prussia. Before any unification could take place, there would have to be a showdown with Austria. Bismarck wanted Stieber to observe and report upon Austria's military preparedness.

The most commonly told story about Stieber is that, following Bismarck's request, he went into Austria disguised as a harmless pedlar. By day he rode from village to village selling religious statuettes; at night he frequented inns, discretely selling pornographic cartoons to drinkers. Months later, having toured the country and built up maps of the military defences and stores, he returned to Berlin to make his report. So accurate were his findings that Bismarck and General von Moltke were able to confidently plan a lightning campaign which saw Austria defeated in seven weeks.

The story is a good yarn and is perhaps based on some elements of truth. However, it grossly over simplifies the true scale of Stieber's operations and downplays his true genius, which was the organization of intelligence gathering. After asking him to spy on Austria, Bismarck gave Stieber ten days to formulate a plan for establishing a network of spies there. Undaunted by the scale of the task, Stieber applied the same patient methodology common in police detective work to military espionage.

Through analyzing past methods, Stieber realized that traditional methods of espionage had produced only limited results. Amateur spies did not have the technical knowledge to collect intelligence of real relevance. Also, in previous wars only small numbers of spies had been employed, making it easier for enemy counter-espionage services to concentrate their resources and pick them up or to feed them false intelligence. Stieber wanted to flood Austria with an 'army' of observers, draining police resources to the point where surveillance became unfeasible. If a single agent was caught they would know almost nothing about the other spies and even if several were caught they would have so little idea of the grand scheme of things that the damage would be negligible.

Austria would be divided into districts, each with a 'home base' set up and controlled by a 'resident spy'. To avoid suspicion, 'resident spies' would not be foreigners, but natives of the district. Their districts would also be quite small so they would not have to make any unusual travel which might be noticed. Their first duty would be to recruit a network of informers throughout their assigned district and collect their reports. These reports would be sent to a central headquarters in Prussia where they would be assessed. Always kept up to date, the processed data would be passed on to the appropriate political or military authorities, enabling them to respond accordingly. However, when very important information came in from the resident spies, special agents would be sent into Austria to investigate it further. With the groundwork already done by resident spies, the job of these special agents would be much easier.

Wherever possible Stieber wanted the 'resident spies' to be recruited from among local journalists. If this was not possible, then the resident spy was to attempt to at least use journalists among his informants. While generals in the Crimean and American Civil Wars had been frustrated by the interference of the press, Stieber had recognized how powerful journalists were becoming and how they had a right to ask questions without causing suspicion. Through their profession they would have already made contacts in government and military circles – contacts that were like a tap waiting to be turned on. But why would normally reputable journalists spy for Prussia? Stieber knew that the weak point of most journalists was that they were always short of cash.

Bismarck approved of the plan and went one step further, allowing Stieber to form a Press Bureau. The king had already expressed concern how the London-based Reuter's Telegraph Company had a monopoly on the news and as such controlled public opinion. He wanted a Prussian news service and so Stieber entered the perhaps yet murkier world of news management.

The observation service began in Austria under cover of 'press activities'. One immediate problem was in funding the rapidly growing network of spies. In solving this issue, Bismarck proved himself as wily as Stieber, telling him to recruit captured forgers and counterfeiters from Berlin prisons. They were careful not to print so much Austrian money the economy would be destabilized, but just enough for funding never to be a problem.

With Austrian counter-espionage duties handed over to inept, retired police officers, Stieber's agents were able to uncover a great deal of important facts, namely:

- Austria also desired a united Germany, with a federation of states and them at the head. They believed this was achievable partly because most of the independent German states were, like them, Catholic, while Prussia was largely Protestant.
- Austria did not expect a war and was totally unprepared for one.
- The Austrian people were against war.
- Austria would take two weeks longer than Prussia to mobilize its armies.
- Austrian weapons were outdated and no match for the new Prussian 'needle guns'.

Armed with these facts, Bismarck asked Stieber to stir up the Austrian population by spreading false stories in the Austrian press. The idea was to make the Austrian government so unpopular at home that it provoked them into declaring war on Prussia. At the same time, Bismarck asked Stieber to stir up trouble among the many different ethnic groups in the Austrian empire. Stieber hired 800 agitators from among Czech and Slovak dissidents who would start uprisings in Hungary, Dalmatia and Moravia should war be declared. He also made plans for a 'Hungarian Freedom Legion' made up of Austrian army deserters who would attempt to break Hungary away from Austria.

With war looming, Bismarck ordered Stieber to shut down his intelligence service in Austria so that there would be no clues that

Prussia had spied on Austria in peacetime.[5] Stieber's concluding report to Bismarck included the allegation that Austrian emperor Franz Joseph had begun using a double on public occasions because of his fear of assassination. Additionally, two of the emperor's closest advisors were highly paid Prussian agents and his wife was in love with an 18-year-old stable groom, while many members of his court had become opium addicts.

On 23 June 1866, ten days before the outbreak of the war, Stieber was placed in charge of protecting the king, Bismarck and the supreme Prussian headquarters on campaign, ensuring its safe movement through occupied terrain. To this end he formed a 'Secret Field Police' which accompanied headquarters through the war.

Although Stieber's intelligence went a good way to deciding to go ahead with the war, it perhaps proved less effective during the actual conflict. The Austrians, Stieber noted, showed unexpected resolve and the Hungarian uprising was quickly quashed. If anything, the victory over the Austrians at the battle of Sadowa on 3 July 1866 was more due to the superiority and rapid-fire of the new Prussian rifles than any great intelligence coup. At the end of the war, although Stieber was officially appointed a 'privy councillor', his failure to raise a Hungarian rebellion greatly rankled him.

The bitter tinge left after failure in Hungary would not fester for long, as Stieber was given even greater scope to build on his successes and failures during the Franco-Prussian War (1870–71). After defeating Austria, Bismarck decided upon the need for war against France and asked Stieber to spy on the country, primarily to warn of any French first strike. Bismarck told Stieber that money would be no object this time, as he had secretly confiscated funds from the Kingdom of Hanover, one of a number of smaller states incorporated into Prussia's German empire, or Reich. Euphemistically dubbed the 'funds of the Central News Bureau', the use of the Hanoverian money meant that the costs of Stieber's operations would not appear on the official Prussian defence budget and therefore his entire operation would remain secret from everyone.

In November 1869 Bismarck sent Stieber to Paris and had him investigate the new French Chassepot rifle and the much-dreaded *mitrailleuse* – an early form of machine gun. Stieber quickly learned the Chassepot rifle worked on the same principles as the Prussian needle gun and did not constitute as much a leap in technology as the French were boasting. The same applied to the *mitrailleuse*, which appeared to have been based on existing models dating back several decades. The *mitrailleuse*, Stieber reported, required a crew of three who could attain a rate of fire in the region of 1,000 rounds in three minutes with 66 per cent accuracy at 1,000 paces. However, the gun was prone to jamming and there was a high rate of misfire with its cartridges. Stieber also had serious doubts about its effectiveness against moving targets. His report concluded that the Prussians should fear it less than had previously been supposed.

While in Paris, this time posing as a journalist named Schmidt, Stieber began setting up a network of spies across France. Helping him with this task were several of the best agents from the war with Austria. Although Stieber knew that the easiest way to recruit spies was through the use of blackmail, he found this type of spy to be the least reliable. Instead he targeted officers and officials who needed large sums of money to pay off gambling debts and those who had been passed over for promotion, dismissed or otherwise disgraced. By making a systematic investigation into the finances of people with access to sensitive information, Stieber was able to draw up a list of those most in need of cash. He then arranged for them to receive a loan through a Hanoverian banking house with irresistible terms of credit. Once they accepted the terms of the loan agreement, they were well and truly in Stieber's pocket.

Through these means, perhaps the most important piece of intelligence Stieber gained was that French troops were scattered round the globe defending the colonies or protecting the Papal States from the Italians. If France went to war, it would take time to recall these soldiers. Stieber predicted it would take France two full weeks to mobilize just 100,000 men against Germany. Bismarck told Stieber his information represented an 'invitation to the German soldier's boot.'[6]

Stieber returned to Berlin, where his records office received thousands of dossiers on Frenchmen who might, with the right inducements, betray their homeland. Investigating other prominent people, Stieber began to build up detailed pictures of their lives, colleagues, wives, mistresses, secretaries, friends, house servants, recruiting as many as possible as spies. Stieber's agents in Berlin also pored over lists of military and civil service promotions, always on the alert for those passed over time and time again. Once a potentially disgruntled candidate was identified, Stieber would send one of his undercover agents to recruit him.

Several of the major espionage coups were performed by an agent Stieber identified only by the initials 'FM'.[7] This agent reputedly made contact with and recruited a group of elite spies, all high-ranking opponents of the reign of French emperor Napoleon III. Stieber gave FM a free hand in running these spies and was rewarded with faith in the agent's abilities when FM gained a copy of the French army's deployment plans in the event of a war with Prussia. Having learned the location of these plans, FM obtained them by posing as a decorator and bluffing his way into the War Ministry with a ladder and a tin of paint. Once in the room, FM set up his tools and made a copy of plans in between decorating the walls.

The infiltration of agents into France proved much easier than with Austria. The operation was so successful even Stieber was surprised how many Frenchmen appeared willing to pass secrets to Prussia. He realized that these Frenchmen did not view their actions as treasonous, but saw themselves as liberators speeding up the end of an unpopular imperial regime. He boasted that even with agents in every significant military and political office in France, not a single one was discovered.

When hostilities commenced on 17 July 1870 Stieber took a very active role in the war and was given greater authority and more resources than during the Austro-Prussian War – including French-speaking officers. Bismarck again asked him to create a 'field security police force' to protect the king and his advisors. Added to this would be his duty to provide the German army with information on the enemy, to counteract the threat of enemy spies and to supervise what we might now call 'embedded reporters' – journalists travelling with the army. Stieber was also responsible for the supervision of postal traffic, which gave him a means to practise censorship.

A typical day for Stieber would begin with the arrival of couriers with reports and questions for him to answer. He could not neglect the news management of the war – press publications had to be supervised and foreign journalists provided with stories portraying the Prussian cause in a sympathetic light. Letters had to be checked and censored so as not to spread alarm at home, and all personally addressed mail arriving for the king, Bismarck and others had to be opened, looking for bombs or poison. During the night, or very early in the morning, reports from secret agents in the field would arrive, forcing Stieber to survive on an average of just two hours' sleep a night with whatever he could snatch during the day. Twice a week he met with the king who asked for a summary of reports from agents in enemy territory. These reports were usually evaluated by comparing them with reports in the French press – other agents sending the French newspapers for Stieber's scrutiny. Lastly, as suspected enemy spies were picked up, Stieber would interrogate them.

As the Prussian military juggernaut rolled into France, something of Stieber's ruthless character is revealed in a letter to his 'dear good wife' dated 18 August 1870. In it he explained how French partisans were dealt with by the Prussian army:

> Yesterday a French peasant fired on a wagon carrying Prussian wounded. But the joker was unsuccessful: two of the wounded still had good legs; they rushed into the house from where the shot had come and took the lad. They hung him from a rope suspended under his arms and slowly fired 34 times until he was dead. He was left there the whole day as an example.[8]

Stieber began to use his spies to observe enemy troop movements. French soldiers, the spies reported, were extremely confident and expected a swift victory, so much so that their generals had not issued them with French maps, only ones of Germany. Spies were established in Paris, Bordeaux, Lyons and Orléans, with others kept nearby so that Stieber could send them to where they were most required.

Stieber had a spy on Marshal MacMahon's staff, who reported the French move to raise the siege of Metz. This information allowed Prussians under von Moltke to set a trap, which when sprung saw the French shut up in the fortress of Sedan. Here Stieber's agents related the incredible news that Emperor Napoleon III was trapped inside the fortress with his soldiers. The French emperor was forced to surrender on 2 September along with 104,000 men. While Napoleon III went into exile in Britain, the Prussian king headed for Versailles to await the surrender of Paris, which was put under siege on 19 September.

Arriving at Versailles on 5 October a large crowd of 'idle folk' came out to meet the Prussian king, having been rounded up by Stieber.

Among the onlookers were several curious foreigners, but the majority were Prussian secret police agents. From that time on, Prussian agents multiplied in the town with extraordinary abundance. Bismarck's quarters were placed under strict guard, with police agents patrolling the street night and day.[9] Stieber oversaw the surveillance of the town and began arbitrary and brutal arrests using the secret police. His officers and spies were notorious, searching and maltreating even the most upstanding of Versailles' citizens.[10]

On 13 and 14 October Stieber made detailed enquiries into the organization of the French police. His intention was to incorporate French police sergeants into the Prussian police with their wearing an armband in Prussian colours. Although the police sergeants did collaborate, they insisted on wearing armbands in the French tricolour for identification. Better assistance came from the local prostitutes Stieber protected in return for information. Stieber asked the prostitutes to inform on Prussian soldiers as much as on their French clientele.[11]

Throughout their stay in Versailles the abuses continued. One of Stieber's most trusted men, Lieutenant Zernicki, caused a scene when he asked the mayor of Versailles for 11lb (5kg) of candles to be taken to Stieber's quarters at 3 Boulevard du Roi. When the candles did not arrive, Zernicki went to the town hall and threatened to put the mayor and the rest of the municipal council in prison. When one of the councillors asked Zernicki who he thought he was, the Prussian drew his sabre and called in some guards. Two of the councillors were seized and dragged off and were only saved when the local French commander went directly to Bismarck. Although Zernicki was told to keep clear of the town hall in future, he was soon promoted to captain for his activities in Versailles.[12]

During the siege of Paris, Stieber faced and thwarted French attempts at aerial espionage. French balloons leaving the city had to be stopped because they were carrying messages to unoccupied parts of the country. For example, one balloon, the *Galilée*, was brought down by troopers of the Prussian 14th Hussars. Onboard were found 924lb (420kg) of letters and newspapers from the besieged city. The balloon's *aeronautes* were taken to prison and then sent to Prussia to face a court martial. Because the balloons traversed the Prussian forward posts, the occupants were deemed technically to be spies and thus faced the death penalty. When dealing with balloons, Stieber found the newly invented

Krupp anti-balloon cannon a double-edged sword. The guns proved so effective the balloonists were now almost always killed and were thus unavailable for interrogation. Later, when carrier pigeons replaced the balloons, the Germans sent hunting hawks after them and many messages were retrieved from round the necks of dead birds.

More decisive was Stieber's investigation on secret communications between Versailles and Paris. His spies tracked down an extensive system of underground passages, which were being used to supply Paris with food. Every night up to 300 wagons passed through these tunnels with their wheels wrapped in cloth to prevent them making a noise. This discovery explained spy reports from inside the city that Paris had ample provisions for a siege. Stieber reported his findings to Bismarck, also pointing out that morale at home was plummeting because of the stalemate. With no end to the siege in sight, the order was given to open fire and bombard Paris. Until then the Prussians had refrained from indiscriminate firing on the city, but when they did results were almost instantaneous. After 5 January Prussian heavy-calibre artillery fired 10,000 shells into the city, destroying over 200 buildings. Stieber's spies in the city reported that the storehouses had burned and people were killing cats and dogs for meat – they even reported the establishment of a rat market.[13]

On the night of 23/24 January, Stieber's agents inside Paris reported that a high-ranking person was coming out to negotiate. Stieber galloped back to his quarters and made arrangements to host the expected negotiations. After disguising his agents in civilian clothes, he prepared overnight lodgings for the French. 'We lit a good fire,' he wrote, 'prepared two beds and, as the French believed that, like Versailles, we were dying of hunger, I did everything possible to procure some good food, desserts, pastries and so on.'[14] When the vice-president, Jules Favre, arrived at Stieber's lodgings to spend the night, he had his agents watch him through the night, spying on Favre through a hole in the wall.

On 26 January an armistice was signed with very stiff conditions for the Parisians. Their forces had to disarm, abandon their fortifications and make a payment of 200 million francs within two weeks. When the Prussians entered the city, Stieber took French hostages whom he made walk ahead of the soldiers as 'human shields'. Worse was to follow for France. On 1 March the treaty of Bordeaux was ratified, with France agreeing to pay a levy of 5 billion francs, and giving Alsace and parts of Lorraine to Germany. It was a disastrous conclusion to the war, which ultimately paved the way for further conflicts in the 20th century.

On 6 March the business was over. Stieber handed police matters back over to the French authorities and set out for home. For his much underrated part in the campaign Stieber received the Iron Cross. Schulmeister would have understood his pride in receiving it. On 17 March Stieber arrived in Berlin with the emperor and continued to manage the 'Central News Bureau'. Although his attention was primarily fixed on the Social Democrat movement, he nonetheless expanded his espionage networks at home and abroad. As word of Stieber's activities began to come to light after the Franco-Prussian War, so began the popular fear of 'the German spy menace'.

The German secret service leading up to and during WWI was described by one of the most successful Allied spies during the war – a Netherlands-based businessman named Charles Lucieto. He considered the espionage system established by Germany as 'gigantic'. Based in the Thiergarten in Berlin, the service consisted of three separate branches: political, naval and military.

The political branch was directly attached to the kaiser's cabinet and was broken down into sections, each dealing with a single country. As its name implies, the function of the political branch was to gather intelligence on the political world that might be used to the profit of the Reich. The directors of this service had direct access to the kaiser, who maintained a lively interest in affairs of espionage. Its agents were the elite, usually drawn from the military and naval branches. Although it included members of the nobility, agents originated from all classes and sometimes even the criminal world. Agents were expected to obey selflessly and punctually and if for any reason the agent was 'scorched' – that is to say exposed – he could count on no official protection or acknowledgement. Because of this, such agents were paid extremely well from a 'Black Chest' for which the directors of the service were never called to account.

The intelligence arm of the Imperial German Navy was composed of four separate sections, including an Intelligence Branch, which was responsible for running agents and making reconnaissances. It also contained a Military-Political Branch, a Foreign Navies Branch and an Observation and Cryptanalytic Service, which, as the importance of radio interception became realized in the run-up to the First World War, grew into a large 458-man organization based in Neumünster.[15]

The military branch of the secret service came under the direct supervision of the secretary of war and was responsible for supplying all military intelligence required by the German general staff. The service was divided into sub-divisions, each possessing both civilian and military agents. The agents were themselves divided into three classes.

The 'Directors of Operations in foreign lands' were the highest type of spy. Often retired officers, these were able to speak several languages fluently and were educated in technical and military matters, including topography, fortification and strategy. The Directors of Operations were expected to go after key enemy personnel, using blackmail to obtain the secrets desired by the general staff. In addition they were to supervise 'Resident Agents', corroborating and evaluating their reports, and maintaining contact through messenger spies, who ferried questionnaires and responses to and from the directors.

Separate from them were the 'agents charged with special missions'. On entering the secret service, these agents were given a crash course of technical and engineering training by officers of the general staff. Once they had passed a stringent examination the agents were given posts in German embassies abroad. Independent from other spies, they were given great freedom to carry out their mission as they saw fit. The information they collected was encoded and sent to Berlin either with the diplomatic mail or by the embassy's military attaché.

The 'Resident Agents' were the most numerous type of secret agent employed by the Germans. They were German nationals placed at the head of businesses or were self-employed and thus free to go off without attracting the attention either of friends or employers. Their commercial enterprises served as 'cloaks' for their espionage operations. Their businesses were often subsidized by the German secret service, which, by means of bogus business deals, was able to make payments to the spy. Although the intelligence they brought in was generally of low-grade importance, the sheer scale of it ensured the German military was kept informed of troop movements, fortification building and so on.

After the Franco-Prussian War, Stieber is said to have flooded France with such resident spies, with at least 15,000 operating there before the outbreak of WWI in 1914. The first wave came in the guise of farm hands who began purchasing land and setting themselves up as farmers in their own right, by preference situated in the regions along the German border. More spies arrived as domestic servants, school teachers, professors and travelling salesmen. With money provided by the general staff, Stieber bought into the hotel industry, ensuring the largest and most prestigious international hotels were in German hands. Attracting a clientele of politicians, diplomats, generals and other members from the cream of society, German agents posing as hotel workers or prostitutes were in a prime position to overhear, steal or copy their secrets.

Stieber was behind the much publicized disgrace of the four-times French Minister of War, General de Cissey (1810–82). The general had been captured during the Franco-Prussian War and taken to Hamburg, where, although a prisoner of war, he enjoyed considerable day-to-day freedom. While captive, de Cissey took a German lover, the Baroness de Kaulla. After being repatriated at the end of the war, de Cissey became minister of war. A short time later Mademoiselle de Kaulla arrived in Paris to reignite the love affair. Unknown to the general, the baroness was working for and receiving funds from Stieber, who was very interested in de Cissey's plans for restructuring the French army.

The matter came to a head in 1880 when the radical newspaper *Le Petit Parisien* accused de Cissey – now a senator – of communicating information to the Germans through his mistress, who they exposed as a spy. Although the editors were convicted of criminal libel and charges of treason could not be proved, it was shown that de Cissey had misappropriated the secret funds of his ministry and he was forced to resign. The great irony in this affair was that de Cissey had been the prime mover in creating a special section to counter German espionage and prevent a surprise attack.[16]

One of Stieber's most notorious achievements was the 'Green House', a high-class bordello in Berlin. Stieber staffed the 'resort' with police agents who monitored their patrons, drawn as they were only from 'people of consequence'. Pandering to every imaginable vice, depravity and perversion, patrons were only admitted by invitation. However, these gratifications came at a price. Stieber would keep a file on each patron and when a favour was required, he would blackmail them by threatening to reveal their indiscretions.[17]

A rare blip came late in Stieber's remarkable career and involved a journalist. It concerned the news management of the Congress of Berlin in 1878 – a conference set up to agree the balance of power in the Balkans. The topics of debate were delicate and Bismarck wanted to keep them out of the newspapers. Not to be thwarted, the editor of *The Times*, John Delane, sent his Paris correspondent, Henri de Blowitz, to cover the story. Despite the presence of Stieber's agents, who kept everyone under surveillance, a series of detailed 'scoops' began appearing in *The Times*. They began with the first day's agenda and finished when a full copy of the agreement (the Treaty of Berlin) was published in *The Times*, almost as it was being signed.

Although Blowitz was suspected from the start, the secret police could not find any evidence of him meeting with anyone present at the debate. The truth did not come out until Blowitz's memoirs were published in 1903. Before the conference opened, the journalist made an arrangement with one of the clerical staff. This 'mole' would write reports of the day's proceedings and conceal them in the lining of his hat. He was then to hang the hat on a hat rack in the Kaiserhof Hotel. Blowitz – wearing an identical hat – would simply walk in, hang up his hat, dine and afterwards pick up the other hat on leaving.[18]

Having succeeded where Pinkerton failed, by making the shift from police detective to military intelligence gatherer, Stieber must be viewed as one of the great spymasters in history. However, like so many other practitioners of the secret services, Stieber has been to a large degree demonized both at home and abroad. Despite his successes and although he was decorated many times, Stieber was an embarrassment to the Prussian military establishment. As early as 1867 von Moltke had established a rival intelligence bureau of his own. Many recognize in him the beginnings of the Nazi police state and more still have compared him to the propagandist Joseph Goebbels (1897–1945). He is routinely portrayed as a deviant and proverbial Bogeyman. The distaste he routinely inspires led one author to describe his rise to prominence as being 'like some mushroom growth, up the backstairs of fashionable Berlin.'[19] When Stieber died, stricken by arthritis in 1892, his funeral, they say, was very well attended – not from well wishers, but by people who wanted to make sure he was really dead.

9

SPY FEVER

For anyone who is tired of life, the thrilling life
of a spy should be the very finest recuperator!

Founder of the Boy Scout movement and
occasional spy, Sir Robert Baden Powell

Britain at the end of the 19th century was the Earth's greatest colonial superpower. With as much as a quarter of the planet's landmass her dominion, Victoria (ruled 1837–1901) was both queen and empress. While the Royal Navy ruled the seas, always maintaining double the strength of its two largest rivals, soldiers were the rock stars of their day. London's docks were jammed with the fruits of a bountiful globe, rewards for an unparalleled projection of national will on so many, by so few. At the height of this imperial prowess, who better to hold up as a shining example of British pluck and gifted amateurism than Sir Robert Baden Powell (1857–1941).

Somewhat a maverick, Baden Powell was very much in the mould of Wellington's 'exploring officers'. As a soldier, Baden Powell had seen service in India and South Africa, where he learned from Zulus much of the bushcraft that formed the basis of his scouting movement. He then progressed into the secret services and spent three years based in Malta, conducting operations in Algeria and Dalmatia. Baden Powell found himself back in South Africa at the beginning of the Boer War (1899–1902) where he was one of just ten volunteer intelligence officers in the country.[1] His most notable contribution in that war came not as a scout but as the garrison commander during the defence of Mafeking (October 1899–May 1900), during which he became a national celebrity. By 1910 Baden Powell retired from the army to promote his fledgling Boy Scout movement. In 1915, while Britain was caught in the grip of an anti-German spy fever, Baden Powell published a short work entitled *My Adventures as a Spy* in which he gave a number of anecdotes on his secret service work.[2]

Throughout his book he distinguishes between espionage carried out by soldiers, which he considered admirable, and the selling of secrets by traitors, which he found despicable. Baden Powell complained that the word 'spy' had degenerated into a term of contempt and that popular belief held every spy to be a 'base and despicable fellow'. Spies, he argued, were 'like ghosts' because although people had a general idea such things might exist, they did not believe in them and did not come into contact with them.[3] Instead, when dealing with wartime military espionage, he asks us to use the terms 'investigator' or 'military agent' rather than spy. After all, in most cases the spy was in fact a scout in disguise and the act of spying a 'reconnaissance in disguise'.

Spies had to be brave because they would be under constant mental strain, knowing full well their government would wash their hands of them if captured and leave them to face almost certain death by execution. The qualities necessary for an effective spy therefore were 'a strong spirit of self-sacrifice, courage, and self-control, with the ability to act out a part, quick at observation and deduction, and blessed with good health and nerve of exceptional quality'. They had to have remarkable powers of observations, the ability to become 'a veritable Sherlock Holmes', deducing the meaning of what they observed. They would often require some scientific training, enabling them to record the structures of forts and bridges and, for demolition purposes, even the geological formation of the ground they were constructed on. With these technical qualities in mind it is easy to understand why Baden Powell shared the long-held preference for using trained military personnel over civilians as spies. He did, however, admit that there was a drawback of using such 'officer spies' – simply it was difficult to find military men who were good actors or masters of disguise.

Baden Powell placed great emphasis on the ability of a spy to use disguises. In fact it is probably fair to say that Baden Powell's enthusiasm for dressing up and performing in vaudeville-style reviews caused him to be the subject of some suspicion among his brother officers.[4] Nevertheless, Baden Powell revealed the key to a spy's survival was his ability not only to wear disguises but to assume totally different identities, changes in voice and mannerism and, in particular, gait in walking. He explained how people did not recognize facial features as much as they might remember a particular necktie or hat the spy wore. One of Baden Powell's most well-known ruses, which he used against a German sentry while observing the testing of a new machine gun, was simply to douse himself in brandy and act like a drunkard.

One of the reoccurring themes throughout this history of espionage has been the different classification of spies – from Sun Tzû to Thiébault and beyond. According to Baden Powell the distinctions were:

Strategical Agents: In peacetime, these study the political and military conditions in countries which might one day become enemies. They also create political disaffection and organize civil unrest, which would draw off troops in wartime. Baden Powell gives examples of how in the lead up to World War I, German agents tried to unsettle the British Empire by targeting disaffected Muslim groups in Egypt and India; the Boers in South Africa and closer to home, Irish republicans.

Tactical Agents: These look into military details about a country, its preparedness for war, transport infrastructure, the tactical features of enemy terrain, probable sites of battlefields and artillery positions etc.

Field Spies: These are disguised scouts who report on enemy movements in wartime and conduct reconnaissance missions.

Residential Spies: This type is comprised of agents resident in foreign countries. Although some were important businessmen and members of the *nouveaux riches* anxious for decorations and rewards, the majority were of insignificant backgrounds, working as spies for pay. While collecting intelligence themselves, their principal duties were to act as go-betweens with other spies, passing on instructions and returning reports to headquarters. Baden Powell said this type of spy was known to the Germans as a 'post-box'.

Commercial Spies: Apparently, this type of spy was initially a German phenomenon. According to Baden Powell young Germans were sent to work in British businesses without salary in order to pick up the language. This provided them for a cover to pick up secrets on the manufacture and trade of goods.

In addition to the procurement of information, the spy must of course deliver it secretly. In the Boer War, Baden Powell revealed that his spies used native runners, in particular cattle-thieves, to bring dispatches to him. To thwart the Boers, messages were always coded or in cipher, British officers using either Latin or, for those having served in India, Hindustani, written phonetically in the Roman alphabet. When passing through enemy lines, the dispatch-runners carried the messages rolled into tiny balls and coated with sheet lead. These balls were worn round the runner's neck on a string: if they were in danger of being intercepted, they would drop the balls onto the ground where they would look like small stones. The runner would then take a bearing of the site and return to collect the balls when the danger had passed. Other tricks of the trade included inserting the messages into hollow walking sticks, sewing them into the lining of clothing or placing them between the soles of shoes. Perhaps the simplest and most ingenious technique was to hide the secret message in the bowl of a pipe under the tobacco so if necessary it could be burnt without suspicion.

But for all these excellent anecdotes and first-hand insights into spying, Baden Powell's adventures cannot disguise the fact that Britain was lagging far behind in the espionage stakes around the turn of the century. During the Boer War these weaknesses – and many others – were highlighted and came as a very timely wake-up call to Britain's armed forces. Britain found itself outmatched by a secret service that was taken very seriously by the Boers. Following the surprise Jameson Raid of 29 December 1895 – a botched coup d'état by Uitlander (foreign) businessmen – the South African Republic had realized the need to expand its secret service – the De Geheime Dienst. Initially recruitment proved problematic, as the people of the Transvaal had little or no experience in such matters and few spoke English fluently enough for them to be of service.[5]

Instead the South Africans were forced to rely on foreign recruits. Before the Jameson Raid, State Secretary W. J. Leyds had travelled to Europe. Two weeks after the raid he was cabled to find three secret service agents and to offer them a significant salary. Two Rotterdam customs officials were selected and sent for training in Paris and then Berlin, before arriving in Pretoria during May 1896. It is alleged that Leyds also formed links with the German secret service against Britain and became a paid agent in his own right.[6]

In the six months leading up the Anglo-Boer War, De Geheime Dienst at last became a truly professional service. This was in large part due to

Attorney General Jan Smuts, who impressed upon the government the need for more funds. Agents reported directly to Smuts, his confidential clerks or through local officials who posted their reports disguised as routine correspondence. Agents were by and large detectives, but occasionally other officials were employed, including traders, customs officials, post masters and railway employees.

Initially the agents were employed to monitor anti-republican activities, prominent British politicians and other potential insurgents. In early 1899 two British subjects, Nicholls and Patterson, were arrested on charges of espionage and conspiracy. At the same time the service was aware that British officers were moving about the Transvaal in disguise with cameras and sketchbooks – Baden Powell among them.

By the time war commenced in 1899, De Geheime Dienst was very well funded. The South African Republic is reckoned to have spent £286,000 on its secret service in comparison with Britain's annual budget of £20,000, only £2,000 of which was spent on South Africa.[7] The organization found itself working on three fronts. Sections were detailed to remain in Pretoria and Johannesburg, as large numbers of British subjects were permitted to stay in the Republic because of their commercial importance. Despite such a large pool of potential foreign agents to police, the South Africans were generally successful in preventing sabotage attempts. A large number of British spies infiltrated the republic through Mozambique, which was a Belgian colony at the time. To counter this movement, the South Africans sent spies of their own over the border, making the city of Lourenco Marques a stomping ground for spies.

A Field Intelligence Branch was formed, placing agents with local knowledge onto the staffs of senior commanders and ensuring field security, press censorship, anti-sabotage measures and safeguarding telegraphic communications. However, after the fall of Pretoria on 5 June 1900, with no central bureau to receive reports De Geheime Dienst ceased to exist. In the same breath, as soon as the war ended so too did the fledging British Field Intelligence Service. At the beginning of the 20th century Britain did not even have a means of putting land-based spies into Europe, let alone South Africa.

In pre-war France, the fear of German spies, accompanied by deep-rooted institutional racism and religious intolerance, resulted in one of the most infamous miscarriages of justice in history – the

Dreyfus Affair of 1894. The affair centred on an intelligence officer, Major Walsin-Esterhazy (1847–1923). Having amassed large debts, this officer attempted to rebuild his fortune through gambling and stock exchange speculations, with predictably disastrous results. When faced with his creditors, Walsin-Esterhazy resorted to treason and in August 1894 sold secrets to Colonel Maximillian von Schwartzkoppen, the German military attaché in Paris.

Since 1850, foreign embassies had been allowed to place military personnel on their staff to observe and monitor the armed forces of that country and enjoy the privacy of the diplomatic pouches to transmit their findings secretly. The functions of these military attachés were another form of legitimate, or at least agreed, spying.[8] In this case Schwartzkoppen was provided with details of a new French 120mm Baquet howitzer fitted with a short-recoil mechanism and manuals describing the organization of France's field artillery.

Next in the chain of conspiracy came Marie Bastian, a cleaning lady working at the German embassy. Bastian was also employed by French military intelligence and claimed to have retrieved a torn-up document from Schwartzkoppen's wastepaper basket. When reassembled, the pieces formed a list or *bordereau* detailing the information provided to Schwartzkoppen. A hunt for the traitor began, which should have led to Walsin-Esterhazy. But it didn't.

In order to protect their man, French intelligence pointed the finger of guilt at a certain Captain Alfred Dreyfus. Completely innocent of the charges, Dreyfus was arrested on 15 October. Much was made of how Dreyfus came from Alsace, which was now in German hands, and that even though he had attempted to disguise the writing on the bordereau from his normal style, the two handwritings matched, which of course was a complete nonsense. What really put Dreyfus into trouble was the simple fact that he was Jewish. At his court martial Dreyfus was found guilty and was sent to Devil's Island, a penal colony off the coast of French Guyana. As in Pichegru's time a century before – 'life' in that part of the world did not amount to very much.

That would have been the end of it, except by 1898 the new chief of French military counter-intelligence, Colonel Picquart, realized that the author of the bordereau was in fact Walsin-Esterhazy. When Picquart presented his discoveries to the French high command, he was ordered to forget about the case. For show, Walsin-Esterhazy was put in the dock between 10 and 11 January 1898 and all charges were dismissed. Picquart, who refused to testify on Esterhazy's behalf, found himself on trial on 13 January for communicating official documents and received 60 days' close arrest. He was then expelled from the army on 26 February 1898.[9] The cause was then taken up by the novelist Émile Zola, who famously began his public denunciation of the army with the headline: 'J'accuse!' For his efforts, Zola was found guilty of libelling the army and had to flee to England to escape imprisonment.

It was only when Picquart's successor, Lieutenant-Colonel Hubert Henry, tried to forge a document to prove Dreyfus' guilt that the conspiracy came unstuck. The forgery alleged itself to be a note from the Italian attaché, Colonel Panizzardi, to Schwartzkoppen discussing their 'relationships' with Dreyfus. In August 1898, Henry confessed he had made forgeries, was arrested and committed suicide in his cell. Amazingly, despite this revelation, Esterhazy was still not found guilty, but was dismissed from the army and settled in England.

In 1899 the Dreyfus case came up for appeal, but he had been so demonized by the army, church and politicians that he was inexplicably still found guilty, albeit with a reduced sentence of ten years' imprisonment. Ten days after the trial, a new government pardoned Dreyfus. Even so, it was not until 1906 that Dreyfus was properly restored to the army, given the rank of major and awarded the Legion of Honour for his troubles.[10]

Back in Britain, the notion of secret service was pulled out of hibernation by another development in the history of espionage: the popularity of spies in fiction. The James Bond phenomenon is nothing new. In Britain, books such as Erskine Childers' *The Riddle of the Sands* (1903) created an anti-German 'spy fever' that caught the public imagination. Perhaps more than anyone else, the popular author William Le Queux was a veritable production line of espionage pulp fiction, with such inflammatory works as *The Invasion of 1910* (1906) and the popular *Spies of the Kaiser* (1909). Le Queux convincingly claimed that Britain was full of German agents. He was supported by Lord Northcliffe's popular newspaper, the *Daily Mail*, which warned that German waiters and barbers were agents of the kaiser – the *Weekly News* went so far as to run a 'spy-spotting' competition.

This media-driven spy fever led to thousands of reports filed at police stations about suspected acts of espionage. It was all terribly inconvenient. At this time in Britain, although some attempts were being made to address the shortfalls of field intelligence services, nothing was in place to root out German spies. In certain quarters of the establishment, the traditional enemy of the British Empire was France and there was a reluctance to antagonize Germany. However, the clamour grew so loud that the government felt moved to deny the existence of 66,000 German soldiers secretly working in England and their supposed arms cache, rumoured to be within a quarter of a mile of London's Charing Cross. In the War Office's Directorate of Military Operations, Colonel Edmonds joined in the call for something to be done about this new threat. Prime Minister Asquith ordered the Committee of Imperial Defence to look into it and acted on its recommendation to establish a secret service bureau, expressly for countering the German spy menace.[11]

This bureau had the most humble of beginnings, consisting of a single junior captain, a clerk and a small office hidden in the lofty reaches of the War Office. Known as MO5, this one-man band would one day become MI5, the counter-intelligence service. The captain was Vernon Kell (1873–1942), a unique individual with a gift for languages. He spoke fluent French, German, Italian, Polish, Russian and, since being employed as an interpreter during the Boxer Rebellion, Chinese. Ill health had put paid to his active career so he joined the German section of the War Office in 1902, before being given the MO5 job.

There was no rulebook for Kell to follow, except perhaps that he should liaise with Scotland Yard's Special Branch to see if they had any leads. Originally formed in 1883 as the Special Irish Branch of London's Metropolitan Police, it had been created to counter Irish republicans at work in the capital. One of Special Branch's founder members was William Melville (1850–1918), who had been advocating the creation of a counter-espionage service since 1903. This union of civilian police and the military would bear happy fruit.

In 1910 the German kaiser, Wilhelm II (1859–1941), came to London for the funeral of his uncle, King Edward VII. In his retinue was a captain believed to be the acting head of German naval intelligence. One day this captain took a cab and was followed to a barbershop in the Caledonian Road. Why on earth, pondered Superintendent Patrick Quinn, was a high-ranking German travelling so far to visit this nonentity of the hairdressing world? He called in Kell.

The barber in question was Karl Gustav Ernst. Kell obtained permission to open Ernst's mail and discovered letters from a Gustav Steinhauer and Fraulein Reimers in Potsdam. It was immediately obvious what was going on. Ernst was a 'post box'. In other words, he received a package from German Intelligence containing letters for him to forward on to other agents and vice versa. For this service he was paid the sum of £1 a month. Like Walsingham before him, Kell showed his genius for counter-espionage by not arresting Ernst, but by watching him to see how far the conspiracy went.

At this point Kell needed help and it came in the guise of Captain Mansfield Cumming, who in 1912 went on to head Britain's fledgling overseas secret service, MI1C, later MI6.[12] Through Cumming, Kell learned that Steinhauer was director of German espionage in Britain and that his real name was in fact Reimers.[13] A former member of the Pinkerton detective agency and a self-professed 'master spy', Steinhauer was efficient at matters of counter-espionage but lacked certain qualities as a spymaster himself.[14]

In addition to the discovery of the postman, one of Kell's officers found another lead from a conversation he overheard on a train. Stanley Clarke was listening to two men speak, when one of them – the proprietor of the Peacock Hotel in Leith – declared that he had received a strange letter from Potsdam in Germany. Clarke approached the hotelier who told him the letter was from someone called Reimers who was asking for information on Britain's preparations for war. With this new lead, Kell was able to make further interceptions and Steinhauer's network of agents was yet more fully revealed.[15]

Still Kell would not arrest the spies. Instead, if as he suspected war with Germany would come sooner than later, he would leave all the German agents in place until the declaration of war itself, then arrest them in one hit. If he arrested them before, they would be replaced by other agents and other postmen and perhaps next time Kell would not be so lucky in detecting them. Only on certain occasions did it become absolutely necessary for Kell to order the arrest of a German spy.

In 1902 German naval intelligence had set up an agent as the landlord of the Queen Charlotte public house in Rochester High Street, a short distance from Chatham Naval Base. Using the alias of Frederick Gould – his real name was Schroeder – this agent passed a steady stream of information back to Germany, which Kell began intercepting.

In addition to his correspondence, Gould was also known to make periodic visits to Ostend from where he went off to meet his German controllers. Kell was happy to continue the waiting game with Gould, until in February 1914 Mrs Gould was arrested on a train bound for the coast. In her baggage was found detailed plans of coastal and anti-submarine defences, a gunnery manual and the address of her contact in Brussels. Kell ordered Gould arrested too and was happy to see him sent to prison for six years followed by deportation.[16]

A few months later, with war imminent, Steinhauer sent all his agents in Britain a warning, then departed the country. This action is extraordinary because Steinhauer later claimed that he knew the British were intercepting some of his agents' messages. Why then did he risk sending a warning? Certainly three of his spies, Kronauer in Walthamstow, Weigels in Hull and Schappman in Exeter, all returned to Germany, feeling they had been compromised by Steinhauer's actions. The rest waited, probably with little idea they were soon to be taken into custody.[17]

On the day war was declared, all Kell's plans to 'paralyze' German espionage came to fruition. The night before, on 3 August 1914 – the day Germany declared war on France – MO5 was secretly given 12 hours' notice of Britain's declaration of war on Germany. A pre-arranged coded telegram was sent out to police forces across the country, telling them to arrest the remaining 22 suspected German spies, including the postman Ernst. The arrests went like clockwork and by the end of 4 August the German secret service had lost every one of its spies in the United Kingdom.

Without German spies watching the ports, the British Expeditionary Force (BEF) was able to cross over to Belgium without the knowledge of the German high command. Their arrival caused a severe dent in the German attempt to turn the French left flank and attack Paris. On 23 August at the battle of Mons, General Alexander von Kluck's German First Army unexpectedly blundered into the BEF, whose rifle fire was so accurate and rapid that the German 'parade ground' formations were shot to pieces; the fire was so intense they thought they had come under machine-gun attack.

Back in Germany the Kaiser was furious to learn that there had been no warning because there were no longer any operational spies in Britain. His ire forced German intelligence to send agents to Britain who were poorly trained and had little chance of avoiding capture. Of these spies, perhaps the most famous was Carl Hans Lody, the first German spy to be executed during the war. Lody was a German naval reserve officer who had emigrated to New York and married an American. Unfortunately he had returned to visit his parents in Hamburg just before war was declared and, as a fluent English speaker, was recruited as a spy by Walter Nicolai, head of German intelligence throughout the war.[18]

Lody landed in Scotland posing as Charles Inglis, an American tourist, and almost immediately drew attention to himself. Sending a telegram to his controller in neutral Stockholm, Lody finished his message with a line he hoped would reaffirm his cover: 'Hope we beat these damned Germans soon.' A copy of this telegram ended up on Kell's desk because something about the last line triggered the suspicions of the local postmaster.

While Kell began his investigation, Lody made a mistake the results of which some have said cost Germany the war. In Edinburgh on 4 September, Lody sent a telegram to Berlin saying he had been informed that large numbers of Russian troops had landed in Aberdeen two days before. These troops were being transported south by rail with the carriage windows covered.[19] Lody was in fact responding to a rumour, which, if the legend is correct, came about because of a misunderstanding of the Scottish dialect. Trains full of Scottish troops were heading south and the story goes that one southern railway worker asked the troops where they had come from. One called back 'Ross-shire', which the railwayman interpreted as 'Russia'. Before long a ridiculous rumour went around that Russians had landed with 'snow on their boots'.

Lody was also aware that Winston Churchill (1874–1965), the First Lord of the Admiralty, had considered a plan to transport Russian troops to the Western Front via Scotland to take the pressure off British troops after the battle of Mons. Having transmitted his telegram, the intelligence was passed to General von Moltke (nephew of Bismarck's general), who held back two German divisions from the battle of the Marne (5–10 September 1914) in case the Russians landed. After an allied counter-attack, the Germans were put on the retreat, halting the advance on Paris and causing the beginning of trench warfare.[20]

With no other German spies in the country, Lody was forced to travel frequently, which again raised suspicion. He visited London,

Liverpool, then crossed the Irish Sea to Dublin, where he was arrested by the Royal Irish Constabulary. He was tried in London on 13 October and shot in the Tower of London on the morning of 6 November.

The capture of the German spies was by no means the only early British intelligence success story of the war. On the second day of the war, 5 August, the British cut the German undersea communication cable. The cable-laying ship *Teleconia* cut the cable in two places and removed a sizeable section, making repair impossible. The Germans were now forced to rely on radio signals to communicate and these could be intercepted by radio-listening posts. Chief of Naval Intelligence, Admiral 'Blinker' Hall, had built a team of codebreakers known as 'Room 40' who began attacking these signals.

Three weeks later, on 26 August, the German light cruiser *Magdeburg* ran aground and was attacked by two Russian warships. Among the German survivors picked up by the Russians was a mortally wounded sailor clinging onto the German naval codebook. The Russians offered the book to the British Admiralty, allowing Room 40 to read the German code until it was changed early in 1915. Cumming's MI6 sent an agent into Germany to investigate the new code. The agent reported that an Austrian national called Alexander Szek was working on the new code. Szek had actually been born in Croydon where his family still lived. First MI5 contacted the family, then Hall's Naval Intelligence, who were a little more persuasive. Unless the family wrote to Szek and asked him to obtain a copy of the new code, British intelligence would put them into an internment camp.

Szek had no choice but to comply, and at considerable risk, spent several months copying small pieces of the code onto paper which he then smuggled into a lavatory and concealed upon his person – internally. Afterwards he would pass the information to an MI6 agent who would bring it to London. In a sign of how ruthless the British could be, once Szek finished his work, to prevent him ever becoming a security risk he 'disappeared'. Although the official verdict was that he died of a car accident in Belgium, Szek's father would have none of it. A more likely version is 'Blinker' Hall had him pushed off a ship mid-Channel.[21]

Another German codebook was picked up from Wilhelm Wassmuss, the German consul to Persia in 1914. Known as the 'German Lawrence', Wassmuss had organized local tribesmen to fight a guerrilla war against

British oil interests in the Persian Gulf. Evading capture after a raid, Wassmuss lost his baggage to British troops. The papers therein were sent to London and found to contain a copy of the German diplomatic code. The seeds had now been sown for perhaps the greatest secret-service triumph of the war.

On 16 January 1917 the German Foreign Secretary, Artur Zimmermann, sent a telegram to the German ambassador in Mexico, via the German embassy in Washington. The telegram was intercepted and passed on to Room 40 where it was partly decrypted by codebreakers Nigel de Grey and William Montgomery. The message was passed quickly on to Admiral Hall – it was pure dynamite, so much so it might bring America into the war. How, though, could Hall reveal the contents of the telegram without letting the world know that the British could read the German codes?

There was also another problem. US President Woodrow Wilson (1856–1924) was at the time engaged in peace talks with Germany. In order to encourage these talks, Wilson had allowed Germany to use the American diplomatic telegraph which went from the US embassy in Berlin to Copenhagen then via a transatlantic cable to the United States. To reveal the contents of the message would reveal that the British were actively listening to US diplomatic traffic.

The British guessed the German embassy in Washington would forward the message to Mexico using a commercial telegraph company. Therefore, if the British could obtain a copy of this telegram in Mexico City, they could claim to have discovered it through agents in Mexico rather than through signals interception as was the case. To Admiral Hall's relief the message had been sent through the company Western Union and, as an added bonus, the Germans had used the same diplomatic code used in the captured Wassmuss papers. The now fully decoded message was taken to the British Foreign Minister Arthur Balfour, who passed it to the US ambassador in London on 23 February. Two days later the message was sent to the president. It read:

> We intend to begin on the first of February unrestricted submarine warfare.[22] We shall endeavor in spite of this to keep the United States of America neutral. In the event of this not succeeding, we make Mexico a proposal of alliance on the following basis: make war

together, make peace together, generous financial support and an understanding on our part that Mexico is to reconquer the lost territory in Texas, New Mexico, and Arizona. The settlement in detail is left to you. You will inform the President of the above most secretly as soon as the outbreak of war with the United States of America is certain and add the suggestion that he should, on his own initiative, invite Japan to immediate adherence and at the same time mediate between Japan and ourselves. Please call the President's attention to the fact that the ruthless employment of our submarines now offers the prospect of compelling England in a few months to make peace [Signed] Zimmermann.

This message arrived in the United States at a time when American sailors were dying as a result of German torpedoes and when Mexico was supporting Pancho Villa's raids across the US border. The president made the telegram public on 1 March, but against all Admiral Hall's expectations it was declared a fraud designed to bring America into a war. However, in an inexplicably stupid move, Zimmermann came out on 29 March and publicly confirmed the telegraph's authenticity and attempted to justify his reasons for sending it. On 6 April the US Congress declared war on Germany.

One of the most successful French spies during WWI was a Netherlands-based businessman named Charles Lucieto, who obtained information on German poison gas. First employed by the Germans on the evening of Thursday 22 April 1915, the gas was described by a *New York Tribune* reporter as being 'a cloud of vapor, greenish gray and iridescent' which 'settled to the ground like a swamp mist and drifted toward the French trenches on a brisk wind. Its effect on the French was a violent nausea and faintness, followed by an utter collapse. It is believed that the Germans, who charged in behind the vapor, met no resistance at all, the French at their front being virtually paralyzed.' The following day, a similar attempt was made on Canadian positions, but with less success due to wind conditions.[23]

Lucieto was given the perilous mission of going into Germany to find out about this new German weapon. He set out for Rotterdam from where he secretly entered Germany and travelled to Mannheim where he had an informant. From this person he obtained the chemical formula of the chlorine gas C12 used on 22 April and formulas of four other poison gases that would be used in future operations. Lucieto transmitted this information back to France.

Since the first gas attack it was also believed the Germans had developed 'asphyxiating bombs' which could be fired from artillery. Lucieto believed the gas-filled artillery shells were being manufactured at the Krupp munitions factory, so he travelled to Essen in a bid to find out. Arriving in the city he found the Krupp plant heavily guarded by a private police force. Instead of a direct approach he trawled the bars and restaurants frequented by skilled foremen and mechanics. Before long Lucieto had overheard enough technical details being discussed to draw a fairly accurate impression of the new shells – but he still wanted proof.

He was very frustrated that it was taking so long to discover which gas was being put inside the shells. All the while he loitered in bars, men were dying in the trenches. Luckily his barfly existence paid off when he became drinking buddies with one of the factory's special policemen. Over a beer the policeman confided in Lucieto that a new type of shell had been developed, which would win the war for Germany. The less Lucieto appeared to believe his companion, the more the policeman felt the need to justify his claims. In the end a 2,000 mark wager was put on the existence of the shells and Lucieto was smuggled into the test ground with a camera.

The spy watched as shells exploded in a field full of sheep. A yellowy-green smoke billowed up and wafted through the flock. When the gas had passed the sheep were dead and the grass appeared to have burned. Asking for a souvenir, his policeman gave him a fragment of the shell, which contained enough trace of the chemical for it to be identified when he arrived in Paris three days later. From his investigation a gasmask was designed, thwarting the German plan.

It is ironic how the most famous spy of WWI was also one of its least successful. Before the war, exotic dancer Mata Hari (1876–1917) had attracted a string of lovers, including royals, high-ranking politicians and soldiers. It was her endless desire to acquire the attention of power-broking men that ultimately led her into trouble.

Performing in Germany just a few months before the outbreak of war in May 1914, her risqué show provoked a number of complaints to the police. In response, a police officer named Griebel went to see the performance for himself. Through Griebel, Mata Hari was introduced to and had an affair with Berlin police chief Traugott von

Jagow. On the day war was declared, French spies in Berlin apparently saw Mata Hari driving to lunch with von Jagow, a suspected member of the German secret service. In addition to von Jagow, the French secret service learned of Mata Hari's affairs with the German crown prince and the Dutch premier. Then, on her return to Paris, she was believed to be a mistress of the minister of war and an official high up in the Department of Foreign Affairs. Her activities bore all the hallmarks of an active, busy spy.

Despite her being under constant surveillance, the French could find no evidence against her, nor her 'letter box' for reporting the intelligence she was no doubt collecting on behalf of Germany. In the absence of proof, the French Deuxième Bureau (counter-intelligence) deduced that she might be using the legation of a neutral country to transmit messages to her German employers. It appears not to have occurred to them she might not be a spy at all.

Mata Hari then met a 21-year-old Russian pilot in French service, Captain Vladmir Masloff. Their affair – Mata Hari claimed it true love – was cut short when Masloff returned to the front and was wounded, losing the sight in his left eye. Hearing the news, Mata Hari applied for a pass to travel to Vittel where Masloff was recuperating. This set more alarm bells ringing in the Deuxième Bureau: a new aerodrome was being built at Vittel and from questionnaires found on captured spies, it was clear the Germans were trying to find out about it. Was Mata Hari using Masloff's injury as a front for her mission, or were her intentions purely innocent? The French decided not to take a risk and refused her permission to travel.

Friends recommended that Mata Hari should take up her case with Georges Ladoux, head of the bureau. Some friends! In return for a pass, Ladoux asked Mata Hari to spy for the French. She agreed, so she claimed, in order to obtain an income to support herself and Masloff through his convalescence. Ladoux sent Mata Hari on a mission to Brussels, where, through a mutual contact, she would be introduced to General von Bissing, who in turn might be able to renew Mata Hari's acquaintance with the crown prince of Germany.

To enter Belgium, Mata Hari would return to her native Holland, which was neutral in the war. To reach Holland, she had to travel via Spain and England, where she was taken into custody by the British secret service. Some claim that the British suspected her of being a

German spy named Clara Benedix, others that the head of the Special Branch, Sir Basil Thompson, warned her to stop what she was doing before it was too late. In any case, the British would not allow her to cross over to Holland, but instead, after consulting with Ladoux, sent her back to Spain.

Alas, Mata Hari paid no heed to Thompson's advice. In Madrid she began an affair with the German military attaché in Madrid, Major Kalle, who was a member of German intelligence. Although never clarified, it is possible that Mata Hari was trying to extract information from Kalle, but if so, the German was too wily for her. Mata Hari returned to Paris and went to see Ladoux with the information she had gleaned from Kalle. Ladoux was unimpressed and refused to pay her. At the same time Kalle sent a radio message to Berlin which implicated Mata Hari as a German spy, known by the codename *H-21*. Quite why Kalle chose a code he knew the French had broken has never been proven. Some have suggested Kalle had found the perfect means to dispose of an expensive mistress.

The intercepted message provided the French secret service with all the information they required. The very codename H-21 suggested that Mata Hari had been recruited before the war, those recruited afterwards having the codename prefix 'AF' (for Antwerp-France). Mata Hari's trial came at a time when the French government was under heavy criticism for its management of the war, and also when there were widespread mutinies among soldiers in the field.

Without any corroborating proof and despite Mata Hari being a citizen of a neutral country (Holland), she was found guilty of espionage and sentenced to death. The sentence was carried out on 15 October 1917 in the moat at Vincennes, the same place the Duc D'Enghien met his fate in 1804. It is said that Mata Hari faced death bravely, albeit after a fortifying shot of rum. After the firing squad had administered justice, an officer provided the customary *coup de grace* by firing his pistol into her ear. The former dancer's body, once so much in demand, went unclaimed and was sent to a medical school for dissection. Did she really deserve such a fate?

It should be remembered that there were many far more effective female spies than Mata Hari active in WWI. While Mata Hari had been digging a grave for herself in Madrid, agent Marthe Richer had succeeded in penetrating German intelligence by becoming mistress to the German naval attaché in Madrid, Baron Hans von Krohn. Known by the codename *l'Alouette* (the Lark) Richer actually met Mata Hari in Madrid while she was living with Kalle, but did not realize that she was also working for Ladoux. Although Richer succeeded in locating German U-Boat refuelling points on the Spanish coast and the routes taken by German agents across the Pyrenees, she was snubbed at the end of the war because of her affair with a German. She moved to England, remarried and only became a member of the Legion of Honour in 1933.

On the German side was Elsbeth Schragmüller, better known to the French as 'Mademoiselle Docteur' or to others as 'Tiger Eyes'. Schragmüller was a senior figure in the German intelligence service (Nachrichtendienst) based in Antwerp. Because of her lofty position, never before obtained by someone of her gender, Schragmüller was the subject of sensationalist claims. This is the result of a largely fictional account of her wartime deeds written in 1929 by Hans Rudolph Berndorff. The fictional Schragmüller lived a life of lost love, espionage and high adventure, which culminated in her being committed to a lunatic asylum at the end of the war.

In reality Schragmüller was highly intelligent and had gained her doctorate in political sciences with honours from Freiberg in 1913. Born on 7 August 1887 she belonged to the first generation of female students to obtain high qualifications. Her involvement in espionage did not derive from some sinister deviancy, but from a sincere desire to serve her country in war. To that end she obtained a modest position in intelligence in Brussels, working in the postal censorship department. Here she checked intercepted letters between Belgian soldiers and their families, from which she was able to deduce the intentions of the BEF. This piece of analysis brought her to the attention of a Captain Kefer, who offered her a permanent position with the general staff's secret service division.

After the fall of Antwerp, Schragmüller was sent to spy school. The Nachrichtendienst had three such academies – one at Lörrach near Freiberg, another at Wesel and the third at Baden-Baden. Students at the schools were never acquainted with one another. During lectures, each trainee sat at an individual desk wearing a mask covering the upper part of the face. Schragmüller excelled and was considered too valuable to risk on operations in the field. Instead she was assigned to the Antwerp station located at 10 Rue de la Pepinière, where she was instructed to pass on what she had learned to new recruits.[24]

One of the most productive female agents of the war was the Frenchwoman Louise de Bettignies (1880–1918) who worked for the British under the nom-de-guerre 'Alice Dubois'. A native of Lille, Bettignies had escaped the German onslaught and travelled to Britain as a refugee. An excellent linguist, she was recruited by a Major Cameron, one of the joint heads of GHQ's intelligence service. Screening refugees arriving in the Channel port of Folkestone, Cameron and his colleague Major Wallinger ran their own spy networks in the occupied territories, using French and Belgian agents inserted through Holland.[25]

Bettignies returned to Lille where she began to assemble her own network of sub-agents. Chief among these was a chemist who could produce secret inks and forge passports. Her principal co-conspirator was Marie-Léonie Vanhoutte, who became 'Charlotte', a cheese vendor. Once a week she would pass into Holland to deliver her intelligence reports, playing a dangerous cat-and-mouse game with the watchful German occupiers.

After some months the Germans began to clamp down on the routes to Holland. After several close shaves, in September 1915 'Charlotte' was lured into a trap by the Germans. A similar fate awaited Bettignies on her return from Holland. Both women were confined in a Brussels prison and sentenced to death on 2 March 1916. They were spared this sentence, however, on account of the bad publicity the Germans endured after shooting the nurse Edith Cavell. Instead the two agents were sentenced to a life of penal servitude. Charlotte survived until the end of the war, but Bettignies was treated extremely harshly by the Germans and died on 27 September 1918, less than two months before the end of the war. Gone, but not forgotten, Louise de Bettignies' remains were returned to Lille after the signing of the armistice and buried with full military honours.

The final word in this spy-rich era goes to a German agent who, although self-taught in the dark arts of espionage, was perhaps the perfect spy. Working in the British censorship bureau, Julius Silber was a German who had spent most of his adult life away from home, mostly in South Africa and America. When war broke out, Silber's first loyalty remained to Germany, so he travelled to Britain and obtained a job in censorship with a view to committing espionage.

On reflection it was the perfect cover for a spy. Silber had access to all manner of sensitive information passing round the country, including the reports sent in by MI6 agents abroad. These agents, Silber noted, never used cover addresses, but sent their information in letters to friends, knowing it would be recognized by the censorship department and forwarded to the proper authorities. Silber was also privy to the work carried out to net German spies through mail censorship. But in both cases, Silber never took the risk of warning Germany about the MI6 agents or the German spies under surveillance. He reasoned, probably rightly, that this would only lead investigators to him.

Instead he carried on photographing such documents as he could smuggle out of the office overnight. Careful not to arouse the suspicion of his landlord, he copied the documents at a separate address to his apartment and collected used theatre ticket stubs, which he left around his lodgings to explain his absence. Once the documents were copied Silber was able to send them on to the Continent without scrutiny.

Only once did Silber come under suspicion when a shopkeeper wondered what he was doing with all the photographic supplies he purchased. With the shopkeeper following him, Silber coolly went to his employers and asked them to investigate the shopkeeper. With Silber an important censor, the shopkeeper was told to back off and mind his own business.

In his career Silber took one big, calculated risk. He opened a letter from a woman which mentioned that her brother was working on important modifications to merchant ships. Eager to find out more, Silber actually visited the woman, put the frighteners on her for flouting the censorship laws and through the course of the interview managed to extract the full story about her brother. Thus Silber learned the secret of the Q-ship, a ruse to help combat the U-boat threat. Merchant ships were fitted with concealed armament, so when U-boat surfaced to attack what appeared to be a normal, undefended merchantman, down would come the false compartments revealing the artillery. Such information was worth a risk.

At the end of the war Silber was thanked for his sterling work – for he was never suspected of any wrongdoing by the British authorities. He later returned to Germany and published his memoirs in 1925. Needless to say, his revelations were not well received by his former, wartime employers.

10

EASTERN PERIL

With the Japanese samurai all means are permissible as long as they lead to the end in view. To them it is smart to lie, to cheat, to deceive, to intrigue, to be double-faced, hypocritical, provided it pays or brings power. It is in their nature to be false.

Amleto Vespa – former secret agent for Japan[1]

In 1853 the United States sent four warships under Commodore Matthew Perry to barge open trade relations with Japan. The Japanese stalled and so Perry returned to Tokyo Bay a year later with more ships and hinted at war if an agreement was not reached. For centuries Japan had isolated itself from the world and until the coming of Perry it existed in an introspective, feudal cocoon. No one was allowed to leave Japan and no one could visit, with few exceptions. Perry's arrival changed everything and Japan soon embraced the modern, industrial era, with Western experts advising on everything from postal systems to army reform.

The arrival of so many foreigners caused a schism in Japanese society that affected political life. Although Japan was nominally ruled by an emperor, since the 1600s military dictators known as *shoguns* had run the country. After several revolts, in 1868 imperial power was restored to the young Emperor Meiji (1852–1912), who passed a series of laws heralding a policy of Westernization and tolerance to foreigners.

While Japan eagerly embraced everything the West had to offer, few Westerners realized the bitterness felt by many Japanese toward foreigners. A philosophy known as *Hakko Ichiu* (Eight Corners of the World under One Rule) took hold of Japan, which preached a doctrine of racial superiority and the divine right of the Japanese people to do pretty much as they pleased. Japan was said to be at the centre of the world and the *tenno* (emperor) was a divine being directly descended from the Goddess of the Sun. The Japanese people, furthermore, were protected by their gods and were thus superior to all others. The Hakko Ichiu also had a profound impact on foreign policy, Japan having been given a divine mission to bring all nations under the beneficial rule of the tenno.

To realize these divinely inspired ambitions, Japan needed a modern espionage system. Adopting the German model, Japanese officials were sent to study under Wilhelm Stieber in the mid-1870s. Over the next decade Japan built up separate army and naval intelligence services, each with an accompanying branch of secret military police (Kempeitai for the army and Tokeitai for the navy). These latter organizations also provided an excellent counter-espionage service. However, where the Japanese were unique was in the use of spies belonging to unofficial secret societies working alongside or independently of the official intelligence agencies. These shadowy institutions were ultra-nationalist by nature, drawing their membership from a cross-section of Japanese society, including the military, politics, industry and Yakuza underworld. Under ruthless leadership, their henchmen would spy on, subvert and corrupt Japan's Far East neighbours.

Perhaps the biggest losers in the Meiji Restoration were samurai warriors – the knights of the shogunate era. As Japan modernized and built an army based on universal conscription, the samurai found themselves an unwanted anachronism – even banned from publicly carrying their swords. Known as *ronin*, masterless samurai gravitated towards new urban centres where, unwilling to give up their martial way of life, they turned to crime. Realizing their potential, gang leader Mitsuru Toyama (1855–1944) organized the ronin into an effective force of hired muscle specializing in strikebreaking and assassination. Demand for Toyama's services saw doors opened for him to the highest levels of society. Soon he was one of the most influential figures in the ultra-nationalist underworld, known to many by the sinister appellation 'Darkside Emperor' or 'Shadow Shogun'.

An exponent of Japanese expansion, Toyama became the guiding hand of the Genyosha or Dark Ocean Society formed in 1881 by Kotaro Hiraoka – a rich samurai mine owner with an eye on business opportunities in Manchuria. To collect intelligence on the region and its

Triad gangs, Toyama dispatched a hundred Genyosha agents to China. The most effective front for their espionage operations came through activities in the vice trade, with the Genyosha setting up bordellos in Hankow, Shanghai, Tientsin, Pusan and Russian-controlled Central Asia. The most noted of these was the 'Hall of Pleasurable Delights' at Hankow.[2] Based on Stieber's 'The Green House', this brothel was extremely popular among Chinese politicians and Triad bosses. While providing a safe house for Japanese spies, it brought in funds for the Genyosha's clandestine activities and provided ample means to blackmail clients or find potential allies among the growing number of Chinese revolutionaries.

The name 'Dark Ocean' referred to the *genkai nada* – the stretch of water between Japan and Korea, hinting at the location of the group's first major operation. The close proximity of the Korean peninsula to the Japanese islands gave it considerable strategic value as a springboard into East Asia and as a defensive buffer against China and Russia. At the behest of the minister of war, Soroku Kawakami, Toyama and another leading Genyosha member, Ryohei Uchida, set up the Tenyukyo, a group of 15 hand-picked *agent provocateurs* sent into Korea as agitators.[3]

Once inside the country the Tenyukyo established contact with the Tonghaks, a radical Korean terrorist group. Together they waged such a campaign of terror that the Korean emperor was compelled to ask China for help. As obliging Chinese troops gathered on the border, Japanese hawks were presented with the excuse they had been hoping for. After condemnation of China's 'aggressive' intervention (the Chinese had not actually entered Korea yet), Japanese troops were landed and, claiming to be acting in defence of Korean sovereignty, they seized the royal palace in Seoul on 23 July 1894. The ensuing conflict, which was declared a few days later on 1 August, saw a quick succession of Japanese victories against the Chinese on land and sea, leaving part of Manchuria and the island of Formosa (Taiwan) in Japanese hands.

Despite the victory, war had stretched Japan's resources to the limit and rival nations were quick to detect the scent of vulnerability. Pressure from France, Germany and in particular Russia obliged Japan to give up its mainland gains in China. Russia formed an alliance with China against Japan in 1896, which gave it important strategic gains including the lease of Port Arthur (1898) and rights to extend the Trans-Siberian Railroad across Manchuria to the Russian seaport of Vladivostok.

It was clear to the Genyosha leadership that this growing Russian influence would have to be checked. However, after the Korean episode, the society's activities had come to the attention of headline writers. The unwanted publicity increased after Toyama's disciples assassinated the Korean princess Bin and terrorized the Korean emperor into seeking refuge in Russia.[4] Its high profile made the Genyosha unsuitable for conducting further secret operations, so in 1898 the group dissolved. Toyama instead formed the East Asia One Culture Society, a pan-Asian group with the ambition of formulating a common system of writing in the region. To help accomplish this, the group formed the Tung Wen College in Shanghai. Still operational in 1945, the Tung Wen College had thousands of graduates working from India to the Philippines. Of course the whole project was a sham front for espionage operations – the Chinese always referred to the Tung Wen as 'the Japanese Spy School'.[5]

In 1901, under Toyama's direction, his Black Ocean comrade Ryohei Uchida formed the Kokuryu-kai, or Black Dragon Society. Like the Genyosha before it, the clue to the group's ambitions lay in its name, which really implied 'Beyond the Amur River', the river separating northern Manchuria and Siberia. In Chinese the Amur translates to Black Dragon River, hence the origin of the society's most common name.

Initially the group recruited its *soshi* (lit. brave knights) from patriotic ronin and avoided the criminal types increasingly predominant in the Genyosha.[6] As word of their activities spread, other crusaders for the Japanese imperial cause sought membership. Although the society quickly boasted members in upper governmental and military circles, the group was not always in line with government policy, nor did it receive official sanction.

As war with Russia approached, the group successfully lobbied for the appointment of Colonel Motojiro Akashi as military attaché to St Petersburg. Akashi was an excellent intelligence officer sympathetic to the Black Dragons' aims. He had previously served as military attaché at Japanese embassies in Sweden, France and Switzerland. In these posts he established that Western Europe would not come to the aid of tsarist Russia if it were attacked by Japan.

While fulfilling his duties, Akashi made secret contact with anti-tsarist revolutionary cells inside Russia and around Europe. In return for financial aid, these groups provided Akashi with intelligence on the Russian military and secret services. He also made contact with Abdur Rashid Ibrahim, a Tartar Muslim who provided important information on the Russian fleet at Port Arthur. More intelligence came out of Port Arthur from the British agent Sidney Reilly who had met Akashi in St Petersburg. Reilly had set up a sham company in Port Arthur to provide him with a cover story while he spied on Russian defences for Akashi.

In addition to Akashi's work, Japanese spies posing as coolies and dockworkers infiltrated Russian bases in Manchuria. The Black Dragons were at the forefront of these actions. They sent agents into Manchuria and Siberia – and even opened a ju-jitsu school in Vladivostok to provide a front for their operations against the Russians. They observed troop and naval movements, building up detailed information on the Russian order of battle and logistics. They also had an agent in the north of Manchuria, Hajime Hamamoto, who ran a general store near to a Russian army base. By seducing wives of Russian officers, Hamamoto was able to glean important information from them, which was passed on to Military Intelligence in Japan via an agent in Vladivostok.[7]

These secret operations gave Japan a major advantage in the war, which began on 8 February 1904 with a Japanese surprise attack on Port Arthur, two days before a formal declaration of war was made. Moving to Stockholm, Akashi stretched Russian resources, stirring up Russian and Finnish revolutionaries. On a more practical level, Black Dragon agents acted as interpreters and guides for the Japanese army, organizing guerrilla operations with allied Manchurian warlords such as Marshal Chang Tso-lin.

Japan slowly wore down the Russian opposition, capturing Port Arthur and Mukden (now Shenyang). The Russians were finally forced to agree terms with Japan after its fleet was smashed at the battle of Tsushima (27–29 May 1905). A conference was held in Portsmouth, New Hampshire, resulting in Japan gaining control of Port Arthur and the South Manchurian railroad. Russia evacuated southern Manchuria, which was restored to China, and Japan's dominance of Korea was recognized.

With Russia out of the way, the Black Dragons turned their focus to China. Having met the revolutionaries Sun Yat-sen (1866–1925) and Chiang Kai-shek (1887–1975) in Tokyo during 1905, the Black Dragons subsidized the 1911 overthrow of the Manchu Dynasty, which made China a republic.[8] However, this assistance was given only to destabilize China and facilitate Japan's seizure of Manchuria – a long-term ambition of the Black Dragons.

The hunt began for a stooge in whose name the seizure of Manchuria would be justified and world opinion placated. One candidate had been identified by the Black Dragon Naniwa Kawashima, an old samurai and veteran of the Russo-Japanese war. After the war Kawashima found himself chief of police in the Japanese section of Peking. In the course of his duties he befriended his opposite number, Prince Su Chin Wang, head of Peking's Chinese police force. Prince Su was one of eight princes of the Iron Helmet, traditionally the emperor's closest companions, which in Kawashima's opinion gave him the right pedigree. Prince Su agreed to the plan, but it did not receive support from the Japanese government and floundered, much to the Black Dragons' disappointment. Su went on to form an anti-Republican army in the northeast together with the Mongol general Babojab. When this army was defeated, Su retired to Port Arthur where he died in April 1922. The search for a suitable puppet shifted from Su to the deposed Chinese emperor.

Pu Yi (1906–67), the last emperor of the Qing Dynasty, had ascended to the throne in 1908 before his third birthday. Since 1925 Pu Yi had lived in a villa – the Chang, or Quiet, Garden – inside the Japanese concession of Tientsin, where he enjoyed a playboy lifestyle with his increasingly opium-addicted wife 'Elizabeth' Wan Jung.[9] Faced with the crippling cost of maintaining his royal trappings, Pu Yi was desperate to regain the throne and hoped he might find support among the Black Dragons. He was well informed of their activities, recording in his memoirs how the society had taken hold in China:

[It] started out with bases in Foochow, Yentai (Chefoo) and Shanghai and operated under such covers as consulates, schools and photographers … its membership was said to have reached several hundred thousand with correspondingly huge funds. Toyama Mitsuru was the most famous of its leaders and under his direction its members had penetrated every stratum of Chinese society. At the side of Ching nobles and high officials and among peddlers and servants, including the attendants in the Chang Garden. Many Japanese personalities were disciples of Toyama's.[10]

Pu Yi agreed to discuss his restoration with a Black Dragon agent named Tsukuda Nobuo. However, because the Black Dragons' policy was not shared by the Japanese government, when Nobuo learned the local Japanese consul had also been invited to the interview, he pulled out and promptly disappeared. Puzzled at the agent's behaviour, Pu Yi sent his advisor and tutor, Chang Hsiao-hsu, to Japan to make contact with the Black Dragons directly.[11]

In the meantime, plans were set to seize Manchuria and its vast, unexploited resources. Since the war with Russia, Japan controlled the South Manchurian Railway, which it protected with a body of troops known as the Kwantung Army based in the Japanese concession at Mukden. Before Manchuria could be seized the powerful Manchurian warlord Marshal Chang Tso-lin had to be eliminated. A former Japanese ally in the war against Russia, the marshal opposed the growing Japanese influence in the region. In 1928 the Japanese assassinated the marshal by bombing his train, leaving Manchuria ripe for the taking. The following year intelligence specialist Colonel Seishiro Itagaki was posted to the Kwantung Army to make the final plans for the seizure of Manchuria. His plan was a masterpiece of ruse and treachery.

On the evening of 18 September 1931, Japanese sappers secretly planted explosives near to the track of the South Manchurian Railway. The objective was not to destroy the tracks, but to give the impression that Chinese saboteurs had attempted to derail a passing train. The Japanese quickly condemned the 'attack' and launched a 'retaliatory' attack against the Chinese in Mukden. To ensure a successful outcome, two heavy-calibre guns had been hidden in a 'swimming pool' constructed at the Japanese officers' club. One gun was trained on the Chinese constabulary barracks, the other at the air force base at Mukden airport. When news of the 'attack' on the railway reached the Japanese garrison, the guns opened fire on the sleeping Chinese. It was a massacre.

News of the 'battle' quickly travelled to Port Arthur, where Lieutenant-General Honjo ordered an all-out attack by the 20,000-strong Kwantung Army. In a feat of unparalleled military efficiency, Honjo's men were already mobilized before his orders arrived. The rival Chinese troops were caught on the back foot and, under general orders not to engage Japanese forces, were pushed back to the Sungari River. This attack left most of southern Manchuria in Japanese hands for the loss of just two men.

The outside world condemned the 'Mukden Incident' as a blatant case of Japanese aggression. However, Pu Yi saw it as an opportunity to take up the throne of his native Manchuria. Eight days after the incident, Colonel Itagaki arrived in Tientsin and offered Pu Yi the throne. To his surprise, the former emperor's advisors urged caution, suspicious that a 'mere colonel' was making the offer rather than Japanese politicians. Pausing for thought, Pu Yi wrote to Toyama asking him to clarify the situation.

Three weeks later, Pu Yi was introduced to a senior member of the Kwantung Army, Colonel Kenji Doihara (1883–1948). Another of Toyama's acolytes, Doihara was an intelligence officer and had been active in northern China and Siberia for some considerable time. Even among the pantheon of villains that were his contemporaries, Doihara stands out as a particularly loathsome individual. His rise to infamy began with tricking his 15-year-old sister into posing nude for some photographs. Armed with the developed pictures, the loving brother touted them to a Japanese imperial prince who was so impressed he made her his number one concubine. In return for this favour, Doihara was posted as an assistant to General Honjo, military attaché to Peking.[12]

Doihara must not be dismissed as a simple thug. He had a deserved reputation as a linguist, claiming to speak nine European languages and four Chinese dialects faultlessly. He enjoyed the attention of Western journalists who dubbed him the 'Lawrence of the East' for the way he adopted Chinese costume on his many travels round the country recruiting spies and seeking out potential allies. In 1928 he became military advisor to Marshal Chang and was almost certainly involved in his assassination, after which he was promoted to colonel. In 1931 Doihara was head of the Japanese Special Service Organ in Mukden and was declared mayor of the city after the attack on 19 September.

Doihara arrived at the Quiet Garden villa and offered Pu Yi the throne of Manchuria. Pu Yi knew that Doihara was a 'disciple' of Toyama and recorded his opinion of the colonel in his memoirs. Although at first taken in by him, Pu Yi came to realize – too late – the full depth of Doihara's mendacity:

Because of the mysterious stories that were told about him the Western press described him as the 'Lawrence of the East' and the Chinese papers said that he usually wore Chinese clothes and was fluent in several

Chinese dialects. But it seems to me that if all his activities were like persuading me to go to the Northeast [Manchuria] he would have had no need for the cunning and ingenuity of a Lawrence: the gambler's ability to keep a straight face while lying would have been enough.[13]

Doihara asked Pu Yi to travel to Mukden from where he would be placed on the Manchu throne. His sovereignty would be guaranteed by the Kwantung Army, which of course said it had no territorial ambitions in Manchuria. Eager for power, Pu Yi agreed in principle, but sought assurances from Doihara that he would not be merely a Japanese puppet. Doihara assured, but still Pu Yi dithered. It appeared that the empress did not trust the Japanese and would not agree to leave Tientsin. Frustrated, Doihara needed help and so called on Itagaki for advice. The author of the Mukden Incident answered Doihara's call by playing the joker in the Japanese pack – the Manchu-born agent known as 'Eastern Jewel'.

The daughter of the pro-Japanese prince Su Chin Wang, Eastern Jewel was born in 1907. In 1913 she was given to the Black Dragon Naniwa Kawashima for adoption as a mark of friendship between the two men. Arriving in Japan, she was renamed Yoshiko Kawashima and educated at the Matsumato school for girls. She was a thrill seeker and tomboy, with a voracious sexual appetite which she claimed was awakened by her adoptive grandfather at 15. After a string of affairs, an arranged marriage was set up for the 21-year-old Eastern Jewel with the Mongol prince Kanjurjab, son of her biological father's ally, General Babob.

The marriage – which took place in Port Arthur during November of 1927 – was seen as a means of cementing influence in Mongolia, where Japan held territorial ambitions. However, Eastern Jewel claimed that the marriage was never consummated and she quickly ditched the prince. She plunged headlong into the depths of Tokyo's wild, bohemian underbelly. Outgrowing her adopted land, she travelled widely and even turned up as a houseguest of Pu Yi and the empress at Tientsin in 1928. With similar family backgrounds, Elizabeth and Eastern Jewel struck up an improbable relationship, the closeted empress in turns captivated by and envious of Eastern Jewel's lurid and exotic exploits.

Eastern Jewel was in seedy Shanghai, having just walked out on a Japanese politician who had run out of money. On the prowl for a new sponsor she daringly set her sights on Major Tanaka, the head of the Shanghai secret service – or Special Service Organ. Attending a New Year party she ushered Tanaka to a discreet location and attempted to seduce him. Tanaka resisted the advances of the Manchu princess, explaining that it would be disrespectful for him – a commoner – to take her to bed. Eastern Jewel was not so easily deterred and dishonoured herself by borrowing money from Tanaka, finally breaking his resistance through a shared fetish for leather boots.[14] Tanaka was impressed by Eastern Jewel's forward manner and put her on the secret service payroll to fund her whims. Tanaka also paid for her English lessons, believing she might one day prove useful as a spy.

Returning to the matter of Pu Yi and the throne, Itagaki sent a telegram to Shanghai ordering Tanaka to report to Mukden. Fearful of being disgraced for lavishing official funds on his mistress, Tanaka left for Mukden on 1 October 1931. At the subsequent interview Itagaki revealed Doihara had been sent to get Pu Yi and that the Japanese forces were planning the next stage of their advance into Manchuria with the capture of Harbin. Tanaka was charged with keeping the League of Nations' attention fixed away from Manchuria by provoking a disturbance in Shanghai. Tanaka told Itagaki he had the perfect agent in mind and was surprised – not to mention worried – when Itagaki said he knew all about Eastern Jewel. He then revealed the trouble Doihara was having with the implacable Elizabeth and mentioned he might need to borrow Eastern Jewel. Itagaki gave Tanaka $10,000, which he used to clear Eastern Jewel's debts and begin the preparations for his Shanghai diversion.

Subsequent to this interview, Doihara wired Shanghai for Eastern Jewel. Calling in a favour from a pilot boyfriend, she flew to Tientsin that same evening. Anxious to make a lasting first impression on Doihara, Eastern Jewel disguised herself in the robes of a Chinese gentleman. She arrived and immediately caused a stir by refusing to divulge her name to the desk sergeant at Doihara's headquarters. Suspecting treachery was afoot, Doihara placed a revolver on his desk and opened the inquisition.

'Your name, please?' he asked. 'My name is of no importance,' replied Eastern Jewel, 'I have come to help you.' 'You speak like a eunuch,' Doihara retorted. 'Are you one of Pu Yi's men?' Eastern Jewel simply laughed in reply. Doihara grabbed his samurai sword. 'Very well then, if you won't tell me who you are, let us see what you are.' Drawing the sword, he began to away cut the ties to her robe. Eastern Jewel did not move, but continued to stare at Doihara provocatively. Doihara flicked open the robe and 'with a guttural samurai yell' cut open the silk scarf she bound her breasts with. 'I saw that she was a woman' Doihara later confessed, 'so I conducted a thorough investigation and determined that I had not put even the smallest scratch on any part of her white skin.'[15]

Next day, Eastern Jewel visited the Quiet Garden and heard Elizabeth's views on the proposed move to Mukden.[16] She was able to report to Doihara that the empress was implacably opposed to any move to Mukden and it would take extreme measures to convince Pu Yi to travel alone. Growing impatient, Doihara resorted to terror tactics. He told Pu Yi that a price had been put on his head by Chang Hsueh-liang, the son of the murdered Marshal Chang. To lend credence to Doihara's warnings, Eastern Jewel placed some snakes in Pu Yi's bed. On 8 November bombs were hidden in a basket of fruit delivered anonymously to the Quiet Garden. Pu Yi recalled: 'an assistant came running into the room shouting "bombs, two bombs". I was sitting in an armchair and this news gave me such a fright that I was incapable of standing up.'[17] Eastern Jewel called the Japanese guards who came rushing in led by one of Doihara's henchmen. He took the bombs away and then later revealed they had been manufactured by stooges of the late marshal's son.

More was to follow. Along with warning letters, Pu Yi received a telephoned tip-off from 'a waiter' at his favourite Victoria Café that men with concealed weapons had been enquiring after him. Doihara then arranged for a crowd of Chinese agents to make trouble in the Chinese-administered part of the city. On 10 November martial law was declared and Japanese armoured cars surrounded the Quiet Garden to defend Pu Yi, whose nerve began to crack.[18] Scared out of his wits, Pu Yi at last agreed to go to Mukden, travelling without the empress on Eastern Jewel's advice. After dark he was bundled into the trunk of a car and driven to the docks by his Japanese interpreter. Elizabeth, meanwhile, was comforted by a heady mix of Eastern Jewel and opium until reunited with Pu Yi in Port Arthur six weeks later.

Eastern Jewel returned to Shanghai and began preparations with Tanaka for what became known as the Fake War. She hired gangs of Chinese street thugs and provided them with lists of Japanese business and residential addresses to attack. After the attacks began on 18 January 1932, Tanaka stoked up indignation in the Japanese community. Outraged by two more days of attacks, an ultimatum was delivered by the Japanese consul general to the Chinese mayor to stop them. However, with Eastern Jewel controlling the thugs, the Chinese mayor had little chance of success. In the face of Chinese impotence Admiral Shiozawa felt justified in landing his Imperial Marines to protect Japanese nationals. Tanaka's mission was accomplished.

While engineering the arrival of the Japanese troops, Eastern Jewel had been busy in her now familiar role of seductress extraordinaire. The son of the Chinese republican Sun Yat-sen happened to be in town and soon fell victim to Eastern Jewel, confiding in her the rivalries in the Chinese camp. She also acted as a weathervane on international reaction to the Japanese actions. Putting her English lessons to good use, she took a British military attaché as a lover. From his pillow talk she was able to tell Tanaka that the West was unlikely to back its vigorous condemnations with any real action.

After the Shanghai incident, Eastern Jewel took up with a string of lovers. Her extravagance became so great that Tanaka offloaded her to Pu Yi's chief military advisor, Major-General Hayao Tada. She was also indulged with the command of 5,000 Manchu 'rough riders', the captains of which she selected personally to her own exacting criteria of manhood. During the Japanese bombing of Shanghai in 1937, Eastern Jewel caused outrage among the Chinese when she was seen walking through the ruined streets laughing with Japanese officers. It was rumoured she had even flown over the city in a bomber. When Peking fell to the Japanese in 1937, Eastern Jewel formed part of the administration. She abused her power by blackmailing wealthy Chinese with false accusations of assisting the enemy. Once noted for her beauty, Eastern Jewel's debauched lifestyle began to weather her looks, although her libido remained undiminished. She found it increasingly harder to attract men and had an actor arrested on trumped-up charges of theft because he spurned her advances. Instead she increasingly began to explore her fantasies with local sing-song girls. Even Tanaka was moved to describe her later conduct as 'beyond common sense'. At the end of the war Eastern Jewel declined an offer to return to Japan and went into hiding. Acting on a tip-off, Chiang Kai-shek's counter-intelligence officers picked her up in November 1945. On 25 March 1948 Eastern Jewel was led to a wooden block and decapitated by a swordsman.

After the Pu Yi drama, Doihara began recruiting agents in the newly conquered territories. He broadened the Special Service Organ's network of spies throughout southern Manchuria, utilizing large numbers of Russian refugees who had fled the Soviet Union. Desperate for employment, the men worked for Doihara as hired thugs, while women filled the brothels. European women were much in demand and acted as opium peddlers, receiving a free pipe for every six they sold.

One of Doihara's converts was Italian-born spy Amleto Vespa, a one-time agent of Marshal Chang who had since managed a cinema. A fascist sympathizer and former member of the Mexican Revolutionary Army, Vespa had travelled extensively, coming to work with Marshal Chang Tso-lin in 1920. To avoid trouble with the Italian authorities, Vespa had obtained Chinese citizenship. Because of this, after the Mukden Incident Vespa found himself under the Japanese yoke without the usual protection afforded to Westerners. He was forced to work for the Japanese, running the spy service in Harbin until 1936 when he managed to get out of China with his family. Vespa wrote a remarkable book detailing Japan's brutal clandestine activities in Manchuria. He was taken to meet Doihara on 14 February 1932, an encounter described in his book. Vespa disliked the man intensely:

> Foreign journalists had referred to colonel Doihara as the Japanese 'Lawrence of Manchuria'. I suspect, however, that if his sister had not been concubine of a Japanese Imperial Prince most of his success would have been still in his imagination.[19]

Doihara left Vespa under no illusions about where his future loyalties belonged. If Vespa disobeyed, Doihara would shoot him. Vespa was told to return the following day and be introduced to the chief of the Japanese secret service in Manchuria. Vespa never discovered the true identity of this man, but many believe he must have been a Japanese prince close to Emperor Hirohito. The ensuing interview revealed the true extent of Japanese secret operations in Manchuria. In perfect English the mysterious chief told Vespa:

> 'If Colonel Doihara has told you anything unpleasant, please pay no attention to it. Since, in other countries, they call him the Japanese Lawrence, he delights in showing his greatness by his

hectoring manner. He has worked under me for many years, however, and I have no hesitation in saying he is much less of a Lawrence than he thinks he is.'[20]

With remarkable candour, the chief explained how it was Japanese policy to make colonies pay for themselves. The Japanese system was to secretly grant certain monopolies to trusted individuals. Naturally the monopolies changed hands for enormous sums, in return for which the holder gained Japanese protection. The principal monopolies were the free transportation of goods by railway under the guise of Japanese military supplies; the monopoly of opium smoking dens, the sale of narcotics, poppy cultivation, the running of gambling houses and the importation of Japanese prostitutes – 70,000 Korean and Japanese prostitutes were shipped to Manchuria in the year after the Mukden Incident.[21]

Although very strict on drug abuse at home, the Japanese flooded Manchuria with narcotics. Throughout the 1930s Manchurian streets were littered with wasted addicts and the corpses of emaciated overdose victims. To meet the demand, soya-bean farms were turned over to poppy production and drug-processing plants were set up along with 'shooting-galleries' for those too poor to enjoy the comforts of an opium den. Vespa revealed:

In Mukden, in Harbin, in Kirin etc., one cannot find a street where there are no opium-smoking dens or narcotic shops. In many streets the Japanese and Korean dealers have established a very simple and effective system. The morphine, cocaine or heroin addict does not have to enter the place if he is poor. He simply knocks at the door, a small peep-hole opens, though which he thrusts his bare arm and hand with 20 cents in it. The owner of the joint takes the money and gives the victim a shot in the arm.[22]

The Japanese didn't need bullets to kill Chinese; the drugs would do it for them – and at a profit.

By 1938 Doihara was the commander of the Kwantung Army. Based in Shanghai he successfully penetrated Chang Kai-shek's headquarters with spies. Operating under the pseudonym of 'Ito Soma' and posing as a Japanese financier, Doihara managed to befriend the republican leader's personal assistant, Huang-sen. His hook, improbable as it may sound, was a shared passion for goldfish, Doihara being an authority on the subject. In return for information and the procurement of rare goldfish, Huang-sen spied for Doihara. His information was used to foil a Chinese plan to attack Japanese shipping in the Yangtse River. The failure of the plan led to an investigation, after which Huang-sen was exposed and executed by the republicans. A follow-up investigation led in 1938 to the execution of eight Chinese divisional commanders, all of whom were found working for Doihara.[23]

Later, as an air force major-general, Doihara sat on Prime Minister Hideki Tojo's Supreme War Council. Doihara was present at the session of 4 November 1941 when the attack on Pearl Harbor was decided. He went on to command the army in Singapore (1944–45) and ran brutal POW and internee camps in Malaya, Sumatra, Java and Borneo. Doihara was tried at the Tokyo war crimes trial and executed on 23 December 1948 by hanging. He was joined by Seishiro Itagaki, the author of the Mukden Incident, and Prime Minister Tojo, the former Kwantung Army leader. Eastern Jewel's case officer, Tanaka, was more fortunate, surviving to tell the tale. Having opposed the decision to attack America, he retired in 1942. After the war he was an aide to the tribunal's chief American prosecutor, Joseph Keenan. Tanaka claimed he even procured girls for the American.[24]

As for the Black Dragons, their reputation as sinister arch-plotters meant that they were not ignored in the round-up of war criminals in 1945. General MacArthur banned the group on 13 September 1945 and ordered the arrest of seven leadership figures. He need not have bothered. Of the seven, two had never been members, a third had died of old age in 1938, while a fourth had committed suicide in 1943. The other three suspects had once been members but had renounced their membership long before.[25]

In truth the Black Dragons had long since fallen out of favour and had ceased to be a force in Japan. Their last public meeting was held in October 1935 when Toyama protested at Mussolini's invasion of Ethiopia – another episode of white aggression against men of colour, as he saw it. The Japanese police used the meeting as a pretext for a crackdown on the Black Dragons and thereafter the society dwindled to a handful of forgotten diehards working out of a dingy, backstreet Tokyo office.[26]

While Toyama and his disciples continued to view Russia as the main enemy, a new group rose to prominence – the Strike South faction. This group called for expansion into Southeast Asia and Indonesia, rich areas abundant in the resources Japan was lacking. After an undeclared border war with Russia, which culminated in Japan's defeat at the battle of Khalkhin Gol in August 1939, Tokyo began to favour the new option. There was just a one slight problem with their plan. If a strike south occurred, Japan would inevitably clash with Western interests, particularly those of the British Empire and the United States of America.

As Japan paused to take breath before its next move, we should return to Europe where a sequel to the Great War of 1914–18 was about to erupt.

11

DOUBLE AGENTS & RADIO GAMES

*By means of the double agent system we
actively ran and controlled the German
espionage system in this country.*

J. C. Masterman. Chairman of the British XX
Committee in World War II[1]

After World War I, in 1919 the British Admiralty's code-breaking department – 'Room 40' of the Zimmermann telegram fame – was merged with its army equivalent (MI1b) to form the Government Code and Cypher School (GCCS). Under the command of Alastair Denniston, GCCS was initially controlled by the Admiralty, but then came under the Foreign Office in 1922, reflecting its focus on diplomatic traffic. As war with Germany moved closer and the fear of aerial bombing grew, GCCS was moved out of London so it could continue operating. In 1939 it moved to a mansion 50 miles (80km) north-west of London called Bletchley Park.

Although a closely guarded secret for 30 years after the war, the work carried out at Bletchley Park is now so legendary that it almost needs no introduction. In short, German coded wireless traffic was intercepted by a series of 'Y' stations dotted around Britain and abroad. In their raw state, the intercepted Morse code messages were then sent to Bletchley. The first part of the decryption process was to decide the origin of the message: German navy, army, air force, the Gestapo, and so on. Once its origin had been established the message would be passed on to the relevant hut specializing in the particular code of that branch and would be decrypted, then passed on for analysis. At its height Bletchley had over 10,000 personnel working in it, mostly young women aiding an eccentric band of mathematicians and academics working round the clock, searching for clues to break into the various German codes, of which Enigma was only the most famous. At good times messages were being read almost as fast as they were by their German recipients; during bad times – and there were many of them – the codes remained unbroken.

From the work of Bletchley Park the Allies were able to win the Battle of the Atlantic and blunt the menace of the German U-boat wolf packs, eventually sinking U-boats faster than new ones could be launched. Bletchley allowed the Allies to throttle Rommel's Afrika Korps by sinking supply ships in the Mediterranean. The German secret service spent huge resources hunting informers in Italy because, according to one of its chiefs, Walter Schellenberg (1910–52): 'Until the capitulation of the Afrika Korps in May 1943, there was not a single German tanker, troopship or aerial transport whose position was not reported to the western Allies.'[2] Of course, Schellenberg had no idea about Bletchley Park and instead suspected treachery in high places. Montgomery's victory at El Alamein in 1942 now seems all the more logical given the intelligence he received. By knowing the thoughts of German high command and at times Hitler himself, Bletchley is widely believed to have shortened the war by several years.

What must not be forgotten is that the success of Bletchley was in large part due to the pre-war efforts of Polish cryptanalysts, French intelligence and a German spy. This is not to say the British would never have worked out how to break the German codes on their own, but to recognize the actual series of events as they happened.

In the early 1920s German engineer Arthur Scherbius patented a complex rotor encryption machine known as Enigma, which by 1927 was used commercially in a number of countries, including Britain, the United States, France and Poland. This machine was adapted by both the German navy in 1926 and the army in 1928. The army version of Enigma (Wehrmacht Enigma) included a variation that greatly increased the security of the machine and it was this version which was adopted throughout Germany's armed forces during the 1930s and into World War II.

The science of the Enigma machine is bafflingly complicated, but broken down into the most basic terms it works as follows. Before sending or receiving a message the operator would set the machine up in a prearranged manner. The operator would choose three from five wheels, which were inserted into the top of the machine. Then, using a plug-board at the front of the machine (this was the army's adaptation), the operator would vary the machine's circuitry. When the operator typed a letter, the machine would encrypt it through this combination of mechanical and electrical means. Each time a letter was pressed the right-hand wheel would rotate one place, thus altering the settings for next letter. After 26 inputs, the second wheel would also rotate one place, followed 25 inputs later by the rotation of the third wheel. By alternating the wiring and the starting position of the wheels, 159 million, million, million basic combinations were possible. Quite simply, Enigma was thought to be unbreakable.

Nevertheless, doing just this became a long-term priority for the Poles. In 1928 a select group of mathematics students in Poznan University were chosen to undertaken lessons in cryptology. By 1932 the German section of Polish intelligence under Major Maksymilian Ciezki was ready to attack the German code.

As the Poles were struggling with Enigma, in Berlin a disgruntled German was pondering his lot in life and coming up with some very negative conclusions. Hans-Thilo Schmidt (1888–1943) had served his country in WWI, but his career in soap manufacture had been wrecked by the super-inflation of the Great Depression. Unable to feed his family, Schmidt had been forced to go to his elder brother Rudolf for help. Whereas Schmidt had left the army, Rudolf had stayed and by 1925 had become head of the Signals Corps. Through his brother's contacts, Schmidt gained a position in the Chiffrierstelle, or cipher bureau. He travelled to Berlin, leaving his wife and two children back in Bavaria. Isolation from his family left him depressed and, coupled with resentment against his more successful brother and bitterness towards the nation of his birth, he set out on the path to treachery.

On 8 November 1931, Schmidt met a French agent in Belgium codenamed *Rex* and Captain Gustave Bertrand from the French cryptological section. For 10,000 marks, Schmidt arranged for Rex to photograph several documents, which gave the operating instructions for using an Enigma machine. Under the codename *Asché*, Schmidt had 18 other such meetings with Rex over the coming decade.

Bertrand was unable to use the material provided by *Asché* – as were the British when Bertrand offered it to them. Only in December 1932, when Bertrand passed it onto the Poles did the information come into its own. In addition to operation manuals, *Asché* provided copies of the Enigma settings for several months. Although these were now out of date, the Poles were able to check back through their records of German intercepts for those same months. Now knowing the original key settings, the cryptologist Marian Rejewski was able to deduce the elusive wiring system for the machine. For the next seven years, the Poles were able to produce their own Enigma machines and read a large percentage of the Wehrmacht traffic – somewhere in the region of 75 per cent by January 1938.

In September 1938, the Poles were suddenly put out of the game by a change in the Enigma set-up. Suspecting the changes in some way marked a countdown to war, the Poles went to Bertrand who set up a meeting with French, Polish and British codebreakers. Bertrand's solution to the problem was simple: announce to the world that the Enigma had been broken and that Germany's radio traffic was an open book. The Germans would realize that their plans were common knowledge and be forced to halt their military build up while a new communication system was put in place. Fortunately for the long-term success of the Allies, the Polish did not agree to Bertrand's scheme and the conference ended up being little other than a polite getting-to-know-you session.

But war was coming and a solution needed to be found quickly. The Poles were initially reluctant to share their findings with the British, but this changed after 31 March 1939 when Prime Minister Neville Chamberlain announced that Britain would declare war if Germany attacked Poland. This created a new climate of trust and at a conference held in Warsaw on 25 July 1939 the Polish delegation revealed they had built their own Enigma machines. In the new spirit of co-operation, both France and Britain would receive a machine each, plus diagrams of all the other devices the Poles had so far invented, including an electromechanical device called *bomba kryptologiczna* – quite literally a cryptological bomb. This device would inspire mathematician Alan Turing to design the Bletchley Park *bombe* which drastically sped up the time it took to work out new Enigma settings each day.

Bertrand was put in charge of transporting the machines using a diplomatic pouch from the French embassy. The Frenchman duly arrived in London's Victoria Station on 16 August and handed the machine over to Stewart Menzies, head of MI6, who was apparently dressed in evening attire and on his way out to dinner. Just 15 days later, Germany invaded Poland and WWII began. It had been a very close shave indeed.

With WWII in its infancy, now is a prudent time to introduce the two secret intelligence services of Nazi Germany against whom the Western Allies were faced. The Abwehr (lit. defence) was the secret intelligence service of the armed forces. This organization was created in 1921 under the command of Major Friedrich Gempp, a former deputy to Walter Nicolai, the head of German intelligence during the Great War. In 1928 it merged with the German naval intelligence service, which led to it being commanded by Rear Admiral Patzig between 1932 and 1935, then most famously by Admiral Canaris (1887–1945) who remained in control until the organization was disbanded in 1944.

During WWII, the Abwehr was divided into three principal branches. Under the command of Colonel Piekenbrock, Abwehr I controlled espionage operations, while Abwehr II was under the command of Colonel Erwin Lahousen and was employed in sabotage operations and in targeting military objectives behind enemy lines. Lastly was the organization's security and counter-espionage branch under Colonel von Bentivegni – Abwehr III.[3] From the start one should always bear in mind that Canaris and the bulk of his organization – especially his number two, Hans Oster – were confirmed anti-Nazis, although Canaris was not, as many have since believed, a British spy.

Abwehr headquarters were located at 76/78 Tirpitzufer Strasse in Berlin, adjacent to the offices of the Oberkommando der Wehrmacht (OKW), the supreme high command to which it reported. There was a network of 23 stations within Germany called *Abwehrstellen*, or *Asts*, which in turn operated subsidiary stations, or *Nebenstellen*. For example, the Hamburg Ast was responsible for gathering intelligence on the United Kingdom and the United States, but also naval and shipping matters through Nebenstellen in Bremen, Flensburg and Kiel. Outside of the Reich, Abwehr stations operating in neutral countries were called *Kriegsorganisationen* or KOs. The most senior of the ten KOs was Madrid. At the height of Nazi Germany's power, others were found in Lisbon, Berne, Stockholm, Helsinki, Zagreb, Ankara, Casablanca, Bucharest and Shanghai. In many cases, these too had their own Nebenstellen, thus the KO in Ankara also had stations in

Istanbul and Tehran, with the network reaching as far as a Nebenstelle in Kabul responsible for monitoring India.[4]

Running parallel to the Abwehr, or rather in direct competition with it, were the intelligence, counter-intelligence and law-enforcement agencies of Heinrich Himmler's SS – the armed wing of the Nazi Party. One part of this organization was the Sicherheitsdienst – or SD. This was the Nazi Party's intelligence-gathering arm and was charged with seeking out enemies of the Party. There was then the security service, the Sicherheitspolizei – or Sipo – which was divided into the Reichs Kriminalpolizei (Kripo) and the Geheime Staatspolizei (Gestapo). Shortly after war broke out a central organization was formed by Heinrich Himmler called the Reichssicherheitshauptamt or RSHA, which survived throughout the Second World War. Under the command of Reinhard Heydrich until his assassination in 1942 and then Ernst Kaltenbrunner, the RSHA was itself divided into seven departments, or *Amter*, the most relevant ones being:

Amt III, Inland-SD, which was responsible for intelligence
and security within Germany and was sub-divided into five
departments concerned with issues as diverse as culture,
law, ethnicity and commerce.

Amt IV, or Geheime Staatspolizei (Gestapo), headed by Heinrich
'Gestapo' Müller. The role of the Gestapo was to investigate and
combat 'all tendencies dangerous to the state'.
It had the authority to investigate treason, espionage and
sabotage cases, and cases of criminal attacks on the Nazi Party
and on Germany. Again it was composed of a number of
sub-departments with a wide range of concerns, including
assassinations, combating opponents of the regime in occupied
territories and counter-intelligence. Perhaps most notorious of
all the departments of Amt IV was B4 under Adolf Eichmann,
which carried out the identification and transportation of Jews
to concentration camps.

Amt V, Kriminalpolizei, (Kripo) was a detective service which
dealt with serious crimes of a non-political nature.

Amt VI, Ausland-SD, the foreign intelligence service of the SS.

Despite their rivalry, Amt VI worked closely with the Abwehr on many issues. Together they had a number of very high-profile successes during WWII, many of which were recorded in the memoirs of Walter Schellenberg, who commanded Amt VI after 1941. Reminiscent of Stieber's infamous 'Green House' was a brothel dubiously named 'Salon Kitty'. Set in a large Berlin house in a fashionable district, the Salon Kitty was targeted at foreign diplomats and businessmen. In each room technical experts had constructed false walls behind which microphones were installed. Through automatic tape recorders every word spoken in the house was recorded and assessed for potential blackmail use. According to Schellenberg one of its most noted victims was the Italian foreign minister, Count Ciano, who had been against an alliance between Italy and Germany.

Although Walter Schellenberg provided the technical services, he would not supply the hostesses, claiming his female agents were far too valuable to be used as whores. Schellenberg's boss, Heydrich, passed this duty to Kripo head Artur Nebe, formerly of the Berlin vice squad. According to Schellenberg, Nebe rounded up 'the most highly qualified and cultivated ladies of the *demi-monde,* and, I regret to say that quite a few ladies from the upper crust of German society were only too willing to serve their country in this manner.' Apparently Heydrich took a very hands-on approach to running Salon Kitty and missed no opportunity to make 'personal inspections'. On these occasions Schellenberg was given strict orders to ensure the bugging devices were switched off.[5]

On the operational front, a Sudeten German in Czechoslovakia provided a complete set of plans for the Czech fortification construction programme.[6] In 1938 blueprints of the top-secret American Norden bombsight were passed to the Abwehr by a German sympathizer in the United States, Herman Lang. This sight was far superior to the one used by the RAF and although Lang did not want anything for his troubles – he had even gone to Germany to check on the development of a prototype – Hermann Göring is said to have given him 10,000 marks.[7]

Before the invasion of France, German agents had infiltrated the cement factories at Nancy, Sarreguemines and Metz. These agents were able to provide 'precise information' about the construction of the Maginot Line – the French fortifications along the German border. Agents were also at work inside the Schneider-Cruesot armament factories, providing up-to-the-minute information on French artillery and tanks. Nazi spies even managed to secure copies of orders and operational plans from France's Deuxième Bureau intelligence agency.[8]

Returning to the invasion of Poland, on the eve of war the SD conducted secret operations in an attempt to gain justification for the German invasion of Poland. Shortly after 8.00pm on 31 August 1939 a German radio station on the Polish border at Gliwice broadcast the message 'Attention! This is Gliwice. The broadcasting station is in Polish hands...' In fact the radio station had been attacked by members of the SD under the command of Sturmbannführer Alfred Naujocks. This squad had earlier obtained Polish uniforms and false papers from the Abwehr.[9] Once at the station a Polish Silesian named Franciszek Honiok became the first victim of WWII. He had been arrested the day before, drugged, then shot at Gliwice so that his corpse would provide further evidence of a Polish attack. This phoney attack was only the most famous of a number of such missions that night.

After the Gwilice raid, Schellenberg was involved in his first cloak-and-dagger operation against the much-vaunted British secret service. In an action known as the Venlo Incident, the SD was able to knock Britain's Secret Intelligence Service (SIS) European operation out of action in a single blow. For several years before the war, German agent 'F479' had been working in Holland posing as a political refugee. In this guise F479 made contact with the British secret service and let it be known he had links with a group inside the Wehrmacht conspiring to overthrow Hitler's regime. The British took the bait and asked the German agent to arrange a meeting with the plotters.

Schellenberg adopted the identity of Captain Schaemmel from the transport department – the real person of this name had been sent on a long journey in the East. On 21 October 1939 Schellenberg and another agent met two British SIS agents and a member of Dutch intelligence in Arnhem. Their game plan was to string the British along and hopefully uncover any real anti-Hitler plots in Germany. A second meeting took place on 30 October, in which discussions took place along the lines of a peace treaty in which Germany would regain much of the overseas territory it had lost in 1918. The two SIS agents gave the German delegation a brand new radio transmitter and codes, which were eagerly received by German codebreakers.

Meanwhile on 8 November Hitler was due to give his annual speech to Nazi Party members at Munich's Bürgerbräukeller. Hitler normally spoke at some length, but due to a change in travel arrangements he left the meeting shortly after 9.00pm. Minutes after leaving the hall a bomb exploded in a pillar close to where Hitler had stood. Eight people died and 63 were injured in the explosion, which was the work of dissatisfied German named Johann Georg Ester who thought killing Hitler would prevent a major war. Although Ester was picked up by the Gestapo trying to cross into Switzerland, Hitler refused to believe he had acted alone and blamed British intelligence. In retaliation, SS Chief Heinrich Himmler (1900–45) ordered Schellenberg to arrest the British agents he had been 'negotiating' with. A team led by Alfred Naujocks was assembled to kidnap the British and bring them into Germany.

The next meeting with the British had been arranged for 9 November. Their Dutch intelligence contact, Lieutenant Klop, had chosen the Café Backus in Venlo, which although on Dutch soil was in fact situated between the Dutch and German border posts. Klop and the two British agents, Captain Sigismund Payne Best and Major Richard Stevens, along with their Dutch driver, Jan Lemmens drove from their base in a passport control office in The Hague to Venlo. Schellenberg was waiting outside the café and watched the British agents' car pull to a stop. As it did so, an open-top car drove through the German border post with Naujock's gang of SD hijackers hanging from the runner boards. Klop fired at the German car's windscreen and a brief gunfight ensued, during which Klop was mortally wounded. The rest of the group surrendered and were dragged across the German frontier.

Best, Stevens and Lemmens were sent to Berlin. In Stevens' pocket they found a list of MI6 agents and other important assets that were to be pulled out of Holland in case of German invasion. Under interrogation the two British agents revealed enough for the Germans to mop up the whole MI6 operation in Western Europe, leaving London without a secret service just at the point Germany looked set to launch its attack. They also obtained the names and addresses of senior intelligence figures in Britain, all of which was included in a secret report on the British secret services – *Der Britische Nachrichtendienst*.[10] When the Dutch government asked for the return of Klop's body, Hitler claimed this proved Dutch neutrality was a sham and he was justified in invading. Best and Stevens were sent to Sachsenhausen concentration camp and then Dachau, where they were liberated by US forces in April 1945.

After this brilliant success, Germany nearly threw away its advantage in an inexplicable act of stupidity. Early in 1940, a Wehrmacht officer was carrying copies of the secret plans to attack Holland and Belgium. With another officer, this courier stopped off in Munster to meet a friend who was a major in the Luftwaffe. This congenial reunion led the two Wehrmacht officers to miss their train to Cologne. The Luftwaffe officer offered to fly them, but mid-flight became lost in poor visibility. The plane actually came down in Belgium, where the three officers were arrested before they had a chance to destroy the invasion documents. The Belgians seized the documents, translated them but decided they were a plant and the whole business was some dastardly Nazi ruse. In Germany both Hitler and Field Marshal von Manstein guessed that this would be Belgium's conclusion and played a double bluff by not altering the plans in the slightest.

When the battle of France began in May 1940, Schellenberg was involved with a number of deception operations in conjunction with experts from the Propaganda Ministry. Together they broadcast a number of false news items, purportedly from the French media, with the intention of causing panic. In addition to these radio broadcasts, a small pamphlet was dropped in large numbers from German aircraft. This document claimed Nostradamus had predicted the German attack and that only south-east France would be spared from it.[11] Coupled with military action, these various schemes helped put thousands of refugees onto the road, blocking military traffic and using up manpower trying to control them.

When France fell on 25 June, only Britain was left to face the Nazi onslaught. The huge demand for information on the British Isles appears to have taken the Abwehr somewhat by surprise. Their key agent in England was a Welsh nationalist codenamed *Johnny*, around whom the Abwehr had been slowly building a network of sub-agents since the outbreak of war. Unfortunately for the Abwehr, what they and nobody else in Germany realized was that *Johnny* was in fact a double agent known to the British as *Snow*.

Snow/Johnny was in fact a Welsh-born electrical engineer named Arthur Owen who worked for a firm with Admiralty contracts. In the course of his work Owen also did business with the German navy. While doing so he passed information to the British Naval Intelligence Directorate (NID) and then to SIS and Special Branch. In 1936 it transpired that Owen had also been passing intelligence to a known Abwehr address in Germany: PO Box 629, Hamburg. Owen admitted he had been recruited by the Germans under the codename *Johnny* and was controlled by *Dr Hantzau*, in fact the alias of Major Nikolaus Ritter. He managed to convince the sceptical British authorities that he was playing a double game with the Germans for their benefit.

In January 1939 *Snow* – as Owen was henceforth codenamed by the British – revealed that the Germans were sending him a wireless transmitter and he soon received a cloakroom ticket for Victoria Station, where it was hidden inside a suitcase. In August 1939 *Snow* visited his Abwehr controllers in Hamburg and disappeared until 4 September when he telephoned Special Branch to offer his services. By now the authorities were unsure quite whom *Snow* was working for, so as a precaution they interned him in Wandsworth Prison.

Once in custody, *Snow* revealed the whereabouts of his radio which was returned to him in his cell on 12 September. In order to play him as a double agent MI5 allowed *Snow* to return to neutral Belgium for a meeting with the Abwehr. At this meeting *Snow* was told to recruit a contact in the Welsh Nationalist Party who would be trained to perform sabotage operations. MI5 nominated a retired Welsh police inspector named Gwilym Williams to pose as the saboteur. Under the codename *GW*, the new recruit travelled with *Snow* to Rotterdam and met with Ritter.

Snow was then introduced to a German-born photographer working for the Abwehr in England under duress due to threats made against his brother still in Germany. This agent was turned by MI5 and codenamed *Charlie*. In addition to his primary mission of reporting on shipping, *Charlie* was able to miniaturize *Snow*'s reports, which were then hidden under postage stamps. *Snow* was also informed that he would receive money via a woman in Bournemouth who was laundering money through Selfridges. The British authorities subsequently discovered she was Mathilda Krafft and imprisoned her in Holloway.

In April 1940 *Snow* again travelled to Belgium for a meeting with Ritter. The Abwehr wanted *Snow* to obtain a trawler for a rendezvous off England's east coast. The idea was for *Snow* to hand over another sub-agent who would go on to Germany for training. For this mission MI5 chose a former smuggler turned police informant named Sam McCarthy whom they codenamed *Biscuit*. On 19 May 1940 the trawler *Barbados* left Grimsby, but during the trip *Snow* and *Biscuit*

An extraordinary photograph of Pinkerton's secret service agents at Foller's House, Cumberland Landing, Virginia, in 1862. Pinkerton can be seen seated in the centre-background of the picture, behind the group of figures seated at the table.

Rose O'Neal Greenhow and daughter imprisoned in Old Capitol Prison in Washington, DC, after being caught passing secrets to the South by Pinkerton.

Mata Hari dancing at a garden party in Paris, accompanied by a Javanese orchestra.

Marthe Richer (codenamed *Alouette* – the 'Lark'), accomplished aviatrix and spy.

Fraulein Doktor: Elsbeth Schragmüller (1887–1940)

Kenji Doihara (1883–1948)
the so-called 'Lawrence of
Manchuria', shown here,
*c.*1940.

'Henry' Pu Yi and 'Elizabeth' Wan Jung seen here in 1933.

German general Heinz Guderian in his command vehicle in France, June 1940, showing an Enigma machine being used at bottom left.

Abwehr chief, Admiral Wilhelm Canaris (1885–1945) c.1940.

SD Chief, Walter Schellenberg (1910–53).

US codebreaker William F. Friedman (1891–1969). The strain of breaking the Japanese 'Purple' code in 1940 caused Friedman to suffer a breakdown.

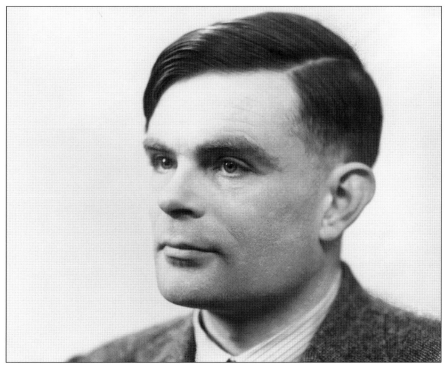

Alan Turing (1912–54), mathematical genius, codebreaker and one of the founding fathers of the computer age. Turing committed suicide in 1954 by eating an apple laced with cyanide after the police discovered his homosexuality.

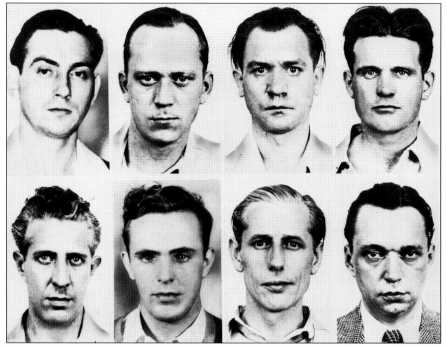

The 'Pastorius' Nazi saboteurs. From the top (left to right) Herman Neubauer, Henrich Harm Heinck, Werner Thiel and Edward John Kerling; bottom, Richard Quirin, Herbert Hans Haupt, George Dasch and Ernest Peter Burger.

Chart used by Japanese pilot in Pearl Harbor attack. The chart identifies ship mooring locations and is entitled at upper left: 'Report on positions of enemy fleet at anchorage A'.

FBI Chief J. Edgar Hoover demonstrates how to use a machine gun to baseball legend Mickey Cochrane, then manager of the Detroit Tigers.

Felix Dzerzhinsky, the first head of the
Soviet secret service, *c.*1920.

Lavrenti Beria, photographed in 1953.

Richard Sorge.

Atomic spy Klaus Fuchs.

Reinhard Gehlen (1902–79), the former head of German intelligence on the Eastern Front during WWII.

Oleg Penkovsky hears he has been sentenced to death in Moscow's Soviet Supreme Court on 11 May 1963.

Director of Mossad from 1952 to 1963, Isser Harel was responsible for the 1960 capture of fugitive Nazi war criminal Adolf Eichmann.

fell out violently, both accusing each other of being a real German agent. The true details of what happened were never satisfactorily explained, but *Biscuit* claimed a German plane had flashed the trawler at a different time to the agreed rendezvous. Suspecting *Snow* had double-crossed him, *Biscuit* ordered the trawler to turn back.

When *Snow* was searched he was found to be carrying papers which had not been provided by his MI5 case officer, the inference being that he was a triple-cross agent still working for the Germans. The source of this information turned out to be a London restaurateur named William Rolph. *Snow* had secretly recruited Rolph, who was given the Abwehr number A3554. MI5 interviewed Rolph, who admitted he was the author of the report and would co-operate fully. This situation left MI5 in a fix, for if they prosecuted Rolph or *Snow* the double-cross operation would be blown. While deliberating what to do, Rolph pre-empted everyone by sticking his head inside a gas oven and committing suicide. Even this caused more problems than it solved. If the Abwehr realized that their agent had committed suicide they would probably suspect he had been blown. The coroner was ordered to record that Rolph had died of a heart attack.[12]

After a long interrogation MI5 decided to continue with *Snow*'s case. To the Germans *Snow* explained that the trawler had not been able to find the submarine in the fog, but that *Biscuit* would travel to Portugal instead. Arriving on 27 April 1940, Ritter provided *Biscuit* with a radio of his own, an Abwehr questionnaire and $3,000. What the British did not quite yet understand was that these few double agents were in fact the sum total of German agents operating in the United Kingdom.

Between April and September 1940 only sporadic attempts were made to infiltrate more agents into Britain. Six Abwehr agents were picked up and arrested in the Irish Republic, two of whom at least were under orders to rendezvous with *Snow* in Britain. A British double agent in Lisbon codenamed *Sweetie* had recruited two Czechs for the Abwehr, who were sent on to London and became *Giraffe* and *Spanehl*, but were only of limited effect. In early September a four-strong Abwehr team was landed on Britain's south coast only to be picked up and arrested. Because of the publicity their arrests received, none of the agents were suitable for double-cross work. Therefore the authorities made an example and executed three of them, the fourth being interned for the rest of the war. The execution of some German agents was very much a necessary evil. On one hand it was good for civilian morale, but more importantly it reinforced the credibility of the double agents. If no German agents had been caught, the Abwehr would surely have become suspicious of their easy success.

Meanwhile *Snow* was alerted to the arrival of agent '3719' who was dropped by parachute in Northamptonshire on 4 September. The agent was a Swedish national named Gösta Caroli. He was arrested and taken to the MI5 interrogation centre at Latchmere House in Ham, Middlesex, codenamed 'Camp 020'. This was a specially designed detention centre for enemy spies. The building had been modified to prevent communication between inmates, with listening devices placed in cells and pipes buried within masonry to prevent prisoners tapping signals to one another. Typically the first interrogation would take place a few days after capture so that information could be compiled. The interrogators refrained from torture, but attempted to break the spy by impressing on them the hopelessness of his position and the 'omniscience and omnipotence' of the British security service. Later in the war, if a prisoner refused to co-operate they would be shown the obituaries of executed prisoners. As a last resort, the prisoners would be put in solitary confinement and have all privileges removed, including their daily ration of three cigarettes.[13]

In this case Caroli co-operated very quickly and revealed that two other agents, Hans Reysen and Wulf Schmidt, were soon to follow him. Caroli agreed to work for the British and received the codename *Summer*. He radioed Hamburg claiming he had injured himself landing and had been unable to report at once. There then followed an entirely notional 'rescue' mission in which *Snow* sent *Biscuit* to collect *Summer* and bring him to a safe house in London.

On 19 September Wulf Schmidt parachuted into Cambridgeshire and was picked up by the local Home Guard, who thought he was acting suspiciously. He arrived at Camp 020 on 21 September but would not co-operate and even taunted his interrogators how they would all soon be prisoners of the German army, which was preparing to invade. After 13 days of interrogation, Schmidt changed his tune and agreed to co-operate, receiving the codename *Tate*.

The acquisition of these and other double agents presented a problem to MI5. If they were to be exploited to the full they had to maintain their credibility with the Abwehr by delivering plausible answers to their questionnaires. The trouble was in deciding exactly what to tell the Germans. Until this point, running the double agents had been the preserve of MI5's 'B' Division, which was under the control of Guy Liddell (1892–1958) throughout the war years. Although 'B' Division had proved itself very adept at capturing and turning spies, it was ill suited to providing them with suitable intelligence. This information could only come from the armed services and other government bodies. For example, if an agent was asked 'should the Luftwaffe continue bombing London or switch to targets in the Midlands' – who was qualified to make such life and death decisions? Such decisions needed to be made by a special body of all the interested parties, and such was the origin of the celebrated Twenty Committee, which met for the first time on 2 January 1941.

The Twenty Committee was so named because the numeral '20' in Latin is formed by a double cross – XX. It was chaired by the Oxford don John Masterman (1891–1977), who among other things had written a detective novel in 1933 called *An Oxford Tragedy*. Present at the first meeting were representatives from the War Office, GHQ Home Forces, Home Defence Executive, Air Ministry Intelligence, Air Ministry Deception, NID (Naval Intelligence), MI6 and, of course, MI5 itself. Masterman presented the meeting with a memorandum defining the problems faced with running double agents. Unless the services were prepared to provide the agents with traffic containing enough truth to stand up under German scrutiny, the double agents would be lost. If, however, they could be maintained, MI5 would not only control German intelligence's picture of Britain, but also gain intelligence on the German secret services and divert German secret service funds into British coffers. Perhaps most fundamentally, once established, the double agents could then be used to deceive the Germans over Allied operations.[14]

It cannot be emphasized enough how the keystone to the success of the double-cross system lay in the security of the British Isles. If uncontrolled German agents reported differently to the double-cross agents the Abwehr may have realized the dupe. It was vital therefore that all active German agents were under MI5 control. At the outbreak of war the British had formed a Radio Security Service (RSS) to watch out for transmissions by German agents. In fact RSS had picked up

Snow's radio transmissions from Wandsworth Prison. If there had been more agents at large there was a good chance RSS would catch them.

However, the key to security came from the operations of the GCCS at Bletchley Park. A special section at Bletchley studied all Abwehr traffic not passing through Enigma machines. The radio sets and codes used by *Snow* and *Tate* helped this section break into Abwehr traffic by December 1940, the decrypts of which were codenamed *ISOS*. It was another 12 months before Bletchley broke into the Abwehr's Engima traffic, which became designated *ISK*. Unfortunately for MI5, Bletchley was considered so secret that only the head of MI6 received the Abwehr decrypts. Much to MI5's dismay, MI6 would only feed it the information it considered strictly relevant for MI5's purposes. Inter-service rivalry was not a problem limited to Germany.

At the same time as the Twenty Committee was being formed, trouble flared up with *Summer*. The Swedish agent had begun suffering from depression. In one gloomy session he let slip a piece of information he had not previously told his interrogators. *Summer* was sent back to Camp 020 where he slashed his wrists in a suicide attempt. In order to relieve the pressure on him, *Summer* was transferred to Hinxton where he had spent Christmas with *Tate*. On 13 January the pressure finally became too much for *Summer* who half throttled his guard to death – apologizing profusely to him for having to do so – then escaped on a motorcycle in the direction of the east coast. If *Summer* made it back to Germany the double-cross game would be blown, so a major manhunt ensued. *Summer* was spotted and shot in the leg while trying to escape. He was returned to Camp 020 and thereafter detained. In the meantime *Snow* radioed Hamburg that *Summer* was under suspicion and had gone to ground at an unknown location.

Also in January 1941 plans were made for *Snow* to visit Ritter in Lisbon. With him was a new recruit given the cover name *Celery*. The new agent was introduced to Ritter as Jack Brown of the RAF, who had been refused a commission because of a criminal conviction. In fact *Celery*'s real name was Dicketts and he had served in air intelligence during WWI. He had blundered into the world of espionage after spotting *Snow* meeting with 'Tar' Robertson, head of B1a, the division responsible for the day-to-day management of the double-cross agents. Being the upstanding citizen he was, Dicketts reported *Snow* and Robertson to the police for acting suspiciously. When he met Ritter in

Lisbon, *Celery* put up such a good performance that he was sent to Hamburg for three weeks of further interrogation, which he luckily survived.

When *Snow* and *Celery* returned to the UK, the case finally fell apart. While being debriefed, *Snow* claimed that he had told Ritter everything while *Celery* was in Hamburg. This confession puzzled the British authorities – if *Snow* had confessed everything, why had *Celery* been released? It was clear *Snow* wanted out and his case was run down by March 1941, explaining to the Germans he was suffering a serious illness. *Snow* was afterwards interned at Camp 001, a hospital wing in Dartmoor prison. Unfortunately, with *Snow*'s demise the cases of *Celery*, *Biscuit* and *Charlie* also came to an end.

Of Snow's network only *GW* still remained operational. In September 1940 *GW* had received a postcard from a Spaniard named Del Pozo who wanted a meeting. At the rendezvous, Del Pozo handed over £4,000 in return for *GW*'s latest reports. MI5 investigated Del Pozo and found he was working at the Spanish embassy for the press attaché, Alcazar de Velasco – a known Spanish secret agent. Del Pozo was recalled to Spain in February 1941, but *GW* managed to contact Luis Calvo who had replaced Velasco as press attaché. Through Calvo *GW* was able to pass a number of bulky intelligence reports and secret documents unsuitable for radio transmission to the Abwehr using the embassy's secure diplomatic pouches. However, in February 1942 he too was forced to close down after Calvo was arrested.

The star performer through early 1941 became *Tate* who, while dutifully completing the intelligence questionnaires sent to him from Hamburg, signalled that he was badly short of funds.[15] Hamburg replied that two parachutists would bring money with them. Josef Jakobs landed on 29 January followed by Karel Richter on 14 May. Both these agents were caught and sentenced to death. The Abwehr then arranged for Mitinory Yosii, the assistant naval attaché at the Japanese embassy, to deliver money to *Tate* on a London bus.

A long-term solution to funding *Tate*'s operation was worked out by MI5 – codenamed *Plan Midas*, which centred around the flamboyant Yugoslav double agent Dusko Popov (1912–81), codenamed *Tricycle*. Popov was recruited to the Abwehr in 1940 by a student friend in the service, Johann Jebsen. Popov reported this advance to the British embassy at Belgrade and was advised to play along, but to keep the embassy informed. With British approval, Popov came to Britain via Lisbon and in addition to a supply of secret ink and his Abwehr questionnaire, he brought the information that Jebsen was an anti-Nazi Anglophile who might make a good double agent himself.

Tricycle returned to Lisbon to report to a Major von Karstoff – in fact Colonel von Auenrode, the Abwehr station chief – who advised him to recruit some assistants in London. *Tricycle* then went to Madrid to meet his friend Jebsen who was later codenamed *Artist* by the British. Returning to London *Tricycle* was given two assistants codenamed *Balloon* – a former officer turned arms dealer – and *Gelatine*, the codename of Friedle Gaertner, an apparent pro-Nazi Austrian who had been used by MI5 as an *agent provocateur*.

Like *Tate*, *Tricycle* needed a secure means of obtaining funds. In a second meeting with von Karstoff in March 1941, *Tricycle* revealed he was acquainted with a rich Jewish theatre agent who was eager to build up a cash reserve in America in case Britain lost the war. The deal was for the Germans to pay *Tricycle* a sum of money he would deposit in a New York bank. The theatre agent would then pay £20,000 to *Tricycle*'s nominee in England. This person would be chosen by the Germans and was of course *Tate* who by now was their principal agent. The most important outcome of *Plan Midas* was MI5 could see how much confidence the Abwehr placed in both *Tate* and *Tricycle*. On the Abwehr's part, their trust in *Tricycle* was secured because they too gained from *Plan Midas* by taking a percentage cut of the money that went straight into their own pockets.

In August 1941 *Tricycle* was sent by the Abwehr to America to set up new networks and complete a questionnaire on the defences at Pearl Harbor. The details of this mission are given in the next chapter, but needless to say it was a fiasco. *Tricycle* was by anyone's standards a playboy, which put him at odds with Hoover's puritanical FBI. Worse, the FBI had no intention of allowing *Tricycle* to set up networks of double-agents *à la* Twenty Committee, but instead wanted *Tricycle* to help them catch Nazi spies and make headlines. The mission was so badly mismanaged it almost blew *Tricycle*'s standing with the Abwehr. Nor did it help that MI6 initially failed to inform MI5 that ISOS decrypts showed the Abwehr was suspicious of *Tricycle*. By the summer of 1942 *Tricycle* returned to Lisbon for a face-off with his Abwehr control. London did not think their agent would survive the interrogation, but *Tricycle* went on the offensive, accusing Lisbon of not providing him with enough funds to accomplish his mission. Von Karstoff apologized and provided *Tricycle* with a new questionnaire and £25,000.[16]

Despite the Allies' growing success, it was not all one-way traffic in their favour. As Venlo proved, the German secret services could be just as effective. Since the beginning of the war German navy codebreakers had successfully broken the Allied merchant shipping code, which greatly assisted the U-boat wolf packs and led to the deaths of over 30,000 merchant sailors, not to mention the loss of more than 2,200 ships in the North Atlantic alone. Late in 1939 codebreakers had also noticed the solo voyage of the *Automedon* on a mission to the Far East. A disguised German commerce raider, *Atlantis* intercepted the *Automedon* on 11 November and found it carrying top-secret mail for the British high command in the Far East, and on the defences of Singapore. These documents were shared with the Japanese and proved most interesting to the Strike South faction: London basically told its forces in the Far East that if Japan attacked, they could expect no help at all.

Also in the field of signals intelligence, Schellenberg revealed how they had 'tapped' the main cable between England and America using shortwave instruments and were able to listen in on telephone conversations. Most of these concerned requests for reinforcements and materials, which proved useful for planning U-boat raids on convoys. In early 1944 a five-minute conversation between Churchill and Roosevelt was deciphered concerning the forthcoming invasion and ended in Roosevelt telling Churchill: 'Well, we will do our best – now I will go fishing.'[17]

Probably the most successful German spy in World War II was Ilyas Bazna, codenamed *Cicero*. Employed as the valet to British ambassador Sir Hughe Knatchbull-Hugessen (nicknamed 'Snatch') in Istanbul, *Cicero* photographed documents from his safe and sold them to the German ambassador, Franz von Papen. Through *Cicero* the Germans first learned the codename for the Allied invasion of France – *Overlord* – and details of secret negotiations held in conferences between Stalin, Churchill and Roosevelt. Although Schellenberg believed *Cicero's* information was correct, he was highly suspicious of the spy's motives. When certain photographs suggested *Cicero* had an accomplice – a hand could be seen holding one of the pages photographed by *Cicero* – Schellenberg wondered if in fact the spy worked for the Turkish secret service.

In the spring of 1944, the British finally learned a spy was at work in their embassy, through information provided by Fritz Kolbe, a German providing intelligence to Allen Dulles, the American in charge of the Office of Strategic Services (OSS) mission in Switzerland. Kolbe had intercepted a message from von Papen to the German Foreign Office mentioning that information was being taken out of the British embassy in Ankara by a spy named *Cicero*. Bazna learned an investigation was on the way and promptly disappeared along with the £300,000 in cash he had been paid by the Germans. There was a bitter sting in the tail of this story, although Bazna is said to have laughed it off at the time. Heading for a life of luxury in South America, the £300,000 turned out to be composed entirely of counterfeit notes![18]

Of all the German secret operations against the Western Allies, perhaps the most telling came in 1942. While the British were building their deception operations, the Abwehr was playing one of its own against Dutch members of SOE, which it codenamed *Nordpol* (North Pole). Somewhere between spy and commando, the Special Operations Executive (SOE) was a brainchild of Britain's prime minister, Winston Churchill, who directed SOE agents to 'set Europe ablaze' by organizing local resistance and sabotage. They were active from 1941 and carried out a number of highly important coups, including the assassination of RSHA chief Reinhard Heydrich in 1942 and the destruction of the Norwegian heavy water plant at Vemork in 1943, which effectively ended the Nazi atomic bomb programme.

In Holland, however, the organization met with disaster. On 6 March 1942 Dutchman Huub Lauwers was about to transmit to England from an apartment in The Hague when four black cars pulled up outside. Lauwers asked the landlady to drop his radio from the back window while he tried to escape. As Lauwers walked away, one of the black cars pulled up and two Abwehr officers arrested him. His radio set was also recovered, as it had inconveniently landed on a washing line.

Lauwers was captured carrying a list of ciphered texts, which the Germans quickly broke because one of Lauwers' colleagues had betrayed the network to the Abwehr. Lauwers was offered a stark choice: either continue transmitting normally back to London on behalf of the Germans or be handed over to the Gestapo. All SOE agents had been warned that there was a high chance of capture and according to Lauwers he had been told to carry on transmitting for the Germans if captured, but to omit a special security code. With the code missing, his controllers in London would know their agent was in enemy hands.[19]

However, when Lauwers therefore began transmitting without the security code his controllers in London carried on as usual. To Lauwers' horror they continued to transmit back and announced the arrival of another agent whom the Germans subsequently picked up. For the next 18 months Abwehr major Hans Giskes played what was called *Englandspiel* – the England game. Firmly the victor, Giskes was able to infiltrate the SOE's 'N' Section – the Dutch division – and capture over 50 of its agents. The fact that SOE ignored Lauwers' lack of radio security for so long was such a monumental oversight that many have wondered if the British continued to send their agents in as a double bluff to the Germans – making it look as though they were more interested in Holland than was really the case. Others have argued against this and blame the whole thing as a tragic blunder.[20]

In fact, back in Baker Street, London – of Sherlock Holmes fame – Leo Marks was in charge of the codes used by SOE agents. He began to suspect something was wrong in Holland because the messages received from there were always perfectly delivered. Elsewhere, SOE radio operators were working in such extremely stressful conditions that messages were often garbled, hurried or stopped halfway through, as the operators tried to evade detection by the German detector vans outside. This was never the case in Holland.[21] Separately from Marks' investigation, another radio operator was suspicious of the Dutch traffic. At the end of receiving one message, the London operator typed out the letters 'HH' for *Heil Hitler*, which is how German agents signed off. Back came the same reply 'HH' from Holland.

In March 1943 Marks presented his evidence to Colin Gubbins, head of SOE operations and training. Although unconvinced, Gubbins set up an internal enquiry, which resulted in no more agents being sent to Holland after July 1943. Around the time of the March meeting, Dutch SOE agent Pieter Dourlein (codenamed *Sprout*) was dropped into Holland. He too was arrested on landing, but later managed to escape from Haaren prison with fellow SOE agent Johan Ubbink (*Chive*), a radio operator who had been parachuted into Holland the previous November. When the two men reached Switzerland they informed the Dutch military attaché how the Germans had been forewarned of their arrival. When the two eventually got back to England via Spain they were arrested by the British, who suspected them of being double agents![22]

Returning to the affairs of the British Twenty Committee, while *Tricycle* had been away in Lisbon a new star performer had emerged. The Spaniard Juan Pujol had an inherent dislike of the Nazis and of his own volition decided he would play his part, however small, in helping to defeat the fascists. After discussing the business with his wife, Pujol decided to offer his services to the British as a spy. In January 1941 his wife went to the British consulate in Madrid and said she knew someone who would be willing to spy for Britain. The consular official told her that Britain was not interested in such offers. Rather than be discouraged, Pujol decided he would prove his worth before going to the British again. He went to the German embassy and volunteered to travel to Lisbon as an informant, or even to England if they could find a means of getting him there.

Pujol travelled to Lisbon and spent the next nine months in Portugal writing letters to the Germans, pretending he was in Britain and actively spying. Pujol was remarkably inventive. Because the letters he sent were not franked by the British post office, Pujol explained how he had recruited a KLM pilot on the Lisbon–London route as an unwitting courier. For information on Britain – a country he had never visited – he bought himself a 'Blue Guide' to England, Bradshaw's railway timetable and a large map of the country.

His first message was written in October 1941 and revealed that he had recruited three sub-agents: one in Glasgow, another in Liverpool and one from the West Country. Later Pujol claimed the BBC had offered him a job and that there were landing-craft manoeuvres being conducted on Lake Windermere. Despite a complete lack of awareness of day-to-day information, including how to add up his expenses in British currency and claiming that Glasgow dockers would 'do anything for a litre of wine', Pujol was fully believed by the Germans who codenamed him *Arabel*. All the while, Pujol had been trying to gain the attention of the British authorities, but to no avail.

Bletchley Park had been reading about *Arabel* on the Madrid–Berlin wireless and passed the information on to MI6 who did not disclose it. MI5 only learned about the existence of *Arabel* in February 1942 when a Lisbon-based intelligence officer returned to London and mentioned him in passing. At a subsequent meeting of the Twenty Committee MI6 came clean about *Arabel* and by 12 March contact had been made with the Spaniard through the offices of the US naval attaché in Lisbon, to whom Pujol had gone out of frustration. Again the lack of co-operation between MI6 and MI5 had almost caused the double-cross system irreparable damage. If *Arabel* had reported things as very different to the deceptions being concocted by the Twenty Committee, the whole project would be blown. It was decided to bring Pujol to Britain and have him operate under MI5 control. Pujol arrived in England on 24 April 1942 and received the codename *Garbo*.

He was taken to London and given over to his case officer, the Spanish-speaking Tomás Harris, with whom he formed a brilliant partnership.[23] Between them, Pujol and Harris wrote hundreds of letters each heavily padded with long and deliberately confusing passages of verbose nonsense. Together *Garbo* and Harris dreamt up an entirely fictitious network, which by its peak in 1944 had included 27 highly believable sub-agents. These included five immediate contacts:

J1, the KLM pilot courier who carried letters to Lisbon
J2, an RAF officer at Fighter Command HQ
J3, an official in the Spanish section, Ministry of Information
J4, an official in the Censorship department, Ministry of
    Information
J5, a girlfriend employed as a secretary in the Ministry of War

In addition there were the following agents and sub-agents:

Agent 1, Carvalho, a Portuguese commercial traveller based
    in South Wales
Agent 2, Gerbers, a German-Swiss businessman located in Bootle
    by the River Mersey
Agent 2:1, Gerbers' widow recruited after his 'death' in
    November 1942
Agent 3, a Venezuelan in Glasgow with three sub-agents forming
    the *Benedict* network:
Agent 3:1, an NCO in the RAF
Agent 3:2, a lieutenant in the notional 49th Infantry Division

Agent 3:3, a Greek sailor and communist based on the Scottish east coast

Agent 4, Fred, a Gibraltese waiter later working in a munitions depot at Chislehurst caves

Agent 4:1, a radio ham who transmitted *Garbo*'s messages after March 1943

Agent 4:2, a guard at Chislehurst caves

Agent 4:3, an American sergeant in the US supply service

Agent 5, the brother of Agent 3, based in Canada

Agent 5:1, an American commercial traveller and cousin of Agent 5

Agent 6, Dick, an anti-British South African working in the War Office

Agent 7, Stanley, a Welsh Nationalist and leader of the *Dagobert* network, comprising:

Agent 7:1, a British soldier in the 9th Armoured Division

Agent 7:2, David, a Welsh nationalist and founder of the 'Brothers in the Aryan World Order'

Agent 7:3, Theresa Jardine, mistress of Agent 7:4 and secretary to 7:2's movement

Agent 7:4, 'Rags', an Indian poet living in Brighton

Agent 7:5, an unnamed member of the 'Brothers in the Aryan World Order' group

Agent 7:6, an unnamed member of the 'Brothers in the Aryan World Order' group

Agent 7:7, the treasurer to the 'Brothers in the Aryan World Order' group[24]

Believing *Garbo* had such a huge network, coupled with *Tate*, *Tricycle* and a number of others, the Germans did not see the need to infiltrate any more agents into the UK. Therefore, as the tide began to turn against the Nazis, MI5 controlled every German agent operating inside Britain. This allowed the organization to cause Germany untold damage.

From its inception, the Twenty Committee's aim had been to build up confidence in the double agents to the point where they could be used to deceive the Germans over Allied strategy. The first of these deceptions came in support of the Allied *Torch* landings in North Africa in 1942. *Garbo* strongly hinted that an attack might in fact be made against the French coastline around Normandy or Brittany, which put the German forces in north-west France on high alert. To cover the deception, *Garbo* actually sent the Germans a warning of the *Torch* landings. It was ensured that this warning arrived too late for it to be of any use to the Germans, who were nonetheless impressed by *Garbo*'s attempt to alert them.

Having established the credibility of the double agents, the climax of the Twenty Committee's plan came to fruition in Operation *Fortitude*. The Germans knew that the Allies would invade Europe in 1944 and looked to their agents for details. To protect the invasion – codenamed *Overlord* – the Allies used the double agents to deliver a series of plausible untruths, the main ones being *Fortitude North*, a bogus plan that an amphibious landing would take place in Norway, and *Fortitude South*, that the main landings in northern France would take place in the Pas de Calais, not Normandy as was the case.

In addition to the double-cross agents, false radio traffic and physical deceptions (including dummy landing craft and tanks) would indicate the presence of the large First US Army Group (FUSAG) in the south-east. This subsidiary of *Fortitude South* was codenamed Operation *Quicksilver*. FUSAG was an entirely notional formation placed under the command of US general George S. Patton (1885–1945), consisting of 11 non-existent divisions.

The key part of the plan was to take place after the landings in Normandy. *Garbo*'s network was to convince the Germans to hold back reserves in the Calais region. To do this *Garbo* transmitted a warning signal at 3:00am on 6 June, just a matter of hours before the first assault troops hit the beaches. Unfortunately Madrid was off the air at the time and did not receive the message until 6:08am. This mistake on Madrid's part further reinforced *Garbo*'s credibility, which was crucial when the Spaniard sent what was perhaps his most important message of all.

Around midnight on the 8/9 June, *Garbo* sent an urgent message for the attention of German high command (OKW). This reported that Patton's FUSAG had not moved from south-east England and that all indications were that the Normandy landings were only diversionary, with the main blow still aimed at Calais. This message reached OKW on the evening of 9 June, a few hours after a separate source had claimed the same thing. This separate source was an uncontrolled Abwehr agent in Stockholm, Karl Heinz Kraemer, codenamed *Josephine*. On this evidence

OKW halted the movement of 1st SS Panzer Division towards Normandy and diverted it to reinforce the German Fifteenth Army in Belgium, which consisted of 19 infantry and two armoured divisions – all of which were held back from the battle of Normandy in expectation of FUSAG's attack.

The deception continued into July when General Patton took command of the US Third Army to lead the Allied breakout from Normandy. To explain how Patton ended up in a subordinate command to General Bradley, *Garbo* came up with a typically imaginative cover story which he transmitted on 20 July. The Spaniard revealed how Patton was furious that his best units were being sent to reinforce the Normandy front and after a bitter argument had been demoted by Eisenhower on the spot. FUSAG was still being spoken of well into September. On 29 July 1944 *Garbo* was informed that Hitler had awarded him the Iron Cross for his services.

Also working on the FUSAG deception had been a number of other agents including *Tate* who was notionally doing agricultural work in Kent where much of Patton's phantom army was based. Seen as much more valuable by the Germans was *Tricycle*, who took a large amount of information with him on a trip to Lisbon in March 1944. Another key double agent involved with the build-up to D-Day was *Brutus*. This was the codename of Polish Air Force captain Roman Czerniawski. After the fall of France he had set up an espionage/resistance network in France known as Interallié. He was joined by the nurse Mathilde Carré who took the codename *La Chatte* (The Cat). In November 1941 Interallié was penetrated by the Abwehr's Hugo Bleicher with both *Brutus* and Carré arrested. *Brutus* agreed to work for the Germans and travel to England, but as soon as he arrived in the country he went to the authorities and explained what had happened to Interallié. He then began to work as part of the double-cross system. Mathilde Carré also agreed to work for the Germans and was sent to London in February 1942 in order to penetrate SOE. She was arrested by MI5 and spent the rest of the war in Holloway prison. *Brutus*, meanwhile, had the good fortune to be posted as a Polish liaison officer to FUSAG, allowing him to deliver notional intelligence.

One of the more flamboyant double agents was Eddie Chapman (codenamed *Zig-Zag*), who provided the inspiration for the 1967 film *Triple Cross*. Imprisoned on Jersey for safe breaking and burglary before the war, Chapman was recruited after the German occupation of the island and codenamed *Fitzchen*. Highly trained in sabotage, parachuting and radio operation, Chapman was parachuted into Britain in December 1942. His mission was to sabotage the production of Mosquito bombers at the De Havilland factory in Hatfield, Hertfordshire. Instead Chapman went straight to the authorities on landing, which is just as well, because they already had detailed information on him, including ISOS intercepts of his wireless transmissions while training.[25]

With Chapman in custody MI5 decided to carry out his sabotage mission 'notionally' and ensure it was well reported in the newspapers, which were provided with photographs purportedly showing damage to the aircraft factory. After receiving guarantees that his daughter would be provided for if he did not return, Chapman returned to the Germans who awarded him the Iron Cross for bravery. Chapman then spent 15 months as an Abwehr instructor living the high life on his earnings. He was sent back to Britain late in June 1944 to report on damage being inflicted by the V1 flying bombs. However, *Zig-Zag*'s tendency to talk about himself and the fact he had revealed his true identity to a Norwegian girlfriend meant the case was wound down.[26]

While the Twenty Committee was enjoying its greatest success, the Abwehr was in ruins and Canaris was under house arrest. Himmler had long been waiting for the opportunity to topple Canaris and had been building a dossier on his failures, for example not having warned Hitler of the Allied landings in North Africa, Sicily or Italy. Canaris had also encouraged a secret operation to save Jews from the Holocaust – he put his overtly anti-Nazi deputy Hans Oster in charge of Operation U-7, a scheme to infiltrate Abwehr agents into the United States disguised as Jewish refugees. In fact the agents were Jewish friends of Canaris and Oster, something which eventually became known to Himmler. The final nail in the coffin came after an Abwehr official named Erich Vermehren defected to the Allies in February 1944. Himmler pounced and Canaris was sacked.

From the outset, the Abwehr had suffered from a number of major handicaps. First, it had no means of analyzing the intelligence data it received from the field. Instead the raw information was circulated to whichever recipient appeared the most interested party. Second, when information was presented by the Abwehr it was often viewed with extreme scepticism. The German army preferred its intelligence to originate from more trustworthy sources – signals interception, captured documentation, POW interrogation, air reconnaissance and so on. Then of course was the crossover of duties between the Abwehr and RSHA – the lesson of history, which the Germans ignored, was that intelligence gathering has to be centralized. Fundamentally the Abwehr and SD were singing from different hymn books throughout the course of the war.

As an organization the Abwehr was anti-Nazi and in general opposed to Hitler and his cronies. Canaris surrounded himself with like-minded subordinates, including Oster, who had taken a lead role in several plots to topple Hitler and gathered evidence on Nazi atrocities. The head of Abwehr I, Piekenbrock, was so anti-Nazi that he appeared to encourage inefficiency in his department, which may help to explain why his department's agents in Britain were not scrutinized carefully enough. Piekenbrock was replaced in March 1943 by Colonel George Hansen.

Although Hansen made a good first impression, he was in fact an active conspirator in the 20 July 1944 plot to kill Hitler. Just a month before the end of the war, Hitler signed his execution order, which was carried out at Flossenbürg concentration camp. On 9 April 1945 Canaris, Oster and several other figures behind the 20 July plot were led naked to their place of execution before a crowd of jeering SS troops. Canaris was cruelly hanged by the neck on piano wire and his corpse left unburied to rot. As will be seen, the irony is that far bigger traitors than Canaris, much closer to Hitler, were at work inside the Third Reich.

12

AXIS SPIES
AGAINST AMERICA

*'The Japanese for many years had the reputation,
and the facts bore out that reputation, of being
meticulous seekers for every scrap of
information, whether by photography or by
written report or otherwise.'*

Admiral Wilkinson, *Report of the Joint Committee on the
Investigation of the Pearl Harbor Attack*[1]

In 1931 a book was published entitled *The American Black Chamber*
by Herbert Yardley, former chief of America's Cipher Bureau. This
book told the story of how, following World War I, the US Army and
State Department formed a cryptanalytic organization known as MI-8.
Disguised as a commercial business in New York City, it was MI-8's job
to break foreign diplomatic codes. It was then shut down in 1929 after
Secretary of State Henry Stimson declared, 'Gentlemen do not read each
other's mail.'

The organization's moment of glory had come during the Washington
Naval Conference on Naval Limitation, which opened on 12 November
1921. This conference was headed by the world's three main naval powers:
the United States, Britain and Japan. The key negotiation revolved around
the ratio of battleship tonnage allowed between them. US Secretary
Hughes proposed a ratio of 5:5:3, with Japan receiving the smaller share.
His argument was that if Japan was allowed an equal tonnage it would
dominate the Pacific, as both Britain and America required ships to protect
their interests in other waters. The Japanese negotiators did not agree and
held out for a ratio of 10:10:7 or at worst 10:10:6.5.

Yardley described how his staff broke the Japanese ciphers and read
Tokyo's secret instructions to its negotiators. At all costs they were to

avoid a clash with Britain and America and, if necessary, agree with Hughes' demands. This information was passed on to Hughes who, armed with his best poker face, held out, knowing the Japanese would eventually buckle to American demands.

Yardley was never prosecuted for this leak, for to do so the American government would have to admit the cipher bureau had indeed existed. Yardley's book became an international bestseller, shifting 33,119 copies in Japan alone. Needless to say, the Japanese government was furious at the revelations. Tensions had already developed between the two countries following the US 1924 Immigration Act, which barred Japanese immigration to the United States. The law provoked widespread anti-Americanism, which was only fuelled by the Yardley revelations. In 1934 Japan denounced the Washington agreement and began unlimited naval construction. When the Sino-Japanese conflict escalated with the bombing of Shanghai and the infamous 'Rape of Nanking' in 1937–38, relations with the United States deteriorated still further. Japan joined the Axis with Germany and Italy in 1940 and was allowed to occupy French Indo-China following the fall of France. In retaliation America froze Japanese assets and put an oil embargo on Japan. Japan now reached its Rubicon. It could pull back from its conquests, or go to war with America.

Although the Japanese had been spying in North, South and Central America for years, in early 1941 they began enlarging their espionage activities in the United States. According to one Japanese spy active at the time, Japan's policy was to maintain two distinct espionage systems in America.[2] The first was centred on the Japanese embassy and regional consulates. Agents operating in them would collect information without compromising their diplomatic status, gathering intelligence from newspapers or on visits to unrestricted sites. The other system saw the use of individual agents with no ties to any Japanese organizations performing illegal activities, including trespassing, theft, paying informants and so on. Working alone, these individuals proved very hard to pick up and even harder to convict. Better still, Japanese officials could deny all knowledge of them and claim the person was nothing more than a misguided individual acting on their own initiative.

To recruit agents in the United States, Japan had the advantage of a large ex-pat Japanese community in North America. US intelligence calculated that as many as 3 per cent of these ex-pats – approximately

3,500 people – had been deliberately placed in the US to act as saboteurs or agents. The most dangerous were considered those of Japanese ancestry born in the United States and who thus qualified as American citizens, but who had been educated in Japan. It was estimated that there were between 600 and 700 in the Los Angeles metropolitan area alone, with at least that many again in other parts of southern California.

Japanese commercial organizations were suspected of spying, but US intelligence was more concerned with the plethora of Japanese 'cultural' societies. Some were clearly organized on paramilitary lines; organizations like the 'Southern California War Veterans' in Los Angeles and San Francisco's 'Association of Japanese in North America Obligated for Military Duty' must have caused concern. Members were suspected of being veterans or reservists in the Japanese army. They were certainly suspected of being ultra-loyal to Japan and important in espionage and sabotage functions. However, to a certain extent these organizations proved a red herring. The bulk of intelligence gathering was done by Japanese diplomatic staff.[3]

On 30 January 1941 a coded message from Tokyo gave the Washington Japanese embassy new directives in light of the deteriorating political situation. The message mapped out a large-scale programme of intelligence gathering. A digest of the message includes the following directives:

- Establish an Intelligence Organ to liaise with private and semi-official Intelligence Organs.
- Determine the political, economic and military strength of the United States.
- Discover all persons or organizations openly or secretly in opposition to the war.
- Investigate anti-Semite, Communist, Black activist, and Labour movements.
- Utilize second-generation Japanese and resident nationals.
- Cooperate with German and Italian Intelligence Organs in the USA.
- Make arrangements to transfer all intelligence operations to Mexico in the event of war with the USA.
- Set up an 'international intelligence route' between Mexico and the USA, Brazil, Argentina, Chile and Peru.

- Cable copies of these instructions under the cover of
  'Minister's orders' to Canada, Mexico, New York, New
  Orleans, Chicago and San Francisco, from where further
  copies should be sent to Honolulu, Los Angeles, Portland,
  Seattle and Vancouver.

This directive was followed by a more comprehensive list sent to
Washington on 15 February 1941. Tokyo wanted specific information on:

- The strengthening or supplementing of military preparations
  on the Pacific Coast and the Hawaii area.
- Ship and plane movements, in particular large bombers and
  sea planes.
- The requisition and modification of merchant vessels.
- Calling up of army and navy personnel, their training,
  manoeuvres and movements.
- 'Words and acts' of minor army and navy personnel.
- Whether Black Americans were being drafted, and, if so,
  under what conditions.
- Those enrolling and graduating as pilots.
- Troop transports to the South Pacific.
- Developments in the manufacture of arms and planes and
  the increase of the labour force.
- Plane movements and shipment of military supplies to
  Alaska and the Aleutian Islands.
- An outlook on US defence measures.
- Travel routes to Central and South America and the South
  Pacific. In particular the shipment of military supplies to
  those areas.

In reply to these requests, on 9 May 1941 the Los Angeles consulate
reported to Tokyo that they had formed close connections with the
Japanese Association, the Chamber of Commerce and newspapers.
They had already established contacts with reliable Japanese in the
areas of San Pedro, San Diego and along the US/Mexican border, who
monitored shipments of aircraft and war materials. They also had
contacts with second-generation Japanese Americans working in
aircraft plants, had prominent people in the 'Negro movement' and

contacts in the movie industry (Hollywood) passing on information about anti-Jewish movements.

The Seattle consulate reported similar success on 11 May 1941. Employers were passing on a steady stream of intelligence on the construction of ships and aircraft, zinc and aluminium production and the yield of tin cans and lumber. Their agents had made contact with anti-Jewish movements, German communists and union members in the Boeing aircraft factory and Bremerton Naval Yard – the key US Pacific naval facility. They also reported that arrangements had been made to collect information from second-generation Japanese-American draftees on matters dealing with troop 'speech and behaviour' – a reference to morale issues.

On 19 May the Japanese embassy in Washington sent a request to Tokyo asking for more funds to spend on intelligence. Their intelligence budget had been $30,000, only $3,900 of which was available for 'developing intelligence', with another $1,800 left over for entertainment and receptions. In the light of the need for more intelligence, they figured they would need $500,000 that year alone. They also requested more staff, asking for at least one-third the number of intelligence personnel they had in Shanghai. They announced the intelligence officer responsible for gathering and investigating secret information would be titled 'press attaché'.

One setback to mainland operations occurred in May 1941 when the FBI reported that they had uncovered espionage activities of Japanese Lieutenant-Commander Itaru Tachibana. Since 1939 Tachibana had been operating as a nightclub owner under the cover name of Mr Yamamoto, spying on US naval technological improvements and heading the biggest West Coast spy network. With echoes of Black Dragon tactics in Manchuria, Tachibana funded his activities through vice – notably the sale of narcotics.[4]

After a tip off, the FBI knew Tachibana was actively spying. However, Tachibana still managed to keep one step ahead of the FBI, getting agents into Seattle, Portland, San Francisco and Los Angeles. He was only caught out by a mistake made by Torchichi Kono, one of his prime agents. Kono emigrated to the United States from Hiroshima around the time of the Russo-Japanese War to study law. In 1916 he was hired by movie star Charlie Chaplin as a valet and can be seen as an 'extra' in some Chaplin movies, including The Circus (1928). In

1934 Kono fell out with Chaplin's third wife and was dismissed. After turning down a managerial job at United Artists Japan, Kono became a lawyer in Los Angeles. At this point the FBI identified him as a possible Japanese spy, but nothing could be proved until Kono attempted to recruit an American named Al Blake.

Kono knew Blake from 1917, when the American appeared in the movie *Shoulder Arms*. In 1940 the two men were reunited at the San Francisco World Fair where Blake was running the 'Candid Camera Artist's Model Studio' – a peep show for amateur photographers. Since they had last met, Blake had served a brief stint in the navy but had subsequently worked as a mannequin-like mime artist with the stage name 'King of the Robots'. Kono expressed an interest in Blake's naval career and told him it was a pity he had left the service as he could have made some money.

A year later, in March 1941, the two had dinner together. Hard-up for cash and remembering Kono's interest in his navy days, Blake lied when he told Kono he was thinking of rejoining the navy. Kono suggested that Blake meet him next day on Hollywood's Santa Monica Boulevard – Blake obliged and was picked up by Kono and Tachibana.[5] Although uncomfortable at being sounded out to spy for the Japanese, Blake played along. He mentioned – falsely – that he had a friend named Jimmy Campbell serving on the battleship USS *Pennsylvania* then stationed at Pearl Harbor. Kono's ears pricked up at this and he offered Blake $2,500 up front if he was prepared to go to Pearl Harbor and ask his friend Jimmy some questions. On completing the mission, Blake was promised another $5,000.

Blake agreed, but then went to the Office of Naval Intelligence (ONI) with the story. ONI quickly realized that they were onto a major case, something confirmed when the FBI revealed their investigation into 'Mr Yamamoto'. Blake was told to play along with the Japanese. When Blake sailed out to Hawaii at Japanese expense, the part of Jimmy Campbell was played by an intelligence officer carrying several papers, mostly on the results of target practice. Blake took the papers and flew back to the West Coast and handed them back to the Japanese.

As a result of this sting, Tachibana and Kono were arrested and accused of 'conspiracy against the United States on behalf of a foreign state'.[6] However, no action was taken. At the personal request of Japanese ambassador Nomura in Washington, the State Department intervened and

Tachibana was returned to Japan. On arriving in Japan he joined the Third Bureau – the intelligence service of the Naval general staff. At the time this bureau was focused on the strength and disposition of the US Pacific Fleet and in particular aircraft carrier construction.[7] However, it would soon turn its attentions to preparing for the attack on Pearl Harbor.

The US Pacific Fleet had arrived in Pearl Harbor in May 1940. Although Pearl Harbor was considered a safe anchorage, there were several key and unique circumstances making it ideal for observation by hostile agents. The first was the island's geography. The port was overlooked by a large mountain, allowing sightseers and spies alike to get good views of the harbour and the boats within it. As will be seen, most scouting missions of the harbour would be carried out by agents 'sightseeing' from the back of taxis. Closer still were the homes and buildings overlooking the harbour.

Much like West Coast America, Hawaii had a large Japanese community, estimated as 160,000 strong in 1941. As was the case in California and other areas, large sections of this community were sympathetic, even enthusiastic, supporters of Japanese expansion. Many subscribed to Japanese war bonds to help finance the war against China, while others shipped recyclable material back to Japan. The Japanese community even raised enough money to buy a warplane for the Japanese navy, which was christened 'The Spirit of Hawaii'.[8]

For 20 years before the outbreak of WWII, the Japanese consulate had appointed so-called *toritsuginin* (consular agents) to assist illiterate Japanese residents with forms required by Japanese national law. In 1941, there were approximately 240 such consular agents active in the Hawaiian Islands, mostly Japanese priests, school teachers and hotel proprietors. Although nothing could be proved, US intelligence and the FBI believed they were responsible for a substantial amount of information collection. However, with just 30 to 40 FBI and ONI investigators available, detailed surveillance of these activists was virtually impossible. Referring to the Japanese community, one American simply said: 'We suspected all of them.'[9]

Although the authorities suspected the consular agents, they were rarely able to press charges against them. Even with an airtight case there were still loopholes for the Japanese to exploit. Admiral Smith had been told that many of the Japanese priests were ex-army officers. When the Americans tried to deport one of these priests 'it was found nothing could be done because of an old agreement between the United States and Japan, based upon our missionary activities of the past, that once a man in the religious status arrived in the country, if he chose to undertake other activities, nothing could be done about it.'[10]

In June 1940 it was discovered that one consular agent on the island of Maui had been requested to report on the presence of the US Fleet including when and if it departed. Following this incident the FBI investigated a number of consular agents. The FBI reports were sent to Washington but it was thought the arrest and prosecution of several hundred Japanese consular agents would create tension between the American and Japanese communities at a time when the US Army was trying to gain the confidence of Japanese residents. The matter was dropped.

Hawaii's large Japanese community was periodically swelled by the arrival of visiting Japanese naval personnel. Until the autumn of 1939, Japanese naval training squadrons regularly visited the Hawaiian Islands on training cruises. It was also common to see Japanese naval oil tankers stop at Honolulu en route between Japan and California. The Americans suspected that personnel from the tankers were left behind in Honolulu on reconnaissance missions, returning to Japan on the next tanker passing through. Although the tanker visits were stopped in 1940, passenger liners of the Japanese-owned NYK (Japan Mail Steamship Company) made frequent stops at Honolulu. Under the guise of sightseeing trips, crews from these ships were as active as the Japanese naval personnel before them.

The navy also worried about the Japanese sampan fleet based at Kewalo Basin, 12 miles (19km) from Pearl Harbor. The fleet was almost entirely manned by Japanese aliens, many of whom were believed to be former naval personnel. The sampans were suspected of smuggling narcotics and there were rumours of their rendezvousing with Japanese submarines operating off the islands of Hawaii. What is more, some of these boats were suspected of being radio equipped and it was not difficult to imagine the crews were actively scouting out the coast and waters round the harbour. American commanders also noted how these boats routinely appeared near naval units taking part in exercises or engaged in target practice.

However, behind this fog of suspects, the real centre of espionage activity on Oahu was the Japanese consulate in Honolulu, located just

7 miles (11km) from Pearl Harbor. Since the arrival of the US Pacific Fleet in May 1940, Consul General Kiichi Gunji had been sending regular reports to the Japanese Foreign Ministry, which were drawn largely from information taken from Honolulu's newspapers. However, it was the acting vice consul, Otojiro Okuda, whom the Americans rightly suspected of heading espionage operations.[11]

Okuda continued reading newspapers for information but made sure agents verified the accounts. Interestingly given American fears, Okuda refrained from recruiting local Japanese as agents and instead relied on his embassy staff to carry out operations. There are several possible reasons for this, but one Japanese intelligence officer discounted the consular agents and natives as being too poorly educated to offer any assistance.[12] Principal among Okuda's agents was the consulate's treasurer, Kohichi Seki. Armed with a copy of *Jane's Fighting Ships*, Seki set to work. Without breaking any US laws, he hired a taxi and began observing the fleet from its window.

Seki passed his reports to Sainon Tsukikawa, the consulate's code man. Once encoded, the messages were sent to Tokyo using the various commercial telegraph communication companies. This means of communication was used because the US government had self-imposed restrictions guaranteeing the privacy of its citizens and residents. The Roberts Commission (18 December–23 January 1941) revealed how the FBI was hampered in uncovering the consulate's activities:

> The United States being at peace with Japan, restrictions imposed prevented resort to certain methods of obtaining the content of messages transmitted by telephone or radio telegraph over the commercial lines operating between Oahu and Japan.[13]

Able to send messages as telegraphs, the Japanese often bypassed the efforts of American codebreakers reading Japanese diplomatic traffic. Following the publication of former codebreaker Yardley's *The American Black Chamber*, the Japanese had made major changes to their code systems. Having introduced an Enigma-type machine codenamed 'Red', in 1937 the Japanese Foreign Ministry switched to an even more sophisticated machine, which the Americans dubbed 'Purple'. This machine was used to convey the most sensitive diplomatic traffic and was mistakenly considered, like the German Enigma, to be unbreakable.

The task of breaking Purple fell to the Signal Intelligence Service (SIS), which had been formed in May 1929 as a part of the Army's Signal Corps. Head of this unit was William Friedman, who in 1939 was told to concentrate on breaking Purple. It was not until August 1940 that Friedman was able to read Japanese messages, by which time he had suffered a nervous breakdown and was forced to retire from service. The information derived from intercepted Foreign Ministry traffic was codenamed 'Magic' and, in an attempt to preserve the secrecy of its source, was restricted to only a few high-level US officials, which did not always include President Roosevelt. Thus Magic intercepts became a double-edged sword. Although the Americans could read what the Japanese were up to, they could not use Magic evidence directly without revealing the source.

Returning to events on Oahu, on 14 March 1941 a new consul, Nagao Kita, arrived onboard the NYK liner *Tatuta Maru*. Following him on 27 March, a Japanese intelligence officer arrived onboard the liner *Nitta Maru* under the pseudonym 'Tadashi Morimura'. His real name was Takeo Yoshikawa, a 28-year-old naval ensign who was to head intelligence operations. Yoshikawa had been forced out of active service due to ill health and had instead moved into naval intelligence. After four years of study, he took the Foreign Ministry's English examination and qualified as a junior diplomat, which provided him with a cover for his real mission on Oahu.

His arrival marked a stepping-up of intelligence gathering on Oahu. Unlike Seki, Yoshikawa was a trained intelligence officer and although he was entirely lacking in any field experience he was an expert on the US Pacific Fleet. To act as a cover, Consul Kita soon gave Yoshikawa the title of Chancellor. Unaware of his real purpose, most of his colleagues inside the embassy viewed Yoshikawa with suspicion and thought him a lazy, hard-drinking womanizer.[14]

Yoshikawa began his secret mission by taking sightseeing trips round the island. Like Seki before him, Yoshikawa conducted many of his fact-finding missions from inside a taxi. By end of April 1941 he had identified a number of vantage points for observing the harbour. Kita had introduced him to a Japanese teahouse called Shuncho-ro, located on the Alewa Heights, a second-floor room overlooking Pearl Harbor and Hickham Field airbase. Dressed as a labourer, Yoshikawa would sometimes work in the cane fields at Aiea, from where he had an excellent view of the naval installations. From sightseeing trips to Pearl City, Yoshikawa noticed how American ships were moored in pairs, which would limit the effect of torpedo attacks. He also noticed that large numbers of ships were in harbour at the weekend and made notes on the direction and duration of air patrols, noting with interest that hardly any of them went in a northerly direction.[15]

When visiting Kaneohe, Yoshikawa invited two female consulate staff out for a boat trip. Having heard rumours that the Americans were looking at Kaneohe as an alternative anchorage, Yoshikawa made sure his pleasure boat had a glass bottom through which he could gauge the depth of the water. From this he saw it would be too shallow for large ships. On 6 August there was a public open day at Wheeler airbase. Although cameras were banned, Yoshikawa attended and gained a lot of information on the base, P-40 aircraft, their pilots and how three aircraft could take off simultaneously.[15]

Yoshikawa lived in constant fear that the FBI might be tapping his telephone or the restaurants he dined at. In fact US intelligence had been suspicious of Yoshikawa from the start. His young age for a diplomat and the fact he was not listed in the official Japanese Diplomatic Registry caused him to be thoroughly investigated. However, despite promptings from the FBI, who had Yoshikawa tailed and had his telephone tapped, the US government could not approve his arrest, as Yoshikawa had been careful not to do anything actually illegal.

At this stage Yoshikawa was unaware of the plans to attack Pearl Harbor, and was merely carrying out the requests sent by Tokyo. He had no feedback from Tokyo concerning his efforts and did not know how he was performing.[17] Unknown to Yoshikawa, in September his reports and other intelligence were the subject of close scrutiny by the Third Bureau. Between October 1940 and June 1942, Japanese naval intelligence was headed by Rear-Admiral Minoru Maeda. He was ably assisted in matters relating to America by Captain Kanji Ogawa, who joined the bureau in 1940 having been assistant naval attaché in Washington. Working with Ogawa on the Pearl Harbor project was Commander Itaru Tachibana, recently returned from his arrest after the Al Blake fiasco.

Ogawa and Tachibana noted how the fleet routinely left harbour on either Monday or Tuesday and returned Saturday or Sunday. From monitoring US radio traffic, they concluded that the American fleet conducted its manoeuvres within 45 minutes' flying time of Pearl

Harbor. Tachibana realized that the success of Admiral Isoroku Yamamoto's plan rested on knowing if the fleet was actually going to be in harbour at the time of the attack. It would be of equal importance to know the exact location of each individual ship so that specific planes could target them. Therefore on 24 September the Foreign Ministry sent message No.83 to Honolulu, which divided the harbour area into sections. This infamous message was intercepted by Magic and later became known as the 'Bomb Plot' message.[18]

The receipt of this message caused a stir in the embassy and at last convinced Yoshikawa that Japan was planning to attack Pearl Harbor.[19] The message called for the waters of Pearl Harbor to be divided into five sub-areas:

Area A, waters between Ford Island and the Arsenal
Area B, waters adjacent to the south and west of Ford Island
Area C, East Loch
Area D, Middle Loch
Area E, West Loch and the communication water routes

The message then asked for Honolulu to report on the warships and aircraft carriers at anchor, tied up at wharves or buoys and in docks. Following Yoshikawa's earlier reports, the message also highlighted the need to mention when two or more vessels were tied up alongside one another.

In reply to this message Yoshikawa reconfigured the areas and assigned codenames to each of them, sending them to Tokyo through Kita on 29 September. The new codes for identifying the locations of vessels were:

KS, Repair dock in Navy Yard
KT, Navy dock in the Navy Yard (the Ten Ten Pier)
FV, moorings in the vicinity of Ford Island
FG, alongside in Ford Island (with east and west sides
    differentiated by A and B respectively)[20]

With a growing sense of urgency, Yoshikawa continued to monitor the comings and goings in the harbour. He decided to get an aerial view of the island, so, dressed in his brightest Hawaiian shirt, he took a geisha girl on a tourist flight over Oahu. He noted the directions of the runways at Wheeler Field and estimated the number of planes by counting the hangers. On 13 October Yoshikawa made another commercial flight. The purpose of this was to confirm that the Americans were not dispersing their fleet into other anchorages – they weren't. He also took time to check on some of the army installations.[21]

The day before Yoshikawa's flight, on 12 October, Japan announced that the three NYK liners would depart Japan heading for the United States. Many suspected that this was in order to evacuate Japanese citizens before the outbreak of war. What nobody appears to have guessed is that their real purpose was to scout the route which would soon be taken by Admiral Yamamoto's carrier force en route to Pearl Harbor.

On board the *Tatuta Maru*, which sailed from Yokohama on 15 October, Captain Sakao Kimura carried a sealed envelope to give to the Japanese Consul General in Honolulu. It was a high-priority message asking Kita for a detailed map showing the exact location of every military installation on Oahu. The ship arrived in Honolulu on 23 October and Kita went aboard to receive the sealed envelope.[22] Kita was also given a sum of cash to be given to a foreign 'sleeper' agent resident on Oahu.

Yoshikawa was sent to meet this sleeper and pass on instructions received from the *Tatuta Maru*. Dr Bernard Julius Otto Kühn was a resident German alien and had been under contract with Japanese naval intelligence since 1935. Kühn had served in the German Imperial Navy during WWI, during which he spent some time in England as a prisoner of war. In 1930 he joined the Nazi Party and became a close friend to Heinrich Himmler, who offered Kühn an appointment with the Gestapo. Kühn's eldest son, Leopold, became private secretary to Joseph Goebbels and Kühn's daughter, Ruth, became Goebbels' mistress.

When this affair became public, Goebbels looked for a way to sweep the embarrassment under the carpet. Opportunity raised its head in the guise of General Haushofer, head of the Geopolitical Department at Berlin University. Haushofer had maintained links with Japanese intelligence since 1914 and was asked to acquire some Europeans for their espionage operations. At Leopold's suggestion, Goebbels put forward the whole Kühn family as a candidate, with the exception of his private secretary. In August 1935, the Kühns found themselves in the unlikely setting of Hawaii.[23] Given a radio transmitter by Okuda in March 1939, Kühn was instructed to lay low and, in the event of war between Japan and the United States, he was to use the transmitter to signal Japanese submarines operating off Oahu.

On 25 October 1941, Yoshikawa took a note to Kühn asking him to make a radio transmission on a certain wavelength to test the equipment. He also instructed Kühn not to engage in any intelligence activities before the outbreak of war, nor contact the Japanese consulate. Finally he told Kühn to simplify his code and paid the German over $14,000 for his troubles.[24]

Privately Yoshikawa thought the German a dubious choice for a spy. Although Kühn had eagerly taken the money, he appeared to panic at the thought of making the radio test. Most people predicted Kühn would attract suspicion, which was true. For over a year the District Intelligence Officer had thought Kühn a suspicious character and probable Nazi spy who might also be working for the Japanese. This was extremely worrying from a Japanese point of view, as Kühn had been lined up to replace Yoshikawa as head spy once war began.

Back in Tokyo, the Third Bureau wanted to check the information being sent from Honolulu by Kita and to have experienced naval personnel observe the actual conditions at Pearl Harbor. A three-man team was put together, which included Commander Toshihide Maejima, an expert on submarines, Sub-lieutenant Keiu Matsuo, a midget-submarine expert who would examine the possibility of using mini-subs in the attack, and Lieutenant-Commander Suguru Suzuki, an expert on US air power and carrier warfare. These three officers would travel onboard the NYK liner *Taiyo Maru*, which was scheduled to leave Yokohama on 22 October. The day before departure the three officers were given their final instructions. As the ship would be taking the route to be followed by Yamamoto's carriers, they were to report all ship movements in the northern Pacific sea lanes and keep a daily record of weather.

The *Taiyo Maru* arrived at Honolulu on the morning of 1 November 1941. With rising tensions, US Customs enforced a series of measures they hoped would prevent secret information being taken onboard. Shore leave was restricted to those Japanese personnel certified as being ashore to carry out maintenance on the vessel. No visitors from shore would be allowed aboard the vessel, and once aboard the departing passengers were not allowed back on the dock. Eager to prevent mail or messages being carried out of Hawaii, intelligence and customs officials made searches of people leaving Honolulu and their luggage.

In view of these countermeasures the three Japanese officers decided not to leave the ship. However, Kita came to visit them, probably deciding it was too risky to send Yoshikawa to brief them as he was already suspected of being a spy. Onboard, Suzuki gave Kita a questionnaire prepared by the Third Bureau, which he subsequently turned over to Yoshikawa to complete. Meanwhile Maejima and Matsuo concerned themselves with submarine-related problems. In particular they were looking for a safe haven from where they could operate and pick up midget-submarine crews and aviators after the attack. For this, they both agreed that the island of Niihau was most suitable.

Before answering the questionnaire, Yoshikawa took a ride round his usual vantage points in a taxi. Once completed, the questionnaire and maps previously requested by the captain of the *Tatuta Maru* were smuggled aboard without much difficulty. Although the FBI was watching the boat the whole time, the material was smuggled onto the ship hidden in newspapers. On the evening of 5 November, the *Taiyo Maru* departed from Honolulu, the last Japanese liner to leave before the outbreak of war.[25]

On 15 November Tokyo sent Kita a message saying that relations between the United States were 'most critical'. In response to this situation, Kita was to send his 'ships in harbour' report twice a week, at irregular intervals. Kita was cautioned to 'take extra care to maintain secrecy'. Yoshikawa stepped up his surveillance and formulated a daily graph. He also began burning his records.[26]

Two days later, on 17 November, the *Taiyo Maru* arrived back in Japan just as the task force departed. Against this backdrop the three agents presented the questionnaire and made their report. Suzuki concurred with Yoshikawa that the Americans could be taken by surprise, a key component of the planned air attack.[27] On 22 November Suzuki gave an intelligence briefing onboard the carrier *Akagi*. For props he had a scale model of Pearl Harbor and Oahu, plus the map that Kita had provided him.

Both Yoshikawa and Suzuki had overestimated the number of American planes on the island. Even so, Suzuki reported that the Americans were lax with their aircraft patrols and so, if large numbers of aircraft were spotted on the day of the attack, it would be an indication that the element of surprise had failed and that the Americans had been alerted. The only grey area – and it was a vitally important one – concerned the American aircraft carriers. Suzuki had to admit not seeing any himself, but three flat-tops had been reported.[28]

On 24 November Honolulu reported on American fleet manoeuvres. Battleships exercised in groups of three or five accompanied by lighter craft, conducting manoeuvres for a week at sea, either to the south of Maui or to the south-west. The aircraft carriers manoeuvred by themselves. Meanwhile, the heavy cruisers operated in groups of six, carrying their operations over a period of two to three weeks and were suspected of going to Samoa. When in Pearl Harbor they usually remained at anchor for four or five days at a time.

On 28 November, Tokyo warned Honolulu that they were anticipating the possibility of telegraphic communication being severed. In a separate message they asked Kita for more intelligence, which they classed as being of 'major importance'. Tokyo was concerned that reports of battleships leaving harbour were being received only once a week. They wanted reports on the entrance and departure of all capital ships and the length of time they spent at anchor. The following day, on 29 November, Tokyo sent an even more important message: 'We have been receiving reports from you on ship movements, but in future will you also report even when there are no movements.'

On 30 November a minor bombshell arrived at the Japanese consulate in the form of Dr Kühn who, for reasons known only to him, had taken it upon himself to become active. Operating totally against his brief, some time on the 28/29th he had visited the navy yard to check on the US ships. On the 30th he delivered his code to the embassy. The embassy considered his code too elaborate, so Kühn was again sent to rework it.

On 1 December the Americans finally appeared to gain a lucky break. During November the Japanese consulate had been using the Mackay Radio Company to send its coded messages, but when they switched to RCA on 1 December, copies of the messages were made available to American intelligence services. Here the luck ended – because the messages were in code and there were no code-breaking staff on Hawaii, the messages had to be sent elsewhere for decryption. Therefore the vitally important content of the next few days' messages were only learned after the attack.[29] The importance of this inability to decode the Japanese messages is highlighted by a transmission sent by Tokyo on 2 December, still five days before the attack. If given the chance to read it, one suspects Admiral Kimmel, the US naval commander at Pearl Harbor, would have understood the Japanese intentions quite clearly:

> In view of the present situation, the presence in port of warships, airplane carriers, and cruisers is of utmost importance. Hereafter, to the utmost of your ability, let me know day by day. Wire me in each case whether or not there are any observation balloons above Pearl Harbor or if there are any indications that they will be sent up. Also advise me whether or not the warships are provided with anti-mine nets.[30]

Following this chilling message, on 3 December Kühn produced his simplified code, which Yoshikawa prepared to send to Tokyo. The message was sent from 'Fujii' – Kühn's Japanese codename being *Ichiro Fujii*. The new set of codes was a complex mixture of flashing light signals from attic windows and classified radio ads to be broadcast, including 'Chinese rug etc. for sale, apply P.O. box 1476' or 'Beauty operator wanted etc. apply P.O. box 1476'. Kühn also handed over the fruits of his mission to the naval yard, which even he later admitted contained a purely fictional number of ships.

Having received Tokyo's urgent request for information on the US fleet, the Honolulu consulate had bad news for Tokyo on Friday 5 December. Although three battleships had arrived, in the afternoon the aircraft carrier *Lexington* and five heavy cruisers left port on the same day. The total count of ships remaining in harbour on the afternoon of 5 December included eight battleships, three light cruisers and 16 destroyers.

The day before the attack, Saturday 6 December, it is probable that Kita, Yoshikawa and the rest of the Honolulu consulate really had no idea how close they were to war. Yoshikawa spent the latter part of the morning at Pearl Harbor checking up on the presence of barrage balloons and torpedo nets. His report described how the army had begun training barrage-balloon troops at Camp Davis, North Carolina. Four to five hundred of these balloons were on order and it was understood they would be used in the defence of Hawaii and Panama. At the present time, in Hawaii there were no signs of barrage-balloon equipment and it was unlikely any existed. Yoshikawa then delivered the killer punch: 'I imagine that in all probability there is considerable opportunity left to take advantage for a surprise attack against these places.' Yoshikawa was vaguer about the existence of torpedo nets, but reported that he did not believe the battleships had them.

A message then arrived from Tokyo asking Kita to 'please wire immediately the movements of the fleet subsequent to the fourth [of December].' This prompted Yoshikawa to take a taxi at three in the afternoon and make what would be his last check on the fleet. He returned and gave Kita the report to check over. At 6.01am it was sent from the telegraph office to the Foreign Ministry in Tokyo. The message read:

> The following ships were observed at anchor on the 6th: 9 battleships, 3 light cruisers, 3 submarine tenders 17 destroyers, and in addition there were 4 light cruisers, 2 destroyers lying at docks (the heavy cruisers and airplane carriers have all left). It appears that no air reconnaissance is being conducted by the fleet air arm.[31]

From the Foreign Ministry, Yoshikawa's message was forwarded to the Naval general staff, who passed it on to Admiral Yamamoto onboard his flagship. Despite the positive news confirming the absence of barrage balloons, torpedo nets and air patrols, the confirmation that there were no carriers in Pearl Harbor must have been a bitter disappointment to him. At first he considered radioing the task force commander, Admiral Nagumo, onboard the carrier *Akagi* and asking him to make an aerial search for the American carriers, but then thought better of it. Instead Yamamoto sent the message 'NO CARRIERS REPEAT NO CARRIERS IN PEARL HARBOR' and left Nagumo to decide his own course of action. When Nagumo received the message he threw it down on his chart table in disgust. He felt there was no option but to press on and sink the battleships.[32]

While this sombre drama was being played out, earlier in the day the FBI thought it had made a breakthrough. At 2.00pm the FBI's Honolulu-based Japanese translator finished the transcript of a telephone call between a Japanese journalist in Tokyo and Mrs Motokazu Mori, wife of a Honolulu dentist. The journalist asked Mrs Mori questions about the number of planes flying daily, how many sailors there were on the island and then went on to discuss weather conditions and made references to 'hibiscus' and 'poinsettias'.

These references to flowers were thought to have a hidden meaning and it was suspected that pre-arranged codewords had been exchanged. The text was shown to the head of the local FBI, Special Agent Robert Shivers. Knowing Dr Mori was on the FBI suspects list, Shivers became alarmed and was convinced the telephone call had a military significance. Shivers spoke to Colonel George W. Bicknell, assistant G-2 of the Hawaiian Department in charge of counter-intelligence matters. Bicknell concurred with his views. Because of the complexities of the Japanese language, it was agreed to give a transcript of the tape recording to Japanese-speaking Lieutenant Carr, in order to study any possible hidden meanings that might be concealed in the inflections of the voice. For some reason the FBI were unable to release the tape immediately and told Carr it would be available for study at 10.00am the following day – 7 December.

Mori was later cleared of any wrongdoing, but it appears there was a hidden purpose to the telephone call. If the Americans had got wind of the attack, they would surely have cut all telephone lines to Japan. Tokyo was probably testing the lines to Honolulu in order to check this. This call might not have been made in isolation: at 1.50am on Sunday morning the fleet received a message that telephone contacts with Japanese residents on Oahu indicated the island was calm and no blackout was in force.[33]

It went down as a day of infamy, but on the morning of Sunday 7 December the members of Honolulu's consulate staff carried on with life as usual. Kita was planning to play golf. With the sound of explosions in the distance, Yoshikawa asked Kita if he could go and see what was happening – but he was refused permission. It was all too obvious. When a late-edition copy of the *Star-Bulletin* was shown to the embassy confirming a Japanese attack, Yoshikawa raced off to the code room and began burning evidence. By 11.00am a police guard had assembled to protect the consulate and its staff. The police entered the consulate and found a wash tub filled with burning papers, salvaging what they could.

Dr Kühn, meanwhile, whose part in the drama has long been overplayed, was unable to remain still during the attack. He seems not to have realized what was meant by the term 'sleeper agent'. Instead of remaining quiet, waiting for the incident to die down before resurfacing at a later date, Kühn was spotted by an intelligence officer trying to send signals to the Japanese consulate from the roof of his house overlooking the harbour. This was reported to the FBI who arrested him and his daughter Ruth at 9.30am.

In the immediate aftermath of the raid, Yoshikawa and the rest of the consulate staff were held prisoner for ten days. They were then taken under heavy guard to a US Coast Guard vessel which took them to San Diego. In March of the following year they were taken to an internment camp in Arizona, before the FBI took them to New York City from where they were sent back to Japan under the arrangements for exchanging diplomats between warring nations.[34] As for the bungling Nazi, Dr Kühn, he was sentenced to death, but the sentence was later commuted to 50 years' imprisonment after he agreed to spill the beans on the Japanese espionage system. In 1946 he was released and returned to Germany with his family.[35]

In the subsequent investigations after the raid and with the benefit of hindsight, the meaning of the intercepted Japanese messages appeared all too obvious. However, at the time they were lost in the 'noise' created by Japanese activities elsewhere. There was so much Japanese espionage going on, Pearl Harbor did not stand out as any different from other major naval centres or strategic points. This view was confirmed by Admiral Wilkinson during the *Report Of The Joint Committee on the Investigation of the Pearl Harbor Attack, Congress of the United States.* In his testimony Wilkinson testified:

'The Japanese for many years had the reputation, and the facts bore out that reputation, of being meticulous seekers for every scrap of information, whether by photography or by written report or otherwise. Japanese naval officers had been caught on the west coast investigating ship movements around Seattle, Bremerton, Long Beach, and San Diego. The Americans also knew that Japanese agents were active in the Philippines with Tokyo requesting detailed information on airfields, air strength and activity, strength and activity of land forces, location of antiaircraft guns, and other items of defence. The Japs in the Philippines also looked for ship movements. Messages were also sent to Singapore requesting details on fishing boats and air forces stationed in Malaya. Other requests concerned the strength of the air force in the Dutch Indies with specific information requested on training, combat methods and organization.'[36]

Others have downplayed the role of Japanese espionage in the Pearl Harbor attack. This is understandable, and to a degree correct. Although great havoc was caused by the air raid, a collective sigh of relief must have been heard when the Japanese missed the oil storage facilities. In some respects the loss of such huge fuel reserves would have been a far bigger blow than the loss to shipping and harbour facilities. How, if the Japanese spy system had been so effective, had such a target opportunity been missed?

On balance, however, almost every report and investigation confirmed widespread espionage activity on the Hawaiian Islands. For example, from 9–14 December 1941 Secretary of the Navy Knox was sent to Pearl Harbor to make a report for the president. In it Knox recorded:

> It cannot be too strongly emphasized that there was available to the enemy in Oahu probably the most efficient fifth column to be found anywhere in the American possessions, due to the presence of very large numbers of alien Japanese. The intelligence work done by this fifth column before the attack provided the Japanese Navy with exact knowledge of all necessary details to plan the attack. This included exact charts showing customary position of ships when in Pearl Harbor, exact location of all defenses, gun power and numerous other details. Papers captured from the Japanese submarine that ran ashore indicated that the exact position of nearly every ship in the harbor was known and charted…[37]

The subsequent Hewitt Inquiry concurred with Knox:

> Japanese espionage at Pearl Harbor was effective and, particularly during the critical period 27 November to 7 December 1941, resulted in the frequent transmission to Japan of information of great importance concerning the Pacific Fleet, the movements and locations of ships, and defense preparations.[38]

In a different vein, many have wondered how much the British knew before the attack. Had Churchill warned Roosevelt, or, perhaps more pertinently, did Churchill know and not say anything, hoping America would be drawn into the war? These are high-level conspiracies that may never be resolved without the release of classified papers, but certainly Churchill breathed a huge sigh of relief when he heard of the Japanese bombs falling.[39] One deeper mystery, which is less spoken about, concerns the spy Dusko Popov, *Tricycle*. In his memoirs, which were first published in 1974, Popov alleged that he told the FBI about Japanese plans to attack Pearl Harbor in August 1941.

Popov had met his Abwehr contact Jebsen in Lisbon at the end of June 1941. According to Jebsen, the Japanese Foreign Minister Yosuke Matsuoka had gone to Berlin at the end of March and asked for the Abwehr to provide the Japanese with details on the Italian naval base at Taranto, which had recently been attacked by British carrier-based torpedo planes. Canaris nominated Jebsen for the mission – the Japanese, he said, were very curious about the effectiveness of the torpedo nets. Furthermore, Jebsen had learned how much the American oil embargo was hurting Japan from Baron Gronau, the German air attaché in Tokyo. According to Gronau, the Japanese navy was down to 18 months' oil reserve and would need to strike before that reserve fell below 12 months. Doing the maths, the Japanese would have to attack before the end of December 1941.[40]

Following this meeting, Popov met with his controller, von Karstoff. He instructed Popov to gather information on ammunition dumps and mine depots on the island of Oahu. Popov asked von Karstoff if this had any connection with Jebsen's investigations at Taranto: 'So one would presume,' the German replied. Popov left the meeting and communicated with MI6: instructions from London were for Popov to go to America as instructed by the Abwehr and deliver this intelligence directly to the Americans.[41]

The double agent arrived in New York in August and was met by the FBI. Popov was carrying a questionnaire relating to Pearl Harbor, which had been shrunk down to a microdot in size. This he handed over to the Americans. Unfortunately, no one seemed quite sure what to do with Popov and much of his time was spent at leisure. For his extracurricular activities he was labelled a 'playboy' by the FBI and, to skip over the details, when he did finally get to meet J. Edgar Hoover (1895–1972) six weeks later, the two fell out immediately. Popov offered to help the FBI set up a double-cross system modelled on the British one. Hoover said he did not need his help catching spies. Popov was instead sent on a mission to South America. On his return he learned of the Pearl Harbor attack. Popov was furious and put the blame squarely at Hoover for not passing on the information he had provided.

This version of events is backed by a report written by John Masterman at the termination of the war in 1945. Masterman included the text of Popov's questionnaire, a large proportion of which asked for specific information on Pearl Harbor, including the power installations, workshops, petrol installations, dry-dock facilities and torpedo protection nets. Masterman confirmed the FBI was in possession of all the information carried in the questionnaire, which he described as 'a sombre but unregarded warning of the subsequent attack on Pearl Harbor'.[42]

Moving on from the Pearl Harbor attack, at the beginning of this chapter it was shown how the Japanese had planned to transfer their espionage operations to bases in Central and South America. This policy may explain the FBI's bizarre 'Doll Woman' case. In February 1942 the FBI was alerted to an unusual letter it had intercepted from an address in Portland, Oregon, to Buenos Aires, Argentina. At first glance the letter appeared to be about collectable dolls. Suspicions were alerted by the mention of a 'wonderful doll hospital', of three 'Old English dolls' sent for repair, not to mention 'fish nets' and 'balloons'. FBI laboratory cryptographers examined the letter and correctly guessed the terms were in fact a code relating to naval installations on the West Coast.

Over the coming months four more letters sent to the same Buenos Aires address began arriving at homes across America, marked 'Address Unknown'. In each case, the people these letters were returned to had no knowledge of them. They were alarmed to find the letters contained accurate information about them and that their signatures had been forged. Again each letter contained information on dolls. One had a mention of a Mr Shaw, who having been ill would soon be back at work. The FBI quickly concluded this was a reference to USS *Shaw* which had been repaired following the Japanese raid. Other comments appeared to relate to ship movements and repairs to an aircraft carrier.

The FBI quickly established a connection between the four addresses: they all shared a hobby in doll collecting. An FBI laboratory examination of the five letters in their possession confirmed the signatures were forgeries made by someone copying an example of the original signature. A further lead was provided when one of the addressees suspected that the forger may have been a New York doll shop owner named Velvalee Dickinson. It turned out that Dickinson was the common denominator between all addressees.

The FBI turned their attention to Dickinson and established that she had been a member of the Japan-American Society in the early thirties while living in San Francisco. In addition to meetings with members of the Japanese Consulate in San Francisco, the FBI learned she had dealings with the Japanese community after moving to New York City. In tracing her movements during the time the five letters were sent to Argentina (January–June 1942), it was confirmed that Mrs Dickinson and her husband had visited each of the areas the letters were postmarked from. Furthermore, four of the letters were found to have been written on hotel typewriters in these areas. Until the outbreak of war Mrs Dickinson appeared to have had money troubles, but had come into a large number of $100 bills. Four of these bills were recovered after transactions and were traced back to Japanese sources.

Based on this detailed investigation, Velvalee Dickinson was arrested by the FBI on 21 January 1944. A safety deposit box disclosed $13,000 traceable to Japanese sources. Mrs Dickenson claimed the money came from a savings account, insurance companies and from her doll business. The FBI knew a sizeable portion of the money in fact came from Captain Yuzo Ishikawa of the Japanese Naval Inspector's Office. Dickinson claimed she found the money hidden in her husband's bed after his death in from a heart ailment, on 29 March 1943.

Eventually Dickinson admitted she had typed the letters and promised to furnish information in her possession concerning Japanese intelligence activities in return for lesser charges than espionage. The content of the letters had been based on conversations with people in the Seattle and San Francisco areas. The code had been given to her husband in November 1941 by a Japanese naval attaché, Ichiro Yokoyama. In return for spying for the Japanese he received $25,000 in $100 bills. In court the FBI proved Mr Dickinson had not known the Japanese naval attaché and that Mrs Dickinson alone was guilty. On 14 August 1944 she was sentenced to the maximum ten-year term with a $10,000 fine. She was conditionally released in 1951.

Two of the FBI's biggest WWII successes were the discovery and conviction of a major Nazi spy ring and the capture of Nazi saboteurs.[43] The first case predates Pearl Harbor. It involved the so-called Duquesne spy ring, which was discovered through the co-operation of an American citizen of German origin. William Sebold was born in Mulheim, Germany, and had served his country of birth during WWI. In 1921 he settled in the United States, working in industry and aircraft manufacture before becoming a naturalized American citizen in 1936. When he returned to Germany to visit relatives in February 1939 he was approached by the Gestapo and told he would be contacted. An interview took place in September 1939 with a Dr Gassner, who asked him about military places and equipment in the United States. Subsequent to this, Gassner and 'Dr Renken', the alias of Abwehr agent Major Nickolaus Ritter, persuaded Sebold to return to the United States as a spy. Sebold agreed, fearing reprisals against his family in Germany if he did not.

Sebold then visited the American consulate in Cologne, ostensibly because his passport had been stolen. While there he told consulate staff that he had been recruited as a German spy, but wanted to co-operate with the FBI. He was told to play along with the Germans and so went to Hamburg where he was trained in coded messages and microphotographs. He was also given instructions on the type of information he was to report on and to deliver similar instructions to three German agents already working in the United States.

Using the alias 'Harry Sawyer', Sebold arrived in New York City on 8 February 1940. The FBI had been notified of his desire to work for them and they helped him establish an office on Times Square, which provided him the 'cover' of working as an engineer. FBI agents set up a short-wave radio transmitter on Long Island and established contact with the Germans. This radio station would serve as the main channel of communication between German spies in New York City and their superiors in Germany for the next 16 months. In that time the FBI transmitted and received over 500 messages to and from Germany.

The messages given to Sebold by the Abwehr led him to Frederick Joubert Duquesne, a native of South Africa who had left the country at the end of the Boer War. Fiercely anti-British, Duquesne claimed he was behind the sinking of HMS *Hampshire* in 1916 and the death of Earl Kitchener – a story told in the 1932 book *The Man Who Killed*

Kitchener by Clement Wood. Sebold managed to gain acceptance into Duquesne's large spy ring, and became Duquesne's chief radio operator. In January 1941, this role expanded to passing on messages from Abwehr agents in Mexico City to Germany. This allowed the FBI to meddle with the text of German spies coming out of Latin America.[44]

When the Mexican authorities stopped German agents transmitting to Sebold in June 1941, Hoover decided it was time for the Duquesne spy ring to be rounded up. In all 33 German agents were arrested on the charge of espionage and 19 pleaded guilty. The other 14 men were brought to trial in New York on 3 September 1941 and were all found guilty by jury on 13 December 1941. The 33 agents received sentences totalling more than 300 years; Duquesne was sentenced to serve 18 years in prison on espionage charges, as well as a two-year concurrent sentence and payment of a $2,000 fine for violation of the Registration Act.

Following the Pearl Harbor attack, on 11 December 1941 Germany and Italy declared war against the United States. Unable to strike with conventional forces, the Nazis planned a sabotage campaign against American industry to hamper and reduce war production. The project, codenamed *Pastorius*, was placed in the hands of Abwehr lieutenant Walter Kappe, who had spent time in America before the war and who had kept in touch with many of those returning to Germany from the United States. From this number, 12 trainees were recruited and sent to a sabotage school near Berlin where they were instructed in bomb-making, secret writing and concealment techniques. They were taken to industrial plants, railway sheds, canals and other important sites in order to familiarize themselves with the types of targets they were going to attack and to study their vulnerabilities.

Their training completed, on 26 May 1942 a group of four saboteurs left from the U-boat base at Lorient, on the west coast of France. This group consisted of George John Dasch, aged 19; Ernest Peter Burger, 36; Heinrich Harm Heinck, 35; and Richard Quirin, 34. Their targets were the hydroelectric plants at Niagara Falls, the Aluminium Company of America factories in Illinois, Tennessee and New York, a cryolite plant in Philadelphia and the locks on the Ohio River between Louisville and Pittsburgh.

In the early hours of 13 June the four were landed on a Long Island beach. Wearing German uniforms to ensure they were treated as prisoners of war, not spies, if caught while landing, the group almost met with immediate disaster. Having just buried their equipment and uniforms, the group was discovered by a coastguard. Suspicious, but not armed, the coastguard accepted a bribe from the saboteurs to turn a blind eye to them. The coastguard reported the incident to headquarters, and a patrol was sent out. Although the patrol did see a submarine out in the fog, Dasch and his group were long gone, having taken the train to New York City. By early morning the coastguards had dug up the saboteurs' supplies and immediately notified the FBI, which began the largest manhunt in its history.

Shaken by their close shave on the beach, once in New York, Dasch indicated to Ernest Burger that he wanted to go to the authorities. Burger had a choice – kill Dasch or, the choice he opted for, go along with him. On 14 June, using the alias *Pastorius*, Dasch telephoned the FBI's New York office. He told them he had recently arrived from Germany and would call FBI headquarters in Washington, DC, the following week. Meanwhile a second group of saboteurs landed on 17 June at Ponte Vedra Beach, south of Jacksonville, Florida. This group included Edward John Kerling, aged 33; Werner Thiel, 35; Herman Otto Neubauer, 32; and Herbert Hans Haupt, 22. They landed safely and took the train from Jacksonville to Cincinnati, where they split up. Neubauer and Haupt went on to Chicago and the other pair to New York City.

On 19 June, FBI headquarters received the call from *Pastorius* who gave his location and allowed himself to be taken into custody. Dasch gave the identities of the other saboteurs and their possible locations. The three remaining Long Island saboteurs were arrested in New York City on 20 June, followed by Kerling and Thiel of the Florida group on 23 June. The remaining two saboteurs were picked up in Chicago on 27 June. All eight were tried before a military commission between 8 July and 4 August 1942. All of them were found guilty and sentenced to death by the electric chair. Attorney General Biddle and J. Edgar Hoover appealed to President Roosevelt to commute the sentences of Dasch and Burger. Dasch received a 30-year sentence and Burger life imprisonment. In 1948 Dasch and Burger were granted clemency and deported to the American zone of Germany.

Only one more attempt was made to land saboteurs in America by submarine, but not until the summer of 1944. This time agent Erich

Gimpel had been provided with an American accomplice named William Curtis Colepaugh who had defected to Germany from the United States. Landing in Maine, Gimpel evaded capture for five weeks before the FBI caught him: he had been betrayed by Colepaugh.

13

<hr style="width:15%">

SPIES OF THE SOVIET ERA

I'm pretty sure that the intelligence services on the whole, and the spies both in the East and the West, tended towards a more realistic assessment of the balance of power than that of politicians and military leaders

East German secret service chief, Markus Wolf[1]

Secret service in Russia goes back to a contemporary of Sir Francis Walsingham, Tsar Ivan IV (1530–84). Following the death of the tsar's wife in 1553, there followed a period of repression and murder so cruel it earned Ivan the nickname Grozny – 'Terrible'. In 1565 Ivan created the Oprichnina. These were territories under his absolute control, policed by the Oprichniks – a private army notorious for murder and torture. The whole experiment was a complete disaster. People fled Ivan's lands to escape the Oprichniks and tax revenues fell well below the national average. In 1573 the tsar disbanded the Oprichniks, executed their leaders and went so far as to deny that the organization had ever existed. In so doing, he set a bloody precedent for Russian leaders of later years.

Directly before the 1917 Revolution, the Russian secret police was known as the Okhrana. Formed in 1881 following the assassination of Alexander II by Nihilists,[2] the Okhrana's primary mission was to protect the tsar and the royal family. However, to do this, the Okhrana had to find a way to infiltrate the large numbers of ex-pat radicals sheltering abroad. In 1883 the Okhrana therefore formed a foreign bureau in Paris, which at its peak employed 40 detectives and 30 agents working across Europe.[3]

The presence of the Russian secret service was not entirely welcomed by the French or British police. This led the Okhrana to make use of *agents provocateurs* to further their cause. In 1890 one such *provocateur* operating in Paris, Arkadiy Harting, armed a team of 'bomb-throwers', then betrayed them to the French police. Their arrests caused a scare among Parisians and forced the Paris police to take the threat of Russian dissidents more seriously. A similar tactic was used in London where there are several notable cases of Russian agents at work. Special Branch's Basil Thompson even suspected that the infamous serial killer Jack the Ripper was in fact Okhrana *agent provocateur* Mikhail Ostrog, a former inmate at asylums in both France and the United Kingdom.[4] Perhaps a better example of Okhrana agitation came in the 1911 'Battle of Stepney' – a failed jewellery heist and shootout in London's East End between Latvian anarchists and the Coldstream Guards. The ringleader behind the attempted robbery, a mysterious figure known only as 'Peter the Painter', has long been suspected of having links with the Okhrana.

The *agent provocateur* tactic was also used successfully on the Okhrana's home turf in Russia. The most famous of its agents was a Jewish radical named Evno Azef (1869–1918) who fled to Germany in 1892 to escape arrest for embezzlement. Studying electrical engineering in Karlsruhe, Azef funded his studies by spying for the Okhrana on fellow exiled members of the Russian Social Democratic Party. His peers thought him an out-and-out terrorist, but in fact, although Azef did organize several bank robberies and assassinations, he very quickly betrayed those who carried them out. By 1899 Azef had become so useful that the Okhrana's Moscow chief, Sergei Zubatov, brought him to back to Russia to work under his direction. Azef quickly joined the Socialist Revolutionary Party and became head of its Combat Organization. Again, Azef would plan an assassination and then betray the perpetrators to Zubatov.

It is claimed that in order to make the Okhrana appear indispensable, Azef was given the nod to arrange the assassination of Vyacheslav Plevhe, the unpopular minister of the interior. Acting under Azef's orders, Yegor Sozonov threw a bomb into Plevhe's carriage on 28 July 1904, blowing the minister to pieces. On 1 January 1905, Azef struck again, this time against the Moscow military commander, Grand Duke Sergei Alexandrovich, the tsar's uncle.[5]

In addition to Azef's infiltration of radical groups, the Okhrana secretly funded trade unions. In his youth, Zubatov had dabbled with revolutionary causes and understood workers had genuine grievances and needed an outlet for them. He introduced what became known as Zubatovism or police socialism. By installing Okhrana agents as the leaders of trade unions, Zubatov hoped that the workers' discontent would be directed against rich industrialists, rather than against the tsar. However, after Zubatov was blamed for a series of strikes, he was expelled from the Okhrana in August 1903. The new figurehead chosen to lead the trade unions was Father Gapon (1870–1906), a Russian Orthodox priest with a reputation for defending workers' rights.

Unfortunately Gapon took his role too seriously. In the middle of the war with Japan, which was going badly for Russia, Gapon announced he was bringing several hundred thousand protestors to the Winter Palace to present the tsar with a petition calling for an eight-hour day and a minimum wage. On Sunday 22 January 1905, Gapon appeared at the head of over 100,000 workers, dressed in full religious garb, surrounded by icons, flags and pictures of the tsar. Rather than a benevolent ruler, the marchers encountered troops with fixed bayonets barring the way ahead. Before long a shot rang out and the government troops charged. In the ensuing chaos at least 92 protestors were shot dead, with hundreds more wounded. This 'Bloody Sunday' was the Tiananmen Square of its day. It marked the beginning of the end for the Romanov dynasty and set in motion the events ultimately leading to the revolution of 1917.

Gapon was beside himself with rage. He had truly believed that the tsar would listen to the petition, but now he denounced the tsar as a tyrant with blood on his hands. Gapon also denounced the Okhrana and named Azef as one of its agents. He fled to London, then Paris, before finally coming to rest in Monte Carlo where he indulged himself in every luxury. Azef, meanwhile, had to plead for his life in front of panel of fellow revolutionaries. He managed to talk his way out of trouble, pointing out that he would hardly have organized the assassination of the tsar's uncle if he was a police agent.

Gapon returned to Russia a year after Bloody Sunday and attempted to pick up from where he had left off. By now Azef had learned of Gapon's extravagancies on the Riviera and so made a little denunciation of his own. Gapon, Azef claimed, was an agent of the tsar and had been directly responsible for the Bloody Sunday massacre, leading the workers into a pre-arranged trap. On 28 March 1906 Gapon was lured to a cottage across the Finnish border where he was savagely beaten and strung up from the rafters. Azef, meanwhile, claimed he was planning to assassinate the tsar. Whether this was true or not we shall never know. In February 1909 Azef's double game was discovered by a revolutionary named Vladimir Burtsev and the Okhrana agent again fled to Germany where he died in 1918.

The first nail in the coffin for the Okhrana came with the assassination of the Russian prime minister Pyotr Stolypin in 1911 at the Kiev Opera. Stolypin had come to office in 1906 and had been responsible for a heavy-handed clamp down on revolutionaries. Thousands were sent to the gallows after summary trial and sentencing by military tribunals. His assassin was Dmitry Bogrov who, it turned out, had been working as an Okhrana double agent since 1906.

This revelation, combined with the dealings of Azef and Father Gapon, led to the Okhrana being scaled back. In 1913 the Okhrana stations were closed down except in Moscow, St Petersburg and Warsaw. Abroad, pressure from the more radical elements of French politics had the Paris office shut down in 1913. However, the Okhrana formed a private detective agency – the Agence Bint et Sambain – to front its operations.[6] Although its methods would live on in organizations such as the Cheka and KGB, the Okhrana came to an end with the fall of the tsar in March 1917.

As with the French Revolution 13 decades before, the Russian Revolution underwent a number of increasingly bloody phases. The initial revolution was almost bloodless and came about in March 1917 when soldiers based in Petrograd (St Petersburg) joined protestors complaining about food shortages and the mismanagement of the war. The tsar abdicated on 15 March and a provisional government was formed with the promise of elections. In the meantime, the provisional government maintained Russia's commitment to the war with Germany. After a summer of strife, on 7 November 1917 the 'October Revolution' took place.[7] This was led by supporters of the communist Vladimir Lenin (1870–1924) and brought the Bolshevik Party to power. Russia then made peace with Germany before plunging into civil war and political terror. Needless to say, secret services were hard at work throughout.

In his history of the Russian Revolution, Leon Trotsky (1879–1940) has a lot to say about the provisional government's use of dirty tricks against Lenin, in particular an incident known as 'the Great Slander'. In early July 1917 a rumour claimed that Lenin was associated with the German army general staff. According to Trotsky, the source of the rumour was a Russian agent named Ermolenko. In 1914 Ermolenko had allowed himself to be captured by the Germans in order to spy on Russian prisoners of war. However, when incarceration proved incommodious, Ermolenko offered his services to the Germans. He was sent back to Russia as a saboteur and spy 'agitating for peace' and was told that Lenin would be working 'in the same direction'.[8] On his return to Russia on 25 April, Ermolenko provided himself with a second pay day by going to the provisional government and denouncing Lenin. Initially these allegations were dismissed by the provisional government. However, by July, when Lenin was growing more powerful, Ermolenko was recalled for his evidence to be heard a second time.

The provisional government's intelligence service was hard at work with enemies both in the Bolshevik camp and among those still loyal to the tsar. In the middle of a war with Germany, the new intelligence service was very quick to denounce its enemies as German spies. When the ship carrying Britain's Lord Kitchener to Russia sank in mysterious circumstances, the tsarina was accused of betraying the voyage to Germany. The intelligence officers manipulated the press, exaggerating reports of Russian defeats, which they blamed on German spies. Trotsky's description of the institution was typically venomous:

> In Russia the intelligence service was the very sewer of the Rasputin regime.[9] The scum of the officers, the police, the gendarmerie, together with the discharged agents of the secret police, formed the cadre of that foul, stupid and all powerful institution.[10]

Strangely enough, Lenin was indirectly protected by members of the old tsarist secret service who had little fondness for the new government. The former chief of St Petersburg secret police testified there was no evidence that Lenin was employed by the Germans, and he ought to have known – the Okhrana had been monitoring the Bolsheviks abroad since the party's foundation.

Momentarily thwarted, another approach was taken when a merchant named Burstein surfaced with news of a German spy network in neutral Stockholm headed by an agent called *Parvus*. The alias of Dr Israel Helphand, *Parvus* had known Lenin since 1900 and was a determined advocate of socialist revolution in Russia. He had gone to the Germans and told them there would be no peace with Russia unless they funded a socialist revolution under Lenin. *Parvus* was given substantial financial backing to deliver one.

Separately from *Parvus*, as early as 1915 the German Foreign Ministry had been toying with the idea of funding communists in order to cripple Russia and knock it out of the war. Their chief agent for this was an Estonian nationalist, Aleksander Kesküla, who was based in Stockholm. Kesküla was paid by German intelligence to pass pamphlets to Russian soldiers urging them to mutiny or desert. In return, Kesküla passed on details of conversations with Lenin about the news he was receiving from supporters in Russia. Kesküla's control officer in Berlin was an intelligence officer named Hans Steinwachs, who, by all accounts, considered Lenin an excellent source of information. In September 1915, Kesküla and Lenin met in Bern. At this meeting Lenin agreed to make a separate peace with Germany if his revolution succeeded. It was a marriage of the greatest convenience.

At the beginning of 1917, Germany was about to commence unrestricted submarine warfare against neutral shipping heading for Allied ports. Although this policy might bring Britain to the negotiating table, it was more likely to bring the United States into the war on the Allied side. In preparation for this, Zimmermann had sent his infamous telegram, inviting Mexico to enter the war on Germany's side. Zimmermann also began looking for a way to get Russia out of the war so that the German army would no longer have to fight on two fronts.

After the Tsar abdicated and a provisional government was formed, Zimmermann saw an opportunity to create chaos in Russia. Both *Parvus* and Kesküla had vouched for Lenin, so German intelligence arranged for Lenin to travel in a 'sealed train' from Switzerland to Petrograd, thoroughly expecting the Bolshevik firebrand to plunge Russia into chaos and take it out of the war. Lenin arrived in Petrograd on 16 April 1917 and duly obliged. On 6 March 1918 Russia signed the Treaty of Brest-Litovsk and made peace with Germany.

Once in power Lenin and the Bolsheviks began a secret service of their own. On 20 December 1917 the 'All-Russian Extraordinary Commission to Combat Counter-revolution and Sabotage', or Vecheka, was created headed by the Polish communist Felix Edmundovich Dzerzhinsky (1877–1926). Born into the nobility, 'Iron Felix' as he was known, had been a Marxist since 1895 when he joined the Lithuanian Social Democratic Party. Like many of the Bolshevik leaders he had spent his life either on the run or in prison. When the Russian Revolution broke out, Dzerzhinsky was in prison, having been arrested by the Okhrana in 1912. Released from prison in March 1917, he joined the Bolshevik Party and was quickly promoted by Lenin to head the new organization, which became better known as the Cheka.

In terms of counter-espionage, Dzerzhinsky's main opponent was the British secret service, which had been very active since 1917. The British had a number of agents who could easily pass themselves off as Russian. The first of these was Paul Dukes who had been studying music in Petrograd since 1908 and then went on to work for the Foreign Office during the war. Dukes was recruited by Mansfield Cumming in 1918, trained in the use of secret ink, and then sent to report on the situation inside Russia. While helping to fund anti-Bolshevik espionage, Dukes assisted the rescue of a number of 'White Russians' through Finland. Using a variety of disguises, Dukes joined the Communist Party, the Red Army and even the Cheka. In August 1919 the Cheka arrested a number of White Russian spies who had infiltrated the organization. Dukes' cover was blown, but he managed to escape into Latvia. Arriving back in London, Mansfield Cumming took Dukes to meet King George V who was so impressed with his adventures that he knighted the spy in 1920.[11]

After Dukes came the self-styled 'Ace of Spies', Sidney Reilly (1874–1925). It is difficult to know what to make of Reilly. For decades after his disappearance in 1925 he was celebrated as the most audacious spy in history. Reilly, they say, became a spy after saving British diplomats in the South American jungle; that he infiltrated German high command in WWI; that he was a womanizer, a bigamist with 11 passports and a wife to match each of them; that he was responsible for the Zinoviev Letter, which brought down the first Labour government in Britain in 1924.[12] More than anyone else, Reilly was said to be the influence behind Ian Fleming's James Bond character.

However, in recent times the veil has been lifted on the reality of Reilly, who now appears more of a self-obsessed confidence trickster than a secret agent.[13]

Steering a course through the various legends, Reilly was most probably born in 1874 in Odessa, Russia, and named Sigmund Rosenblum. Although he claimed to have been a secret agent since the 1890s and had sold plans of Port Arthur to Japan before the 1904–5 war, his service only really began in March 1918 when he volunteered to go to Moscow in a bid to assassinate Lenin and overthrow the Bolsheviks. Arriving in Moscow, Reilly tried to meet Lenin, but was instead referred to Robert Bruce Lockhart, the British government's representative to the as yet unrecognized Bolshevik government. The two men saw the situation in Russia very differently. While the gung-ho Reilly wanted to shoot Lenin, Lockhart believed the Bolsheviks were there to stay and wanted to bring them back into the war through negotiation.

With money provided by Cumming, Reilly began bribing Lenin's bodyguards. However, before he could strike someone beat him to it. On 30 August 1918 an attempt was made against Lenin by disgruntled socialist Fanya Kaplan. As Lenin was walking out of a Moscow factory, Kaplan called over to him and when he turned, she fired three shots, wounding him in the shoulder and lung. Claiming Lenin had betrayed the revolution, Kapla refused to answer questions from the Cheka and was shot four days later. In a separate incident on the same day, the leader of the Petrograd Cheka, Moisei Uritsky, was assassinated.

These two events precipitated the 'Red Terror' which began on 5 September. Dzerzhinsky's Cheka ruthlessly clamped down on all opponents, executing 10,000 during the autumn alone, with a further 70,000 sent to the Gulag labour camps. The assassination attempt on Lenin was blamed on the British, and Lockhart was arrested while Reilly went underground. The bodyguards Reilly had bribed betrayed him and revealed how the British agent planned to kill Lenin. While Reilly was smuggled out of the country, a trial was held in which he was found guilty of conspiracy and sentenced to death *in absentia*. Arriving in London, Reilly continued to lobby for the overthrow of the Bolshevik government. Instead he found himself out of favour with the Foreign Office and the new head of SIS, Admiral Hugh Sinclair.

Meanwhile, at the end of the Russian Civil War in 1922, the Cheka was reorganized to form the GPU, which was itself renamed the OGPU when the Soviet Union was formed a year later. From 1924 to 1925 this 'Joint State Political Directorate' masterminded a highly successful sting. GPU agents contacted Russian émigrés and pretended to represent a group – The Trust – working to overthrow the Soviet Union from the inside. Reilly was informed about The Trust in 1925 by Ernest Boyce, SIS chief in Helsinki. Reilly agreed to meet The Trust leadership and crossed the Finnish border on 25 September 1925. Reilly was taken to a villa outside Moscow for a meeting, where he was arrested and told that the longstanding death sentence would now be carried out. According to Soviet sources, Reilly panicked and wrote to Dzerzhinsky, offering to sell out everything he knew on the British and American secret services, as well as the Russian émigrés he had dealt with. Dzerzhinsky made no reply and the sentence was carried out in November 1925.

On 21 January 1924 Lenin died, in part due to the Kaplan assassination attempt. A bullet was still lodged in his neck too close to the spine for doctors to operate on.[14] The leadership passed to the Communist Party's general secretary, Joseph Stalin (1879–1953).[15] Unlike his main rival, Leon Trotsky, Stalin preferred a policy of consolidation and of building socialism in one country, not promoting world revolution. This perspective led to a conflict between the two men, and saw Trotsky expelled from the Communist Party in 1927 and then exiled from Russia two years later.

After Dzerzhinsky died in 1926, the OGPU was expanded to enforce Stalin's policies. Dzerzhinsky was succeeded by Vyachesiav Menzhinsky (1874–1934), who, like Dzerzinsky, was a Pole. The new secret service chief enjoyed high living and surrounded himself with luxury. He was less concerned with intelligence-gathering as counter-espionage, considering everything other than scientific achievements a waste of time reporting. Despite his lifestyle, he appeared to get on with Stalin. When the latter asked for the reform of the overseas intelligence service, Menzhinsky simply invited all the department heads to a conference and then let loose his new deputy, one of Stalin's lap dogs named Genrikh Yagoda (1891–1938).[16]

In 1934, the OGPU became the NKVD (People's Commissariat for Internal Affairs) headed by Yagoda, who had succeeded Menzhinsky and quickly developed a reputation of being a ruthless sadist. Under Yagoda, the NKVD began the infamous 'Great Purge', where thousands of old Bolshevik Party members and high-ranking military officers were liquidated to placate Stalin's paranoia. To cover his tracks, Stalin had Yagoda replaced in 1936 by his deputy, Nicolai Yezhov (1895–1940). Yagoda was put on trial and charged with mass murder and conspiring with the West. He was probably shot some time in 1938.

Meanwhile Yezhov continued the Great Purge, turning on the NKVD itself and executing more than 3,000 officers in 1937. Unfortunately for the new NKVD chief, he knew too much for Stalin's liking. When the Soviet leader appointed his ally Lavrenti Beria (1899–1953) as Yezhov's deputy, the writing was on the wall. On 25 November 1938 Yezhov resigned as leader of the NKVD and was replaced by Beria, who later had him arrested on charges of espionage, treason and homosexuality. His fate is unclear, except that Yezhov was probably killed in 1940. The most popular version of events is that Beria visited Yezhov in his cell, throttled him with chicken wire, strung him up from the ceiling and left him to rot so he could show other prisoners what awaited them if they did not co-operate.

Like Stalin, Beria was from Georgia. He joined the Cheka in the early 1920s and by 1926 was head of OGPU in his native Georgia, then party secretary for Georgia and member of the Central Committee of the Communist Party in 1934. One of his first acts as head of the NKVD was to purge the organization and install men loyal to him. By this point even Stalin realized that the country was suffering heavily from brain-drain as a result of the purges. Once Beria had the NKVD firmly in his grip, the purges against Russians were scaled down and some 'political' prisoners were released. This did not mean that Beria was by any means going soft. When the Soviet forces occupied part of Poland in 1940, Beria oversaw the mass deportation of Poles and also ordered the infamous Katyn massacre of some 22,000 Polish prisoners of war.

It was also under Beria's watch that an NKVD agent hunted down and killed one of Stalin's biggest rivals and most outspoken critics, Leon Trotsky. The founder of the Red Army and Politburo, Trotsky had been deported by Stalin in 1929. After sojourns in Turkey, France and Norway, Trotsky finally settled in Mexico. There in 1938 Trotsky founded an international Marxist organization, which was intended as an alternative to Stalinism. The following year a Spanish-born NKVD agent called Ramón Mercader (codenamed *Gnome*) arrived in Mexico using the alias 'Frank Jacson'. Gaining access through one of Trotsky's secretaries, on 20 August 1940 Mercader planted an ice pick into Trotsky's skull.

Having survived revolution, counter-revolution, anti-counter-revolution, civil war, famine, forced collectivization and purge after bloody purge, the Russian people were next subjected to Nazi invasion. To survive such trials their collective fortitude must have been astounding. If Stalin had not been such a paranoid megalomaniac he would have known the Germans planned to attack in 1941. In fact, his spy networks were so extensive that he would have known the exact timing and strength of the Nazi invasion, had he only listened to the reports coming in from as far afield as Switzerland and Japan. Fortunately for Russia, Stalin came to realize the error of his ways and, as his armies were being pushed back towards Moscow, he began if not trusting then at least listening to the secret intelligence he received.

The scale of Soviet espionage in WWII is astounding. Whereas the British relied most on captured German spies, the Russians were served by spies of their own making, mostly recruited and put in place before the war began. Also, the Russians did not limit themselves to spying on the Axis. True, Germany was the most immediate threat, but Britain and America were not far behind, the latter especially when it began to construct the atomic bomb.

Among the most famous foreign agents were the so-called Cambridge Spies, a coterie of communist sympathizers working their way into the most sensitive reaches of the British establishment. For example, Anthony Blunt (1907–83) was personal assistant to the director of MI5 'B' Division, Guy Liddell, who ran the double-cross agent set-up. Blunt also had access to SIS reports and Bletchley decrypts, which he later admitted passing on to the Soviets. Fellow spy John Cairncross (codenamed *Carelian*) actually worked at Bletchley Park in 1943 and passed Moscow Centre documents, as did Leo Long (codenamed *Elli*), who worked in MI14, the German section. Even before then, decrypts of communications between Moscow and the Soviet embassy in London show that a third, as yet unnamed, agent codenamed *Baron* was passing Bletchley intercepts to the Russians from as early as March 1941 – months before Hitler's attack on the Soviet Union.[17]

A friend of Blunt, Guy Burgess (1911–63), worked in the BBC, then in 1944 joined the Foreign Office as personal assistant to the minister of state, Hector McNeil. Kim Philby (1912–88) was a reporter for *The Times* at the beginning of the war. After the fall of France he joined SIS and then later SOE. He was close to the American OSS and was friendly with Allen Dulles, the future CIA chief. Donald Maclean (1913–83), on the other hand, was blackmailed by Burgess to maintain his loyalty to their NKVD controllers – he photographed a drunken Maclean in a compromising position with another man. Suitably indebted to Burgess, Maclean proved more than useful when posted to the British embassy in Washington, becoming Stalin's chief source on Anglo-American relations.

The only saving grace for the British is that the Cambridge spies were not fully exploited by Moscow Centre, simply because they appeared too good to be true. The Soviets were suspicious of the British secret services and wondered if Philby, Burgess, Maclean and Blunt were actually SIS double agents intent on penetrating the NKVD. None of the priceless intelligence they sent to Moscow was accepted at face value, unless confirmed by other sources.

Trust was in short supply with another of the big Soviet spies of the war years, Richard Sorge (1895–1944). Born in Russia of a German father, Sorge grew up in Germany and served the kaiser in WWI, receiving the Iron Cross after being severely wounded in the legs. His convalescence was a crucial period in Sorge's life. His uncle had been a secretary to Karl Marx and while recovering from his wounds, Sorge became a disciple of communist ideology, joining the German Communist Party (KPD) in 1921. By 1924 Sorge had visited Moscow and returned to Germany as a Comintern agent posing as a journalist.[18] However, his career as an agent did not really take off until after he was sent to Shanghai in 1930, again working as a journalist. In Shanghai he met and cultivated a lasting relationship with Ozaki Hozumi, a Japanese journalist working for the newspaper *Asahi Shimbun*.

Sorge returned to Moscow and announced that he was going to travel to Germany and join the Nazi Party to see what he could learn. He was accepted by the party and managed to secure a position as a reporter with the *Frankfurter Zeitung*. Operating under the codename *Ramsay*, in 1933 Sorge arrived in Japan and began building a network of informants, including Hozumi, who had government connections and was a particularly good source for foreign policy matters. More importantly, Sorge became friends with a German officer, Eugen Ott, an artillery expert seconded to the Japanese armed forces. Through Ott, Sorge built his connections with the German embassy and secured the position of press attaché. Via these contacts, in April 1941 Sorge sent Moscow details of Operation *Barbarossa* – the planned Nazi invasion of the Soviet Union. He even went on to give the correct date for the opening of hostilities, 22 June 1941. But to Sorge's horror, Stalin did nothing. His reports were ignored.

By the autumn, when Moscow was on the verge of falling to the Nazis, Stalin began to take more notice of his spies. Sorge reported that after its defeat at Khalkhin Gol in 1939, Japan had no plans to attack Siberia, but was focused on the navy's Strike South policy. This meant that the Soviets were able to transfer their Siberian troops under Zhukov to face the Germans. They arrived in the nick of time. By 27 November the German advance had almost reached within sight of the Kremlin. However, on 5 December 1941 Zhukov unleashed his winter-equipped Siberians on the freezing Germans, whose equipment had stopped working in obscenely low temperatures. The Germans were pushed back and Moscow was saved. Unfortunately for Sorge, he was not able to dwell long on his success. The Japanese secret services had long suspected the presence of a Russian radio transmitter and Sorge had been under surveillance for some time. His sub-agent Ozaki was arrested on 14 October 1941, followed by Sorge four days later. He spent more than three years in prison before being hanged on 7 November 1944.

In the early stages of the war, the Soviets had a number of spy rings in occupied Europe and within Germany itself. German intelligence labelled these networks *Rotte Kapelle* – Red Orchestra – and named the two principal agents in it *Grand Chef* (Big Chief) and *Petit Chef* (Little Chief). Big Chief was Leopold Trepper (1904–82) who used the alias 'Jean Gilbert'. Trepper was from Poland but had spent time in Palestine living in a kibbutz. Chased out of Palestine by the British for being a communist, Trepper had spent time in Paris and Moscow where he was recruited by the NKVD. Little Chief was Victor Sukulov, who used the alias 'Edward Kent'. A Latvian Red Army officer, Sukulov was based in Brussels and was Trepper's radio man. They were also in touch with two large anti-Nazi networks inside Germany. The first of these was run by Harro Schulze-Boysen (*Choro* – 1909–42), a figure high up in the Air Ministry and Arvid Harnack (*Wolf* – 1901–42), a civil servant in the Ministry of Economics. Paradoxically, the success of *Rotte Kapelle* was its undoing.

Trepper, *Choro* and *Wolf* all relied on Sukulov to broadcast messages back to Moscow Centre. Although the Germans could not break Sukulov's codes, they could send out detector vans to try and pinpoint his broadcasting location. To begin with, Sukulov ensured he used different locations and remained on the air for just minutes at a time. But when Moscow Centre became greedy for information, Sukulov found himself stuck on air for five hours a night – it was only a question of time before the Germans located his radio.

On 13 December 1941, German soldiers wearing socks over their boots crept up on three addresses in the Brussels suburbs used by Trepper's agents. Bursting in they found the transmitters and all the paraphernalia of a busy spy ring: forged documents, invisible ink and so forth. Three agents were caught red handed, but not Sukulov, who was absent. Just as the Germans were tearing the place apart looking for evidence, Trepper turned up. When a German answered the door, the quick-thinking spy chief pretended to be a salesman who had called at an inopportune time. Taking one last look at the three captured agents gazing back at him, Trepper was sent packing by the Germans. Breathing an almighty sigh of relief, Trepper fled and headed for a safe house in France, warning Sukulov to do likewise.

Of the three agents captured in the raid, Anna Pozanska swallowed a cyanide tablet. The other two, Mikhail Makarov and Rita Arnould, were taken to Gestapo HQ for interrogation. Under torture Makarov insulted his captors so much that they got angry and killed him before extracting any information. In a nearby cell Arnould could hear Makarov's ordeal and was so shaken by the experience that she agreed to talk in return for her life. It gave her false hope. After several weeks of spilling the beans, Arnould was executed when she ran out of information.

While Trepper and Sukulov were on the run, transmissions from Brussels were resumed by radio operator Johan Wenzel. On air a week after the German raid, this broadcast also fell to the Abwehr listening vans on 30 June 1942 when Wenzel was arrested. He turned out to be the prize catch for the Germans. Wenzel betrayed Sukulov, Trepper and the spy rings headed by Harro Schulze-Boysen and Arvid Harnack. In the subsequent interrogations over one hundred other members of the *Rotte Kapelle* were rounded up by the Gestapo. From their interrogations, the Germans were made aware that Trepper used a front company called Simex. Searching the offices of this company, an Abwehr agent noted that the company chief executive had a dentist appointment on 16 November 1942. Sure enough, Trepper was at last caught sitting in the dentist's chair.

Rather than deliver the torture Trepper could reasonably expect, the Abwehr did a deal with him. He agreed to keep his radio channel open, sending false messages to Moscow Centre – known as *Funkspiel*. More interestingly he was told that this line of communication had to be kept open in case of peace negotiations, and Trepper suspected some elements of the Nazi regime might have been actively plotting for such a peace. Moscow saw through the game and asked Trepper for some specific information, which the Germans refused to divulge. When Trepper could not provide an answer, Moscow knew he had been turned. In June 1943, Trepper managed to give his guards the slip and escaped, going into hiding with the French Resistance until after the liberation of Paris in 1944.

A similar game was played by Sukulov, who set himself up in Marseille. The Little Chief was arrested and also turned. This time the Germans tried to use Sukulov to expose a separate Soviet spy ring in Switzerland, codenamed *Rotte Drei* (Red Three) by the Germans. However, one of the radio operators involved in that ring, Alexander Foote, grew suspicious and warned Moscow, which shut down all networks belonging to Trepper.[19]

This Swiss network was better known as the *Lucy* spy ring. Although less celebrated than Sorge or even his contemporaries, *Garbo* and *Tricycle*, Rudolf Rössler (codenamed *Lucy*) was one of the most important spies at one of the most crucial phases of WWII. A German journalist who had moved to Switzerland in 1933, Rössler played a leading part in some of the biggest espionage coups in history. The amazing fact about Rössler is that no one to this day is completely sure of his motivation or background, nor the identity of his principal source, codenamed *Werther*.

What became known as the *Lucy* spy ring had deep roots. Before the war, the Soviet network in Switzerland was controlled by Maria Poliakova of Red Army Intelligence (4th Department), codenamed *Gisela*. When Poliakova was recalled to Moscow in 1937, *Gisela's Family* – as her network was known – passed to her sub-agent, the

Hungarian Alexander Rado (codenamed *Dora*), who became the new station controller.

In May 1940, Rado was put in touch with a separate Soviet spy ring in Switzerland led by Ursula Maria Hamburger (codenamed *Sonia*). Hamburger was destined to leave Switzerland for an assignment in Britain and had been ordered to check in with Rado to see if he required anything. Rado explained he needed a secure source for contacting the Moscow Centre, preferably by wireless. Hamburger obliged, providing two radio operators, Alexander Foote and Leon Buerton.

These two Englishmen were both veterans from the International Brigade fighting against Franco in the Spanish Civil War. Foote had been recruited by a Red Army agent and sent to meet *Sonia* in Geneva. To improve his German, *Sonia* sent Foote to Munich. Once in the Bavarian capital, Foote (codenamed *Jim*) was stunned to see Hitler enter the small restaurant where he was eating. Apparently Hitler and the proprietor were Great War comrades, so the Führer often visited when in town. When Foote contacted *Sonia* with this news she ordered him to plan an assassination attempt and sent him Buerton as an accomplice.

Sure enough, Hitler came back to the restaurant seemingly unguarded. Buerton wondered if there were SS men among the other diners, so reached into his pocket and quickly pulled out a cigarette lighter as if reaching for a pistol. Despite his sudden movement, no one batted an eyelid – Hitler was unguarded. However, just as Foote was waiting for the explosives to arrive, orders came from Moscow to stop all clandestine operations against Germany. The Russo-German non-aggression pact had been agreed on 23 August 1939. Instead of killing Hitler, Foote and Buerton were taught how to operate wireless transmitters.[20]

Foote was later transferred from Rado to being the radio operator for Rössler's case officer, Rachel Dübendorfer (*Sissy*). Having received his information, Rössler would pass it to *Sissy* by a friend named Christian Schneider (*Taylor*). Rössler would provide information on two conditions: he was to be well paid for it and he was never asked to reveal his sources' identities. Much to the annoyance of Stalin and Rado, Dübendorfer upheld the bargain and protected Rössler's identity – if of course she actually knew it.

At first Stalin was mistrustful of *Lucy* and suspected the agent of being an Abwehr plant. Only with time did he come to realize that *Lucy* was the proverbial pot of gold at the end of the rainbow. Through *Lucy*, *Werther* warned about *Barbarossa* and, like Sorge, gave the start date for the offensive but was not heeded. When *Werther* gave the Soviets advance warnings about the German push on Stalingrad, Stalin was less sceptical: the warning allowed the Red Army to redeploy reserves to the south. If this redeployment had not occurred the Nazis would probably have taken the city and cut off the River Volga, throttling Russia's oil supplies. *Werther* then supplied the details of the weak points in the German line, which allowed the Soviet army to break through in a pincer operation and entrap the German Sixth Army inside Stalingrad.

Perhaps *Werther*'s crowning glory was to forewarn Stalin about Operation *Citadel*, the German advance that culminated in the battle of Kursk fought over July and August 1943. Forewarned of the German plans, the Russians were able to spend four months preparing for the battle, laying over 400,000 landmines in the process. When the battle opened on 5 July, the Russians knew the exact time of the German zero-hour, so, ten minutes before it, they opened up on the German positions and launched a massive pre-emptive air strike. Although the Russians sustained enormous losses, they wrested the initiative from the Germans at Kursk.

Alas, all things must come to an end. The Germans knew Russian agents were transmitting from neutral Switzerland and so Walther Schellenberg contacted his opposite number there, Roger Masson, and asked him to shut the Soviet transmitters down. To demonstrate his sincerity, Schellenberg also gave Masson a draft of the German plans to invade Switzerland. Although Schellenberg may have been bluffing, the Swiss took no chances and ordered the arrest of the Rado and *Lucy* networks in 1943.[21] Rössler and Foote were arrested, as was Dübendorfer the following year. Rado on the other hand managed to escape to Paris. This was the end of the *Lucy* network, but not the speculation. Who was *Werther*?

When called upon by Stalin to reveal his sources, Rössler would only say that *Werther* was in German supreme command (OKW) where Hitler, Jodl and Keitel planned the war.[22] In a post-war interview, Rössler continued to be vague, mentioning only that he had several anti-Nazi friends in the Germany military who were able to transmit information to him using German military transmitters, but he refrained from naming names.

Many believed *Werther* was in fact the British secret service, who wanted to find a way of passing Bletchley Park intercepts to Stalin without revealing that they had broken the Enigma code. This theory has been discredited, as *Werther* was able to reply to specific questions set by the Kremlin. The Bletchley Park operation was not that sophisticated. If, as Rössler claimed, *Werther* had access to OKW he must have been a very highly placed traitor inside the Nazi regime itself. When one considers how figures as close to Hitler as Himmler and Göring were trying to make their own deals with the Allies, is it so difficult to believe that *Werther* was probably Hitler's deputy, Martin Bormann? Certainly Reinhard Gehlen, responsible for German intelligence on the Eastern Front, named Bormann as a Soviet spy in his memoirs, but can we be sure?[23] It seems amazing how the identity of probably the most important spy in history remains unknown. In the last days of the war Bormann vanished and, despite the occasional alleged sighting, is presumed to have died in the streets of Berlin in May 1945.

Russia's secret services still had one last act to perform against Nazi Germany. No account of espionage is complete without a mention of the NKVD's counter-intelligence service, 'Smersh'. Formed on 19 April 1943, Smersh is the acronym of the Russian Smert' Shpionam, or 'Death to Spies' – a title allegedly chosen by Stalin himself. It was headed by Viktor Abakumov (1894–1954), a close ally of Beria, and was notorious for machine-gunning retreating Russian soldiers. On the 60th anniversary of its foundation, a Smersh museum was opened on Lubyanka Square in Moscow. Attending the ceremony was former Smersh officer and Moscow counter-intelligence chief, Leonid Ivanov. He recalled how he had taken part in a special Smersh operation to locate Hitler's body and confirm he was actually dead. Going in with the assault troops, the Smersh agents found Hitler's partially burned corpse near the Führerbunker alongside the body of Eva Braun. With that discovery Russia knew it could forget the Nazi menace and concentrate on its future opponent – the United States.[24]

Throughout the war years Russia was particularly interested in the development of the so-called superbomb. President Roosevelt authorized development of an atomic bomb on 9 October 1941, almost two months before the attack on Pearl Harbor. It was not long before the Russians were trying to find out about it. Colonel Peter Bukhanoff was put in charge of atomic espionage in Moscow and began by compiling lists of scientists involved with the project. In 1942 Bukan off came up trumps when he selected two potential candidates – the German émigré Dr Klaus Fuchs (1911–88) and the Briton Dr Alan Nunn May (1911–2003).

Dr Alan Nunn May was yet another communist sympathizer who had come out of Cambridge and sold his soul to the Soviets. In January 1943 May was sent to Canada to continue working on the atomic bomb project. There he became part of a network run by the Soviet military attaché in Ottawa, Colonel Nikolai Zabotin.

Fuchs, on the other hand, was a German Communist Party member who moved to England in 1933, continuing his studies and maintaining his party membership. Recognized as a brilliant physicist, Fuchs worked on Britain's atomic bomb programme under Professor Rudolf Peierls. Fuchs was given full British citizenship, which he repaid by contacting Semion Kremer at the Soviet embassy in London and agreeing to pass on everything he knew about the atomic bomb. Conveniently ignoring the Official Secrets Act he had just signed, Fuchs believed that as an ally in the struggle against the Nazis, Russia had the right to know what Britain and America were up to.

Towards the end of the year, Fuchs was transferred to New York's Columbia University to continue his research. He was contacted by a network run by the Soviet vice-consul, Anatoli Yakovlev. Fuchs was ordered to pass his stolen secrets to Yakovlev's courier, Harry Gold, a pharmacist recruited as a Soviet agent in 1935. Harry Gold was known to Fuchs as *Raymond*. Their first meeting took place in a street corner in New York City. Fuchs was told to carry a tennis ball and that *Raymond* would be wearing a pair of gloves, carrying another pair and holding a green book under his arm.[25] When Fuchs was later assigned to work on the Manhattan Project at the atomic research centre in Los Alamos, New Mexico, Gold moved to Santa Fe and remained in contact with the British scientist who continued passing him atomic secrets.[26]

On 24 July 1945, the new US President, Harry Truman, decided to tell Stalin about the existence of a weapon of 'unusual destructive force' and was curious that the Russian president 'showed no special interest' in the matter.[27] There are two schools of thought on this. The first is that Stalin did not appreciate the significance of what Truman was telling him; on the other hand, there are those who believe that Stalin probably knew more about the project than Truman did. Either way, Stalin reportedly agreed that the weapon should be used on Japan. On 6 August 1945 an atomic bomb was dropped on Hiroshima killing 100,000 people instantly; three days later a second bomb was dropped on Nagasaki killing another 40,000. On 15 August Japan surrendered, bringing an end to the war it had started in Manchuria 14 years before.

In the immediate period of peace, things began to go wrong for the Russian espionage service. Working for Zabotin in Ottawa was an NKVD cipher clerk named Igor Gouzenko, who was recalled to Russia shortly after the Japanese surrender. Gouzenko had been in Canada since 1943 and liked it very much. The people in Canada seemed much better off and happier than those at home in Russia under Stalin's repressive, murdering, totalitarian regime, so Gouzenko and his wife defected. Not only did they defect, but Gouzenko emptied the embassy safe of every sensitive document he could carry and went to the Canadian authorities. The contents of these documents lifted the lid on Soviet espionage against its wartime allies.

At the same time, Allied cryptographers had been trying to break the Soviet 'one-time pad' codes since 1943. These codes were the safest form of encipherment known. The sender and recipient both had copies of the same pad, each sheet of which contained a different code, which was used once, torn out of the pad and then destroyed. During the early years of the war, the Russians ran short of cipher material and began duplicating their one-time pads. In 1946 American cryptanalyst Meredith Gardner began working on the charred remains of a Russian codebook found at a battle site in Finland. Using the information in this document, Gardner began checking back through intercepted Russian radio traffic and realized that the information had been duplicated in some cases. His first break came in the Washington–Moscow ambassadorial channel when he recognized a phrase from a US book on defence strategy. At this point the information was shared with the British and a joint attempt was made to break the Russian traffic which lasted until October 1980. The codename given to the project was *Venona*.[28]

When faced with Gouzenko's documents and *Venona*, Soviet networks began to fall like dominoes. The first major victim was Alan Nunn May, who was sentenced to ten years' imprisonment in 1946. Next to fall was Fuchs, who was implicated by the *Venona* decrypts. After the end of the war, Fuchs had returned to England to work at the

Harwell Atomic Energy Research Establishment. From 1947 to 1949 Fuchs passed information on the development of the hydrogen bomb to his case officer, Alexander Feklisov. When confronted by MI5 in 1950 Fuchs confessed and received a 14-year sentence.

In his confession Fuchs stated that he did not know the true identity of his American contact, *Raymond*. He gave only a few descriptive details of the man, from which the FBI began an exhaustive manhunt. They checked all the locations Fuchs and *Raymond* had met. The breakthrough came when Fuchs' sister and her husband recalled meeting *Raymond* on one occasion. They remembered him mentioning something about chemistry and Philadelphia. The FBI checked and cross-checked and eventually came up with the name Harry Gold.

On 22 May 1950, Gold confessed and then incriminated an American soldier called David Greenglass, who had been posted to Los Alamos in 1944. Gold confirmed he had collected secrets from Greenglass on behalf of his Soviet controller, who was known to him only as *John*, but who was of course Yakovlev. Greenglass was arrested and, in order to protect his wife, cut a deal with the FBI. He blamed his sister Ethel and her husband Julius Rosenberg for getting him involved.

Julius Rosenberg was an electrical engineer who joined the Army Signal Corps in 1940. He was also a confirmed communist and met his wife Ethel through membership of the Young Communist League. In 1943 Rosenberg began providing information first to NKVD agent Alexander Feklisov – who later became Fuchs' case officer after being reassigned to London – then to Yakovlev. When pressed for information on the Manhattan Project by Yakovlev, the Rosenbergs enlisted Greenglass to steal documents on their behalf. Arrested and convicted, both Ethel and Julius Rosenberg were sentenced to death. They went to the electric chair in New York's Sing Sing Prison on 19 June 1953.

The execution of the Rosenbergs has been the source of some controversy. Other spies, especially Fuchs, had done more damage and received lesser sentences, but Fuchs had confessed his crimes whereas the Rosenbergs did not. The decision must also be looked at in the context of its time. In 1948 the first Cold War flashpoint developed when the Soviets blocked all ground corridors to West Berlin, causing the Berlin Airlift. Then in 1950 the Korean War erupted when United Nations troops went to the aid of South Korea, which was being invaded by the Chinese-backed, communist North Koreans. Perhaps most significantly, on 29 August 1949 the Soviet Union tested its first atomic bomb. As former US Secretary State of Defense Robert McNamara said when reflecting on those times: 'Cold War? Hell, it was a hot war!'[29] The death of the Rosenbergs was a clear signal of how serious the US government considered the communist threat to be.

The Soviets were next betrayed by Whittaker Chambers, a former agent turned whistleblower. Chambers had been sent to Moscow in 1933 in order to receive spy training. On his return Chambers became part of the Ware Group, a secret communist cell in Washington DC. His main task was to act as a courier between the group and their Soviet controller, Boris Bykov. However, Chambers quit the communist movement in response to Stalin's Great Purge and, to protect himself, put a collection of incriminating documents away for a rainy day. Chambers went on to become a senior editor at *Time Magazine* where he pursued a strong anti-communist agenda. When Stalin signed the 1939 non-aggression pact with Nazi Germany, Chambers could take no more. He went to Assistant Secretary of State Adolf Berle and passed on everything he knew about Soviet activity in the United States.

Chambers' story was more or less forgotten until it was picked up in 1948 by future US President Richard Nixon (1913–94), then a Representative from California. Eager for scalps, Nixon had Chambers testify before the House of Un-American Activities Committee. Chambers produced a list of people he claimed were communists, including the high-ranking State Department official Alger Hiss. If this was true it was highly embarrassing because in 1945 Hiss had attended the Yalta conference between Roosevelt, Stalin and Churchill and was responsible for negotiating the Soviet Union's three seats on the United Nations. Chambers' claims were initially rubbished and when repeated on a radio show, Hiss filed a libel suit. In defence, Chambers produced the documents he had put away, reduced to microfilm and hidden in a hollowed-out pumpkin. After two trials Hiss was convicted, not of espionage, but of perjury. It was only later that *Venona* transcripts revealed that Hiss had been a Soviet spy since 1935 under the codename *Ales*.[30]

Crossing back to Britain, *Venona* put FBI agent Robert Lamphere on the hunt for the mysterious *Homer*, who was believed to have worked at the British embassy in Washington from 1944 to 1946 and had been passing messages to the Soviets. By a process of elimination a shortlist of possibles was drawn up with Donald Maclean heading the list. While

Lamphere was investigating the case, Maclean's co-conspirator Kim Philby was sent to Washington and was made aware of the *Venona* project. Realizing that Maclean was about to be blown and might confess everything, he ordered Guy Burgess to return to London and get Maclean to defect to Russia. Under additional orders from Moscow, Burgess actually went with Maclean, leaving Britain on Friday 25 May 1951 – MI5 had scheduled his interrogation for the following Monday. News of their defection came like a thunderbolt to the British secret services. Philby immediately came under instant suspicion as the 'third man' who had tipped them off. Although nothing was proven, Philby was forced to resign because of his close ties to Burgess.

On 5 March 1953 Stalin died and was replaced by Nikita Khrushchev (1894–1971). Inevitably there had been a scramble for the top job among Stalin's former lieutenants, including Lavrenti Beria, head of the wartime NKVD, which since 1946 had been become the Ministry of Internal Affairs or MVD. In fact some believed that Beria had been responsible for poisoning Stalin at a dinner on the evening he collapsed four days before dying.

With Stalin dead, Beria adopted a much more liberal approach, outlawing torture, releasing a million political prisoners and encouraging hard-line Soviet satellite states to become more moderate. This populist approach did him no favours among the Soviet old guard who mounted a coup against Beria and arrested him. Leading the revolt was Khrushchev, who accused Beria of being a British spy and wanting to restore capitalism. Worse was to follow. He was accused of having raped teenage girls, of having contracted syphilis from prostitutes, using drugs to get women into bed, and that he enjoyed personally torturing and killing his victims. On 23 December 1953 Beria was sentenced to death and shot along with a number of his top aides.

The following year, on 13 March 1954, the secret service was reorganized so as never to have the same power it had enjoyed under Stalin. This new organization was the Komitet gosudarstvennoi bezopasnosti (KGB) – the Committee for State Security. This organization – perhaps the most synonymous with the Cold War – was responsible for a wide range of activities, from guarding leadership figures and government buildings to international spying and carrying out counter-intelligence, or even *aktivnye meropriiatiia* – active measures, which included undercover and deception operations in support of Soviet foreign policy. Responsible for KGB foreign operations was the First Chief Directorate. This body was in turn composed of three separate directorates:

Directorate S, responsible for espionage abroad

Directorate T, responsible for the collection of scientific and technological intelligence

Directorate K, responsible for the infiltration of foreign intelligence services and surveillance over Soviet citizens abroad

In addition to these divisions, the First Chief Directorate employed three services:

Service I, responsible for analyzing intelligence collected by KGB agents, producing a daily summary for the Politburo and forecasting future world events

Service A, responsible for planning and implementing 'active measures'

Service R, responsible for evaluating KGB operations abroad

The First Chief Directorate was organized into 11 geographical departments which supervised KGB employees assigned to foreign residences. These *rezidenty* officers operated under legal cover much the same as attachés, but were engaged in the illegal activities associated with espionage and other covert operations.[31]

Despite the reorganizations, more Soviet spies were exposed in the 1950s. In June 1953, newspaper delivery boy Jimmy Bozart was making his collections and was given a nickel, which felt lighter than the other coins. He dropped the coin and was amazed to see it split in two, revealing a small photograph inside. The boy told a girl about it and she told her father – a detective from New York City. The detective obtained the coin and passed it to the FBI, which sent it to its laboratory for analysis. The photograph revealed a numerical coded message, which left the FBI puzzled until the defection of a KGB officer in May 1957.

Lieutenant-Colonel Reino Hayhanen had been working in America for five years and had been ordered to return to Moscow. Like Gouzenko before him, Hayhanen decided not to go back. In return for asylum,

Hayhanen was very forthcoming about KGB activities in New York. His controller was known to him as *Mikhail*, whom he communicated with by using dead-letter drops. Two of these were located in the New York area. In one of these 'dead drops' FBI agents found a hollowed-out bolt containing a typewritten message. When questioned about the bolt, Hayhanen revealed that KGB agents used a variety of hollowed-out objects for concealing messages, including pens, screws, batteries and coins. During questioning, Hayhanen provided information on Soviet codes that allowed the message discovered by Jimmy Bozart to be read. Bizarrely, it turned out to be a message addressed to Hayhanen on his arrival in the United States.

The hunt for *Mikhail* began. By showing Hayhanen photos of Soviet embassy staff, the FBI identified Mikhail Svirin as his contact. Unfortunately Svirin had returned to the Soviet Union in 1956 and could not be prosecuted. However, Hayhanen's next controller, *Mark*, was still believed to be active. Of all their various meeting places, Hayhanen remembered a photographic storage room on the fourth or fifth floor of a building near Clark and Fulton streets in Brooklyn. A search led the FBI to an address in Fulton Street and the apartment of a certain Emil Goldfus.

After a stakeout, the FBI showed a photograph of Goldfus to Hayhanen who immediately recognized him. On the morning of 21 June 1957, Goldfus was arrested. With him a whole host of espionage paraphernalia was discovered, including a short-wave radio, cipher pads, cameras and a variety of hollowed-out containers. After initially refusing to co-operate, Goldfus admitted he was a Russian citizen, Rudolf Abel. In October 1957 Abel was tried and convicted of espionage. Because he would not co-operate, Abel was sentenced to the electric chair, but this was later commuted to a 30-year custodial sentence after his lawyer James Donovan argued that Abel might one day prove useful as a hostage. He did.

On 1 May 1960, US pilot Francis Gary Powers took off from an air base in Pakistan in a U2 spyplane. The U2 had been in service since 1956 and was capable of passing over Russian defences to take high-resolution photographs of the Soviet Union. However, during the mission a surface-to-air missile badly damaged Powers' plane over Sverdlovsk, which, incidentally, was the place Tsar Nicholas and his family were executed by the Bolsheviks in 1918. Before bailing out,

Powers failed to activate the U2's self-destruct mechanism, nor did he use his CIA 'suicide pin' that had been issued to U2 pilots to spare them the ordeal of torture.

Four days later the United States released a press statement that a NASA weather research plane had gone missing north of Turkey. The pilot had reported oxygen difficulties and may have passed out leaving the plane on autopilot – it was feared the plane may have accidentally passed into Russian airspace. Khrushchev was having none of it. On 7 May he announced the shooting down of a US spy plane and that the pilot was still alive. The Soviets also announced they had been able to recover the surveillance cameras intact and developed the photographs. This came at a very bad time for US President Eisenhower (1890–1969), who was scheduled to meet Khrushchev at a disarmament summit in Paris on 16 May. Khrushchev attended the summit and then immediately walked out after Eisenhower refused to apologize. Powers was convicted of espionage and sentenced to ten years. However, on 10 February 1962 Powers was taken to East Berlin where he was exchanged for Abel on the Glienicke Bridge.

On Sunday 14 October 1962 a U2 spyplane began its six-minute flight over Cuba. In that short time 928 pictures were taken of an area 75 miles (120km) wide. The film was delivered to the Naval Photographic Interpretation Center (NPIC) in Maryland, where it was analyzed. The photographs clearly showed surface-to-surface missiles, which had been deployed by the Soviet military on Khrushchev's orders. Thus began one of the most tense periods of the Cold War.

The fact that nuclear war was averted and President John F. Kennedy (1917–63) survived with his reputation intact is partly attributable to information passed on by a Soviet traitor, Oleg Penkovsky (1919–63). A colonel in the GRU (Soviet military intelligence), Penkovsky was convinced that Khrushchev was taking the Soviet Union down a very dangerous road that would ultimately result in its destruction. Using MI6 agent Greville Wynne as an intermediary, Penkovsky arranged a meeting with British Intelligence during a visit to London in 1961. He then began passing a large number of high-grade secrets to British intelligence through MI6's station chief in Moscow, Ruari Chisholm, whose wife Janet would meet Penkovsky in a Moscow park and collect documents while playing with her children. Among the documents Penkovsky provided were rocket manuals that allowed NPIC to identify the missiles in Cuba as Soviet SS4 and SS5s.

Penkovsky's information gave Kennedy a tremendous edge. Knowing that the true sum of Soviet missiles was much less than Khrushchev made out, the American president was able to hold his nerve longer than Khrushchev, who 'blinked first'. Not wanting to risk a war, Khrushchev opened what they call a 'back-channel' to Kennedy. The KGB station chief in Washington DC was Alexander Feklisov, the same man who had been involved in the Rosenberg and Fuchs cases. Under the alias of 'Alexander Fomin', Feklisov met the journalist John Scali and, off the record, outlined Khrushchev's terms for a resolution over Cuba. Essentially this was a Soviet withdrawal of missiles in return for a pledge by the United States not to take any hostile action against Cuba. These points formed the basis on which Kennedy negotiated and by this means Khrushchev was able to back down without losing face in front of Soviet hardliners.

Unfortunately for Penkovsky, two Washington-based KGB double agents, Jack Dunlap and William Whalen, sold him out. On 20 October 1962, Penkovsky's apartment was raided and a spy camera was recovered. He was arrested and shot for espionage soon after his trial in 1963. In the wake of the incident the Chisholms were expelled from Moscow and Wynne was arrested in Budapest. He was taken back to the Soviet Union where he was sentenced to eight years in prison. Before serving out his time, Wynne was exchanged in 1964 for a KGB spy in Britain.

After the disaster of Maclean, Burgess and Philby, the British secret service could hardly have thought anything as bad could follow. Unfortunately it did. The treachery of MI6 agent George Blake drove a wedge between the British secret service and the Americans, who found it increasingly difficult to trust the British.

Born in Rotterdam, Blake's real name was Georg Behar. He was a member of SOE during the war, then joined MI6, despite failing the cardinal rule of agents requiring British parents. During the Korean War Blake was taken prisoner by the North Koreans and, although he later denied it, was probably brainwashed by the Chinese.[32] On his return to Europe after three years in captivity, Blake continued to work for MI6 and was sent to Berlin where he was assigned to Operation *Gold*. This was a CIA plan to dig a tunnel into East Berlin and tap into Soviet telephone and telegraph land lines. Since 1951 the Soviets had been shifting military traffic from wireless communication, which could be intercepted, to secure land lines. Work on the tunnel began in

February 1954 and took a complete year before the taps were put in place. Blake told his case officer, Sergei Kondrashev, about the tunnel in February 1954. Initially the KGB's first priority was to protect Blake as a source, so the tunnel was allowed to operate until the tap could be traced. On the night of 21–22 April 1956 a team of Soviet engineers 'accidentally' found the tunnel while digging up cables.

Blake's treachery was exposed by information provided by a mole calling himself *Sniper* – in fact Polish intelligence officer Michal Goleniewski. Blake was arrested in April 1961 and tried. He received the longest peacetime sentence for espionage in British history: 42 years. Amazingly, though, Blake escaped from London's Wormwood Scrubs prison in 1967 and fled to Moscow. In addition to Blake, Goleniewski had mentioned a spy working in the British Admiralty. After a painstaking investigation, MI5 turned their attention to the Underwater Weapons Establishment at Portland, which at the time led the field in submarine detection. By going through all the employees, MI5 noticed a clerk named Harry Houghton, who had been a naval attaché in Poland. Houghton was put under surveillance and this led MI5 to 'Gordon Lonsdale', the alias of Soviet agent Conan Molody.

The Soviet agent had recruited Houghton and his mistress 'Bunny' Gee, who also worked at Portland. After collecting stolen documents from Houghton and Gee, Molody delivered them to a bungalow in the quiet London suburb of Ruislip. There antiquarian book dealer Peter Kroger and his wife Helen would photograph the documents then reduce them down to microdot size. The Krogers were in fact Morris and Lona Cohen who had previously worked as Russian agents in America for Rudolf Abel. Moving to England in 1954, posing as Canadians, the couple's home was a fully equipped Soviet communications centre with a short-wave radio hidden under a trap door beneath the refrigerator. Once MI5 pieced this together they pounced. On 7 January 1961 Special Branch arrested Houghton, Gee and Lonsdale in the act of passing secrets. The Krogers were then picked up in their bungalow. Lonsdale was later exchanged for Greville Wynne while the Krogers were sent back to Russia in 1969 in a separate exchange.

More embarrassment for the British establishment came in the 1963 Profumo Affair. It revolved around a series of parties held by Stephen Ward, an osteopath to the rich and famous. Ward's parties were notorious affairs – perhaps best described as orgies. In 1961 Secretary of State for

War John Profumo was 'introduced' by Ward to showgirl model Christine Keeler. A brief affair ensued, which would have been hushed up if Keeler had not also been sharing a bed with Yevgeny Ivanov, naval attaché at the Soviet embassy. Amidst accusations of a security breach, in March 1963 Profumo stood up in the House of Commons and lied, claiming that there had been no impropriety in his relationship with Keeler. Ten weeks later Profumo again stood up, but this time admitted the truth and resigned. His resignation was followed a month later by that of British Prime Minister Harold Macmillan (1894–1986), on grounds of ill health, in part caused by the stress of the Profumo scandal.

What was truly scandalous about the whole thing was not that Ward's apartment had two-way mirrors or that people went to orgies in Britain, but rather the allegation that MI5 was running a brothel in Church Street, Kensington, which was being used to 'entertain' foreign diplomats. Apparently MI5 also arranged discreet 'home visits' for its more discerning customers. Ward, it seems, played a part in this seedy world as a match maker. He was introduced to Yevgeny Ivanov by MI5 agent Keith Wagstaff and instructed to fix the Russian up with a girl who might cause him to defect. Hence Keeler met Ivanov. When the Profumo scandal blew up, Ward was dropped like a hot potato. In 1963 he was charged with living off immoral earnings – a polite way of calling him a pimp. Nothing was said about his work for the secret service during the trial. Before the jury returned a verdict, Ward committed suicide in his cell.

Another notable British traitor was sex offender Geoffrey Prime. Having offered his services to the KGB while posted to West Berlin, Prime was instructed to apply for a position at GCHQ, the British code-breaking establishment. In September 1968 Prime became a translator for GCHQ and during service was highly trusted. In 1975 he transferred to work on the intelligence provided by Rhyolite spy satellites. The following year he was made section head and became privy to all information on spy satellites, which was extremely important as throughout the Cold War America relied almost exclusively on signal intelligence and reconnaissance satellites to penetrate the Soviet Union. After August 1959, with the first successful *Corona* mission, America had built successively more sophisticated satellites until they were capable of photographing small objects or, as was the case with Rhyolite, eavesdropping on telephone conversations. For selling out the spy satellite programme Prime received just £800. He later quit the spying game and ended up driving taxis. It was only when he was arrested on charges of molesting young girls that Prime's wife informed on his being a spy. Prime received a 38-year sentence, only three years relating to the sex offences. In wartime he would have swung.

Of course the KGB was not alone in the Cold War struggle and was closely involved with the secret services of their Eastern Bloc allies. This involvement was not always in the KGB's best interests, as proved in the 1978 murder of journalist Georgi Markov, an outspoken critic of the communist regime in Bulgaria. Embarrassed by Markov's critical radio broadcasts, the Bulgarian party secretary, Todor Zhivkov, requested KGB help in getting rid of the dissident.[33] The then chairman of the KGB, Yuri Andropov,[34] was initially reluctant to get involved with the Bulgarians but eventually agreed to provide them a choice of weapons. The Bulgarians chose an umbrella, the tip of which fired a capsule impregnated with ricin. On 7 September 1978 Markov was waiting at a bus stop on London's Waterloo Bridge. A stranger jabbed him in the leg with the umbrella, apologized and carried on his way.[35] The ricin went to work, but took three days to kill Markov. The poison capsule was supposed to dissolve in the body within 24 hours, but was discovered during the examination of his body and caused a major scandal.

More independent than the Bulgarian secret service was East Germany's secret police – the Stasi. This organization had been formed in 1950 and was partly recruited from former Gestapo officers. The organization built up a network of some 300,000 civilian informants who helped keep dissidents in check. When the Berlin Wall came down in 1989 the Stasi began shredding its files, but with tens of millions of pages there was simply too much to dispose of. When people began to demand their Stasi files, many were shocked to find that members of their family, close friends and colleagues had been spying on each other for years.

In addition to surveillance on the East German population, the Stasi had an international intelligence-gathering arm known as the HVA. This was headed by Markus Wolf from 1958 to 1987, known as 'the man without a face' by Western intelligence. Wolf's HVA had about 4,000 agents with which it infiltrated NATO headquarters and the administration of West German Chancellor Willy Brandt.[36]

Technology played only a subordinate role in Wolf's service – he preferred to use real spies. One of the most effective ways of running spies was through the 'Romeo method', in which male agents would be sent round the globe seducing women in order to procure secrets. The technique was pioneered by the KGB, who penetrated embassies in Moscow. 'Red Casanovas', as they were sometimes called, would seduce targets and lure them to where the KGB had hidden cameras. The victims were then blackmailed.

Unlike the KGB who used 'worldly' women to train their Romeos, the Stasi were more puritanical in approach. East German Romeos were schooled by politically reliable and 'morally clean' instructors. The Stasi preferred a 'slow burn'. They wanted their Romeos to develop long-term relationships with targets. One case concerned a West German secretary at the American embassy in Bonn, Gabriela Kliem. In the summer of 1977 she was approached in a restaurant by someone she considered her 'dream man'. An introduction and several bottles of wine later, Kliem was unwittingly in love with a Stasi agent. By the following January, Kliem was photographing hundreds of embassy documents for the Stasi agent, never suspecting his true identity, or that he had a wife in East Germany.[37]

While mentioning that East Germany used ex-Nazis in its secret service, it is only fair to point out that West Germany did likewise. Towards the end of WWII the head of German army intelligence on the Eastern Front predicted that America would one day need his expertise in dealing with the Russians. Therefore in March 1945, Major-General Reinhard Gehlen (1902–79) and some of his senior officers began transferring their documents onto microfilm and burying them on the Bavarian Mountains. In May 1945, Gehlen surrendered to the American Counter-Intelligence Corps (CIC) and made them a proposal. He had a ready-made organization which he was prepared to hand over 'for intelligence work against the Soviet Union.'[38] After hard negotiation, Gehlen was able to restart his anti-Soviet operation despite the post-war policy of de-Nazification.

The Gehlen organization was based near Munich, operating under the cover of the South German Industrial Development Organization. Perhaps the most controversial aspect of the organization was its choice of personnel. Gehlen had hundreds of German officers released from internment camps, including at least 100 Gestapo and SD members, with others suspected of war crimes.[39] Gehlen's organization was controlled completely by the US Army until 1948 when it was taken over by the CIA. The basic arrangement was for the CIA to provide material and funding, while Gehlen provided the agents for espionage and other clandestine operations against Warsaw Pact countries. In 1956 the group came under the German federal government and was renamed the Bundesnachrichtendienst (BND) or State Intelligence Service, which is still in existence today.

During the Reagan years (1981–89) there was a perception that the world was again on the brink of nuclear war. Unlike presidents Nixon, Ford and Carter, Reagan decided to take the Soviet bull by the horns and confront it, not militarily, but through economics. His announcement of the 'Star Wars' SDI missile defence screen was the final straw for the Soviet Union – it simply could not keep throwing money onto the table to maintain its hand in the arms race. By the end of the decade, the Berlin Wall had collapsed and the Soviet Union was teetering on the brink of extinction.

Western policy was influenced by the defection of Oleg Gordievsky, a political intelligence officer in the KGB. Gordievsky was recruited by the head of MI6's Copenhagen station in 1974. His most important contribution was explaining how a paranoid Kremlin feared that President Reagan was preparing to launch a first-strike nuclear attack. In 1981 the KGB had instructed all its stations in NATO countries to report preparations for a first strike. When in 1985 Gordievsky was recalled to the Soviet Union he was considered such an important asset that Prime Minister Margaret Thatcher ordered MI6 to bring him out. Gordievsky was smuggled out of Russia into Finland in a car boot, then flown to London. His debriefing led to a 50-page document entitled *Soviet Perceptions on Nuclear War*, which was distributed to British and American policy makers. When Reagan read the document he decided to tone down his aggressive 'Evil Empire' rhetoric, thus calming Soviet nerves.[40] A year after Gordievsky's defection, Reagan went to Iceland for his first meeting with new Soviet Premier Mikhail Gorbachev.

The 1980s has been called the 'Spy Decade', with 1985 figuring as the 'Year of the Spy'. Other than Gordievsky's defection, there were high-profile arrests in the United States that year. Former US Navy communications specialist John Anthony Walker Junior had spied for the Soviets since the 1960s, not for ideological reasons but purely and simply for cash. In serious debt, Walker had turned up at the Soviet embassy in Washington DC and sold the KGB a US Navy radio cipher card. Over the years he recruited his wife, older brother and son as spies and also Jerry Whitworth, a senior chief radioman in the navy. With a spy ring established, Walker retired from the navy in 1976 and became a private investigator as a front for his espionage activities. To further cement this cover, Walker joined the ultra-conservative John Birch Society and the white supremacist Ku Klux Klan. In the meantime he made a million dollars out of spying, passing on secrets about nuclear submarines and naval ciphers. When he divorced and neglected to pay his former wife alimony, Barbara Walker went to the FBI and told them everything.

In November 1985 three more spies were exposed. Naval intelligence officer Jonathan Pollard was arrested spying for Israel. This was a complex case because Pollard claimed he was warning an American ally about Soviet arms shipments to Syria and Iraq. Prosecutors pointed out that espionage is espionage and he was sent to jail. More clear cut and certainly more damaging was the case of Larry Wu Tai Chin, a retired CIA translator and interpreter who had been spying on behalf of communist China since 1952. Chin began by revealing the identities of Chinese prisoners of war during the Korean War and went on to reveal Nixon's plans for negotiating with China in the 1970s. The defection of a Chinese intelligence officer in 1985 led to Chin's arrest. After confessing, Chin committed suicide in his cell by placing a plastic bag over his head. Lastly, in 1985 National Security Agency (NSA) employee Ronald William Pelton, was arrested and charged with selling military secrets to the Soviets. Although no documents were passed to the Soviets, Pelton's colleagues claimed he had a 'photographic memory' and was able to give a full breakdown of the agency's activities. Like Walker, Pelton did it for money. When he first walked into the Soviet embassy in 1980, Pelton was bankrupt and had quit the NSA. In July 1985, KGB officer Vitaly Yurchenko defected to the United States and denounced Pelton, who was arrested and imprisoned with three life sentences.

In a bizarre twist, Yurchenko then re-defected back to the Soviet Union three months later. While having dinner with a CIA agent, Yurchenko got up, walked out a side door and went to the Soviet embassy, claiming he had been drugged and kidnapped by the CIA. There is a theory he was working as a double agent all along, protecting a recent addition to Soviet espionage – Aldrich Ames. In a frank interview, Yurchenko's former KGB colleague, Boris Solomatin, called this allegation a 'fantasy' and declared Yurchenko was nothing but a 'typical son of a bitch' traitor.[41]

Aldrich Ames is recognized as one of the most damaging traitors in US history. In 1985 he secretly made advances to the KGB at the Soviet embassy. Shortly thereafter, the KGB paid him $50,000, the first of many payments totalling $2.5 million. Inside the CIA, Ames' speciality was Russian intelligence and his first overseas assignment in Turkey had been to target Soviet intelligence officers for recruitment. These responsibilities meant that Ames knew the identities of US sources behind the Iron Curtain. He sold them out.

With all that blood money burning a hole in Ames's pocket, it was only a matter of time before he was caught. When the CIA's Russian contacts were being arrested and executed, the agency guessed they had a mole. It was noticed that Ames was enjoying a lifestyle far beyond the means of his salary, so the FBI got involved and launched a 10-month investigation. Although by now the Cold War had come to an end and the KGB no longer existed, Ames continued to spy for Russia's Foreign Intelligence Service. In February 1994 the CIA scheduled for Ames to go to Moscow, but the FBI feared he might defect. Therefore, on 21 February the FBI closed in, arresting Ames and his wife Rosario. On 28 April 1994, Ames was sentenced to incarceration for life with no chance of parole.

And so it ended.

On reflection, the collapse of the Soviet Union was surprisingly swift and remarkably bloodless. It is ironic how, after all the billions spent on weapons, the USSR simply imploded under the weight of its own introspection. The Iron Curtain did not fall because the people behind it were scared of America or the West. It fell because Eastern Bloc citizens realized they were being cheated by their governments – cheated out of prosperity and denied basic freedoms of expression. It was the same realization Igor Gouzenko had come to in 1945. In the end, people craved less for the teachings of Marx than they did for Levi Jeans and the Rolling Stones.[42]

Only in Romania did the old regime try to fight the reforming tide; but within a month TV showed a firing squad shooting dictator Nicolae Ceausescu (1918–89) and his wife. When the Soviet Union began to break up, hardliners no longer had the power to stop it. A coup against Gorbachev was attempted by elements of the military and KGB in August 1991, but it failed in the face of popular protest. On 25 December 1991, the red flag was lowered from the Kremlin and the Soviet era came to an end. The KGB was disbanded for its role in the coup.

Interviewed by CNN in January 1998, Markus Wolf gave a neat conclusion to the role played by the secret services in the Cold War. He said:

> I'm pretty sure that the intelligence services on the whole, and the spies both in the East and the West, tended towards a more realistic assessment of the balance of power than that of politicians and military leaders; so that actions, or even adventurous actions which could easily have led to an escalation or even to a war, would have been desisted from. So, yes, I do claim that my unit contributed to our having had the longest peacetime in modern European history.[43]

With the threat of a toe-to-toe, nuclear slugging match apparently gone, the world breathed a collective sigh of relief and looked forward optimistically to the new millennium. Some went so far as to call it the 'End of History'.[44] In a century of 'isms', democratic, liberal capitalism had outlived fascism and communism – it was the end of the food chain so far as economic and political development went. People had thought like this before of course; at the end of the Napoleonic Wars, when Europe experienced the Great Peace, or after World War I – the war to end all wars. Each time our optimism has been dashed. The end of the Cold War has proved no exception.[45]

WITH NO END IN SIGHT...

SED QUIS CUSTODIET IPSOS CUSTODES?[1]

The cases of espionage and other secret operations encountered so far are by no means exhaustive, but form a summary of the most important or colourful episodes in history. The more open minded might also like to consider the frontier of *ESP*ionage – where secret service merges with the paranormal. There are many claims that the United States used psychic spies or 'remote viewers' to mentally scan buildings in the search for Saddam Hussein during the Gulf War. In addition there are a whole series of related topics, which fall into the category of 'Black Ops', including the quest to create psychic soldiers – as seen with the strange-but-seemingly-true Project *Jedi*.[2]

From the supernatural to the sinister, we have the 'real Dr Strangelove' – the CIA's Dr Sidney Gottlieb (1918–99). An expert in poison, Gottlieb joined the chemical division of the CIA's Technical Services Staff in 1951. Two years later he headed Project *MKUltra* which investigated the possible military uses of psycho-active drugs, including LSD. Research on CIA agents led Chemical Corps Major-General William Creasey to suggest dropping LSD into an enemy city's water supply as a humane alternative to the use of nuclear weapons. Another colleague of Gottlieb's was Dr Frank Olson. When given LSD without his knowledge, Olson suffered a nervous breakdown and was sent by the CIA to a New York City psychiatrist. Once in the Big Apple, Olson fell 13 storeys out of a hotel window. Although the incident was officially blamed on the side-effects of a 'bad trip', Olson's son maintains his father was thrown from the window after threatening to go public about the programme.[3]

Less far fetched has been the long-running conflict between Irish Republicans and the British government. Of all the espionage stories relating to 'the Troubles', perhaps the most startling was that of a 'mole' codenamed *Stakeknife*. Recruited by the intelligence services in 1978 as a low-ranking IRA volunteer, *Stakeknife* became head of the IRA's internal security unit, the so-called 'nutting squad'. His handlers were the FRU (Force Research Unit), an undercover British military intelligence unit, which mounted covert operations against IRA and Loyalist terrorists. In return for his services, Stakeknife was paid via a Gibraltar-based bank account to the tune of £80,000 a year – then comparable to a cabinet minister's salary.

As head of the nutting squad, *Stakeknife* would have been in charge of vetting IRA recruits and seeking out moles working for the British and Irish governments. It is believed that *Stakeknife* had a hand in the murders of up to 40 suspected informers. It is also believed that to protect *Stakeknife*'s identity, his FRU handlers authorized him to kill three FRU agents. It is also alleged that *Stakeknife* supplied the information leading to the ambush of three IRA volunteers in Gibraltar on 6 March 1988. In February 1989 Belfast estate agent Joseph Fenton was murdered, apparently on *Stakeknife*'s orders. Fenton supplied safe houses for the IRA but also acted as a police informant. When Loyalist paramilitaries began to go after *Stakeknife*, it is alleged that the FRU protected their man by fitting up Francisco Notarantonio with false documents and persuading the Loyalist paramilitary group the Ulster Defence Association (UDA) that he was *Stakeknife*.[4] That British intelligence could have been privy to so many murders proved somewhat unpalatable to say the least.

Another spy of note is former MI5 agent William Carlin.[5] A soldier in the Queen's Royal Irish Hussars, Carlin was approached by MI5 in 1974 and asked to return to his native Derry and become involved in the political side of the Republican movement. Over a number of years, Carlin began to work his way into Sinn Fein, the political wing of the IRA, reporting back to his handlers on the activities of activist Martin McGuinness.

In 1980 Carlin became disillusioned with the behaviour of the army and security services in Northern Ireland and quit MI5. However, he found it much harder to disengage himself from his political work with Sinn Fein. In 1981 Carlin re-established contact with the security services after the murder of census-collector Joanne Mathers. Rather than being handled directly by MI5, Carlin was run by the FRU, although he did not know this at the time. Carlin rose through the ranks of Sinn Fein, all the while providing his handlers with detailed information on McGuinness and other political intelligence. Carlin's cover was then blown by one of his former MI5 handlers.

Michael Bettaney was recruited to MI5 in 1982. His erratic behaviour was perhaps best summed up by one MP in a House of Commons debate:

'He was an alcoholic, a misfit, a fantasist, a curious wild and way-out character, whose fatal weakness was alcohol in a big way. He used to be so drunk among his Security Service colleagues that he could not stand up. On one occasion, he even set fire to himself. He had two convictions for criminal dishonesty. At social occasions in the MI5 mess he used to say things such as, "Come and see me in my dacha when I retire". "I am sure the East Germans would look after me better." "I am working for the wrong side."'[6]

Another popular Bettaney story is that having not paid for a rail journey, he was chased through the carriages by a ticket inspector and police, shouting 'You can't arrest me, I'm a spy!' The amazing thing was that Bettaney really was working for the Soviets, copying secret documents and passing them on to the KGB. His treachery was eventually exposed by KGB mole Oleg Gordievsky.[7] Bettaney was arrested and put on remand in Wandsworth prison. There he met Patrick Magee, an IRA member charged with bombing the 1984 Tory Party conference in the Grand Hotel, Brighton. Bettaney is believed to have told Magee that the British had a spy close to McGuinness. Magee passed this news on to the Republicans who began an investigation. Other informants within the IRA warned that Carlin's cover had been blown and so, on 3 March 1985, Carlin's handler telephoned him at midnight and told him it was time to leave. He was taken with his family to a secret location in Britain.

In an unexpected twist to the case, Carlin gave evidence in support of McGuinness in an investigation into the deaths of 14 civilians at the 'Bloody Sunday' civil rights protest in 1972. At the time it was claimed that British soldiers opened fire on the demonstrators after shots were fired at them. It was alleged that Martin McGuinness, then second-in-command of the Provisional IRA in Londonderry, had opened fire on the British troops. According to Carlin, the accusation against

McGuinness was based on a conversation reported by him, but which was being used out of context and wrongly in his opinion.[8]

Dirty tricks are by no means the sole preserve of Anglo-Saxon agencies. In 1985 France grabbed the headlines by sinking the Greenpeace ship *Rainbow Warrior*. In the 1980s France had been testing new nuclear devices on Mururoa Atoll in the Pacific. Greenpeace planned to go to the atoll and disrupt these tests. To prevent this occurring, plans were drawn up for France's intelligence and covert action bureau (DGSE) to sink the Greenpeace ship. Codenamed Operation *Satanic*, three DGSE teams were dispatched to New Zealand where the ship was moored in Auckland Harbour. On the night of 10 July, two small explosions tore into the hull of *Rainbow Warrior*. Four minutes later the ship had sunk. Although the French saboteurs had planted the explosions so as not to harm any of the crew, photographer Fernando Pereira drowned trying to rescue his equipment.

France initially denied any involvement in the attack, but New Zealand's police force arrested two agents, Alain Mafart and Dominique Prieur, who were each found guilty of manslaughter and sentenced to ten years' imprisonment. Both agents were later transferred into French 'custody' in 1986 and were both freed in 1988. It is believed the other saboteurs were picked up by a French nuclear submarine. A story in *The Sunday Times* claimed President Mitterrand knew of the plan and in the subsequent scandal, France's Defence Minister, Charles Hernu, resigned, while Admiral Pierre Lacoste, director of the DGSE, was sacked. Twenty years after the operation, *Le Monde* published a report written by Admiral Lacoste, revealing that President Mitterrand had in fact given him his personal authorization for the operation.

Although the days of the KGB are behind us, their heirs are still at work. Witness the case of the opposition leader Viktor Yushchenko, who was apparently poisoned during the controversial Ukrainian elections of 2004. On 5 September 2004, Yushchenko attended a dinner hosted by Volodymyr Satsiuk – deputy head of the SBU, Ukraine's secret service. Shortly afterwards Yushchenko was taken ill with severe abdominal and back pains. His face then became unusually bloated and pock-marked, a characteristic symptom of dioxin poisoning. It was subsequently alleged that a Russian political scientist, Gleb Pavlovsky, came up with the idea of giving Yushchenko 'the mark of the beast' by disfiguring him and that the poison was administered during the dinner with Satsiuk. Despite these and other 'dirty tricks', Yushchenko was inaugurated President of Ukraine on 23 January 2005.[9]

Another agency no stranger to 'active measures' is Israel's 'Institute for Intelligence and Special Operations' – better known as Mossad. As an active participant in the long-running Arab-Israeli conflict many of Mossad's operations have yet to be declassified. Although a number of high-profile cases are currently in the public domain – that is to say, published on the internet – there is little hard evidence available.[10]

When the State of Israel was declared in 1948 it immediately came under attack by its Arab neighbours. Recognizing that the first line of defence was intelligence, Israel's government formed Mossad on 13 December 1949. The organization is responsible for a wide range of covert activities, from espionage to secretly aiding Jewish refugees reach Israel, the movement of Ethiopian Jews to avoid the famine of 1984 being a good example of this.

Widely recognized as the top spy in Israeli history, Eli Cohen (1924–65) infiltrated the Syrian government in 1962 under the alias 'Kamel Amin Tsa'abet'. To establish his cover, Cohen posed as a Syrian returning from Argentina. One of his more notable achievements was to suggest that the Syrian military should plant trees in front of its outposts facing Israel, to guard them from view. In reality the reverse was true: everywhere the Israeli military saw a group of eucalyptus trees they knew where to find Syrians. In 1965 Cohen was caught sending a radio message. Found guilty of espionage, he was publicly hanged in Damascus on 18 May 1965.

That same year, Mossad lost its top spy in Egypt, Wolfgang Lotz (1921–93). Posing as a West German war veteran recently returned from Australia, Lotz was sent to Egypt to collect information on Soviet arms being supplied to President Nasser's government, including MiG warplanes and SAM missiles. Lotz also provided Mossad with the names of the German scientists working on a missile programme for Egypt. Mossad was then able to intimidate many of the scientists into quitting the project. Unluckily, Lotz was arrested in a Soviet-inspired clamp down on West Germans in Egypt. Wrongly believing the Egyptians had discovered he was a spy, Lotz confessed to everything. He fell back on a cover story of being a German pressed into service by Mossad against his will and was believed. Sentenced to life imprisonment, Lotz was exchanged with other Israeli spies after the 1967 war.

Mossad operatives have also been linked to a number of assassination missions carried out against members of the Palestinian group Black September in retaliation for the killing of 11 Israeli athletes at the 1972 Munich Olympics. In many respects, the Munich killings were to Israel what 9/11 was to the United States. In both cases – whether officially admitted or not – the gloves came off in respect to the government's dealing with the issue of terrorism. The Israeli response was to take the fight to the terrorists in a series of revenge attacks dubbed Operation *Wrath of God* by the media.

The members of the 'Avner' *Wrath of God* group were reportedly told to resign from Mossad in order to cut any trace of Israeli government involvement.[11] They were provided with unlimited money in a Swiss account and a list of 11 targets they were to assassinate.[12] Their first 'hit' was in Rome against Wael Zwaiter, the cousin of Palestine Liberation Organization (PLO) chief Yasser Arafat. Two Israeli agents shot Zwaiter in the lobby of his apartment. Before opening fire the agents were careful to identify Zwaiter properly – their instructions were only to kill when absolutely certain they had the right man and never to risk injuring a third party. This rule led to problems with the next hit, as the suspect had his family living with him. Mahmoud Hamshari was the PLO's official representative in Paris.[13] The assassins broke into Hamshari's apartment dressed as telecom engineers and placed a small bomb inside his telephone. On the morning of 8 December 1972, after the suspect's wife and daughter had left the apartment, one of the agents telephoned Hamshari under the pretext of conducting an interview. Once Hamshari confirmed his identity, the agent detonated the telephone bomb by remote control. Hamshari was mortally wounded by the explosion and died a month later.

The group went on to perform four more successful missions, including one against Zaid Muchassi, who had not been on the original list but had replaced Abad al-Chir as the PLO contact with the KGB. While killing Muchassi the group also shot the PLO man's KGB contact who was waiting outside the building and appeared to be drawing a gun as the group made their escape.[14] In March 1973 Mossad learned that three targets from the original list were meeting in Beirut. These were Mahmoud Yussuf Najjer, Kamal Nasser and Kemal Adwan. An operation to get these three men was launched and codenamed *Spring of Youth*. On 10 April 1973, approximately 40 Israeli commandos landed on a Beirut beach and were met by an advance party of Mossad agents. Together they tracked down and killed the three targets.[15]

Completely independent from the Avner group, another team was sent after Israel's principal assassination target, Ali Hassan Salameh, believed to be the organizer of the Munich operation. On 21 July 1973 this team accidentally shot dead an innocent man in Lillehammer, Norway, whom they believed was Salameh. The actual victim was Ahmed Bouchiki, a Moroccan waiter walking home from the cinema with his pregnant wife. Norwegian police arrested six of the Israeli agents and recovered documents linking them to Mossad. They also passed details of a safe house in Paris to the French authorities who uncovered more evidence linking the Israeli government to the murder of Palestinians. Undeterred by such embarrassing setbacks, Mossad made several more attempts against Salameh, finally killing him in Beirut with a remote-controlled car bomb on 22 January 1979.[16]

Mossad is also believed to have been behind the 1988 assassination of senior PLO figure Abu Jihad in Tunis and is one of several suspects behind the murder of Gerald Bull, a Canadian aerospace engineer. Bull was the designer behind Project *Babylon*, better known as the Iraq 'Supergun', and also worked on a project to build a multi-stage missile for Iraq. In March 1990, as he returned to his Brussels apartment, he was shot five times in the back of the head.[17] Other suspected parties include the secret services of Iran and Iraq itself.

It is widely believed that Mossad kidnapped Mordechai Vanunu, a former nuclear technician who revealed details of Israel's nuclear weapons programme to the British newspaper *The Sunday Times* in 1986. Following this disclosure, an American Mossad agent calling herself *Cindy* began an affair with Vanunu in London and persuaded him to go to Rome with her. It was the oldest trick in the book. Once in Italy, Vanunu claims he was drugged and returned to Israel where he faced treason charges. In 1988 he was sentenced to 18 years' imprisonment. He was released in 2004 under heavy restrictions.

In 1991 the American investigative journalist Seymour Hersh's book *The Samson Option* accused Nicholas Davies, the foreign editor of the *Daily Mirror*, of tipping off the Israeli embassy that Vanunu was giving his story to *The Sunday Times* and had tried to pass it to the *Sunday Mirror*, a title owned by Czech-born media tycoon Robert Maxwell, who was thought to have contacts with Israeli intelligence.

These allegations were not exactly new. Hersh's principal source, Ari Ben-Menashe, had made these allegations before, but no British newspaper would publish them for fear of legal action. Even when repeated in Hersh's book, no one would run the story.

In order to circumvent the threat of legal action, on 21 October 1991, MP Rupert Allason raised the issue in the House of Commons, which enabled newspapers to report the allegations. Allason's early-day motion expressed concern that the *Daily Mirror* and Maxwell had maintained a close relationship with Mossad and that in 1983 Nicholas Davies had gone into partnership with Ari Ben-Menashe and 'negotiated the sale of 4,000 TOW anti-tank missiles to Iran in contravention of the United Nations arms embargo then in force in 1987'. Allason's motion also alleged that Davies had conspired to supply information on Vanunu's whereabouts to the Israeli embassy. Allason asked if the Secretary of State for Trade and Industry would investigate the alleged export of weapons and suspend confidential and Foreign and Commonwealth Office briefings to Mirror Group personnel until an investigation was completed.[18] The following day, Allason asked the Leader of the House, John MacGregor: 'Will he ask the Prime Minister, as head of the security and intelligence services, to order an immediate inquiry into the alleged relationship between the Israeli intelligence service and Robert Maxwell and especially Mr. Nicholas Davies, the news editor of the *Daily Mirror*?'[19]

British newspapers began publishing the allegations, and although Maxwell denied the claims, he sacked Davies soon after. The media tycoon then had Hersh and his publishers, Faber and Faber, issued with a writ for libel. However, on the night of 5/6 November 1991, Robert Maxwell died when he fell off his yacht, the *Lady Ghislaine*, while cruising off the Canary Islands. The official verdict was accidental drowning, but, it is fair to say, there are plenty of theories to suggest otherwise, if one cares to look for them.

By now it should be clear how much of world history has been shaped by unseen hands. In nations of democratic tradition the work of secret services is reprehensible to many, but there is no reason to think such things will go away overnight – nor even in the long term. Few people can really be so naive as to believe that elected governments will never again authorize illegal acts in the national interest. However, a balance must be maintained. Elected politicians must always hold ultimate veto over the actions of the secret services, as politicians can then be held accountable through the ballot box. To allow secret services complete freedom to do as they see fit is a recipe for disaster. However, at the same time, they need to be robust enough to make a difference. It is all a question of balance. As Tolstoy declared in *War and Peace* 'the wolves should be fed and the sheep kept safe'.[20]

ENDNOTES

INTRODUCTION

1. *The 9/11 Commission Report: Final report of the National Commission on Terrorist Attacks upon the United States* (Washington, DC: National Commission on Terrorist Attacks upon the United States, 2004), pp.128–129.
2. Ibid., p.141.
3. See *The Office of Strategic Services: America's First Intelligence Agency* (United States Central Intelligence Agency, 2000) available at www.cia.gov/cia/publications/index.html.
4. *The 9/11 Commission Report*, p.89.
5. Steve Coll, *Ghost Wars* (New York: Penguin, 2004), pp.378–379.
6. Ibid., p.411.
7. *The 9/11 Commission Report*. See also Steve Coll, *Ghost Wars*, p.410, for evidence of ISID warning the Taliban, p.123.
8. Ibid., p.140.
9. The following excerpt is from an official statement on the Chinese embassy attack by Bill Harlow, Director of Public Affairs, on 10 April 2000:

   > One of the key findings of the Inspector General's investigation of this matter was that the CIA lacked formal procedures for preparing and forwarding target nomination packages to the U.S. military. We have taken several steps to address the systemic organizational problems that contributed to the accidental bombing of the Chinese Embassy. These steps are classified and we cannot discuss them further.
   >
   > With regard to individual officers involved in the process that led to the bombing, the principal shortcoming the IG investigation identified was the fact that numerous CIA officers at all levels of responsibility failed to ensure that the intended bombing target – the Yugoslav Federal Directorate of Supply and Procurement headquarters – had been properly identified and precisely located before CIA passed a target nomination package to the U.S. military for action.

10. *The Times*, Wednesday 10 August 2005, p.8.
11. House of Commons Foreign Affairs Committee, *The Decision to go to War in Iraq, Ninth Report of Session 2002–03*, Vol. I (The Stationery Office Limited: 7 July 2003), pp.25–26.
12. Ibid., p.10.
13. Ibid., p.24
14. Ibid., p.22.
15. Stephen Grey, 'America's Gulag', *New Statesman* (May 2004). The article quotes former CIA agent Bob Baer as follows: 'If you want a serious interrogation, you send a prisoner to Jordan. If you want them to be tortured, you send them to Syria. If you want someone to disappear – never to see them again – you send them to Egypt.'
16. Charles Bremner, 'Britain accused of turning blind eye to torture flights', *The Times* (25 January 2006).
17. *Parade Magazine* (1 August 2004).

1. IN ANCIENT TIMES

1. Ralph T. H. Griffith, *Rámáyan of Válmíki* (London: Benares, 1870–74) p.442.
2. A scene depicted on the Great Tableau at the Temple of Abû-Simbel.
3. Amelia B. Edwards, *Pharaohs, Fellahs and Explorers* (London: Osgood and McIlvaine, 1891) pp.203–204.
4. Genesis 42:10 (New International Version).
5. Deuteronomy 1:22.
6. Numbers 13:17–20.
7. Numbers 21:32.
8. Joshua 2:1.
9. See Chaim Herzog and Mordechai Gichon, *Battles of the Bible* (London: Weidenfeld and Nicolson, 1978), p.27.
10. Joshua 2:2.
11. Joshua 2:8–10.
12. Joshua 7:2–5.
13. Judges 1:23.
14. Judges 16:5.
15. The other three 'beauties' included Wang Zhaojun, a concubine during the reign of Emperor Yuan (49–33 BC), who was so startlingly attractive, that it is said a flock of geese forgot how to fly and fell from the sky after seeing her. The second beauty was Diao Chan, a singer during the Eastern Han Dynasty (AD 25–220), who, again, was so beautiful, that the moon was said to have hid in shame behind a cloud. Lastly, there was Yang Guifei (AD 719–756), a singer and dancer to whom flowers would bow their heads.
16. Sun Tzû (trans. Lionel Giles), *Sun Tzû on the Art of War: The Oldest Military Treatise in the World* (London: Luzac & Co., 1910), chapter 1.18.
17. Ibid., chapter 13.3.
18. Ibid., chapter 13.4–13.6.
19. Ibid., chapter 13.21–13.25.
20. Ibid., chapter 13.15.
21. Ibid., chapter 13.17.
22. Henry Graham Dakyns (trans.), *Cyropaedia – The Education of Cyrus' by Xenophon* (J. M. Dent: 1906).
23. Aubrey de Sélincourt (trans.), *Herodotus – The Histories* (Harmondsworth: Penguin Books Ltd., 1972), p.491.
24. Ibid., p.513.
25. Xenophon, 'The Cavalry General', from H. G. Dakyns, *The Works of Xenophon* (MacMillan: 1897).
26. See Dr Kedareswar Chakraborty, *Art of Spying in Ancient India* (Kolkata: Sanskrit Book Depot, 2002).
27. Hymn LXXXVII, Varuna, from Ralph T. H. Griffith (trans.), *The Hymns of the Rig Veda* (Benares: E.J. Lazarus & Co., 1896).
28. *Mahabharata*, Book 12, *Santi Parva*, section LXIX, trans. by Kisari Mohan Ganguli (1883–96).
29. Ibid., section CXLII.
30. R. Shamasastry (trans.), *Kautilya's Arthasástra* (Bangalore: Government Press, 1915).

31. Ibid., for more information see Book I, chapters XI–XII, 'The Institution of Spies'.

32. Ibid., see book XIII, *The Strategic Means to Capture a Fortress*.

33. Also see S. M. Hali's 'RAW at War – Genesis of Secret Agencies in Ancient India' (www.defencejournal.com).

34. *The Kama Sutra of Vatsayayana*, Part 1, Chapter 3, trans. Sir Richard Burton, (Cosmopoli: for the Kama Shastra Society of London and Benares, and for private circulation only, 1883).

35. Luke 20:25.

36. Matthew 26:4.

37. Matthew 26:8–9.

38. John 12:3–6.

39. Matthew 26:14–15.

40. Matthew 27:5. An alternative ending is offered in Acts 1:18, in which Judas buys a field, then 'fell headlong, his body burst open and all his intestines spilled out'.

2. THROUGH THE DARK AGES

1. Titus Livius (trans. Rev. Canon Roberts), *The History of Rome* (London: J. M. Dent & Sons, 1912), Vol.2, Bk.10, section 10.10.

2. Titus Livius *The History of Rome*, Vol.3, Bk.22, section 22.33.

3. Polybius, *The Histories* (Loeb Classical Library, 1922–27), Book XIV, section 3.

4. Livius, *The History of Rome* Vol.5, Bk.30, section 30.4.

5. William G. Sinnigen, 'The Roman Secret Service' in *Classical Journal* (1965).

6. Rose Mary Sheldon, 'Toga & Dagger: Espionage in Ancient Rome' from www.historynet.com.

7. Procopius (trans. R. Atwater), *The Secret History of the Court of Justinian* (reprinted Ann Arbor, Michegan: University of Michigan Press, 1961), chapter 30. Text available at *Internet Medieval Sourcebook,* www.fordham.edu/halsall/sbook.html.

8. Ibid., chapter 9.

9. Ibid., chapter 16.

10. Cited in C. W. C. Oman (ed. John H. Beeler), *The Art of War in the Middle Ages* (Ithaca and London: Cornell University Press, 1953) p.39.

11. A. I. Akram, *The Sword of Allah: Khalid bin Al-Waleed: His Life and Campaigns* (Karachi, Dacca: National Publishing House, 1970), p.3, Chapter 29.

12. Oman, *The Art of War in the Middle Ages*, pp.34, 43.

13. From the Sahih Collection of al-Bukhari, www.sunnipath.com/.

14. Oman, *The Art of War in the Middle Ages*, pp.37–38.

15. Akram, *The Sword of Allah*, p.11, Chapter 30.

16. Andrew Sinclair, *The Sword and the Grail* (London: Random House, 1993), p.21.

17. Ronald Latham, *The Travels of Marco Polo* (London: The Folio Society, 1958) p.56.

18. James Chambers, *The Devil's Horsemen – The Mongol Invasion of Europe* (London: The Book Club, 1979), p.142.

19. David Morgan, *The Mongols* (Oxford: Basil Blackwell, 1986), pp.68–69.

20. Chambers, *The Devil's Horsemen*, p.10.

21. Ibid., p.25.
22. Stephen Turnbull, *Ninja: The True Story of Japan's Secret Warrior Cult* (Poole, UK: Firebird Books Ltd, 1991) pp.14–15.
23. Ibid., pp.35–36.
24. Ibid., p.86.
25. Stephen Turnbull, *Warrior 64: Ninja AD 1460–1650* (Oxford: Osprey Publishing, 2003) p.53.

3. SPY, BRITANNIA

1. Francis B. Gummere (trans.), *Beowulf*, The Harvard Classics, Volume 49 (P. F. Collier & Son, 1910).
2. Richard Tomlinson, *The Big Breach – From Top Secret to Maximum Security* (Edinburgh: Cutting Edge Press, 2001). His claims relating to the Diana case were made in the public domain in the form of an affidavit to French judge Herve Stephan.
3. Piers Morgan, *The Insider* (London: Ebury Press, 2005), p.419.
4. Ibid., p.361.
5. S. A. Handford (trans.), *Caesar – The Conquest of Gaul* (Harmondsworth, Middlesex: Penguin Books Ltd, 1959), p.119.
6. Geoffrey of Monmouth (trans. Aaron Thompson), *History of the Kings of Britain* (Cambridge, Ontario: In Parentheses Publications, Medieval Latin Series, 1999), p.96.
7. There are numerous references to spies in: Samuel Laing (trans.), *The Heimskringla or The Chronicle of the Kings of Norway translated from the Icelandic of Snorro Sturleson* (London: Longman, Brown, Green and Longman's, 1844).
8. Geoffrey of Monmouth, *History of the Kings of Britain*, pp.147–148.
9. David Howarth, *1066 The Year of Conquest* (London: Collins, 1977), p.105.
10. Ordericus Vitalis, *Historia Ecclesiastica* can be found at the *Internet Medieval Sourcebook*, www.fordham.edu/halsall/sbook.html.
11. Perhaps better known as *Longshanks* or *Scottorum malleus* – quite literally 'Hammer of the Scots'.
12. J. Haswell, *Spies and Spymasters* (London: Thames and Hudson, 1977), p.26.
13. R. Holinshed, *Chronicles of England, Scotland and Ireland*, Vol. 6 (London: 1807–08), p.445.
14. Ian Arthurson, 'Espionage and Intelligence from the Wars of the Roses to the Reformation', *Nottingham Medieval Studies Journal*, Vol.35 (1991), p.135.
15. Haswell, *Spies and Spymasters*, p.26.
16. Arthurson, 'Espionage and Intelligence', p.141.
17. A. W. Wishart, *A Short History of Monks and Monasteries* (Trenton, New Jersey: Albert Brandt, 1900), pp.310–311.
18. Ibid., p.315.
19. Ibid., pp.323–324.
20. Niccolò Machiavelli (trans. Peter Whitehorne & Edward Dacres), *Machiavelli Volume 1* (London: David Nutt, 1905), p.322.
21. Machiavelli, *Machiavelli*, pp.218–219.
22. In another of his works (*Art of War*), Machiavelli gives a simple yet brilliant piece of advice on counter-espionage: 'When thou wilte see if in the daie there be comen

anie spie into the Campe, cause everie man to goe to his lodgynge.'

23. Simon Singh, *The Code Book* (London: Fourth Estate, 1999), pp.27–28.

24. Charles Nicholl, *The Reckoning* (London: Cape, 1992), p.175.

25. Properly known as the Society of Jesus, the order of Jesuits was formed by Ignatius de Loyola (1491–1556) in 1522. Born in Spain, Loyola was a soldier until severely wounded at the siege of Pamplona in 1521. While convalescing he dedicated himself to a career devoted to God and founded the Society of Jesus, which received the sanction of Pope Paul III for the 'defence and advance of the faith'. In real terms this meant bringing about an end to Protestantism and maintaining Papal authority. Jesuit missionaries were constantly active in Britain, secretly working to keep alive the hope of a Catholic revival.

26. Alan Haynes, *The Elizabethan Secret Services* (Stroud, UK: Sutton Publishing, 2004), pp.85–86.

27. The letter survives in the British National Archives and can be seen online at www.nationalarchives.gov.uk/spies/.

28. Nicholl, *The Reckoning*, p.186.

29. William Camden's *Rerum Gestarum Angliae et Hiberniae Regnante Elizabetha*, 2 vols (London: 1615 and 1627), 1586, paragraph 42.

30. Trial quotes from Camden, Rerum Gestarum Angliae.

31. Richard Deacon, *A History of the British Secret Service* (London: Muller, 1969), p.30.

32. Ibid., p.33.

33. Haynes, *Elizabethan Secret Services*, p.101.

34. Alan Haynes, *Walsingham – Elizabethan Spymaster & Statesman* (Stroud, UK: Sutton Publishing, 2004), p.201.

35. Ibid., p.202.

36. Ibid., p.101 and Deacon, *History of the British Secret Service*, p.35.

37. Richard Hakluyt (Edited by Edmund Goldsmid), *The Principal Navigations, Voyages, Traffiques, and Discoveries of the English Nation imprinted at London by George Bishop, Ralph Newberie and Robert Baker, Anno 1599* (Edinburgh: E. &. C. Goldsmid, 1884), Vol.VII, Chapter 2.

38. Haynes, *Walsingham*, p.203.

39. Ibid., pp.213–214.

40. Ibid., p.203.

41. See Nicholl, *The Reckoning*.

42. Deacon, *History of the British Secret Service*, pp.54–55.

43. R. Rowan, *The Story of Secret Service* (London: John Miles Ltd, 1938), p.106.

44. It is fascinating to note that this method of concealing firearms had been thought of 400 years before Hollywood mobsters made it their own.

45. Antonia Fraser, *Cromwell – Our Chief of Men* (London: Weidenfield and Nicholson, 1973), pp.584–585.

46. Fraser, *Cromwell*, pp.594–595.

4. ESPIONAGE IN THE AGE OF REASON

1. T. Foster (trans.), *Military Instruction from the late King of Prussia to his Generals* (Sherborne: William Cruttwell, 1797).

2. Presumably Count Raimondo Montecucculi (1609–80), an Italian general in Austrian service and author on military subjects.

3. Maurice, Comte de Saxe, *Mes Rêveries*, Vol. 2, (Paris: 1757), pp.136–137.

4. Charles E. Lathrop, *The Literary Spy: The Ultimate Source for Quotations on Espionage & Intelligence* (New Haven, CT: Yale University Press, 2004), p.256.

5. Prince Charles Alexander of Lorraine (1712–80) was one of the principal Austrian military commanders.

6. Prince Eugène of Savoy (1663–1736) – the French born, principal general in Austrian service during the War of Spanish Succession, 1701–14.

7. François-Henri de Montmorency-Bouteville, Marshal of Luxembourg (1628–95), general for Louis XIV.

8. The location of the incident is not recorded.

9. Foster, *Military Instruction from the late King of Prussia to his Generals*

10. Leroy de Bosroger, *Principes de l'art de la guerre* (Paris: Cellot & Jombert, 1779), pp.104–105.

11. *aide-maréchal général des logis.*

12. Arthur Machen (trans.), *The Memoirs of Jacques Casanova...* (London: Privately printed, 1894), vol. 2a, chapter II.

13. Ibid., vol.2a, chapter II.

14. Ibid., vol.2a, chapter II.

15. Edna Nixon, *Royal Spy – The strange case of the Chevalier d'Eon* (London: Heinemann, 1966), p.37.

16. Ibid., p.38.

17. On the same theme, apparently Thomas Jefferson drafted the 1776 US Declaration of Independence on hemp paper.

18. Dr Church's actual enciphered letter can be found among the 'George Washington Papers (1741–1799)' on the Library of Congress website: http://memory.loc.gov/ammem/.

19. G. J. A. O'Toole, *Honorable Treason* (New York: Atlantic Monthly Press, 1991), p.23; see also Richard Rowan, *The Story of Secret Service* (London: John Miles Ltd, 1938).

20. Arnold continued in the service of the British Crown and died heavily in debt in 1801. He was buried in the crypt of St Mary's Church, Battersea, London. Full of remorse on his death bed, he was buried in his Continental Army uniform.

5. VIVE LA RÉVOLUTION?

1. Rowan, *The Story of Secret Service*, pp.166–169.

2. Elizabeth Sparrow, *Secret Service – British Agents in France 1792–1815* (Woodbridge, UK: The Boydell Press, 1999) p.33.

3. Ibid., p.35.

4. Ibid., p.39.

5. Ibid., p.15.

6. Ibid., p.41.

7. Ibid., p.42.

8. Ibid., p.53.
9. See J. G. M. de Montgaillard, *Mémoires Secrets* (Paris: les Marchands de Nouveautés, 1804).
10. Sparrow, *Secret Service*, p.53.
11. Louis de Fauche-Borel, *Mémoires de Fauche-Borel*, 4 vols (Paris: Crapelet, 1825), Vol.1, pp.235–249.
12. Sparrow, *Secret Service*, p.52.
13. Klinglin, *Correspondance trouvée le 2 Floréal An 5e a Offembourg.* (Paris: L'imprimerie de la République, Pluviose an VI), p.23.
14. Klinglin, *Correspondance*, p.175. This extract is from a letter, the 61st piece of the captured correspondence, dated 26 February at 9.00am.
15. Some of the other codewords from this conspiracy included: *Poinsinet* for Pichegru; *la partie de billard* (the billiards party) for 'the counter-revolution'; *un peuplier* (a poplar tree) for 'a spy'; *Sauveur* (Saviour) for the Rhine; *dez* for 'espionage' or 'secret correspondence'; *les Grelots* (the sleigh-bells) for the Swiss; *la Foüine* ('the stone marten' or more colloquially 'the nosey parker') for Britain; *une lanterne* (a lamp) for 'an army'. In addition to those already met, other personalities appearing in the letters were codenamed and included: *Grand Bourgeois* (a member of the upper middle class) for Louis XVIII; *César* (Caesar) for Austrian General Wurmser; *la Mariée* (the Bride) for Moreau and *Antoine* for Archduke Charles. Characters on the periphery of the plot usually had their names enciphered numerically, for example the republican General Desaix appears simply as 4452941199470.
16. Fauche-Borel, *Mémoires*, Vol.2, pp.80–81.
17. Ibid., Vol.2, p.84.
18. Sparrow, *Secret Service*, p.62.
19. Fauche-Borel, *Mémoires*, Vol. 2, pp.86–87.
20. Ibid., Vol.2, p.89.
21. Ibid., Vol.2, pp.90–91.
22. Ibid., Vol.2, p.112.
23. Sparrow, *Secret Service*, pp.76–77.
24. Fauche-Borel, *Mémoires*, Vol.2, p.116.
25. Colin Duckworth, *The d'Antraigues Phenomenon – The making and breaking of a Revolutionary Royalist Espionage Agent* (Newcastle upon Tyne, UK: Avero Publications Ltd, 1986), p.231.
26. Klinglin, *Correspondance*, p.15.
27. Sparrow, *Secret Service*, p.129.
28. Ibid., pp.273–274.
29. Ibid., p.289.
30. Ibid., pp.291–293.
31. Ibid., p.228.
32. Ibid., p.336.
33. Richard Deacon, *A History of the Russian Secret Service* (London: Frederick Muller Ltd, 1972), pp.35–37.
34. Sparrow, *Secret Service*, p.347.
35. Philip John Stead, *The Police of France* (New York: MacMillan Publishing Company, 1983), pp.41–48.

6. NAPOLEON'S 'SECRET PART'

1. Josiane Bourguet-Rouveyre, 'La Liberté en Italie – La présence française en Italie du Nord vue par les Piémontais: liberté ou servitude?' This article appears on www.Napoleon.org.
2. Alain Montarras, 'La Liberté en Italie – Le problème du renseignement pendant la première campagne d'Italie.' This article appears on www.Napoleon.org.
3. Ibid.
4. Baron General Paul Thiébault, *Manuel Général du service des États-majors généraux et divisionnares dans les armées* (Paris, 1813).
5. Ibid., p.96.
6. Ibid., p.96.
7. Ibid., pp.97–98.
8. Ibid., pp.98–99.
9. Ibid., p.99.
10. Ibid., p.99.
11. Jean Landrieux, *Mémoires de l'adjudant-général J. Landrieux 1795–1797* (Paris: A. Savine, 1893), pp.107–111.
12. Ibid., pp.110–111.
13. Jean Savant, *Les Espions de Napoléon* (Paris: Hachette, 1957) pp.19–20.
14. Ibid., p.31.
15. Landrieux, *Mémoires*, p.111.
16. Ibid., p.111.
17. Ibid., p.81–82.
18. Savant, *Les Espions de Napoléon*, p.52.
19. Landrieux, *Mémoires*, pp.219–220.
20. Ibid., p.221.
21. Ibid., p.232.
22. Ibid., p.348.
23. Ibid., pp.155–158.
24. Savant, *Les Espions de Napoléon*, p.62.
25. Ibid., p.22.
26. Ibid., p.64.
27. Ibid., p.65–66.
28. Ibid., p.74.
29. Ibid., pp.76–77.
30. Baron Jean Baptiste Louis de Crossard, *Mémoires militaires et historiques pour servir à l'histoire de la guerre depuis 1792 jusqu'en 1815 inclusivement* (Paris: 1829), Vol.2, pp.204–205.
31. Crossard, *Mémoires militaires*, Vol.2, p.206.
32. David Hollins, *Marengo 1800: Napoleon's Day of Fate* (Oxford: Osprey Publishing, 2000), p.19.
33. J. Édouard Gachot, *La Deuxiéme Campagne d'Italie, 1800* (Paris: 1899), pp.152–153.
34. Louis Antoine Fauvaulet de Bourienne, *Memoirs of Napoleon Bonaparte – From the French by John S. Memes* (London: Hurst, Chance & Co., 1831), Vol.2, pp.96–97.
35. Bourienne, *Memoirs of Napoleon*, Vol.2, p.97.

36. Savant, *Les Espions de Napoléon*, p.128.
37. Alexander Elmer, *Schulmeister – l'agent secret de Napoléon*, trans. Lucien Thomas (Paris: Payot, 1980) p.11.
38. Savant, *Les Espions de Napoléon*, pp.135–136.
39. Rowan, *The Story of Secret Service*, p.237.
40. Savant, *Les Espions de Napoléon*, p.137.
41. Rowan, *The Story of Secret Service*, p.236.
42. Savant, *Les Espions de Napoléon*, p.139.
43. Ibid., pp.139–140.
44. Henri de la Neuville (trans. Edward Ryan), 'Karl Ludwig Schulmeister: A Spy for the Emperor', in *Napoleonic Alliance Gazette*, 2001, No.3.

7. UNCIVIL WAR

1. Ridiculous as it may seem, in 2002 Stuart Drummond, the monkey-suited mascot of Hartlepool United Football club (nicknamed by rivals 'the monkey hangers') was elected mayor of the town on the ticket of 'free bananas for schoolchildren'. More recently, in June 2005 the discovery of a 'gorilla bone' on the shore near Hartlepool caused a wave of excitement. Scientists have since dismissed links to the simian spy, claiming the relic was in fact prehistoric.
2. As purists will note, before receiving the title 'Wellington' in recognition of his victory at the battle of Talavera (27–28 July 1809), he should properly be called Sir Arthur Wellesley. Here he is known simply as Wellington.
3. Philip J. Haythornthwaite, *The Armies of Wellington* (London: Arms and Armour Press, 1994), p.157.
4. Elizabeth Longford, *Wellington – The Years of the Sword* (London: Weidenfeld & Nicolson, 1969), p.265.
5. Ibid., p.265.
6. Deacon, *A History of the British Secret Service*, p.127.
7. Longford, *Wellington*, p.183.
8. Ibid., p.183.
9. Ibid., p.265.
10. Ibid., pp.265–266.
11. Michel Molières, *Guerra a cuchillo – la Guérilla pendant la Guerre d'Indépendance Espagnole, 1808–1813* (Paris: Publibook, 2002), p.230.
12. Mark Urban, *The Man who broke Napoleon's Codes – The story of George Scovell* (London: Faber and Faber Ltd, 2001), p.64.
13. Longford, *Wellington*, p.265.
14. Urban, *The Man who broke Napoleon's Codes*, p.188.
15. Ibid., pp.232–233.
16. Peter Hofschröer, *1815: The Waterloo Campaign, Wellington, his German Allies and the Battles of Ligny and Quatre Bras* (London: Greenhill Books, 1998), p.136.
17. This topic is discussed more fully in Hofschröer, pp.136–160.
18. Ibid., p.160.
19. A. F. de Brack, *Avant-Postes de Cavalerie légère*, etc (1834 and many reprints), p.81.
20. Ibid., pp.81–86.

21. Carl von Clausewitz, *On War* (Harmondsworth, UK: Penguin Books Ltd, 1968), pp.162–163.
22. Baron de Jomini (trans. G. H. Mendell and W. P. Craighill), *The Art of War* (Philadelphia: J. B. Lippincott & Co., 1868), p.269.
23. Ibid., p.270.
24. Ibid., p.270.
25. *The Times*, 9 February 1863, p.10.
26. Stephen M. Harris, *British Military Intelligence in the Crimean War 1854–1856* (London: Frank Cass, 1999), pp.67–68.
27. Harris, *British Military Intelligence*, pp.75–76.
28. Haswell, *Spies and Spymasters*, p.83.
29. G. J. A. O'Toole, *Honorable Treason* (New York: Atlantic Monthly Press, 1991) pp.131–133.
30. Rowan, *The Story of Secret Service*, pp.276–278.
31. Margaret Pinkerton Fitchett, *The early Pinkertons*. A full account of Pinkerton and his agents' exploits can be found online at the Pinkerton Resource Page: www.geocities.com/Heartland/Prairie/8980/.
32. Haswell, *Spies and Spymasters*, p.88.
33. Rowan, *The Story of Secret Service*, p.292.
34. Haswell, *Spies and Spymasters*, p.89.
35. P. K. Rose, *The Civil War: Black American Contributions to Union Intelligence*. Available from the CIA website: www.cia.gov.
36. O'Toole, *Honorable Treason*, pp.125–126.
37. Rowan, *The Story of Secret Service*, pp.297–300.
38. Douglas Southall Freeman, *Lee's Lieutenants – A Study in Command, Vol. 3 Gettysburg to Appomattox* (New York: Charles Scribner's Sons, 1944).
39. Conversation cited in ibid., p.49.
40. Ibid., p.49.
41. Douglas Southall Freeman, *R. E. Lee: A Biography*, Vol.3 (New York: Charles Scribner's Sons, 1934), pp.60–61.
42. Harrison is wrongly confused with James Harrison, an itinerant Richmond actor.
43. Freeman, *Lee's Lieutenants*, pp.226–227. More information on Harrison's later life can be found online at the Harrison Homepage members.aol.com/spyharrisn/home/, a site hosted by the spy's great-grandson. It also addresses some of the 'artistic licence' in the portrayal of Harrison in the 1993 film *Gettysburg*.
44. Belle Boyd, *In Camp and Prison* (London: Saunders, Otley, 1865).
45. Edmonds' memoirs are thought to be partly fictional. See: S. Emma E. Edmonds, *Nurse and Spy in the Union Army: Comprising the Adventures and Experiences of a Woman in Hospitals, Camps, etc.* (Hartford, Conn., 1865).

8. THE GODFATHER OF SECRET SERVICE

1. Wilhelm J. C. E. Stieber (trans. Jan van Heurck), *The Chancellor's Spy* (New York: Grove Press Inc., 1980), p.158.
2. Ibid., p.57.
3. Deacon, *A History of the Russian Secret Service*, p.54.
4. Rowan, *The Story of Secret Service*, p.344.

5. Stieber, *The Chancellor's Spy*, p.107.

6. Ibid., p.135.

7. Ibid., p.130.

8. E. Delerot, *Jules Favre et la Police Allemande a Versailles en 1871* (Revue de l'histoire de Versailles et de Seine-et-Oise, Académie de Versailles, 1899), p.235.

9. E. Delerot, *Versailles pendant l'Occupation (1870–1871)* (Versailles: Bernard, 1900), p.151.

10. Ibid., p.151.

11. Ibid., pp.150, 196.

12. Ibid., pp.219–220.

13. Ibid., p.287.

14. Delerot, *Jules Favre et la Police Allemande*, p.236.

15. David Kahn, *Hitler's Spies* (London: Hodder and Stoughton, 1978), p.37.

16. Hervé Coutau-Bégarie, 'Le Renseignement Dans La Pensée Militaire Française', www.stratisc.org/index.html.

17. Rowan, *The Story of Secret Service*, pp.357–358.

18. Henri de Blowitz *My Memoirs* (London: Edward Arnold, 1903).

19. Rowan, *The Story of Secret Service*, p.358.

9. SPY FEVER

1. Haswell, *Spies and Spymasters*, p.109.

2. Sir Robert Baden Powell, *My Adventures as a Spy* can be found online at www.pinetreeweb.com.

3. This thought must still have some currency, as spies are often referred to as 'spooks'.

4. Winston S. Churchill, *Great Contemporaries* (London: Odhams Press Ltd, 1947), p.287.

5. Dr G. N. Van den Bergh, 'Secret Service in the South African Republic 1895–1900', *The South African Military History Society Military History Journal* Vol.3 No.2.

6. Deacon, *History of the British Secret Service*, p.178.

7. D. D. Diespecker, 'British Intelligence Operations in Mozambique in August 1900' in *The South African Military History Society Military History Journal*, Vol.9, No.6.

8. Haswell, *Spies and Spymasters*, pp.83, 102–103.

9. Rowan, *The Story of Secret Service*, p.415.

10. A sting in the tail of this saga is that the information provided to the Germans may have been a deliberate plant by French intelligence to conceal the development of the 75mm field gun. See Jean Doise's *Un secret bien garde: Histoire militaire de l'Affaire Dreyfus* (Paris: Editions du Seuil, 1994).

11. Alan Judd, *The Quest for C – Mansfield Cumming and the founding of the Secret Service* (London: Harper Collins *Publishers*, 1999), pp.65–66.

12. In the service, Cumming was known simply as 'C', the title by which all heads of MI6/SIS have since been known, despite Ian Fleming referring to James Bond's chief as 'M'.

13. Deacon, *A History of the British Secret Service*, p.192.

14. F. T. Felstead (ed.), *Steinhauer, the Kaiser's Master Spy. The story as told by himself* (London: John Lane, 1930).

15. The files on investigating German espionage are found in KV1/39–KV1/41 of the National Archives, Kew.
16. Deacon, *History of the British Secret Service*, pp.213–214.
17. Haswell, *Spies and Spymasters*, pp.114–115.
18. Nicolai produced a memoir in which he complained that the German high command was so confident of victory that it was slow to understand the importance of intelligence. It was translated in *Geheime Machte – The German Secret Service* (London: S. Paul & Co., 1924).
19. National Archives, WO 71/1236.
20. Deacon, *A History of the British Secret Service*, p.131.
21. Ibid., pp.245–251.
22. By 'unrestricted' Zimmermann meant that Germany would begin sinking the ships of neutral countries bound for Britain, including those of the United States.
23. For his many adventures, see the highly readable: Charles Lucieto, *On Special Missions* (New York: A. L. Burt Company, 1927).
24. Rowan, *The Story of Secret Service*, pp.579–580.
25. Judd, *The Quest for C*, p.294.

10. EASTERN PERIL

1. Amleto Vespa, *Secret Agent of Japan* (London: Victor Gollancz Ltd, 1938), p.285.
2. Raymond Lamont-Brown, *Kempeitai – Japan's Dreaded Secret Police* (Stroud: Sutton Publishing, 1998), p.24.
3. David Bergamini, *Japan's Imperial Conspiracy* (London: Heinemann, 1971), p.265.
4. Ibid., p.267.
5. Ronald Seth, *Secret Servants: The Story of Japanese Espionage* (London: Victor Gollancz, 1957), p.63.
6. Richard Deacon, *The Japanese Secret Service* (London: Frederick Muller Ltd, 1982), p.44.
7. Ibid., pp.77–78.
8. Bergamini, *Japan's Imperial Conspiracy*, p.142.
9. Edward Behr, *The Last Emperor* (London: Macdonald & Co, 1987), p.176.
10. Aisin-Gioro Pu Yi, *From Emperor to Citizen* (Oxford: Oxford University Press, 1987), pp.205–6.
11. Ibid., p.203.
12. Seth, *Secret Servants*, pp.106–109.
13. Pu Yi, *From Empeor to Citizen*, p.226.
14. Bergamini, *Japan's Imperial Conspiracy*, p.442.
15. Ibid., pp.450–451. The author verified this story in interviews with Doihara's colleagues.
16. This scene is played out in Bernardo Bertolucci's 1987 film *The Last Emperor*. See also Edward Behr, *The Last Emperor* (London: Macdonald & Co, 1987).
17. Pu Yi, *From Emperor to Citizen*, p.228.
18. Ibid., p.229.
19. Vespa, *Secret Agent of Japan*, pp.37–38.
20. Ibid., p.43.

21. Bergamini, *Japan's Imperial Conspiracy*, p.528.
22. Vespa, *Secret Agent of Japan*, pp.96–97.
23. Deacon, *The Japanese Secret Service*, p.155.
24. Bergamini, *Japan's Imperial Conspiracy*, p.176.
25. Ibid., pp.142–143.
26. Ibid., pp.618–619.

11. DOUBLE AGENTS & RADIO GAMES

1. J. C. Masterman, *The Double Cross System* (London: Yale University Press, Ltd, 1972), p.3.
2. Walter Schellenberg (trans. Louis Hagen), *The Schellenberg Memoirs* (London: Andre Deutsch Ltd, 1956), pp.407–408.
3. Reinhard Gehlen (trans. David Irving), *The Gehlen Memoirs* (London: Collins, 1972), p.53.
4. Michael Howard, *Strategic Deception in the Second World War* (London: Pimlico, 1992), pp.45–52. See also Juan Pujol (with Nigel West), *Garbo – The Personal Story of the Most Successful Double Agent Ever...* (London: Weidenfeld & Nicolson Ltd, 1985), p.72.
5. Schellenberg, *The Schellenberg Memoirs*, p.35.
6. Gehlen, *The Gehlen Memoirs*, p.36.
7. Haswell, *Spies and Spymasters*, p.139.
8. Schellenberg, *The Schellenberg Memoirs*, pp.120–121.
9. From Lahousen's testimony at the Nuremberg Trials. See www.yale.edu/lawweb/avalon/imt/proc/witness.htm for this and Schellenberg's testimony.
10. Deacon, *A History of the British Secret Service*, pp.338–339.
11. Schellenberg, *The Schellenberg Memoirs*, p.123.
12. Nigel West, *MI5: British Security Service operations 1909–1945* (London: Bodley Head, 1981), pp.224–225.
13. In total 14 spies were executed after passing through Camp 020. Long-term prisoners were held at Camp WX, which was located at Stafford Prison, then the Isle of Man and finally Dartmoor. BBC News, 26 January 1999.
14. Howard, *Strategic Deception*, p.9. Also see J. C. Masterman, *The Double Cross System* for a full account of the Twenty Committee's organization and deeds.
15. Quite simply these questionnaires set out the spy's mission and objectives in the field. For example, if Hamburg was interested in aircraft production, the questionnaire would instruct the agent where to go and what technical data to obtain.
16. Howard, *Strategic Deception*, pp.16–18.
17. Schellenberg, *The Schellenberg Memoirs*, p.418.
18. Elyesa Bazna, *I was Cicero* (London: Deutsch, 1962).
19. 'Uncovering the "Game against England"', interview with Lauwers by Jim Fish for BBC News, 3 January 2004.
20. For the standard work on the subject see M. R. D. Foot, *SOE in the Low Countries* (London: St Ermin's, 2001).
21. David Stafford, *Secret Agent: the true story of the Special Operations Executive* (London: BBC, 2000), p.157.

22. For an account of this story: Pieter Dourlein (trans. F. G. Renier and Anne Cliff), *Inside North Pole. A secret agent's story* (London: William Kimber, 1953).

23. For Harris' account of the *Garbo* case see *Garbo – The Spy who saved D-Day* (Richmond; Public Record Office, 2000).

24. Agents 7:5–7:7 were codenamed *Donny, Dick* and *Derrick* by the Germans.

25. The National Archives KV 2/455.

26. After the war Chapman was granted a pardon for his pre-war crimes and given £6,000 for his services. For a long time MI5 was worried what would happen to Chapman when the money ran out. Their biggest fear was Chapman would return to blowing safes and if caught, would try to bargain his freedom against keeping quiet over his top secret wartime experiences. Fortunately the proceeds from the film *Triple Cross* (Chapman was played by Christopher Plummer) kept the wartime double agent out of trouble. He invested in a health farm and died in 1997.

12. AXIS SPIES AGAINST AMERICA

1. *Report of the Joint Committee on the Investigation of the Pearl Harbor Attack, Congress of the United States* (Washington D.C.: Government Printing Office, 1946), p.184.

2. Gordon W. Prange, *At Dawn We Slept – The Untold Story of Pearl Harbor* (London: Michael Joseph Ltd, 1982), p.155.

3. Despite documents being destroyed at the end of the war, an outline of Japanese activities during the build up to Pearl Harbour can be gleaned from surviving *Magic* intercepts.

4. Deacon, *The Japanese Secret Service*, pp.178–179.

5. Ibid., p.180.

6. Ibid., p.183.

7. Prange, *At Dawn We Slept*, p.150.

8. From Proceedings Of The Hart Inquiry, Saturday 15 April 1944, Lieutenant William B. Stephenson, the Japanese Counter-Espionage Desk of the District Intelligence Office in Hawaii, pp.350–362.

9. Admiral Smith in *Report of the Joint Committee*, p.465.

10. Ibid., p.465.

11. Prange, *At Dawn We Slept*, pp.70–71.

12. Ibid., p.154.

13. The Roberts Commission (18 December–23 January 1941), p.12.

14. Prange, *At Dawn We Slept*, p.149.

15. Ibid., p.76.

16. Ibid., p.178.

17. Ibid., p.154.

18. Ibid., pp.248–249.

19. Ibid., p.253.

20. Ibid., p.254.

21. Ibid., p.309.

22. Ibid., p.315.

23. Ronald Seth, *Secret Servants*, pp.14–16.

24. Prange, *At Dawn We Slept*, p.423.

25. Ibid., pp.314–319.

26. Ibid., p.356.

27. Ibid., p.318.
28. Ibid., pp.366–367.
29. *Report of the Joint Committee*, p.477.
30. G. T. A. O'Toole, *Honorable Treachery*, p.376.
31. Prange, *At Dawn We Slept*, p.479.
32. Bergamini, *Japan's Imperial Conspiracy*, p.840.
33. Ibid., pp.478–479.
34. From an interview with Yoshikawa by Ron Layhei, 'The Real Last Samurai' for Edit International (2003) www.editinternational.com.
35. Deacon, *The Japanese Secret Service*, pp.190–191.
36. *Report Of The Joint Committee On The Investigation Of The Pearl Harbor Attack, Congress Of The United States*, p.184.
37. *Hearings Before the Joint Committee on the Investigation of the Pearl Harbor Attack, Congress of the United States* (Washington D.C.: Government Printing Office, 1946), p.1753.
38. Hewitt Inquiry, p.432.
39. See J. Rusbridge and E. Nave, *Betrayal at Pearl Harbor – How Churchill Lured Roosevelt into War* (London: Michael O'Mara Books Ltd, 1991).
40. Dusko Popov, *Spy/Counter Spy* (London: Weidenfeld and Nicholson Ltd, 1974) pp.126–129.
41. Ibid., pp.132–133.
42. J. C. Masterman, *The Double Cross System*, p.79.
43. Further information on these and other famous FBI cases can be found at the history section of the FBI's website: www.fbi.gov.
44. O'Toole, *Honorable Treachery*, pp.353–356.

13. SPIES OF THE SOVIET ERA

1. *The Man Without a Face – An interview with Markus Wolf*, CNN Interactive.
2. Derived from the Latin *nihil* (nothing), nihilism was primarily a youth movement which began in the 1860s. Completely anti-authoritarian, nihilists called into question all aspects of traditional Russian life.
3. After the Russian Revolution of 1917, the Okhrana's Paris office files were secreted to the United States by the last imperial ambassador to France, Basil Maklakov. His only demand was for the files to be remained sealed until after his death, so they remained with the Hoover Institution until opened in 1957, revealing a veritable who's who of the Russian Revolution.
4. Deacon, *A History of the Russian Secret Service*, p.97.
5. Haswell, *Spies and Spymasters* pp.106–107.
6. Ben B. Fischer, *OKHRANA The Paris Operations of the Russian Imperial Police* (History Staff Center for the Study of Intelligence Central Intelligence Agency, 1997).
7. Russia used the Julian calendar and so 7 November was to them 25 October.
8. Lev Trotsky, *The History of the Russian Revolution*, trans. Max Eastman, Vol.2 (University of Michigan Press: Ann Arbor, 1959), p.87.
9. By *Rasputin regime*, Trotsky is referring to the tsarist government, which was held under a sort of spell by the 'mad monk' Gregory Rasputin. When Rasputin was assassinated he too was accused – among other things – of being a German spy.

10. Lev Trotsky (trans. Max Eastman), *The History of the Russian Revolution* (University of Michigan Press: Ann Arbor, 1959), Vol.2, p.99.

11. Sir Paul Dukes KBE, *The Story of 'ST 25.' Adventure and romance in the Secret Intelligence Service in Red Russia* (London: Cassell & Co., 1938).

12. Dated 15 September 1924, the 'Zinoviev Letter' was a document in which Grigori Zinoviev, president of the Comintern (Communist International) called on the Communist Party of Great Britain to intensify agitation in Britain and its armed forces. The letter appeared in the right-wing *Daily Mail* newspaper four days before the 1924 election, which Britain's left-wing Labour government went on to lose. Most believe the document was a forgery sent to the *Daily Mail* by White Russians or MI5 in order to prevent the signing of an Anglo-Russian trade agreement.

13. See Andrew Cook's *Ace of Spies: The True Story of Sidney Reilly* (Stroud: Tempus Publishing Limited, 2004).

14. Before his body was embalmed, scientists removed Lenin's brain and gave it to a German neuroscientist to discover the root of genius. The tests proved inconclusive.

15. Born Iosif Vissarionovich Dzhugashvilli, in 1913 he changed his name to Stalin – or 'Man of Steel.' In April 1956 *Life* magazine published details of a 1913 document called the 'Eremin Letter.' If genuine, the letter indicates Stalin may have been an Okhrana agent from 1906 to 1912.

16. Deacon, *A History of the Russian Secret Service*, pp.191–192.

17. Michael Smith, 'Enigma of KGB's Third Man at Bletchley Park', Electronic Telegraph (26 June 1997) http://www.telegraph.co.uk.

18. The Comintern (Communist International) was an organization formed in 1919 to promote world revolution and the formation of an international Soviet republic. It served as a convenient front for Soviet espionage.

19. Louis C. Kilzer, *Hitler's traitor: Martin Bormann and the defeat of the Reich* (Novato, Calif.: Presidio, 2000), pp.141–146.

20. Ibid., pp.18–19.

21. Ibid., p.187.

22. Ibid., p.4.

23. Ibid., and Reinhard Gehlen's *The Gehlen Memoirs* (London: Collins, 1972).

24. Story from BBC News, published 19 April 2003.

25. Haswell, *Spies and Spymasters*, pp.160–161.

26. Deacon, *History of the Russian Secret Service*, pp.257–258.

27. Harry S. Truman, *Year of Decisions* (Garden City, NY: Doubleday & Company, 1955), p.416.

28. Peter Wright, *Spycatcher* (Richmond, Victoria: William Henemann Australia, 1987), pp.179–180.

29. See Errol Morris' film on McNamara, *The Fog of War* (Sony Pictures Classics, 2003).

30. *Venona* project transcript #1822 dated 30 March 1945. For the official NSA *Venona* site go to: www.nsa.gov/venona/index.cfm.

31. Raymond E. Zickel (ed.), *Soviet Union: a country study* (Federal Research Division, Library of Congress, 1991) at lcweb2.loc.gov/frd/cs/sutoc.html.

32. The term was created in the 1950s and was the translation of the Chinese phrase *Xi Nao* (lit. wash brain). The technique was normally a process of sleep deprivation and intense psychological pressure, which caused behavioural changes in prisoners of war, making them less likely to attempt escape. In some cases the

victims were imbued with a deep allegiance to Marxist doctrine, which lasted beyond their period of confinement.

33. *Inside the KGB – An interview with retired KGB Maj. Gen. Oleg Kalugin*, CNN Interactive.

34. Andropov was head of KGB from 1967 to 1982 when he succeeded Leonid Brezhnev as General Secretary of the Soviet Communist Party. Although his tenure was short lived (1982–84), Andropov was the first head of the KGB to achieve this rank.

35. The killer has since been identified as a bogus antiques salesman named Francesco Giullino, a Dane of Italian origin known to the Bulgarian secret service as Agent *Piccadilly*. Story by Jack Hamilton and Tom Walker: 'Dane named as umbrella killer', *The Sunday Times*, 5 June 2005.

36. Wolf interview, CNN Interactive.

37. 'Sexpionage' from BBC Radio 4's *Sleeping with the Enemy* series. Produced and presented by Linda Pressly. Broadcast 22 November 2004. Kliem was arrested on espionage charges in 1991. She was tried in 1996 and handed down a suspended sentence and a fine. Ashamed by the whole experience, Kliem left Germany and settled in Holland.

38. Gehlen, *The Gehlen Memoirs*, p.21.

39. Richard Breitman, Norman Goda, Timothy Naftali and Robert Wolfe, *U.S. Intelligence and the Nazis* (Washington, DC: National Archive Trust Fund Board, 2004). Source material on Gehlen can be found at The National Security Archive's website: www.gwu.edu/%7Ensarchiv/.

40. Stephen Dorril, *MI6 – Fifty Years of Special Operations* (London: Fourth Estate, 2000), pp.749–750.

41. Interview by Pete Earley at www.crimelibrary.com/terrorists_spies/spies/solomatin/1.html.

42. Shortly after the fall of the Berlin Wall, an East German friend explained to me how he had picked up his excellent English from illegally listening to Mick Jagger on the radio. Apparently Eastern Bloc countries produced their own shoddy version of 'jeans' which didn't fool anyone hankering after the real thing. Such things are surprisingly important to many people.

43. Wolf interview, CNN Interactive.

44. This is a reference to American political economist Francis Fukuyama's *The End of History and the Last Man* (Free Press, 1992).

45. Before closing the door on the Cold War, we should document the defection of Vasili Mitrokhin in 1992. Mitrokhin was senior archivist for the KGB's First Chief Directorate and had overseen the transfer of the KGB archives from the Lubyanka to a new KGB headquarters at Yasenevo. While transferring files, Mitrokhin began taking copies of certain documents. In 1992 Mitrokhin took the copies of these documents to Latvia and visited the US embassy. The CIA decided Mitrokhin was a fake and passed up on his offer. The former KGB man then went to the British Embassy where he was enrolled as an agent. MI6 began a long, painstaking operation to recover the 25,000 sheets of documents in Mitrokhin's possession and bring them to Britain. The papers, some of which dated to the 1930s, led to a host of embarrassing and strange revelations about KGB activities and agents. Mitrokhin died in 2004, but the findings of his 'archive' have been published in two volumes: *The Sword and the Shield: The Mitrokhin Archive and the Secret History of the KGB*, (New York: Basic Books, 1999) and *The World Was Going Our Way: The KGB and the Battle for the Third World* (New York: Basic Books 2005).

14. WITH NO END IN SIGHT...

1. Latin quote attributed to Juvenal, literally 'but who guards the guards?' In a modern context, it might be interpreted as 'who watches over the security services?'
2. See Mandelbaum's *The Psychic Battlefield* (New York: St. Martin's Press, 2000); or for a more sceptical view of this subject and similar, see Jon Ronson, *The Men Who Stare at Goats* (London: Picador, 2004).
3. Ronson, *The Men Who Stare at Goats*.
4. These allegations were part of a speech given by MP Kevin McNamara in the House of Commons on 14 May 2003 (Hansard, columns 74WH–75WH).
5. See statement of William Carlin to Lord Saville's inquiry (www.bloody-sunday-inquiry.org).
6. House of Commons Hansard Debates for 17 January 1989, Column 286, MP Jonathan Aitken.
7. House of Commons Hansard, 15 December 1988, Column 1153, MP Rupert Allason.
8. Richard M. Bennett, *Espionage – Spies and secrets* (London: Virgin Books Ltd, 2002), pp.26–27.
9. From a film by Tim Whewell broadcast by the BBC's *Newsnight* on 22 February 2005.
10. For what Mossad publicly admits to, see its website: www.mossad.gov.il/Mohr.
11. This team forms the subject of a book by George Jonas: *Vengeance: The True Story of an Israeli Counter-Terrorist Team* (New York: Simon and Schuster, 1984) which in itself inspired Steven Spielberg's 2005 film *Munich*. Jonas' principal source was 'Avner' – purportedly the leader of the team. Unsurprisingly, Avner's story has been disputed by official Israeli sources and fellow Mossad agents. See also Aaron J. Klein's *Striking back: The 1972 Munich Olympics Massacre and Israel's Deadly Response* (New York: Random House, 2005).
12. The original list of targets included: 1. Ali Hassan Salameh, who was thought to be the principal planner of the Munich outrage; 2. Abu Daoud – Black September's explosives expert; 3. Mahmoud Hamshari – an intellectual and spokesman for the Palestinian cause; 4. Wael Zwaiter – a poet and spokesperson; 5. Dr Basil al-Kubaisi – a weapons purchaser; 6. Kamal Nasser – spokesperson for the PLO; 7. Kemal Adwan – in charge of sabotage operations against Israel; 8. Abu Yussuf – a high ranking Palestinian; 9. Mohammed Boudia – an Algerian theatre director believed to be involved in terrorism; 10. Hussein Abad al-Chir – the PLO's contact with the KGB; 11. Dr Wadi Haddad, thought to be a terrorist mastermind (Jonas, *Vengeance*, pp.93–94).
13. Jonas, *Vengeance*, p.144.
14. Ibid., p.193.
15. Richard Deacon, *The Israeli Secret Service* (London: Hamilton, 1977), p.258.
16. Ibid. pp.268–283.
17. This accusation against Mossad was made in the House of Commons by MP George Galloway (Hansard, 18 April 1990, Column 1432).
18. Early-day motion 1286 (dated 21 October 1991) Source: http://edmi.parliament.uk/EDMi/Default.aspx.
19. House of Commons Hansard Debates for 22 October 1991, Column 792.
20. The actual quote was from a dialogue between Secretary of State Speransky and Prince Andrei, one of the book's central characters. Speransky said: 'But our idea is that the wolves should be fed and the sheep kept safe.' L. N. Tolstoy (trans. Rosemary Edmonds), *War and Peace*, Vol.1 (Harmondsworth, Middlesex: Penguin Books, 1957), p.506.

SELECT BIBLIOGRAPHY

Alvarez, David, *Spies in the Vatican: Espionage & Intrigue from Napoleon to the Holocaust* (Lawrence, Kan.: University Press of Kansas, 2002)

Baer, Robert, *See No Evil: The True Story of a Ground Soldier in the CIA's War Against Terrorism* (London: Arrow, 2002)

Bennett, Richard M., *Espionage – Spies and Secrets* (London: Virgin Books Ltd, 2002)

Bergamini, David, *Japan's Imperial Conspiracy* (London: Heinemann, 1971)

Chakraborty, Dr Kedareswar, *Art of Spying in Ancient India* (Kolkata: Sanskrit Book Depot, 2002)

Chambers, James, *The Devil's Horsemen – The Mongol Invasion of Europe* (London: The Book Club, 1979)

Cook, Andrew, *Ace of Spies: The True Story of Sidney Reilly* (Stroud: Tempus Publishing Limited, 2004)

Deacon, Richard, *A History of the British Secret Service* (London: Frederick Muller Ltd, 1969)

Deacon, Richard, *A History of the Russian Secret Service* (London: Frederick Muller Ltd, 1972)

Deacon, Richard, *The Israeli Secret Service* (London: Hamilton, 1977)

Deacon, Richard, *The Japanese Secret Service* (London: Frederick Muller Ltd, 1982)

Deacon, Richard, *The Chinese Secret Service* (London: Grafton, 1989)

Doise, Jean, *Un secret bien garde: Histoire militaire de l'Affaire Dreyfus* (Paris: Editions du Seuil, 1994)

Dorril, Stephen, *MI6: Fifty Years of Special Operations* (London: Fourth Estate, 2000)

Dourlein, Pieter (trans. F. G. Renier and Anne Cliff), *Inside North Pole: A Secret Agent's Story* (London: William Kimber, 1953)

Duckworth, Colin, *The d'Antraigues Phenomenon – The making and breaking of a Revolutionary Royalist Espionage Agent* (Newcastle upon Tyne, UK: Avero Publications Ltd, 1986)

Dukes KBE, Sir Paul, *The Story of 'ST 25': Adventure and Romance in the Secret Intelligence Service in Red Russia* (London: Cassell & Co., 1938)

Elmer, Alexander (trans. Lucien Thomas), *Schulmeister – l'agent secret de Napoléon* (Paris: Payot, 1980)

Foot, M. R. D., *SOE in the Low Countries* (London: St Ermin's, 2001)

Gehlen, Reinhard (trans. David Irving), *The Gehlen Memoirs* (London: Collins, 1972)

Harris, Stephen M., *British Military Intelligence in the Crimean War 1854–1856* (London: Frank Cass, 1999)

Harris, Tomas, *Garbo – The Spy Who Saved D-Day* (Richmond: Public Record Office, 2000)

Haswell, J., *Spies and Spymasters* (London: Thames and Hudson, 1977)

Haynes, Alan, *The Elizabethan Secret Services* (Stroud, UK: Sutton Publishing, 2004)

Haynes, Alan, *Walsingham – Elizabethan Spymaster & Statesman* (Stroud, UK: Sutton Publishing, 2004)

Howard, Michael, *Strategic Deception in the Second World War* (London: Pimlico, 1992)

Jonas, George, *Vengeance: The True Story of an Israeli Counter-Terrorist Team* (New York: Simon and Schuster, 1984)

Judd, Alan, *The Quest for C – Mansfield Cumming and the Founding of the Secret Service* (London: Harper Collins, 1999)

Kahn, David, *Hitler's Spies: German Military Intelligence in World War II* (London: Hodder and Stoughton, 1978)

Kilzer, Louis C., *Hitler's Traitor: Martin Bormann and the defeat of the Reich* (Novato, Calif.: Presidio, 2000)

Klein, Aaron J., *Striking Back: The 1972 Munich Olympics Massacre and Israel's Deadly Response* (New York: Random House, 2005)

Lamont-Brown, Raymond, *Kempeitai – Japan's Dreaded Secret Police* (Stroud: Sutton Publishing, 1998)

Lucieto, Charles, *On Special Missions* (New York: A. L. Burt Co., 1927)

Mandelbaum, Adam W., *The Psychic Battlefield* (New York: St. Martin's Press, 2000)

Masterman, J. C., *The Double Cross System* (London: Yale University Press, Ltd, 1972)

Mitrokhin, Vasili (and Christopher Andrew), *The Sword and the Shield: The Mitrokhin Archive and the Secret History of the KGB* (New York: Basic Books, 1999)

Mitrokhin, Vasili (and Christopher Andrew), *The World Was Going Our Way: The KGB and the Battle for the Third World* (New York: Basic Books 2005)

Nicholl, Charles, *The Reckoning* (London: Cape, 1992)

Nicolai, Walter, *Geheime Machte – The German Secret Service* (London: S. Paul & Co., 1924)

Nixon, Edna, *Royal Spy – The Strange Case of the Chevalier d'Eon* (London: Heinemann, 1966)

O'Toole, G. J. A., *Honorable Treason* (New York: Atlantic Monthly Press, 1991)

Oman, C. W. C. (ed. John H. Beeler), *The Art of War in the Middle Ages* (Ithaca and London: Cornell University Press, 1953)

Popov, Dusko, *Spy/Counter Spy* (London: Weidenfeld and Nicholson Ltd, 1974)

Prange, Gordon W., *At Dawn We Slept – The Untold Story of Pearl Harbor* (London: Michael Joseph Ltd, 1982)

Pujol, Juan (with Nigel West), *Garbo – The Personal Story of the Most Successful Double Agent Ever...* (London: Weidenfeld & Nicolson Ltd, 1985)

Ronson, Jon, *The Men Who Stare at Goats* (London: Picador, 2004)

Rowan, R. J., *The Story of Secret Service* (London: John Miles Ltd, 1938)

Rusbridge, J. and Nave E., *Betrayal at Pearl Harbor – How Churchill Lured Roosevelt into War* (London: Michael O'Mara Books Ltd, 1991)

Savant, Jean, *Les Espions de Napoléon* (Paris: Hachette, 1957)

Schellenberg, Walter (trans. Louis Hagen), *The Schellenberg Memoirs* (London: Andre Deutsch Ltd, 1956)

Seth, Ronald, *Secret Servants: The Story of Japanese Espionage* (London: Victor Gollancz, 1957)

Sinclair Andrew, *The Sword and the Grail* (London: Random House, 1993)

Singh, Simon, *The Code Book* (London: Fourth Estate, 1999)

Sparrow, Elizabeth, *Secret Service – British Agents in France 1792–1815* (Woodbridge, UK: The Boydell Press, 1999)

Stafford, David, *Secret Agent: the True Story of the Special Operations Executive* (London: BBC, 2000)

Stieber, Wilhelm J. C. E. (trans. Jan van Heurck), *The Chancellor's Spy* (New York: Grove Press Inc. 1980)

Turnbull, Stephen, *Ninja: The True Story of Japan's Secret Warrior Cult* (Poole, UK: Firebird Books Ltd, 1991)

Urban, Mark, *The Man who Broke Napoleon's Codes – The Story of George Scovell* (London: Faber and Faber Ltd, 2001)

Vespa, Amleto, *Secret Agent of Japan* (London: Victor Gollancz Ltd, 1938)

West, Nigel, *MI5: British Security Service Operations 1909–1945* (London: Bodley Head, 1981)

Wright, Peter, *Spycatcher* (Richmond, Victoria: William Henemann Australia, 1987)

Photograph credits

Page 97, top: The Art Archive / Dagli Orti; page 97, bottom: akg-images; page 98, top: akg-images; page 98, bottom: The Ancient Art & Architecture Collection Ltd; page 99, top: The Ancient Art & Architecture Collection Ltd; page 99, bottom: Kadokawa/The Ancient Art & Architecture Collection Ltd; page 100, top: attributed to John de Critz the elder © National Portrait Gallery, London; page 100, bottom: TopFoto; page 101, top: akg-images; page 101, bottom left: Topfoto; page 101, bottom right: TopFoto; page 102, top: TopFoto / Roger-Viollet; page 102, bottom: TopFoto / Roger-Viollet; page 103, top: TopFoto; page 103, bottom: The Art Archive / Musée du Château de Versailles / Dagli Orti; page 104, top: TopFoto; page 104, bottom: William Salter © National Portrait Gallery, London; page 241, top: Library of Congress; page 241, bottom: Library of Congress; page 242, top: The Art Archive / Musée Carnavalet Paris / Dagli Orti; page 242, bottom left: TopFoto / Roger-Viollet; page 242, bottom right: The Art Archive / Musée Carnavalet Paris / Dagli Orti; page 243, top: Corbis; page 243, bottom: akg-images/üllstein bild; page 244, top: The Art Archive; page 244, bottom left: akg-images; page 244, bottom right: Topfoto; page 245, top: Library of Congress; page 245, bottom: Elliott & Fry © National Portrait Gallery, London; page 246, top: Library of Congress; page 246, bottom left: Official US Navy photograph, Naval Historical Center; page 246, bottom right: Library of Congress; page 247, top left: akg-images; page 247, top right: Topfoto; page 247, bottom left: TopFoto; page 247, bottom right: New York Archives; page 248, top left: Topfoto; page 248, top right: TopFoto/AP; page 248, bottom: Topfoto / AP.

INDEX

References to illustrations are shown in **bold**.